WOMEN, TEXTS AND HISTORIES 1575–1760

The shared aim of these important new critical essays is to make fresh feminist interventions in early modern studies, and to uncover writings by women and about gender from the sixteenth to eighteenth centuries.

Constrained by gendered discourses of the day, the stories of early modern women have been patchily written and interpreted, and silenced in turn by history. New feminist analysis can expose the conditions of production in which stories of the period have been constructed.

This outstanding new collection also uncovers the untold stories which lie behind canonical texts. By beginning to explore women's participation in the history of the period, *Women, Texts and Histories 1575–1760* reveals the significant and fascinating ways in which women's writing can undermine many of the received assumptions on which readings of the period have depended.

The Editors: Clare Brant is Lecturer in English at King's College, London. **Diane Purkiss** is Lecturer in English at the University of East Anglia.

The Contributors: Rosalind Ballaster, Clare Brant, Hero Chalmers, Helen Hackett, Lorna Hutson, Kate Lilley, Bridget Orr, Diane Purkiss and Sophie Tomlinson.

WOMEN, TEXTS AND HISTORIES 1575-1760

WOMEN, TEXTS AND HISTORIES 1575–1760

Edited by

Clare Brant

and

Diane Purkiss

London and New York

First published 1992
by Routledge
11 New Fetter Lane, London EC4P 4EE

Simultaneously published in the USA and Canada
by Routledge
a division of Routledge, Chapman and Hall, Inc.
29 West 35th Street, New York, NY 10001

Typeset in 10 on 12 point Bembo by
Falcon Typographic Art Ltd, Fife, Scotland
Printed in Great Britain by
Clays Ltd, St Ives plc

British Library Cataloguing in Publication Data
Women, texts and histories 1575–1760
I. Brant, Clare II. Purkiss, Diane
809.93352042

Library of Congress Cataloging-in-Publication Data
Women, texts and histories 1575–1760/edited by Clare Brant and
Diane Purkiss.
p.   cm.
Includes bibliographical references and index.
1. English literature – Women authors – History and criticism.
2. English literature – Early modern, 1500–1700 – History and
criticism. 3. English literature – 18th century – History and
criticism. 4. Women and literature – England – History. I. Brant,
Clare. II. Purkiss, Diane.
PR113.W66   1992
820.9′352042′0903 – dc20   91–32120
ISBN 0–415–05369–2   ISBN 0–415–05370–6 (pbk)

'Tis true the first Lady had so little experience that she hearken'd to the persuasions of an Impertinent Dangler; and if you mind the story, he succeeded by persuadeing her that she was not so wise as she should be.

Lady Mary Wortley Montagu,
The Nonsense of Common-Sense, 1738

CONTENTS

CONTENTS

CONTRIBUTORS

Rosalind Ballaster is a lecturer in English literature at the University of East Anglia. She recently completed her doctoral dissertation on the seduction fiction of Aphra Behn, Delarivier Manley and Eliza Haywood, and is currently preparing it for publication. She is co-author of *Women's Worlds: Magazines and the Female Reader*, and has edited Delarivier Manley's *New Atalantis*. Her research and teaching interests lie in eighteenth-century literature and history, popular culture, and critical theory.

Clare Brant is a lecturer in English at King's College, London, and works on eighteenth-century literature, especially letters (both personal correspondence and epistolary fiction) and women's writing. She is currently working on a book on dialogues, and is also preparing a book on women and film with Diane Purkiss.

Hero Chalmers was a Senior Hulme Scholar at Brasenose College, Oxford, from 1987–91. She is currently completing a D.Phil. thesis on the construction of the feminine subject in women's printed writings of the later seventeenth century.

Helen Hackett is a lecturer in Renaissance literature at University College London. She was previously a Junior Research Fellow at Merton College, Oxford, where she completed a D.Phil. thesis on representations of Elizabeth I. She is currently engaged in further research on the relations between the 'cult' of Elizabeth and the cult of the Virgin Mary, and on Lady Mary Wroth's *Urania*.

Lorna Hutson is a lecturer in English at Queen Mary and Westfield College, University of London. She has recently published a study of Thomas Nashe, and is currently working on a study of plot, power and gender in the Renaissance.

Kate Lilley is a lecturer in English at the University of Sydney. She did her Ph.D. on masculine elegy (1987) at the University of London, and was then Junior Research Fellow at St Hilda's College, Oxford (1986–9), where she began working on gender and genre in seventeenth-century women's writing.

Bridget Orr is a lecturer in English at Auckland University. She has previously published on Katherine Mansfield and is currently working on the representation of race in the Restoration.

Diane Purkiss is a lecturer in English at the University of East Anglia. She has published articles on women prophets and women's postwar poetry, and has just completed a book on gender and politics in Milton and seventeenth-century women's writing. She is now working on an edition of Elizabeth Cary and Aemilia Lanyer, and is preparing a book on women and film with Clare Brant.

Sophie Tomlinson is a lecturer in English at Auckland University. Between 1986 and 1990 she was a graduate student at Cambridge University where she worked on a doctoral thesis examining figurations of female performance in English theatre and drama before the Restoration.

ACKNOWLEDGEMENTS

The editors are grateful to Helen Hackett, whose energy and enthusiasm were instrumental in initiating this project, and to Sophie Tomlinson for suggesting the main title and the epigraph. Ivan Dowling's scrupulous word processing, computing expertise and generous support and advice were invaluable throughout. Julia Briggs made helpful comments. We would also like to thank our editor Sue Roe for her confidence in, and our desk editor Jill Rawnsley for her help with, our project.

INTRODUCTION: MINDING THE STORY

Clare Brant and Diane Purkiss

This project originated from the exploration of historical and critical intersections concerning women of the early modern period staged in the Women, Text and History seminars which began in 1988 in Oxford. At those seminars, it became apparent that many of us were doing work which shared premises and problems: this book is a result.

Volumes of essays are expected to offer a rationale for themselves which goes beyond a historical account of their genesis in accidents of acquaintance between various members of academic communities. Yet a community of time and place among contributors may itself explain many of their common critical concerns, because ours is a world in which information, texts and arguments proliferate and circulate in abundance. Our ignorances derive from there being too much to absorb; the impossibility of knowing everything necessitates choices which shape as well as reflect our partialities. We know each other through personal links and the professionalized intimacy of reading and discussing each other's work, and in the mingling and exchange of our own stories, outlines of shared stories emerge – and outlines of difference too.

The synchronic narratives of women in the early modern period, however, are affected by divisions of class, geography and limited access to literacy and print, and by narrative paradigms which have an interest in reducing the complexity of women's lives and representations into a single story. Cultural similarity, then, is more likely to be managed with reference to diachronic continuity, so that women look back through history in order to negotiate speaking positions, be it of submission or resistance. But since women are cut off from their own history through exclusion from print culture and literary traditions, they cannot so easily

1

particularize a historical relation to the archetypes and myths by which representations of them as women are constructed. This limits the means by which they can unsettle such paradigms concerning themselves, but does not foreclose all strategies in exposing representations as constructions, not givens. A story can be unfixed by this act of telling: it may be disturbed in its re-creation precisely because the historical elisions which myths and other paradigms enact can be challenged by those whose actual historical diversity has been elided into totalized figures. Secondly, print's dialogue with oral culture makes it possible to talk about the circulation of stories and figures between orality and literacy; some forms of orality may present fewer barriers to women's entry. Stories representing gender are open to question on the grounds of the gender of the teller. The historical power of masculinity makes culturally sanctioned stories suspect; the gaps between events and discourses, between what women are and what they are made to be, set up both contradictions in discourse and literary possibilities of recognizing and resisting them. Since these contradictions and resistances permeate culture, they operate in women as well as men, as their non-written forms underlie texts through which they are expressed and contended.

Concerns of overdetermined narratives and the gendered politics of representation are exemplified by our epigraph:

> 'Tis true the first Lady had so little experience that she hearken'd to the persuasions of an Impertinent Dangler; and if you mind the story, he succeeded by persuadeing her that she was not so wise as she should be.[1]

Lady Mary Wortley Montagu points to women as vulnerable to discourse but central to its mediation. Textual attentiveness, or minding the story, exposes the concerns at the heart of discursive acts; Eve has to listen and be persuaded. The temptation is tempting because it offers her a new and more knowing position in discourse, a knowledge then denounced as transgressive because of her desire for it. But Montagu goes back beyond the figure of the sinful woman to critique discourse hostile to women which offers them illusory power, and makes that offer depend on an admission of their own inadequacy or lack – a lack strategically articulated for them by misogyny. Yet precisely because such invective exists to invent a lack in women, the story cannot deny it: an uneasy comedy allows Montagu both to claim and disclaim Eve.

2

Lady Mary minds a single story, the story of Eve. This is and is not Eve's own story; it is a story told by men about her and about all women, a story seductive in its collectivity, alienating in its negativity. As perhaps the major story Montagu knows about women, and certainly as the most recognizable, it makes the figure of Eve stand in for what is not available to Montagu politically: the conscious adoption of a position which speaks for a group of women or all women or a history of women. At the same time the story's ambivalence about women and its representation of masculine powers of control make it not a happy story. In Eden, a woman is already placed within an authoritative masculine discourse which is not hers, or in an ancillary position in which her sexuality will be used to disadvantage her. The trope of Eve acts as a synecdoche for all women, fixing them through singularity – a fixity reinforced by the story's focus on the created image with no mention of the image of the creator. In obstructing images of women as creators, the story, despite its enabling possibilities, adds to the difficulties and diffidence of women writers.

This book tells a different story, the story of women beginning to write different stories. The period it covers is a crux for feminist literary history as the first period in which one can point to the emergence of a large and diverse body of women's writing in English. But that body of texts cannot be detached from writings by men. Just as Montagu is caught in the story of Eve, forced to mind it, to bear it in mind, so women writing in the early modern period generally are not telling stories which belong to themselves alone, or can be marked by the storyteller as women's stories.

The present collection makes distinctions between the representation of women and women's writings in order to unsettle existing assumptions and disturb simple projections of their relations. The contributions on women's writing do not concern themselves with a search for women's 'private' or 'authentic' selves revealed in their writings; instead, they explore ways in which women's writings generate and negotiate speaking-positions in discourse. These contributions analyse how women writers can and do internalize and reproduce cultural restrictions and gender limitations; they also refuse simple valorizations of texts because they may have been written by a woman. As Diane Purkiss shows, writing which appears to celebrate women cannot be separated from masculine interests, and can covertly occupy a discursive space otherwise gendered as feminine. Her work marks a distance between representation and metaphor; referentiality and the trace of a historical female subject are evacuated from the discursive scene even as the associative links between women and disorder are reified. The contributions on women's representation map shifts and contradictions in discourses of sexual difference which parallel these negotiations, undoing the notion of a fixed and ahistorical patriarchy. Bridget Orr's chapter, for example, shows how the figure of the female body was implicated in political and class struggles. Other chapters investigate the contingency at different points of women's writing and the representation of women: Rosalind Ballaster's chapter, for example, explores how the construction of literary modes can be imaged through female seduction and vice versa, and Hero Chalmers shows how conflicting discourses of femininity make female identity fluctuate in both material and textual forms. Others engage with the overlap between questions of gender and of genre: Kate Lilley examines women's intervention in the genre of utopian writing, and Helen Hackett looks at their writing of romance in the context of gendered representations of that genre. The question of the publicity of supposedly private genres is reviewed in Clare Brant's examination of the interleaving of legal discourse and scandal, while Bridget Orr examines the place of the female body as site of conflict in overlapping discourses of pornography and cartography. Sophie Tomlinson demonstrates how female theatricality works both as a commentary on stage practices and a metaphor for writing which turns spectators into readers and back again. The unity of these contributions as a volume does not however arise from unifocal practice; sharing involves willingly bringing together different perspectives rather than a prior expectation that all will ultimately agree.

In part, the shared agendas of these works arises from an evolving response to the feminist critical movement of which the contributors are products. The implicit separatism of much of this kind of criticism was originally grounded in a general feminist politics of separation, and could be mapped without too much strain onto women's writings of the nineteenth and twentieth centuries.[2] Elaine Showalter's germinal essay, 'Towards a Feminist Poetics', bifurcated feminist criticism into 'the feminist critique' and 'gynocritics'; the former concerned with men's writings, the latter with women's.[3] Though Showalter admits the ultimate interdependence of the projects, her essay also assumes their provisional separability. Finding out how women write was conceived as tenable and desirable without touching the dubious doings of male writers. This stance was motivated by the political imperative to raise awareness of the large body of women's writing hitherto neglected by the academy; it was enabled by the so-called doctrine of separate spheres which was thought to be a major part of gendered ideology in white, western middle-class society. Leaving for others the question of whether that doctrine fully authorizes transhistorical assumptions about the workings of gender, some limitations of this methodology have become visible. These include its tendency to reify women's separation from the political and public spheres, the risk of essentializing woman as the always already given of the critical project, and the effect of ghettoizing women's writing critically and institutionally.

Another limitation of separatism, one which concerns us more directly here, is its limited applicability to the early modern period. Whereas earlier feminist critics writing on Charlotte Brontë and even Jane Austen could rewrite criticism by locating their texts in a self-conscious and named literary tradition of women's writings silenced or marginalized by the academy, this manoeuvre cannot be performed so easily for Aemilia Lanyer, Margaret Cavendish or even Laetitia Pilkington. Individual chapters in this volume make clear why not; generally, one can point to other factors which make inappropriate a simple backward extension of concepts developed in nineteenth- and twentieth-century texts. For one thing, gender constructs, like the English language itself, are not settled. The doctrine of separate spheres after all supposes an anterior practice of more mixed spheres. Without naïvely supposing we can reconstruct the past in full, or view it free from the effects of present ideologies operating upon critical subjects, it is necessary to acknowledge historical difference and attempt to articulate its differences without the cultural imperialism of assuming exact translation. For these reasons and others, we find the assumed continuities and correspondences of gynocritics troubling. This volume does recuperate women's writing, but it also seeks to bring that area of concern into apposition with more general concerns about the way literature, canonicity, theory and periodicity have been constructed by men and reconstructed by feminists working on men's texts.

Working in this area, we must be careful not to produce an equally proscriptive countercanon with its own totalizing laws, a risk particularly apparent in this period in the overproduction of anthologies of women's writing in comparison with the extremely minute number of editions of their texts made available.[4] Publishers must shoulder some of the blame for this, as any feminist who has tried to persuade them to publish an edition of any single work by a woman in the period covered by this volume could testify; they are currently far more willing to publish yet another essay collection on Shakespeare than an edition of, say, Margaret Cavendish. That is why this volume makes no pretence at coverage; it is not a synopsis of the main events (textual or otherwise) in gender and writing in the period named, but a series of local engagements with particular events which are not intended to be synecdochal of a complete narrative.

There is a real risk, as well, of producing a totalizing narrative which would cover over the differences among or within women in this period, as well as their differences from us. The process of identification implicit in much writing on women in the past can be useful as a strategy, minding the story by adopting it as our own. But it may also elide the specificity of oppression in eras other than our own. Differences of little significance to most contemporary feminists were of serious and divisive concern in the early modern period; religion is only the most obvious of these. We should also be wary of assuming that the same differences operated in the same way; the system by which both class and race were troped in the early modern period appears to have exerted different pressures and created different opportunities for resistance and improvisation. Nor should we overlook Teresa de Lauretis's valuable foregrounding of the differences *within* women. She points out that the consequences of interpellation by ideology may be contradiction, schism and dispersal rather than a single subject which can be named as a construction.[5] As both Hero Chalmers and Rosalind Ballaster show in different ways, the female subject in the early modern period may be less a stable and self-evident identity than the self-conscious staging or negotiation of certain contradictory cultural codes or narratives. Lorna Hutson uncovers the way in which the feminine becomes a dark space to be traversed in the production of masculine virtue through writing, disclosed as a rhetorical problem for the woman writer and her figuration of the woman recipient. The concept of rhetoric as itself a metaphor is explored by Bridget Orr; women as speaking subjects become the vehicle for voicing concerns ungendered by their projection through a feminine body.

6

Taken together, these works address the general failure of main/malestream criticism and theory to respond to feminist attempts to uncover the writings of early modern women. In this respect the new historicism has been if anything worse than the old because of its marked tendency to prefer canonical texts to non-canonical. In her chapter on female utopias and genre theory, Kate Lilley points out that utopian genre criticism and feminist writings have never been brought into apposition; genre criticism obliterates the traces of feminist literary discoveries. In an unintentionally revealing passage in a polemic otherwise sympathetic to feminism, Walter Cohen accepts Showalter's bifurcation of feminist studies, and remarks that feminists doing gynocritics can have little to say to those working on Shakespeare, who can stick with confidence to the feminist critique.[6] Lorna Hutson's chapter in this volume suggests that Cohen's assumption is incorrect; reading the work of women writers over and against the work of Shakespeare can unsettle cherished certitudes about his universality and its basis, while an attentive rereading of Shakespeare may form a pretext for placing the writings of women. Similarly, Clare Brant's chapter shows how from a point of view informed by feminist cultural studies, the cherished Augustan 'balance' of Pope's bathos reads socially and not universally, incidentally showing that a canonical author does not have to be centre-stage to be reviewed.

The careful formulation of the arguments in this volume struggles to resist a tendency to make canonical texts function as familiar backgrounds against which the new can be provocatively staged. The point here is not to add women to an existing state of affairs as a kind of optional extra, but to suggest that beginning to explore this entire period through women's writing as well as men's may undo some of the narratives and assumptions on which existing criticism depends. However, chiastic formulations of production and consumption can cover for a failure to address the theoretical dilemmas that a study of women's writing in this period would pose. If we are to place women's writings as something other than either automatic opposites to or simple receptacles for a gender ideology which in these narratives becomes reified as single and stable, then we must begin to try to theorize new ways to understand the workings of gendered ideology and gendered subjects. The contributions to this volume document a variety of possible points of intervention by women in the gendered discourses of early modern England rather than offering any overarching single answer.

Many of the chapters cover texts which it is tempting to describe as marginal. But that description, besides obliquely authorizing other texts and contexts as central, imposes a kind of quiescence upon them, whereas many of these texts are bizarre, startling, *ex*centric in a manner which replaces the very notion of a centre. In the case of what we usually blandly call pamphlets, we signify by that name the category's ephemerality and consequent exclusion from the timelessness of the literary. Merely by assigning them to this category, we rob them of their power to surprise us, so that their effects can only be topical in the moment of their production, and only relevant to texts within that designation. By disclosing these texts in our own differently politicized context they can be returned to a provocative topicality. Diane Purkiss shows how these two kinds of curiousness can be coextensive in relation to material whose colour has hitherto been taken simply as local.

The essays stage the surprises of their texts in various ways which then produce surprises of their own. Some take together texts of different genre or different status within the institution, revealing unexpected similarities: a poem, a chiliastic utopia, a travel narrative and a polemic on women's education are collocated and show how the boundaries of genre shift when viewed through gender. The botanically complex labels assigned by literary critics to particular kinds of text do little justice to the extraordinary power of those texts which resist such taxonomies, for such texts *remain* unsettlingly in-between, a ceaseless trouble to categorical structures, not excluding feminist ones. Nevertheless, the surprises delivered here are not always pleasurable: the overlap between the pornographic and the cartographic may trouble our own attempts at critical mapmaking, for example, while the return of misogynies to the critical gaze may exert other political pressures.

Merely by writing about texts which are not so much marginal as altogether outside many existing hierarchical schema, this volume necessarily challenges notions of which texts might seem suitable objects of critical attention. We are not making a collective claim for the expansion of the canon on evaluative grounds, but displaying the diversity of discursive resources excluded by the canon. Many of the texts discussed here resist assimilation to the canon or even to the literary, acting instead as disruptive forces which expose the stories told about gender by an interpretative community willing to consult only the canonical as open to question. Yet these contributions may also surprise in their refusal to reify distinctions between high and

8

popular culture, showing the problematics of both terms both in relation to history and in relation to gender.

Using various aids, including theories of genre, the visual, theatrical relations, legal disclosure and other discourses, the individual chapters stage new agendas, not to be confused with the endless atomizations favoured by postmodernism. The most obvious is the dissolution of familiar period boundaries. Rereadings within usual period boundaries tend to be welcomed, whereas those which cut across them unsettle academic specialities and market divisions. The seventeenth century seems a time zone particularly open to disjunctive perspectives; seen from the Renaissance end it reads as a mass of religious and political writing, especially poetry, while seen from the eighteenth century it offers antecedents of drama and prose fiction. Retrospection and anticipation pass like proverbial ships in the night. The dates we have chosen to mark the boundaries of this volume indicate the period in which women's literary production comes fully on stream and responses to it are correspondingly active. But though women's increased entry into print provides a legitimate rationale, several points need to be made. The first is that more does not necessarily mean better. Feminist criticism sometimes seems to have to adopt one of two excuses for its material: that of quantity (all these writers we never knew about) or anteriority (the first woman to write this or thus). This turns the critic into either a Columbus figure, moving through new worlds, or a Scott figure, planting flags in a polar wilderness. We have no wish to be either, for to pose as pioneers would erase the traces of those who have marked the route for us; this collection and all its contributors are part of a general feminist project to reshape perceptions of the early modern period by replacing women in it.[7] Women are always part of a culture, including points at which they are least visible, for how did they come to be made invisible? Second, although print culture is the prime medium by which critics gain access to the past, we do not see print as the past's exclusive *telos*. Publication is but one kind of publicity, and several contributors discuss other forms of self-publicizing which offered equally attractive, and in some cases more accessible, forms. Bodies, theatres, courts and courtrooms could all function as symbolic sites of display. However much more women were writing and publishing, print culture does not create a community so long as men's greater economic power, expressed in patronage and purchasing, limited women's access to it. Market conditions for print culture limit its advantages for women. Our third qualification concerning a teleology of print is that the move from orality to literacy is not a single one, just as culture is more than print culture. Several chapters address other cultural forms, particularly areas of performance, through which women are visible as historical agents and speaking subjects. In supplying material and discursive contexts for texts discussed, the chapters do not reproduce the usual story of foreground and background, because that tends to suggest that a culture is stable and women are not. History is often conflated with the past, the material contexts in which stories are shaped and gendered. But a stricter sense of history would define it as the written residue of the past, and its textual construction. This definition makes texts into histories and thereby allows historical readings to inform critical ones, and vice versa.

None the less, print is important to the critical community, which is constructed around a knowledge of texts, and the texts discussed in this volume are largely absent from current interpretations. As pressures increase on academics to publish more and more, specializations narrow and superficialities spread, critical interventions are simplified into new 'isms' for quicker assimilation. In this period of academic contraction and uncertain employment, both young and established scholars have been affected by reduced funding and market pressures to conform, even in the structuring of their dissent. On the other hand, less time to read may mean more dependence on oral communiqués. Since texts and contexts become part of interpretative communities by being talked about, this volume's concern for the orality within literacy may reflect forces acting on criticism's own history.

Writers of introductions traditionally pay tribute to fellow scholars for fruitful discussions and helpful comments; academic books are themselves an instance of how a text often veils the non-textual discourses which play an important part in its formation. The impact of primary and critical texts alike is affected by how and how much each is talked about, and the terms of those discussions are something which an introduction tries to address. But in its social sense, an introduction is a protocol by which interactions are formally initiated. An introduction between people facilitates conversation: it enables opinions to be formed, debates to take place and ideas to be exchanged. Though this introduction performs the literary equivalent of this social move, we hope that the whole book will act as an introduction, leading to newly informed discussion and newly minded stories.

NOTES

1 Lady Mary Wortley Montagu, *Essays and Poems and Simplicity, A Comedy*, ed. Robert Halsband and Isobel Grundy, Oxford, Clarendon, 1977, p. 133.

2 Recently, those who work on these later periods have initiated the interrogation of a simplistic epistemological separatism; for different approaches to the problem on the terrain of the nineteenth century, see Catherine Gallagher, *The Industrial Reformation of English Fiction*, Chicago, University of Chicago Press, 1985; Nancy Armstrong, *Desire and Domestic Fiction*, New York, Oxford University Press, 1987; Mary Poovey, *Uneven Developments: The Ideological Work of Gender in Mid-Victorian England*, London, Virago, 1988.

3 Elaine Showalter, 'Towards a Feminist Poetics', in Mary Jacobus (ed.), *Women Writing and Writing About Women*, London, Croom Helm, 1979, pp. 22–41. In some ways we regret taking Showalter to be synecdochal of this or that trend in feminism, a role she plays rather too often.

4 Only three of the chapters in this volume are able to draw on published editions of the women's writings they discuss. The Brown University computerization project may ultimately make the texts of women writers more freely available (and may represent the future for academic texts in any case in an age of rising publication costs) but it will not confer on the authors the prestige of a codex, and will effectively confine their consumption completely to the academy. Anthologies tend to favour texts like lyric poems; they tend not to favour the writings of, say, women prophets, though this genre was, as Kate Lilley remarks in chapter 4 of this volume, one of the major points of entry for women writers into the discourses of politics and religion in the seventeenth century. For an exception, see Elspeth Graham, Hilary Hinds, Elaine Hobby and Helen Wilcox (eds), *Her Own Life: Autobiographical Writings by Seventeenth-Century Englishwomen*, London, Routledge, 1989.

5 Teresa de Lauretis, 'Feminist Studies/Critical Studies: Issues, Terms and Contexts', in Teresa de Lauretis (ed.), *Feminist Studies/Critical Studies*, London, Macmillan, 1986, pp. 9–12. See also Denise Riley, *'Am I That Name?' Feminism and the Category of 'Women' in History*, London, Macmillan, 1988.

6 Walter Cohen, 'Political Criticism of Shakespeare', in Jean E. Howard and Marion F. O' Connor (eds), *Shakespeare Reproduced: The Text in History and Ideology*, London, Methuen, 1987, p. 22.

7 Some of the recent publications which have marked out the spaces we also traverse include Margaret W. Ferguson, Maureen Quilligan and Nancy J. Vickers (eds), *Rewriting the Renaissance: The Discourses of Sexual Difference in Early Modern Europe*, Chicago, University of Chicago Press, 1986; Mary Beth Rose (ed.), *Women in the Middle Ages*

and the Renaissance: Literary and Historical Perspectives, Syracuse, NY, Syracuse University Press, 1986; Anne M. Haselkorn and Betty S. Travitsky (eds), *The Renaissance Englishwoman in Print; Counterbalancing the Canon*, Amherst, Massachusetts University Press, 1989; Laura Brown and Felicity A. Nussbaum (eds), *The New Eighteenth Century*, London and New York, Methuen, 1987; Elaine Hobby, *Virtue of Necessity. English Women's Writing 1649–88*, London, Virago, 1988; Janet Todd, *The Sign of Angellica: Women, Writing and Fiction 1660–1800*, London, Virago, 1989.

1

WHY THE LADY'S EYES ARE NOTHING LIKE THE SUN

Lorna Hutson

Everybody who knows anything about Aemilia Lanyer, author of the first original poem by a woman to be published in the seventeenth century, knows that she had black eyes, black hair and a dark past. Her poems are only available to modern readers in complete form in A.L. Rowse's edition which advertises them as *The Poems of Shakespeare's Dark Lady* and prefaces them with pages of repetitive prose, the gist of which is to insist on reading the text, 'rampant feminism' and all, as the Dark Lady's revenge:

> It is obvious that something personal had aroused her anger. Shakespeare's Sonnets had been published, though not by him, in 1609, with their unforgettable portrait of the woman who had driven him 'frantic-mad', dark and musical, tyrannical and temperamental, promiscuous and false, . . . The portrait was defamatory enough. The very next year, 1610, her book was announced and in 1611 published.[1]

For all that he values the text as enabling us to 'read the character of Shakespeare's Dark Lady at last', however, Rowse proves susceptible to the charms of Lanyer's verse. The bits he likes best are, tellingly enough, reminiscent of Shakespeare. He quotes, for example, from Lanyer's exhortation to Anne Clifford to internalize the knowledge of Christ disclosed in the text of her poem: 'Yet lodge him in the closet of your heart,/Whose worth is more than can be shew'd by Art.'[2] In these lines, Rowse contends, we hear the unmistakable accents, and recall the *Sonnets*, where the Bard writes of locking the image of his beloved in his chest.[3] I mention this not so much to argue with the implication of Shakespeare's influence, as to instance the extent to which our understanding of the discursive medium in

13

which sixteenth- and seventeenth-century writers worked is filtered through our familiarity with Shakespeare's deployment of its most fundamental metaphors. It will be one purpose of this chapter to suggest that this sense of familiarity obscures from us the implication of these very metaphors in the humanist project of relocating masculine virtue and honour in the power to authorize meaning. Read in this context, Lanyer's attempt to produce, from a medium so heavily invested in the articulation of masculine virtue, a poem which celebrates woman as an effective reader and agent, rather than offering her as a dark secret to be disclosed, becomes the subject of *Salve Deus, Rex Judeorum*.

First, however, to grapple with the issue of Lanyer's credibility as a poet. Refutations of Rowse's theory mostly turn on the paucity of evidence for positing Lanyer as Shakespeare's mistress; no-one denies that she was promiscuous, but as Samuel Schoenbaum has reminded us, there were no end of promiscuous women about in Elizabethan London. Besides, Schoenbaum argued, we must remember that the *Sonnets* are not an autobiography but a system of moral and poetic meaning: 'the opposition between Fair Youth and Dark Lady' needs no reference to a particular woman to explicate it, he concluded, for it is, 'perfectly comprehensible in terms of moral and poetic symbolism'.[4]

Now, a 'moral and poetic symbolism' that is 'perfectly comprehensible' is one which is still *working*, still creating an evaluative language in which to articulate experience and authorize desire. Yet why should the antithesis between Fair Youth and Dark Lady recommend itself thus as a 'natural' symbolism? Critics of the *Sonnets* make us ashamed to ask such a naïve question. They either read the moral evaluation of the antithesis as referring to the conduct of particular individuals known to Shakespeare, or exploit its signifying potential to consider larger issues, such as the possibility of integrity in poetic representation. This latter position is represented by John Kerrigan's sophisticated introduction to the Penguin edition of the *Sonnets*. For Kerrigan, the *Sonnets* are largely concerned with the unattainable goal of a poetic reproduction that would remain faithful to its object. This involves the apparent rejection of metaphor and comparison, principal devices of sonnet rhetoric. 'Shakespeare', he claims, intriguingly, 'exposes the competitive roots of similitude.'[5] He goes on to explain that similitude is an inherently competitive figure of speech because, in making a topic known to us by analogy with things conceded to be of value (as hair is likened to gold or lips to rubies) similitude implies that value itself is merely a discursive effect, a 'painted beauty'. What is more, similitude transforms its topic into the site of an implied rivalry between author and reader over the concession of value and credibility. Shakespeare, concludes Kerrigan, refuses to embroil his beloved in this invidious marketplace of ingenuity, and aims at a text that is stripped of metaphor. However, one point which this attractive thesis overlooks should help us to understand why, in spite of Schoenbaum's easy dismissal of Rowse's identification of Lanyer as the 'original' Dark Lady, there can be no such easy dismissal of the implications of the 'Dark Lady' symbolism for our reading of Lanyer's text. The point is this: Shakespeare's *Sonnets*, as Kerrigan has argued, achieve their effect of sincerity by discrediting the operations of similitude. But they do so by figuring their own negotiation of value through similitude as the 'dark' or 'black' space of the sonnet mistress, whose value is always conferred, never intrinsic. If we accept this as a symbolism of value, then we are telling the old story of truth's betrayal by metaphor in the form of another old story: the betrayal of a masculine 'marriage of true minds' by the bodily female. This is the story towards which Kerrigan's criticism tends, with its suggestion that Shakespeare's text can reproduce the 'truth' of its relation to a masculine subject. Of sonnet 105, where Shakespeare rejects comparison ('leaves out difference') for identity, with the repetition of the refrain 'Fair, kind and true', Kerrigan writes, 'The text is stripped of metaphor, there are no false comparisons. . . . The friend is coextensive with the text; he really is "all" its "argument".'[6] This ignores a sly subtext of sexual difference; if the usual female friend were to be praised for being 'kind', then she would certainly need a lot of false painting if she were to continue 'fair', let alone 'true'. So the scrupulous rejection of comparison that Kerrigan reads as a quest for integrity is actually an exposition of the extent to which the evaluative power of comparison depends on the mobilization and concealment of a single hierarchical opposition – in this case, that of gender.

The association of the impure motives of a comparative rhetoric, a rhetoric of praise, with the inherent 'falsehood' of woman is so germane to our making sense of Renaissance texts that we should not be surprised to find it informing critical assessment of a real woman poet of the Renaissance. Thus we find that when woman scholars cease to celebrate Lanyer simply for managing to *be* a woman and a poet all at once, their comments on her text display a tendency to account for its embarrassing length, inappropriateness and apparent sycophancy by referring to the lady's notorious past. Thus, Muriel Bradbrook sums Lanyer up scathingly:

> To choose the subject of the Crucifixion and then surround it with several times its own bulk in carefully graded verses of adulation to various ladies, beginning with the Queen – and even interrupting the sacred narrative to bob a curtsey to the Countess of Cumberland, one of the richest women in England, seems to me very practical politics for an ex-mistress of the Lord Hunsden . . . I doubt if 'feminism' or the defence of women was disinterested here.[7]

Barbara Lewalski, by contrast, is persuaded of the sincerity of Lanyer's feminism, but has doubts about her religious conviction:

> Given Lanyer's questionable past, her evident concern to find patronage, and her continuing focus on women, contemporary and biblical, we might be tempted to suppose that the ostensible religious subject of the title poem, Christ's Passion, simply provides a thin veneer for a subversive feminist statement.[8]

The assumption is that a 'true' poem should not be making use of patronage relations, or of a rhetoric of praise; to do so is to betray a dark want of 'disinterestedness' which is in turn associated with a want of moral integrity, or chastity. Actually, Renaissance literary theory assumes the opposite: poetic discourse is never disinterested, but rather seeks to authenticate itself through the devices of rhetoric and the relations of patronage. Yet, as we have seen, our familiarity with a text like Shakespeare's *Sonnets*, which makes a theme of disavowing both these for a more inward source of authenticity, tempts us into easy swipes against the sycophancy of poets who rely on 'rhetoric'. Take sonnet 82, for example, where Shakespeare laments that his true friend should prefer the impurely motivated hyperbole of rival poets to his own plain-speaking sincerity:

> I grant thou were not married to my Muse
> And therefore maiest without attaint ore-looke
> The dedicated words which writers vse
> Of their faire subiect, blessing euery booke.
> Thou art as faire in knowledge as in hew,
> Finding thy worth a limmit past my praise,
> And therefore art inforc't to seeke anew,
> Some fresher stampe of the time bettering dayes.
> And do so loue, yet when they haue deuisde,
> What strained touches Rhethoricke can lend,
> Thou truly faire, wert truly simpathizde,
> In true plaine words, by thy true telling friend.
>   And their grosse painting might be better vs'd
>   Where cheeks need blood, in thee it is abus'd.[9]

I suggested that the naturalness of Shakespeare's *Sonnets* (the comprehensibility of their moral symbolism) depended on the fact that by rejecting as 'false' and 'superficial' the analogical techniques normally used in sonnets, they managed to persuade us of the possibility of a love and a poetry that might remain true to its subject. The possibility is so congenial to our way of thinking that we scarcely feel the need to gloss it, but how is it constructed? Here, in sonnet 82, the subject is described as being 'as faire in knowledge as in hew', so that his inward beauty is identified as a kind of connoisseurship, a capacity to value and to validate the text as a cultural artefact. And this is typical of the beauty ascribed to him. For though we tend to read the *Sonnets* as if they were explorative of an emotional relation between the poet and his masculine subject, an equally prominent feature is the text's exploration of an *interpretative* and *mutually authenticating* relation between the *text* and its *subject*. Indeed, the *Sonnets* enable us to experience the inward beauty of intellectual discrimination which enables the friend – 'as faire in knowledge as in hew' – to judge the text, as itself an effect of the text. In the play of antitheses, we glimpse this authenticating, discriminating subject, the 'friend', in the process of being made up out of a comparative rhetoric which ambiguously privileges the contingencies of gender, of noble birth and a peculiarly 'economic' attitude to the text which is foreign to our assumptions about the purpose of reading. For example: the

17

phrase 'thou art as faire in knowledge as in hew' refers us back to Shakespeare's introduction of this unusual archaism in sonnet 20, where it disturbingly establishes the worth of a masculine as opposed to feminine poetic subject. The colours in the face of the 'Master-Mistres' are apparently authentic because he is 'a man in hew all *Hews* in his controwling'. Here 'hews' means colours in the sense of complexion, but it also bears reading in a rhetorical sense as well, with colours being the equivalent of discursive 'proofs', 'reasons' or 'arguments' for action.[10] 'All *Hews* in his controwling' thus indicates the reader's specifically masculine relation to the text, in which, as he reads, he discovers or 'invents' a store of resources for his own future uses in improvisation, thereby increasing his power to produce emotionally compelling discourse and to control its colours. The relation between masculine author and masculine patron/reader emerges as inherently 'virtuous' (in the Renaissance sense of conducive to good action, rather than to theoretical speculation on the nature of good) by implicit comparison with the relation between masculine author and feminine pretext/reader, since the usual pretext of Petrarchan discourse – love for a woman – can only generate a 'face' or textual surface of rhetorical colours to be exploited by men. For, of course, it was only for men that Renaissance humanism identified the interpretative practices of reading with the prudence, or practical reason, which enables deliberation about action in political life. Only for men could the activity of reading be expected to increase the power to act and speak in emergency, to discover in the emergent moment an argument, a 'colour' for one's own uses.[11] So, since only a man can effectively reproduce from a discourse which celebrates beauty, this power of discursive reproduction becomes his intrinsic beauty, and only a man can therefore be 'truly' beautiful. The sonnet puts this in a cleverly 'moronic' or oxymoronic fashion: only a man can have 'a Womans face with natures owne hand painted'. The oxymoron is developed in the following sonnet, where the ambition to write 'truly' of a masculine beloved is defined against the marketplace comparisons of the poet 'Stird by a painted beauty to his verse' (21.2). All this, of course, is highly ambivalent, since the location of his 'truth' in a capacity to reproduce colours implies (perhaps through a pun on 'hues' and 'use') that the masculine 'truth' which distinguishes itself from feminine 'paintedness' is that eloquence which 'heauen it selfe for ornament doth vse' (21.3).

However, the ascription of authenticity to the friend as a reader engaged in producing an inner self through the rhetorical 'finding out' or 'invention' of the text's colours for his own future hews/uses competes with his ascription of authenticating power as a patron. In sonnet 82, the suggestion of altitude in 'ore-looke' positions him less as a reader engaged in inventing discourse than as a nobleman, who, in the words of Sir Thomas Elyot, should be 'set in a more highe place' where he may 'se and also be sene' by 'the beames of his excellent witte, shewed through the glasse of auctorite' (the 'authority' or 'authorship' of policy making through patronage).[12] Again, in sonnet 20, the authority of the reader-as-patron to irradiate his image in the text is figured as exclusively masculine; the friend has a brighter, truer eye than any woman, an eye that is like the sun, 'Gilding the object where-vpon it gazeth'. Thus, the friend's ability to authenticate and enlarge the text's sphere of influence, figured in his gilding eye and validating hue, sceptically reveals the notion of man's 'truth' or his authentic inner nature, to consist in the privileging of a certain kind of discursive economy. Throughout the *Sonnets* 'truth' and 'inward worth' are articulated as the generative capacity of the text's subject to forestall the dissipation of his own loveliness. What begins as a discourse of natural economy or husbandry – for the first seventeen sonnets the friend is playfully urged to convert his fading beauty to generative 'store' by begetting a son – is apparently superseded by the reproductive economy of the sonnet form itself, which enacts the conversion of beauty into discursive 'store'. This latter is an *economy* precisely because it articulates the pleasurable encounter with the text, the moment of interpretation, as the assimilation of potential for the production of discourse which will stimulate others to take similar pleasure in understanding. If we think of reading in humanist terms as an exercise of the interpretative potential of the text, preparing for the discovery of interpretative potential in practical situations requiring decisive action, then the economy celebrated by the *Sonnets* could be referred to as an economy of 'interpretative power' or 'interpretative virtue'. In his imaging of this economy, Shakespeare conflates a celebration of the friend as inspiration, a storehouse of *copia* or figurative potential for future readers, with a celebration of the friend as exclusive reader, whose invention of colours in the text will furnish him inwardly. Both these concepts derive from humanist ideals about the capacity of published discourse to bring about social change by fostering the political and discursive skills of the nobility, but Shakespeare's comparative rhetoric subverts the humanist fiction of author and patron as authenticating one another in a relation of pure interpretative increase, a pure reproduction of each other's inward worth. The inward worth which did not need painting is revealed to inhere not in the interpretative relation, the encounter with the text, but in the husbandry which appeared to have been superseded, the lines of life which produce noble blood: 'And their grosse painting might be better v'sd,/ Where cheeks need blood' (82.13–14).

From this rather protracted reading of the *Sonnets* we can begin, I think, to see why it is misleading to come to Lanyer's text with the preconception that a poet's sincerity towards his or her subject demands a 'disinterested' rejection of epideictic rhetoric, or a disavowal of dependency on the patron-as-reader. The *Sonnets* play out the moral implications of the assumption, built into humanist claims for the interpretative virtue of analogical rhetoric,[13] that things can only be made known in discourse by being displayed and praised (the very word 'epideictic' means 'adapted for display') so that 'patron' and 'compare' necessarily evaluate or 'authorize' one another. For the humanists, knowledge was not thought of as certain or objective; knowledge was only what was probable, what might be proved in the quasi-forensic and epideictic disclosure of a topic through comparison, simile or analogy, a process which often destabilized itself in an oscillation between hyperbolic and ironic effects. This process of authentication was spoken of as a disclosure or a discovery or invention of what had been hidden; a topic was unfolded to be beheld by the interpreting eye.[14] The beholder thus exercised virtue as a medium of knowledge, and the patron, in his exalted position as potential governor of society, exercised more than most, having eyes like the sun, to bring knowledge to the inferior sight of others.[15]

But could a woman patron, on these terms, have eyes like the sun? Could she gild the discourse that claimed to be a mirror of her virtue by inventing its colours for her own occasions, occasions on which she might speak or act to effect? Shakespeare's text would seem to imply not. Yet Lanyer makes extensive use of this trope in nearly all of her nine dedicatory poems,[16] beginning with a request that the Queen should 'Looke in this Mirrour of a worthy Mind' (p. 42). If, she goes on, the Princess Elizabeth should also deign to lend the text the credibility of an appreciative reading, 'Then shall I thinke my Glasse a glorious Skie,/When two such glittring Suns at once appeare' (p. 44). This is perhaps the moment to point out that Lanyer's poetic project is much more rigorously conceived than it has been represented as being. For it is not that she wrote a narrative of Christ and absentmindedly kept apostrophizing the Countess of Cumberland because she could not keep her mind off the richest woman in England. Her subject, like that of Shakespeare in the *Sonnets*, is reflexive; it is the reading subject, the encounter of the patron's mind with the text, which is celebrated as a textual resource. Lanyer's poem sets itself out to unfold or prove the interpretative virtue of Margaret Clifford's mind through a dramatizing of the female recognition of Christ in the historical moment of his Passion. Hence it is that the narrative of the Passion acquires the status of a rhetorical 'proof', and the argument of the whole is the 'Mirrour of a worthy Mind'. But there are difficulties with the metaphor. For a female author cannot mirror the virtue of a female patron if the space of the gilding, mutually authenticating gaze (the space in which the virtue of the encounter between text and mind is tried and proved) is actually a *homosocial* space – a space of discursive and political opportunity conceivable only between men.[17] I am not trying to say that there were no women patrons in Protestant-humanist England; of course there were, and it has been convincingly argued that Protestant-humanism, with its emphasis on the reformation of society through the education of its princes and the dissemination of texts on rhetoric, marriage and the reformed religion, actually depended on the intellectual participation of women patrons.[18] But the crucial issue here, I think, is the way in which such intellectual participation was assimilated to a masculine monopoly of interpretative increase. Lewalski observes that Lanyer's dedications to women linked through kinship or marriage to the Protestant Dudley faction celebrate 'the descent of virtue in the female line, from virtuous mothers to daughters'.[19] But if the author/text/patron relation which I have been outlining had any cultural significance, then the trouble with Protestant-humanist lines – whether of lineage reproduction or of textual production – is that the female virtue they articulate is assimilable to the masculine economy of interpretative virtue only in terms of chastity – the very virtue that would exclude and discredit Lanyer's text, 'given', as Lewalski says, 'her questionable past'.

Lanyer's poem seems to acknowledge some reservation about its own procedures in its opening, for having announced that her task will be to pen the praise of her patron, Margaret Clifford, the author immediately asks pardon for deferring a poem in praise of the estate of Cookham, which she apparently promised the Countess. Lewalski reads this as an excuse to force a much more substantial poem on the unwilling and unsuspecting Countess,[20] but what is intriguing is the care Lanyer takes, in her apology, to represent the suitability of the absent poem to the rhetorical task she has in hand:

> And pardon (Madame) though I do not write
> Those praisefull lines of that delightfull place
> As you commaunded me in that faire night,
> When shining *Phoebe* gave so great a grace,
> Presenting *Paradice* to your sweet sight,
> Unfolding all the beauty of her face
> > With pleasant groves, hills, walks, and stately trees,
> > Which pleasures with retired minds agrees.
>
> Whose Eagles eyes behold the glorious Sunne
> Of th'all-creating Providence, reflecting
> His blessed beames on all by him begunne;
> Increasing, strengthening, guiding and directing
> All worldly creatures their due course to runne,
> Unto his powrefull pleasure all subjecting:
> > And thou (deere Ladie) by his speciall grace,
> > In these his creatures dost behold his face. (pp. 79–80)

As it happens, this is not at all like the country house poem which Lanyer eventually offers; but what we have here is a deliberate and careful sketch of a rhetorical mode of proceeding which will not be followed. For if the process of making known in language involves the finding out of things by analogy, then the virtue of Margaret Clifford's mind, her capacity to know God, might well have been set forth as a progress of analogical discovery through the estate, which figures the natural economy of Providence as visible beauty. Lanyer expresses the Countess's power to know both as the ability to sustain the utter radiance of full, timeless disclosure (the 'Eagles eye' of the retired mind which is able to behold the 'glorious Sunne' of Providence) while at the same time rendering the temporal process of mediation, the work of interpretation, as the unfolding of an analogical discourse. What makes the incomprehensible radiance of the 'all-creating Providence' a *face* that can be beheld are 'these his creatures', disclosed, in the moment of the poem's inception, before the eyes of the Countess by the light of the moon, 'Presenting *Paradice* to your sweet sight,/ Unfolding all the beauty of her face'. The operation of the moonlight thus establishes a model for the 'praisefull lines' which, by disclosing the estate's loveliness, would reflect the Countess's interpretative virtue or 'inward worth', admirably combining a fulfilment of her patron's request with Lanyer's prescription of the poem as the 'Mirrour of a worthy Mind'. But such a method would tend to the articulation of Clifford's interpretative virtue as an effect of her position within the estate and, in unfolding the estate as a topic of praise, might compromise that virtue by discovering it as a form of 'beauty'.

Lanyer's poem repeatedly impedes its own forward movement with hesitations of this kind. These may be read, I suggest, as attempts to avoid being caught up in a discursive economy that has an interest in gendering as 'female' certain weak points in its projection of an ideally productive political community. The ideal of altruistic productivity, directed towards the profit of the political community, is implicit in humanist methods of education, and in the prominence of 'intelligence gathering' or 'facilitating' as a form taken by patron–client relations in the sixteenth century.[21] The discourse in which this ideal is articulated enjoins men to form relations of interpretative increase for the good of the commonweal. Through these relations, masculine minds become 'treasure houses' or exchanges for the profit of the commonweal. However, as such patron–client relations cannot be forged without the competitive self-advertising that an open market of intellectual ability demands, the altruistic ideal accommodates itself uneasily to an older conceptual model of patronage as 'love' due to lord and kin, and accordingly articulates meritocratic competition as an unspecified 'betrayal' by a 'friend'. But how does this betrayal come to be figured as transgression of the female body? While a full answer would have to go beyond the scope of this chapter, something can be achieved by interrogating, once again, the assumptions behind the humanist metaphor of the text as a mirror for princes. Underlying the metaphor is the classical conception (deriving from Seneca among others) of knowledge as the imitation and mastery of *auctores*.[22] However, this notion was adapted to the humanist enterprise of social reformation through print culture by approximating the idea of the text's circulation to the classical notion of the governor's charismatic and exemplary power.

Thus, as we saw, reforming discourse tends to blur the distinction between the author and the authorizer of social change, allowing the author to claim the power to fashion the nobleman by creating in him interpretative resources which he could not previously command, while the nobleman, being visible and effective in office, could claim the capacity to realize the effects of his reading by conducting affairs with a foresight and eloquence that would move others to imitate him. The theory, then, was that as the patron was modelled on the text, so society modelled itself on the patron or 'pattern' of behaviour. In Elizabethan England it was a peculiar feature of this discourse that the virtue of 'pattern-age' might be ascribed to gentlemen rather than to the prince, since the monarch was, after all, a woman. So Lawrence Humphrey in his reforming book *Of Nobilitye* (1563), after acknowledging God's providence in restoring religion through so weak a vehicle as her Majesty, explains that he is addressing his text to the gentlemen of the Inner Temple because they are more sun-like by virtue of having more contact with more people. Princes 'haue small trafficke with the common people', writes Humphrey, but gentlemen, like licensed texts which 'frely roame and wander eche where', are 'cleare and bryghte, on whom all mens eyes and countenances gaze'; at the other extreme, the common people themselves, 'styll lurke in darkenes, nor almost se anye, nor are seene of others'.23 So gentlemen, the ideal media of imitation, go about, mirroring one another in their 'traffic', as if their encounters took place in a purely interpretative economy, something like the one Jonson describes in the *Epigrams*, where virtuous men bond by 'understanding' and 'knowing' one another like texts:

> When I would know thee, Goodyere, my thought looks
> Upon thy well-made choice of friends and books;
> Then I do love thee, and behold thy ends
> In making thy friends books, and thy books, friends.24

But of what nature are these social encounters, these mutual mediations of knowledge, that make them so productive? The demonized Other of this discourse, as we know from Jonson's *Epigrams*, is the unproductive circulator, the plagiarist, the gamester, the poet-ape or the inactive lord buried in flesh.25 The space in which masculine virtue is proved, then, would seem to be at the nexus of sociability and textual encounter – the truly virtuous man is he who has internalized the power to organize and produce a convincing discourse and can, as Jonson says, 'know' his 'ends', that is, recognize and exploit a social encounter as the occasion of discourse (the 'colour' or the beauty of an opportunity recognized in the discursive moment), or as the space in which to assimilate resources, to 'look with thought' upon the discourse and behaviour of another man. However, in a society where privilege and preferment were theoretically obtained by the demonstration of this virtue, the space of its proof (for example, the published text with its 'dedicated words') was traversed by a gaze not only of cognition and authentication, but also of emulative rivalry and competition. Giles Fletcher the Elder dedicated his sonnet sequence *Licia* to the Lady Mollineux, but prefaced it with an apologia which justifies the publication of such an idle proof of wit on the grounds that such exercises distinguish gentlemen. Accordingly, gentlemen readers are at liberty to construe 'Licia' herself as Lady Mollineux, or as the 'discipline' of learning essential to composition. The crucial process of reflection here, then, is not the textual mirroring of the lover in his lady's eyes, but the mirroring of the published text – proof of the discriminating, interpretative power that distinguishes Fletcher as a gentleman – in the evaluating eyes of gentlemen readers. This has unfortunate consequences for 'Licia', who in sonnet 6, discovers that an image of her naked body is currently circulating among men, since Fletcher has discovered his heart, 'wherein you printed were,/You, naked you'.[26] The poet George Gascoigne dramatized this compromising interpretative 'gaze' of masculine minds across a coveted female body many years earlier, in his fictional account of the *Adventures of Master F.J.* (1573). Here F.J. finds his 'gazing eyes' drawn to admire not his lady's features but the mind of his rival, delineated in a witty rebuff to his conceited exposition of desire. Thus rapt in his rival's authenticating appreciation of his own wit, F.J.'s response replicates the orientation of the published narrative as a whole, which the narrator offers to gentlemen readers as a context from which to appreciate the advantages in amorous and social encounter to be gained by F.J.'s extempore compositions. Minds, of course, cannot gaze admiringly at one another across a vacuum; they require a discursive medium in which to disclose their loveliness. For this purpose, the most common analogical proof of a man's cognitive virtue comes to be the epideixis of the female body. So F.J.'s rival is a *secretary*, whose writing discloses the secret knowledge of his mistress which that virtue has occasioned. His riding to London, however, offers F.J. an 'occasion' to 'lend his mistress such a pen in her secretary's absence as he should never at his return be able to amend the well-writing thereof'.[27]

The mistress's eyes, then, were never like the sun in the discriminating, evaluating sense; they never 'looked with thought'. They merely shared in the play of bright bodily surfaces, the 'blondeness, whiteness, sparkle',[28] which in Petrarchan discourse entangled the male subject, thereby acknowledging the 'superficial' nature of a poetic exercise, the object of which was to practise and display virtuosity at the level of analogical and antithetical invention. 'Of thine eyes I made my mirror,/From thy beautie came mine error', as Lodge put it in his rather lovely sequence, *Phillis*.[29] Serving as the 'occasion' or pretext for such a text, woman is associated with what Kerrigan called the 'competitive roots' of similitude. This is plain from the very earliest English texts advocating eloquence as essential to the mediation of knowledge; thus, for example, William Baldwin's *Treatise of Morrall Phylosophie* (1548) demonstrates by analogy the power of analogical eloquence in stimulating the exercise of interpretation and therefore the *activity* of knowledge:

> Lyke as a louer delyted in the goodly bewtie of his loue, can neuer be satisfyed in beholdyng her, neyther can take any rest until he haue by praysing, enflamed other to delyte in the same, labouryng to the uttermost to set forth hys beloued; euen so the phylosophers rauyshed in the loue of wisdome, haue not only labored to knowe it to the uttermost, but haue also deuysed al maner meanes . . . to set out wisdome in sondry kyndes of wrytyng, that euery man might find wherin to delyte, and so to be caught in his owne pleasure.[30]

But if the humanist ideal of eloquence as a productive exchange of knowledge could be thus disturbingly figured as the analogical unfolding of a female body to arouse forbidden desire, the homosocial rivalry involved could equally be masked in the related metaphor of the female body as the internal organization of the masculine mind, a kind of self-sufficient estate. This metaphor derives from what I call the 'discourse of husbandry', which pervades the entire Protestant-humanist literature of reform, from marriage doctrine to the education of the orator. The function of this discourse in the early reforming texts was to articulate, in an unspecific way, the humanist sense that the reformation of the nobility through classical paradigms would make for an increase in society's productivity. In Humphrey's *Of Nobilitye*, the idle nobleman, 'coasting the stretes' with his 'wauering plumes' and his wasteful 'rout of seruaunts' is a foil to the new style of nobleman who can be productive and organize discourse, but Humphrey can express this productive potential only by way of a discourse in praise of farming (husbandry) among the ancient nobility of Greece and Rome.[31] This *topos* of the virtuous governor as 'good husband' in the commonwealth involves woman as a vital principle of elision, for 'husbandry' articulates the notion of the bourgeois household as a domain which, internally organized and guarded by woman, releases man into the spaces of social encounter which enable him to make productive contacts. The internal organization of the household then becomes analogous to the principle of reading to increase one's *copia* or store of discursive resources 'ready for production'.[32] Thus, as the intimate encounter with the text actually enables men to produce the occasions of competitive social encounter, so the apparent integrity and self-sufficiency of the well-organized household actually demands a mercantile site of contingency and competition to prove the virtue of its well-preparedness. Woman as the cultural product of a husband and a figure of chaste reproduction may be invoked to mask this required space of contingency either in the plot of the outrageous violation of the household's integrity (the rape of Lucrece), or as a fiction of the bountiful independence of its economy. Either way, the female virtue of chastity is subsumed by masculine virtue of good husbandry.

While Shakespeare's *Sonnets* make suspect the fiction of a 'husbandry' of signifying power, shared between the patron and the text, Jonson's *Epigrams* and *The Forest* seem to endorse it, moving as they do from the literary marketplace to the great estate. The *Epigrams* mark out an urban space of social and textual encounter which distinguishes idle haunters and incompetent readers from those who circulate more productively, like well-organized discourses, commanding credit and friends. The second part of the volume, divided off by a kind of waste-disposal section in the voyage down London's sewers, is devoted to the Pembrokes, and two of its poems celebrate the husbandry of great estates. In *To Penshurst* the lady, 'noble, fruitful, chaste withal',[33] is metaphorically elided with the self-replenishing fruitfulness of the estate, which resists any acknowledgement of an exchange relation, even that implicit in the gift-giving of hospitality. The vital contact with the court is thus expressed as the estate's capacity to provide. King James's fortuitous discovery of and entry into the house may be read (through the rhetorical associations of 'forest' and 'found') as a discovery of the contingent extempore space, the 'occasion' for which the masculine virtues of productive reading and good husbandry are always prepared.[34] So the estate's chastity with regard to economic advantage is expressed in its readiness to receive contingency as the guest of a wife who could

> Have her linen, plate, and all things nigh
> When she was far, and not a room but dressed,
> As if she had expected such a guest![35]

The other country house poem, *To Sir Robert Wroth*, uses woman rather differently to mask the dependence of the estate on political and economic contact with the court. Lady Mary Wroth transgresses, as it were, the conceptual boundaries of the book, being praised in the *Epigrams* as a dancer at court masques; specifically, as an index of the language of mythological representation that commands credit at court. Thus she, as David Norbrook has pointed out, implicitly belies Jonson's praise of Wroth's estate as austerely self-sufficient, and of Wroth himself as eschewing participation in the race for favour and economic preferment that contact with the Jacobean court implied.[36]

It is in the context of this discourse of husbandry, I think, that we have to read Lanyer's decision to defer the praise of Cookham. Samuel Daniel had, some years earlier, dedicated to Margaret Clifford *A Letter from Octavia to Marcus Antonius* which implicitly referred to the Countess's own marital situation, George Clifford being a known philanderer and adventurer.[37] Daniel prefaced the poem with an expression of his hope that he might one day be 'secretary' to the Countess, to 'spread' her 'own faire vertues' as he had those of Octavia. But the chief virtues he discloses on Octavia's behalf are those of invisibility and chastity, arguments to redeem Antony as a good husband. 'These walles that here doe keepe me out of sight', she writes, 'Shall keepe me all vnspotted vnto thee'.[38] Lanyer's poem betrays an awareness of the difficulties of negotiating these complex masculine investments in the articulation of female virtue. She, too, hopes to be the secretary of a woman's virtue, but without disclosing it as a secret kept by men. Having deferred the setting forth of Cookham's loveliness, she prefaces the narrative of Christ with a highly problematic 'Invective against outward beauty unaccompanied with virtue' (p. 85) which in our terms appears to be indifferent to the virtue of the women involved, since Lucrece, whom all authorities allow to have been violated as a consequence of her exemplary chastity and huswifery rather than her beauty, is nevertheless incriminated along with the more obvious *exempla* of the evils of seduction, such as Rosamond and Cleopatra. But the beauty and violability of Lucrece's body is a figure for the competitive realignment of homosocial relations in the aspiration to good husbandry. So Vives, in *The Office and duetie of an husband* (trans. 1550) offers Lucrece as an example of how 'strangers and gestes' in a man's house become enemies and how 'the secrets of matrimony' should be kept from other men, to reduce the risk of a wife's 'giftes and vertues' inciting the cupidity of rivals.[39] Rosamond, too, offers an example of how the 'proof' of masculine virtue (i.e. the capacity to disclose the rhetorical potential of an encounter) is displaced and expressed as the transgressive visibility or 'beauty' of a female body. In his influential sonnet sequence, *Delia*, Daniel had the ghost of Rosamond request that he try his skills at narrative, since by telling Rosamond's story, he might move the stony-hearted Delia to the yielding that all his praises of her have been unable to effect. In Daniel's telling, the 'setting forth' of Rosamond's body from 'Countrey . . . to Court', from obscurity to visibility, 'armed . . . With rarest proofe of beauty euer seene',[40] is the cause of her fall; but of course his setting out of Delia's beauty, the proof of his rhetorical skill, is ostensibly motivated by a desire to bring about a similar fall. The ghost of Rosamond ascribes both happy and unhappy consequences to the same cause: beauty. If Daniel's rhetoric succeeds, with her as topic, in moving Delia to show kindness, then 'I (through beauty) made the wofull'st wight/By beauty may have comfort after death'.[41]

Distinguishing 'outward beauty' from inward virtue, then, has its problems, since beauty is a (gendered) way of speaking about the effect of disclosure as a form of textual pleasure and potential for the future; a form of what I have been calling 'interpretative virtue'. Lewalski, referring Lanyer's invective back to the stanzas on the Countess's retirement, reads them as a conventional foil to the 'inward virtue' therein proved.[42] But this would leave no poem to write, for the Countess's virtue would then be taken to have been signified by the enclosure of itself in her estate. What Lanyer is trying to do with the virtue/beauty antithesis is, I think, more complicated. She explicitly refers her invective forward: 'That outward Beautie which the world commends/Is not the subject I will write upon' (p. 85).

So what she will write upon is beauty, and beauty as the expression of her patron's interpretative virtue. But she will avoid the articulation of this virtue as the incriminating display of the female body by avoiding the analogical rhetoric through which such a display is produced, the rhetoric which implicitly strives to match 'those matchlesse colours Red and White' and celebrate its ingenuity in the 'perfit features of a fading face' (p. 85). She returns to this mode of proving knowledge only in the final stanzas of the poem, where a discourse in praise of the Christian martyrs is expressed in terms of disclosing their beautiful features to the sight of the Countess: 'Their freshest beauties would I faine disclose'; 'The purest colours both of White and Red' (p. 136). Having achieved the object of the poem, and dramatized woman as a cognizant subject, Lanyer can afford at this point the gesture of 'Folding up' the beauty of these histories in the breast of her patron, the implication being that they will suffer no discredit, though undisclosed, since their habitation is so radiant. A similar sort of gesture concludes the narrative of Christ's Passion. The Saviour as beloved, made known through a series of comparisons deriving from the *Song of Songs*, and extravagant as any sonnet:

> This is the Bridegroome that appeares so faire,
> So sweet, so lovely in his Spouse's sight,
> That unto Snowe we may his face compare,
> His cheekes like scarlet, and his eyes so bright
> As purest doves that in the rivers are,
> Washed with milke. (p. 120)

This is the climax on which Lanyer abandons her topic to the heart of her patron, begging permission to leave 'This taske of Beauty which I tooke in hand' (ibid.).

But how has she fulfilled the task (a technical term for a dialectical 'trial' or 'proof') of beauty? How has her narrative proved the position of women as the subjects of interpretative experience rather than the analogues and occasions of discursive virtue among men? She organizes the narrative of the Passion so as to give maximum scope to the relation of these problematic metaphors of knowledge as the beholding of beauty. The trial and prosecution of Christ becomes a series of trials in which men's capacity to 'see and know' or to interpret the text of sacred history offered to them by the face of God in persecuted man fails by comparison with the capacity of politically disadvantaged women, whose interpretative virtue is proved by a literalization of the humanist metaphor of textual power as a mutually authenticating reflection when Christ lifts his face to the tears of the daughters of Jerusalem. Lanyer stylizes the movements of Christ throughout the narrative, so as to emphasize her allegorization of the historical moments of his appearance as moments in the experience of rhetorical disclosure as interpretative potential. So the appearances of Christ are treated as interpretative exercises. In Christ lies hidden the meaning of the historical moment; he is the object of the interpreting gaze, the matter to be heard and evaluated, the space in which to 'prove' the colours of argument. Adapting sacred history thus uncompromisingly to the humanist discourse of knowledge as a form of encounter with and trial of discursive potential, Lanyer's work reveals a troubling contradiction in the premises of 'Christian humanism'. For Christian humanism, distinguishing itself from scholasticism on the basis that eloquence is required to set out wisdom, tends towards a definition of knowledge which has the logic of an economy; knowledge is the power to assimilate the resources or exploit the occasions which lie latent in the (sur)face of the text, or in the extempore moment of encounter.[43] So men in Lanyer's narrative apparently mistake the encounter with Christ as a discursive occasion in which to discover potential advantage. But there can be no encounter of God in man under such conditions. God remains obscure to the gaze trained to disclose contingency as the power to determine historical events, revealing his face only to the gaze which comprehends eschatological history in the form of compassionate response to human suffering.

Lanyer's narrative is thus overarched by two moments of suffering which call for compassionate response, one ignored and the other realized. It begins in Gethsemane, where the obscurity of night figures human ignorance of the events to be unfolded. The metaphor of a failure to see articulates both the irony of the disciples' assertions that they will never forsake Christ, and their inability to respond to him in the present hour of need. The contrast is significant: though the foreseeing eyes of Christ ('Wisdom's eyes') might 'looke and checke' Peter's misplaced confidence in his own 'cleare . . . sight' of events to come, we as readers are only invited to judge the disciples' failure to realize the knowledge to which any human being has access; the present and immediate knowledge of suffering which is realized in

31

compassionate response. A failure in compassion is registered as a crucial failure in interpretation, 'Yet shut those Eies that should their Maker see' (p. 92). At this stage, however, Lanyer articulates the failure as human rather than specifically masculine. God, in that moment, is 'farre . . . of Man from beeing pittied' (p. 93). As the narrative goes on, however, this representative use of 'man' is modulated. When events move into the light of the political centre stage and the disciples 'see' Christ on the brink of death, then, 'Though they protest they never will forsake him,/They do like men, when dangers overtake them' (p. 98). The unspoken antithesis of 'men' here signals the absence of women from the official spaces of interpretative encounter, the judicial sphere which produces events as discourses to be interpreted towards the making of history. Christ's emergence into these official spaces is treated as a comedy of redundant labour; his arresters, armed with all the paraphernalia of detection, repeatedly fail to seek out and find the name and face which he repeatedly discloses to them: 'Nay, though he said unto them, I am he,/They could not know him whom their eyes did see' (p. 94). From the arrest as an attempt to discover what needed no special interpretative virtue to disclose, Lanyer stages the trial before Caiphas as an exercise in the ingenious misconstruction of Christ as text, an attempt to 'heare the answere, which he will not make' (p. 100). At this point, when 'Pontius Pilate must the matter heare' (p. 101), the absence of woman from the privileged spaces of interpretative virtue now intervenes in the unheard request brought from Pilate's wife (who remains at home) that proceedings should be stopped on the strength of her knowledge of Christ in a dream. This intervention operates as a sceptical frame for recalling the authoritative account of woman's position in the original trial of interpretative virtue, where Eve, credited with no special 'powre to see', 'simply good' and easily persuaded by the calculated discourse of a serpent, is contrasted with Adam, persuaded by the sight of a fruit:

> If *Eve* did erre, it was for knowledge sake,
> The fruit being faire perswaded him to fall (p. 104)

Lanyer's conclusion

> Yet men will boast of Knowledge, which he tooke
> From *Eves* faire hand, as from a learned Booke. (ibid.)

turns the paradigm of woman's beauty as analogical proof of man's interpretative virtue, his quality of being 'faire in knowledge as in hew', inside out. Through the adjective 'fair', with its connotations of light and disclosure, Eve is metonymically figured as fruit; knowledge, defined by men as the capacity to disclose the 'fair fruits' of a textual or social encounter, here becomes indistinguishable from ignorant appetite. As a gloss on Jonson's ideal of virtuous encounter as 'looking with thought' and 'knowing one's ends' in the text or person before one, Lanyer's rewriting of the Fall defers and ironizes Pilate's decision to overlook his conviction of Christ's innocence in view of the political imperative to remain a friend to Caesar.

Lanyer figures the climax of the narrative as a drama of interpretation, in which women elicit radiance and meaning from the event which had remained mute and indecipherable to masculine exegesis. The Christ who could not be brought, by all the forensic techniques of society's governors, 'To speake on word, nor once to lift his eyes' (this is obviously not naturalistic, since the earlier failure in interpretation is located in Christ's forthcomingness) is accessible to women, whose interpretative power at this decisive moment of human history is brought about by compassion, figured in the suggestion that their reflective knowledge is enhanced by the refraction of light in their tears:

> Most blessed daughters of Jerusalem
> Who found such favour in your Saviors sight,
> To turne his face when you did pitie him;
> Your tearefull eyes, beheld his eyes more bright;
> Your Faith and Love unto such grace did clime,
> To have reflection from this Heav'nly Light:
> Your Eagles eyes did gaze against this Sunne. (p. 110)

Lanyer here picks up the metaphor of full disclosure – the eagle looking directly at the sun – from her earlier refusal to develop the *topos* of Margaret Clifford's retirement as a means to prove it. In the wake of this long-deferred and carefully prepared-for dramatic moment, it becomes possible for the poem to return to a comparative rhetoric, and to express female knowledge of Christ in the blazon of a lover's beauty without solipsism. Here, the text takes its departure from the question in the *Song of Songs* framed by the daughters of Jerusalem in response to a request for help in finding the absent beloved:

What is thy beloved more than another beloved, O thou
fairest among women? What is thy beloved more than another
beloved that thou dost so charge us? (*Song of Songs*, 5:9)

The textual 'finding out' of the beloved in the comparisons that
follow thus works as a shared rather than competitive discourse,
finding its origin in a request to women for help in discovery
rather than a display of secret knowledge designed to arouse
rivalrous desire (as, for example, in Baldwin's model of analogical
rhetoric as the lover enflaming another man to take delight in
his love). The transition to blazon, moreover, enables Lanyer to
return to the interpretative virtue which it has been the object
of the narrative to delineate, to its source in the 'knowing by
heart' of Margaret Clifford. Here it is proved as an internal
spectacle and a daily influence on the Countess's conduct; her
heart is the stage on which knowledge of God sometimes appears
in the figures of protection and power, sometimes in those of
men in need, 'in miserable case', demanding response in compassionate action (p. 120). The representation of the exercise
of female interpretative virtue thus breaks out of its enclosure
in the discourse of husbandry and becomes something more
than the protection of its own violable boundaries. Searching
for analogues for Margaret Clifford's interpretative virtue, Lanyer
finds an approximation in the Queen of Sheba. The 'Ethyopian
Queen' affords an image of woman actively motivated by desire
to interpret, proving the worthiness of King Solomon's mind with
her discourse:

> Yea many strange hard questions did shee frame,
> All which were answer'd by this famous King:
> Nothing was hid that in her heart did rest,
> And all to proove this king so highly blest. (p. 128)

Once again, interpretative encounter is figured as mutual reflection,
'Beauty sometime is pleased to feed her eyes,/With viewing Beautie
in anothers face', but here the experience so figured is active,
stimulated by desire:

> And this Desire did work a strange effect,
> To draw a Queene forth of her native Land,
> Not yeelding to the niceness and respect
> Of Woman-kind; she past both sea and land

All feare of dangers shee did quite neglect,
Onely to see, to heare, and understand
   That beauty, wisdome, majestie and glorie,
   That in her heart imprest his perfect storie. (p. 129)

The Queen of Sheba's going forth to 'proove' in dialectical encounter the qualities which she had 'imprest' as a 'perfect storie' in her
own heart proves herself an image of the ideal reader, exercising
and storing up, in the pleasure of interpreting a text or 'storie', the
potential for argument and decisive action. It is a measure of the
poem's achievement that the cognizant going forth of beauty here
should risk no misconstruction as that casualty of masculine ideals
of intellectual productivity, 'outward beauty unaccompanied with
virtue' which seemed so inescapable in the early stages of Lanyer's
articulation of female agency. Lanyer's poem appears not to have
been received and circulated by the women whose influential
countenances would have made its subject 'fair' with the reflection
of their credibility. But in whose eyes would it have been fair? One
is tempted to say, vaguely echoing the idiom of the *Sonnets*, 'fair
. . . in the eyes of men'. But that is precisely the difficulty. The
description of Cookham which Lanyer eventually wrote emphasizes
the ephemeral and contiguous (rather than metaphorical) relation
of the estate to its Mistress, in the form of a valedictory elegy,
where just for a moment 'all things . . . did hold like similes'
(p. 137), not asking to be taken for the truth at the expense of
the sun.

NOTES

(Place of publication for works printed before 1800 is London unless
otherwise stated.)

1 A.L. Rowse, *The Poems of Shakespeare's Dark Lady: Salve Deus, Rex
Judeorum by Emilia Lanyer*, London, Cape, 1976, p. 20; on the issue
of responsibility for the publication of the 1609 *Sonnets*, see Katherine
Duncan-Jones's account of scholarly attempts to exonerate Shakespeare
and blame his publisher in 'Was the 1609 *Shakespeare's Sonnets* really
unauthorized?', *Review of English Studies*, 1983, new series, vol. 34,
pp. 151–71. Recent feminist scholarship on Lanyer includes Barbara
Lewalski's valuable 'Of God and Good Women: the Poems of Aemilia
Lanyer', in Margaret Patterson Hannay (ed.), *Silent But for the Word:
Tudor Women as Patrons, Translators and Writers of Religious Works*, Kent,
Ohio, Kent State University Press, 1985; and Elaine Beilin, 'The
Feminization of Praise: Aemilia Lanyer', in *Redeeming Eve: Women*

Writing in the English Renaissance, Princeton, N J, Princeton University Press, 1987.

2 Rowse, p. 28. Hereafter references to Lanyer's poetry will be cited from this edition by page number in the text.

3 A.L. Rowse, *Simon Forman: Sex and Society in Shakespeare's Age*, London, Weidenfeld & Nicolson, 1974, p. 111.

4 Samuel Schoenbaum, 'Shakespeare, Dr Forman and Dr Rowse', in *Shakespeare and Others*, London, Scolar, 1985, p. 76.

5 John Kerrigan, Introduction to *The Sonnets and A Lover's Complaint*, Harmondsworth, Penguin, 1988, p. 23.

6 ibid., p. 29.

7 Muriel Bradbrook, reviewing *The Paradise of Women: Writings by Englishwomen of the Renaissance*, ed. Betty Travitsky, in *Tulsa Studies in Women's Literature*, 1982, vol. 1, p. 92.

8 Lewalski, p. 207. Though I take issue throughout this chapter with Lewalski's reading, I am greatly indebted to her fine contribution.

9 I quote from *Shakespeare's Sonnets*, ed. Stephen Booth, New Haven, CN, Yale University Press, 1977, p. 73. Further references to the *Sonnets* will follow the quarto as transcribed in this edition, and will be indicated simply by sonnet and line number in the text.

10 Booth does not include a rhetorical sense in his gloss of 'hues' but as the rhetorical sense of 'colour' itself could not escape a reader with a humanist education, I suggest a synonym such as 'hue' might bear this metaphorical sense without undue difficulty, giving added point to the pun Booth detects in 'hues'/'use', p. 164.

11 See Victoria Kahn, *Rhetoric, Prudence and Scepticism in the Renaissance*, Ithaca, NY, Cornell University Press, 1985, pp. 39–45. Quintilian, *Institutio Oratoria*, X. vi. 5–6. On reading as inventing a store of resources, see Erasmus, *On Copia of Words and Ideas*, ed. and trans. D.B. King and H.D. Rix, Milwaukee, WN, Marquette University Press, 1963, pp. 87–9; Terence Cave, *The Cornucopian Text*, Oxford, Clarendon, 1979, p. 133; Lorna Hutson, *Thomas Nashe in Context*, Oxford, Clarendon, 1989, pp. 38–54.

12 Sir Thomas Elyot, *The Boke Named the Gouernor*, London, Dent, 1907, p. 5.

13 See, for example, the section on the analogical 'opening out' of adages and proverbs in William Baldwin, *A Treatise of Morrall Phylosophie*, 1548, bk 3, ch. 1, sig. M7R.

14 See Erasmus, pp. 67–89; Quintilian, V. ix–xi; Cave, pp. 30, 122; Thomas Wilson, *The Arte of Rhetorique*, 1560, ed. G.H. Mair, Oxford, Clarendon, 1909, pp. 6–12.

15 Hutson, pp. 56–7.

16 Rowse's edition prints all the dedications, but see Lewalski's notes on the omission of certain dedications in extant copies, p. 264n.

17 My use of the word 'homosocial' follows Eve Kosofsky Sedgwick, *Between Men: English Literature and Male Homosocial Desire*, New York, Columbia University Press, 1985. My debts to Sedgwick and to Nancy Vickers, especially '"The blazon of sweet beauty's best": Shakespeare's *Lucrece*', in Patricia Parker and Geoffrey Hartman (eds), *Shakespeare*

and the Question of Theory, London, Methuen, 1985, pp. 95–115, are apparent throughout this chapter.

18 See John King, 'Patronage and Piety: The Influence of Catherine Parr' in Hannay, pp. 43–60. King does not discuss the relation between the patronage of women and the representation of their agency in the reforming works in question; Catherine Brandon's support of Thomas Wilson does not prevent 'woman' from being either a figure of dispraise or part of a discourse in praise of husbandry in a treatise on rhetoric designed to give access to the production of effective discourse exclusively to men (Wilson, p. 13).

19 Lewalski, p. 214.

20 From a discussion following her paper, 'Rewriting Patriarchy and Patronage: Margaret Clifford, Anne Clifford, and Aemilia Lanyer', delivered at Reading, July 1989.

21 William Sherman, '"Official Scholars" and "Action Officers": Research Intelligence and the Making of Tudor Policy in Early Modern England', unpublished research paper delivered at the London Renaissance Seminar, Birkbeck College, University of London, 1990. See also Lisa Jardine and Anthony Grafton, '"Studied for Action": How Gabriel Harvey read his Livy', *Past and Present*, 1990, vol. 129, pp. 32–78.

22 See Richard Peterson, *Imitation and Praise in the Poems of Ben Jonson*, New Haven, CN, Yale University Press, 1981, pp. 3–34; Cave, pp. 39–53.

23 Lawrence Humphrey, *Of Nobilitye*, 1563, sigs A4R–A5R. Humphrey imagines a nobility fashioning themselves through their mastery of paradigms of similarly fashioned classical governors, so 'the auncient Nobilitye, shaped by the Monumentes of auncient writers and drawen from the pattern of Kinges, princes and other auncient nobles, maye be raysed as a mirrour in a hyghe and playne mount to shine and glister to the men of our dayes' to revive 'the auncient discipline and true prayse of their auncestors', sig. B3R.

24 Ben Jonson, *Poems*, ed. Ian Donaldson, Oxford, Oxford University Press, 1978, p. 44.

25 See epigrams 11, 12, 56, 58, 81, 100 in Jonson, *Poems*, pp. 11–55.

26 Giles Fletcher, *Licia: or Poemes of Love, in Honour of the admirable and singular vertues of his Lady, to the imitation of the best Latin Poets and others*, 1593, sigs A2R–B1R, sig. C3R.

27 George Gascoigne, *The Adventures of Master F.J.*, in Paul Salzman (ed.), *An Anthology of Elizabethan Prose Fiction*, Oxford, Oxford University Press, 1987, pp. 10, 15–16.

28 Nancy Vickers, 'Diana Described: Scattered Woman and Scattered Rhyme', in Elizabeth Abel (ed.), *Writing and Sexual Difference*, Brighton, Harvester, 1982, p. 96.

29 See Thomas Lodge, *Phillis*, 1593, sig. H3V. On the importance of Petrarchism as an exercise in technical virtuosity to extend the flexibility of the vernaculars, see Leonard Forster, *The Icy Fire*, Cambridge, Cambridge University Press, 1969, p. 73.

30 Kerrigan, p. 23; Baldwin, sig. M7R.

31 Humphrey, sigs H8V–I8V. Humphrey's discourse derives, by way of Cicero's *De Senectute*, from Xenophon's *Oeconomicus*, a text also at the heart of humanist marriage doctrine.

32 Cf. Cave's discussion of Quintilian on improvisation (Cave, pp. 126–7) with Xenophon on the productive potential of the wife-governed household as an efficient retrieval system (*Oeconomicus*, viii. 2–23).

33 Jonson, *Poems*, p. 91.

34 The part of rhetoric and dialectic called 'invention' takes its name from the Latin *invenio*, 'I find' or 'come upon' or 'discover'. On the metaphor of the 'forest' as the place of invention, where arguments are found, see W.J. Ong, *Ramus, Method and the Decay of Dialogue*, Cambridge, MA, Harvard University Press, 1958, pp. 116–21. Ong quotes Thomas Wilson: 'he that will take profeicte in this parte of Logique, must bee like a hunter. . . . For these places bee nothing elles, but covertes or boroughs, wherein if any one searche diligently, he maie finde game at pleasure', p. 120.

35 Jonson, *Poems*, p. 91.

36 David Norbrook, *Poetry and Politics in the English Renaissance*, London, Routledge & Kegan Paul, 1984, pp. 190–1.

37 Joan Rees, *Samuel Daniel*, Liverpool, Liverpool University Press, 1964, pp. 76–7.

38 Samuel Daniel, *The Complete Works in Verse and Prose*, ed. A.B. Grosart, London, Spenser Society, 1885, vol. i, p. 124.

39 Juan Lodovicus Vives, *The Office and duetie of an husband*, trans. Thomas Paynell, 1550, sigs U4R–X4R. On the significance of Lucrece in the humanist mystification of the dependence of republican virtues on commercial contact and secrecy, see Stephanie H. Jed, *Chaste Thinking: The Rape of Lucretia and the Birth of Humanism*, Bloomington, Indiana University Press, 1989.

40 Daniel, *Works*, vol. i, p. 85.

41 ibid., vol. i, p. 83. In interpreting this text, Kerrigan makes the classic move of translating Daniel's attribution of agency to the 'beauty' of Delia and Rosamond into a form of guilt: 'In Delia, Daniel had shown chastity at two extremes: coldly unyielding in his mistress's case; all too weak in Rosamond's' (p. 17). It is difficult to imagine what kind of conduct could be defined as 'chaste' on these terms!

42 Lewalski, p. 214.

43 Kahn, p. 51: 'The problem for a Christian humanist is that in a Judeo-Christian world . . . there is, in theory, no contingency.'

2

'YET TELL ME SOME SUCH FICTION': LADY MARY WROTH'S *URANIA* AND THE 'FEMININITY' OF ROMANCE

Helen Hackett

In late sixteenth- and early seventeenth-century England, it seems to have been thought that romances were mainly read by women. There is evidence for this in the fact that numerous romances were dedicated to women and included authorial asides addressed to female readers; and in satirical or moralistic writings which held up women's taste for romance to ridicule or opprobrium.[1] Yet the authors of Elizabethan and Jacobean romances were men. The only known exceptions to this were *The Mirror of Knighthood*, translated from Spanish by Margaret Tyler in 1578; and *The Countess of Montgomery's Urania*, written by Lady Mary Wroth, in 1621. These texts, and especially the latter, are therefore of great interest as interventions by women into a form hitherto aimed at women as consumers, but closed to women as writers.

The Renaissance romance was usually a long work of prose fiction, with a highly digressive structure and a highly rhetorical style, concerning improbable events taking place in a fantastic realm. These romances often shared with the modern romantic novel a central concern with love and courtship; but they added to this a concern with chivalry and martial exploits, which, in some cases, was the main narrative theme.[2] Old-established chivalric romances like *Guy of Warwick* and *Bevis of Hampton* circulated among the lower classes in cut-down chap-book form; but most new romances were either dedicated to 'gentlewomen', or, like the *Arcadia*, originated at a courtly level, then filtered down through

39

the gentry and trading and servant classes. The material discussed in this essay under the term 'Renaissance romance' belonged mainly to these aristocratic or bourgeois milieux.[3]

These class distinctions, as well as generally low literacy rates, meant that Renaissance romance differed from the modern romantic novel in that it did not possess a mass market of the size that exists today. However, it was perceived as catering to a growing and commercially important female audience, and resembled modern romantic fiction in being denigrated as a 'women's genre'. For example, Barnaby Rich's *Farewell to Military Profession*, 1581, a collection of romance-type stories, and John Lyly's *Euphues and his England*, 1580, both contained separate dedications to male and female readers. The dedications to women employ irony and a patronizing tone to imply an underlying disdain for this newly lucrative market, to which the author is stooping reluctantly, out of economic necessity. The assumption seems to be that female readers will take the barbed compliments in such dedications at face value, while male readers are more sophisticated and are therefore in on the author's joke. Male readers are addressed 'straight' in their own dedications, as the author's equals and colluders.[4]

Such use of dual dedications suggests that women were not the only readers of romances, but that a professed intention to write for women serves as an announcement to readers of both sexes that the work in question is light and frivolous: 'but a toy', as Lyly puts it; or, in Sir Philip Sidney's words, 'but a trifle, and that triflingly handled'.[5] There may also be an element of voyeurism in play. George Pettie's *A Petite Palace of Pettie his Pleasure*, 1576, another collection of romance-type stories addressed to 'Gentlewomen', has been aptly described by Paul Salzman as follows:

> The Petite Palace has, in effect, two audiences: the gentlewomen created by the narrator, cajoled by him, and spun around by his ambiguous moralizing until they are dizzy; and an invisible audience of fellow young wits, enjoying Pettie's dexterity, his sleight of hand.[6]

Thus the narrative foregrounding of a female audience in romance may be not so much about women reading, as about male readers deriving pleasure from imagining that they are watching women reading. Male readers could enjoy romance as a lightweight entertainment, while simultaneously enjoying a sense of intellectual superiority, knowing that they were distinguished by gender from the kind of foolish creatures who took this nonsense seriously. This was voyeurism in the sense that romance was being presented as a private realm of female literary pleasure into which the male reader was titillatingly invited to gaze unobserved. Such eavesdropping is strongly suggested in Robert Greene's *Penelope's Web*, 1587, a collection of tales presented as if told by Penelope and her female attendants and prefaced by three dedications, one to two female aristocratic patrons, one to ladies and one to gentlemen. In the latter, the author explains, 'I was determined at the first to have made no appeale to your favorable opinions, for that the matter is womens prattle, about the untwisting of Penelopes web.' But he changed his mind because he considered 'that *Mars* wil sometime be prying into *Venus* papers, and gentlemen desirous to heare the parlie of ladies'.[7]

However, despite such evidence of a dual audience, and the anecdotal nature of much evidence of reading habits, so far as we can tell women readers did indeed derive great enjoyment from romance in this period. Caroline Lucas, drawing on theories of the reader's participation in the construction of the text, suggests that Renaissance women may have derived pleasure from romances *in spite of* the restrictive examples of virtuous femininity expounded in many of these texts, and the inherently oppressive nature of the relationship between narrator and reader which many of them construct, by actively reading them against the grain. She draws on recent studies of the modern romantic novel,[8] a genre which resembles Renaissance romance not only in that both have been perceived by the dominant cultures of their time as 'women's reading', of low aesthetic merit, but also in that both genres appear to have appealed to female readers because they offered fantasy and escapism. Louis B. Wright posits this resemblance in conventional sexist terms, when he writes that romances were popular with female readers then as now, 'Since women in general have never subscribed to realism'.[9] While differing considerably from Wright in identifying serious social reasons for this, feminist critics might agree that escapism has had a value for women over the centuries.

In Janice Radway's 1984 study of the avidly romance-reading women of Smithton, a suburban community of the American midwest, her subjects' descriptions of what they enjoyed or valued in romantic novels repeatedly employed the word 'escapism'. Radway discusses how far such escapism is inherently politically repressive, providing women with 'compensatory literature' which distracts them from the injustices of their social situations; and how far it might be politically oppositional, enabling them to 'absent' themselves from their husbands in a realm of self-absorbed pleasure.[10] It is interesting to compare this with Renaissance depictions of women as romance-readers, particularly when the women concerned hold subordinate social positions. In the 1615 edition of Sir Thomas Overbury's *Characters*, 'A Chamber-Mayde' is shown as follows:

> Shee reads *Greenes* works over and over, but is so carried away with the *Myrrour of Knighthood*, she is many times resolv'd to run out of her selfe, and become a Ladie Errant.[11]

Her running 'out of her selfe' is lightly amusing provided it remains merely a distraction and an act of the imagination; but there is a subtext of anxiety that fantasy might not be enough to satisfy her, that the adventurous roles of women in romance might influence her behaviour and encourage her to 'run out of' her socially determined role. Such reading is therefore pre-emptively mocked as over-literal and naïve. The creation of a private female imaginative space has advantages for the patriarchal order, as long as it is marginalized as fantasy and delimited from 'real life'.

An anxiety that enjoyment of romance might lead to non-conformity and disobedience is more openly put in Thomas Powell's *Tom of All Trades. Or The Plaine Path-way to Preferment*, 1631. He gives the following advice on the bringing up of middle-class daughters:

> In stead of Song and Musicke, let them learne Cookery and Laundrie. And in stead of reading Sir *Philip Sidneys Arcadia*, let them read the grounds of good huswifery. I like not a female Poetresse at any hand.[12]

Both gender and class are at issue here: Powell is writing for the trading and professional classes, and he sees such arty pursuits as reading the *Arcadia* and writing poetry as the preserve of 'greater personages', not appropriate for 'a private Gentlemans Daughter'. The reading of romances, and, even more threateningly, literary creation by a woman, are feared as implying aspiration and autonomy, and deviation from the middle-class wife's 'proper' activities of attention and domestic service to a man.

Powell's fears that the female reader might grow into that even more threatening figure, the 'female Poetresse',[13] are striking in that they seem so ungrounded. Although romances were consistently aimed at female readers, by the date of Powell's writing (1631) hardly any of those readers had been fired to create their own romantic reading matter, at least not in published form. This was despite the fact that, besides the apparent existence of a sizeable female readership, romance seems to have been regarded as 'feminine' in other, more metaphoric ways. Patricia Parker has discussed how the 'dilation' of romance, its digressiveness and diffusiveness, were associated by Renaissance writers with the supposed garrulity and irrationality of women, and with the seductive dangers of female sexuality.[14] Roger Ascham, for instance, condemned 'fond books, of late translated out of Italian into English, sold in every shop in London', as being full of 'the enchantments of Circe';[15] they are distrusted as leading the masculine will astray into prodigal paths of pleasure. This was true not only for the male reader, but also for the male writer. Authors like Rich and Lyly in the dedications discussed above imply that they are effeminized and degraded by their excursion into romance. Sidney, for his part, seems virtually to step into female disguise with his hero:

> thus did Pyrocles become Cleophila – which name for a time hereafter I will use, for I myself feel such compassion of his passion that I find even part of his fear lest his name should be uttered before fit time were for it; which you, fair ladies that vouchsafe to read this, I doubt not will account excusable.[16]

The phrase 'I will use' is ambiguous, and can suggest that, in entering the domain of 'fair ladies', an enchanted, enclosed circle where love, courtship and courtliness are chief concerns, the male author performs an act of literary transvestism. It is an effeminization which, it could be argued, is creative and liberating for Sidney, but is represented by Rich and others as a degrading dilution of manhood.

Within Renaissance prose fictions, story-telling was often the role of women. In Gascoigne's *The Adventures of Master F.J.*, Dame Pergo and Dame Frances both tell stories of the uneven course of love as part of the courtly game of *questioni d'amore*.[17] Greene's *Penelope's Web* was a sequence of tales told by Penelope and her nurse and maids as they unravel by night the work she had done on her web by day. The 'endlesse' labour of the web is identified with the 'prattle' by which the loquacious company of women 'beguyle the night'. The unweaving of the web becomes identified with the unwinding of the tales, representing both as women's work: Ismena, one of the maids, is shown 'applying as well her fingers to the web as her tongue to the tale'; and later the other women listen to Penelope, 'setting their hands to the Web, and their eares to hir talke'.[18] Outside fiction, there is evidence of the participation of women of all classes in oral narrative traditions, including the telling of folk-tales, fairy-tales, and bawdy jokes and stories, and the singing of ballads, often at the centre of a circle of listeners and co-participants.[19] The association of rambling or fantastical tales with female tellers persists in the proverbial expression 'an old wives' tale', current in the sixteenth century as now.[20] Yet, despite all these conditions which might have favoured female authorship of romance, it appears that no woman in England took on the role until Margaret Tyler's translation of *The Mirror of Knighthood*, published in 1578. Even then, she was the translator of the work of a male Spanish author, rather than the originator of the text.

Tyler's translation was highly successful and influential. Before it appeared, continental chivalric romances had been little known in England, but it set a trend, including numerous sequels to *The Mirror of Knighthood* itself, produced by other Spanish authors and English translators. It is cited in many of the satirical representations of women as romance-readers: it is the very text which inspired the chambermaid in Overbury's *Characters* to become 'a lady errant'.[21] Tyler's epistle to the reader[22] has become well-known among students of early modern women's writing, partly for its enjoyably feisty tone, but also because it poses exactly the question which occurs to the modern critic, namely: if women were the main readers of romances, why did they not write them? Tyler writes,

> And if men may & do bestow such of their travailes upon gentlewomen, then may we women read such of their works as they dedicate unto us, and if we may read them, why not farther wade in them to the serch of a truth. And then much more why not deale by translation in such arguments, especially this kinde of exercise being a matter of more heede then of deep invention or exquisite learning.

She asserts, 'my perswasion hath bene thus, that it is all one for a woman to pen a story, as for a man to addresse his storie to a woman'.

Yet within the very terms she uses to assert the legitimacy of her role as writer, Tyler proffers some clues as to why other women might have been deterred from emulating her. First, it is notable that she only recommends the translation of books by women; this is acceptable and/or achievable by them because it only requires 'heede', carefulness, rather than 'deep invention or exquisite learning', creative powers or erudition. Second, she finds it necessary to defend her choice of a chivalric romance as her text for translation, which might be regarded as unfeminine material:

> Such delivery as I have made I hope thou wilt friendly accept, the rather for that it is a womans woork, though in a story prophane, and a matter more manlike then becommeth my sexe.

And third, Tyler feels obliged to defend her choice of a secular genre, in a period when the only genre which appears to have been socially sanctioned for women writers was the devotional.[23] She writes,

> But amongst al my il willers, some I hope are not so straight that they would enforce mee necessarily either not to write or to write of divinitie. Whereas neither durst I trust mine own judgement sufficiently, if matter of controversy were handled, nor yet could I finde any booke in the tongue which would not breed offence to some.

Tyler ingeniously employs a modesty *topos*, disclaiming the ability to meddle in religious matters. As with her recommendation of translation as a female activity, she is careful to circumscribe the radicalism of her stance with reassuringly conventional qualifications. Even so, she goes on to make a forceful assertion that romance-reading has moral value: it is pleasure seasoned with 'profitable reading', and the reader will find in her story 'the just reward of mallice & cowardise, with the good speed of honesty & courage'.

It seems clear that female authors were deterred from writing romance because it was seen as morally dubious. The notion of romance as a feminine genre was thus riddled with paradox. Romance was construed as feminine in that it was lightweight, not serious, the sort of thing women were assumed to enjoy; but because it was lightweight it was also morally disreputable, and therefore not fit for women to write. Thus women were fed with romance as consumers, while being simultaneously castigated for accepting it, and categorically excluded from its manufacture.

The Countess of Montgomery's Urania was, so far as we know, the first published romance in English which was authored by a woman. Lady Mary Wroth was the daughter of Sir Philip Sidney's brother Robert; she was born in 1586 or 1587, and married Robert Wroth in 1604. In her early adulthood she played a prominent part in court life: she danced twice before Elizabeth I, and she seems to have enjoyed the favour of Anne of Denmark, with whom she performed among other ladies in *The Masque of Blackness* in 1605. However, in 1614 Robert Wroth died, leaving his widow with enormous debts from which she never fully recovered. Her social as well as financial status now went into decline, and she seems to have fallen from her central place at court. She became involved in a long-running affair with her cousin, William Herbert, the third Earl of Pembroke, by whom she had two illegitimate children. Herbert was both married and notorious at court for his promiscuity. [24]

It was during this less fortunate period of her life that Wroth wrote the *Urania*. The published volume contains a romance in four books, 558 pages long, followed by a sonnet sequence. The central narrative thread is the love of Pamphilia for Amphilanthus, and her constancy in the face of his inconstancy. Amphilanthus' name, we are told, means 'the lover of two', [25] and we are shown Pamphilia's heroic patience as he repeatedly deserts her for chivalric quests and other mistresses. It was published in 1621, also the date of a new edition of Sir Philip Sidney's *Arcadia*. The *Arcadia* by now was an established best-seller, and it may have been that Wroth, or her publisher, hoped to cash in on its success by presenting the *Urania* as a companion volume. [26] Certainly Wroth's Sidney identity was hammered home on the title-page:

> The Countesse of Mountgomeries URANIA. Written by the right honorable the Lady MARY WROATH. Daughter to the right Noble Robert Earle of Leicester. And Neece to the ever famous, and re:nowned Sr. Phillips Sidney knight. And to the most exelent Lady Mary Countesse of Pembroke late deceased.

It may be that Wroth's Sidney credentials gave her a confidence unavailable to other women writers, since she could lay claim to a legitimate identity as an author of romance as Sidney's literary heir.

However, the Sidney name did not protect Wroth from scandal. The *Urania* was widely construed as a *roman-à-clef* whose characters were based on Wroth's friends and acquaintances at court. In particular, Edward Denny, Baron of Waltham, was convinced that one of the *Urania*'s many sub-narratives was a slander upon himself and his family. An arranged marriage had taken place between Denny's daughter, Honora, and Lord James Hay, one of James I's favourites. When she was found to have continued an existing love affair after her marriage, Denny had threatened to kill her. Wroth's story of Sirelius was almost identical to this in its events, and it described the father as 'a phantastical thing, vaine as Courtiers, rash as mad-men, & ignorant as women' (p. 439). There was an exchange of bitterly sarcastic letters between Denny and Wroth, and, although Wroth vehemently denied any intended reference to the Denny family, their standing at court obliged her to withdraw all copies of the *Urania* a few months after its publication. Even so, twenty-seven copies are known to have survived.[27] Wroth also continued the story in manuscript, in a sequel of another two books.[28]

Although this scandal did not arise specifically from the supposed impropriety of a woman's writing a romance, such terms did enter Denny's attack on Wroth. His first letter to her contains some biting verses, which open, 'Hermophradite in show, in deed a monster/As by thy words and works all men may conster.' In his desire to retaliate against his perceived injury, Denny evidently finds easy ground in the assertion that Wroth's act of authorship was unfeminine and unnatural, and seems able to assume that his peer group, the Jacobean court, will concur. His verses conclude 'leave idle bookes alone/For wise and worthyer women have writte none.' Wroth's invocation on her title-page of her illustrious female literary forebear, the Countess of Pembroke, famous for her religious translations, is made to rebound on her by Denny: he urges her to 'repent you of so many ill spent yeares of so vaine a booke', and to:

> redeeme the tym with writing as large a volume of heavenly layes and holy love as you have of lascivious tales and amorous toyes that at the last you may followe the rare, and pious example of your vertuous and learned Aunt.[29]

Denny suppresses the fact that the Countess, as the dedicatee of the *Arcadia*, was also famous as a connoisseur of romance.[30] He perpetuates the view that, whereas religious writing by women was socially respectable, and women's reading of romance was a social fact, female authorship of romances was unfitting and immoral.

Despite Wroth's heated denials of any intention of personal reference to Denny, the story of Sirelius was uncannily close to recent Denny family history, and it is hard to resist the conclusion that the *Urania* was indeed a *roman-à-clef*. Other contemporaries who construed it as such included John Chamberlain, who reported that many people at court believed that Wroth 'takes great libertie or rather licence to traduce whom she please'; and George Manners, seventh Earl of Rutland, who, in a letter of 1640 to his 'noble cosin', very probably Wroth, seems to ask for authorial confirmation of his attempt to draw up a key:

> heere meetinge with your Urania I make bold to send this enclosed and begg a favor from you that I may read with more delight. If you please to interprete unto me the names as heere I have begunn them, wherein you shall much oblige me.[31]

There are numerous analogies between events and personages in the fiction and events and personages in the Sidney and Herbert families and at court.

This intersection of the genres of *roman-à-clef* and romance complicates the relation between fantasy and 'real life' in the text: this romance could not easily be dismissed as wholly fantastic. In this it followed one or two recent precedents. Gascoigne's *The Adventures of Master F.J.* contained a number of hints that the story and characters referred to recognizable real events and people; Gascoigne denied any 'scandalous' intent, but even so issued a revised version.[32] More recently, John Barclay had composed two romances which were self-evidently *romans-à-clef*: the *Euphormionis Lusinini Satyricon* of 1605, and the *Argenis* of 1621. The latter found great favour at court; its Latin text circulated with a manuscript key, while the English translation was provided with a key by the printer.[33]

The *roman-à-clef* stands at a crucial point on the boundary between romance and novel. Lennard Davis has argued that the novel differs from romance in its use of frames and prestructures to set up ambivalence about the nature of the text as fact or fiction. In the late seventeenth- and early eighteenth-century novel, such frames often took the form of an assertion that the story was true, an assertion which was itself a falsehood, thereby setting up this radical ambiguity. By contrast, Davis posits the romance as uncomplicatedly fictional.[34] This is clearly not so of the *roman-à-clef*; yet, equally clearly, the *Urania* remains, in its far-fetched plot structures, exotic settings, high-born characters, rhetorical style, and concerns with love and chivalry, a romance rather than a novel. At the same time, although it does not explicitly contain a frame or prestructure of the type Davis describes, there is an implicit one: Wroth's announcement of her Sidney identity. Sir Philip Sidney's *Astrophil and Stella*, and features of the *Arcadia* such as his insertion of himself into the text as Philisides, had established a family tradition of the creative mingling of fact and fiction.[35] Continued popular interest in the private lives of the Sidneys, and in decoding the real identities behind Sidney texts, was evidenced by the appearance some time after 1607 of two anonymous verse epistles, 'Sir Phillipe Sidney to the Lady Penelope Rich' and 'The Lady Penelope Rich to Sir Phillipe Sidney'. These imagined Sidney's reaction to the news of the marriage of the woman generally taken to be his 'Stella', and her defence of her actions.[36] A new text by another Sidney might offer to readers a promise of more pleasure in unravelling textual clues and seeking out revelations of Sidney family affairs. One function of the author's assertion of her Sidney identity would thus have been to place her text on a fluid boundary between fact and fiction, private and public, inviting the reader to puzzle out where life and art met without holding out any guarantees of veracity.

Beyond the title-page, there are numerous other details which keep Wroth's Sidney literary heritage in view. For instance, the romance opens with the appearance of the shepherdess Urania, possibly filling in the suggestive narrative absence which opens the revised *Arcadia*, where Claius and Strephon lament the fact that Urania is lost; and it ends, like the revised *Arcadia*, in broken mid-sentence. The inclusion of a sonnet sequence looks back to a form which, by 1621, was out of fashion and was associated with the Elizabethan period, and specifically with Philip Sidney's *Astrophil and Stella*.[37] Wroth's Sidney lineage is clearly important to her not only in legitimating her act of authorship, but also in defining generic conventions for her writing. Yet at the same time she appropriates and adapts Sidneian traditions in ways related to her gender. For instance, the sonnet sequence, entitled 'Pamphilia to Amphilanthus', innovates in being addressed from a woman to a man.[38] The full title of the whole volume, *The Countess of Montgomery's Urania*, is clearly imitative of Sidney's full title, *The*

Countess of Pembroke's Arcadia, but with the significant difference that Wroth's book is dedicated to a woman by a woman, placing writer and reader on a level.[39] It is notable that Wroth's narrative voice is never explicitly gendered; though she sometimes steps forward to make authorial comment, and frequently exhibits sympathy with female characters, she never steps forward to identify herself overtly as female. Apart from the dedication, her audience is not explicitly gendered either; we do not find in the *Urania* Sidney's chivalrous asides to 'fair ladies', nor the patronizing or flirtatious addresses to their female readers of other male authors of romance. The relationship between author and reader in the *Urania* is an unusually asexual one.

Wroth was influenced by *The Faerie Queene*, *Orlando Furioso*, and other romances besides the *Arcadia*.[40] She was writing within a genre whose conventions had hitherto been shaped by male writers – yet one of those conventions was a concept of romance as 'feminine'. What happens, then, when a woman writer enters this 'feminine' genre, stepping into an already feminized authorial role? Does it produce a text which evinces a strongly feminine point of view? – perhaps, even, an early feminist text?

The contextual evidence which we have already considered indicates that Wroth's authorship was in itself a radical act. It is tempting on these grounds alone to lay claim to Wroth as a proto-feminist. Carolyn Ruth Swift is one critic who has sought a distinctively female and feminist consciousness in Wroth's works: she asserts that the theme of the *Urania* is that 'society limited women unreasonably and harmed them in the process'. In her view, Wroth's characters 'embody their author's awareness of real societal injustice to women'.[41] Maureen Quilligan, while acknowledging that we might have anachronistic expectations of the *Urania*, reads it as being primarily a critique of 'the traffic in women', the exchange of women in marital alliances by patriarchal authorities, whether fathers or brothers, which acts as the 'cultural glue' between men.[42]

However, there are difficulties in seeking our own kind of feminism in texts from earlier centuries, as other contributions in the present volume show. We may wish to read the *Urania* as an exposé of the patriarchal iniquities of Jacobean aristocratic society, but in doing so we are deploying a consciousness which Wroth may not share. The *Urania* is certainly concerned with women's sufferings; but the cause to which these are most often attributed is not patriarchal oppression, but men's inconstancy. This inconstancy is presented as a timeless and irremediable feature of male nature. Although women's sufferings are shown to be inflicted by men, they are not given an explicitly political interpretation or blamed on a particular social system. In Book III, a lady advises Amphilanthus' latest mistress:

> take heed brave Lady, trust not too much; for believe it, the kindest, lovingst, passionatest, worthiest, loveliest, valliantest, sweetest, and best man, will, and must change, not that he, it may bee, doth it purposely, but tis their naturall infirmitie, and cannot be helped. (p. 375)

There is radicalism here in the contradiction of the usual stereotypical association of fickleness with femininity; but in this ahistorical world of romance, the possibility of change or reform is not addressed. In the *Urania*'s own terms, women's chief remedy for the suffering inflicted upon them by men is to develop noble resignation and self-sufficiency, which is what Pamphilia does.[43]

However, even if the *Urania* is not an explicitly political social critique, this very representation of Pamphilia's self-sufficiency does open possibilities for a new, though limited, form of female autonomy. Pamphilia is determined to keep her love a secret, even, at first, from Amphilanthus. This secret is something which she prizes and takes pride in; as a possession which is hers alone, it gives her a sense of identity. She habitually resorts to deserted forests or her private chamber to muse upon her love; to a great extent, her primary affective relationship is with her own emotions, abstracted and held up to regard, rather than with Amphilanthus. Most importantly, Pamphilia derives not only a sense of selfhood, but also creative power from her secret passion: reading and, more significantly, writing figure largely as private forms for her emotional expression.

In her solitary wanderings in the woods, Pamphilia is frequently moved to carve sonnets on the bark of trees, a motif which alludes to the frequent inscribing of poems on natural objects in the *Arcadia*. But reading and writing specifically by female characters is of particular importance in the *Urania* as demarcating a private female space. For instance, in Book I, Pamphilia retires to her chamber alone to 'breath out her passions, which to none shee would discover'. She goes to bed, taking a little Cabinet with her, wherein she had many papers, and setting a light by her, began to reade them, but few of them pleasing her, she took pen and paper, and being excellent in writing, writ these verses following. (p. 51)

Here female reading engenders female writing, and both provide a private and autonomous space for Pamphilia's free and unconstrained expression of her emotions. Later, when Pamphilia and Amphilanthus declare their mutual affection, their companions leave them and they go 'into the next roome, which was a Cabinet of the Queenes, where her bookes and papers lay; so taking some of them, they passed a while in reading of them' (p. 217). Their love is consummated by Pamphilia's admittance of Amphilanthus to her private literary domain.

The incident reveals not only the prevalent literariness of the *Urania*, but also the importance in the text of the selective disclosure of secrets and the selective admission of chosen individuals to private spaces. Pamphilia takes on agency as a writer, and as arbiter of the boundary between concealment and revelation. In this the inner themes of the text mirror its outward form, as a female-authored *roman-à-clef*. A secret which is completely secret can have no value; it is through its partial disclosure that it becomes powerful, just as the factual referents behind a *roman-à-clef* must be concealed but also partly revealed for it to have any force.[44]

In so far as Pamphilia's pride in her secrecy, and her literary pursuits, provide a model of female authority and self-expression, it is one which is circumscribed, fully enabled only in chambers and cabinets, in isolation from society. In her presentation of women's public roles, Wroth conforms with seventeenth-century prescriptions of silence as a feminine virtue. In public, Pamphilia is 'generally the most silent and discreetly retir'd of any Princesse' (p. 50). At the beginning of Book I, Perissus describes his visit to his mistress Limena and her family:

Being there ariv'd . . . her Father, a grave and wise man, discoursed with mee of businesse of State: after him, and so all supper time, her husband discoursed of hunting. . . . Neither of these brought my Mistris from a grave, and almost sad countenance, which made me somewhat feare, knowing her understanding, and experience, able and sufficient to judge, or advise in any matter we could discourse of: but modestie in her caus'd it, onely loving knowledge, to be able to discerne mens understandings by their arguments, but no way to shew it by her owne speech. (pp. 6–7)

This positive evaluation of feminine modesty and discretion is reinforced by the depiction of countertypes to Pamphilia. One of these is Antissia, who believes herself to be Amphilanthus' mistress when the story opens, but is abandoned by him for Pamphilia. Antissia suffers from bouts of emotional confusion, when she is 'a meere Chaos, where unfram'd, and unorder'd troubles had tumbled themselves together without light of Judgement, to come out of them' (p. 95 [numbered 85]). Intrinsic to Pamphilia's admirability as a heroine is her ability to govern her emotions; indeed, images of government are frequently employed, translating her public authority as a queen into a metaphor for her private self-control (e.g. pp. 188, 398). Antissia, on the other hand, eventually goes mad in the manuscript continuation of the *Urania*, and in her madness she produces raving and rambling poetry, in direct contrast with Pamphilia's elegant versifyings.[45]

A further countertype to Pamphilia is Nereana, who is in love with Steriamus, who in turn is unrequitedly in love with Pamphilia. Nereana makes the long journey to Pamphilia's father's court to inspect her rival. After being received there, she wanders in the woods, but, unlike Pamphilia who derives calm and solace from her solitary musings, Nereana drives herself into a frenzied rage. The main feature of her character is pride and a lack of self-knowledge, 'all good thoughts wholy bent to her owne flattery'; she therefore rails at others whom she blames for her predicament. She loses herself in the woods, and this is linked metaphorically to her emotional confusion and lack of self-direction. She encounters Allanus, a shepherd turned mad by love, who decides she is the goddess of the woods, ties her to a tree, and dresses her up in buskins and a quiver. This incenses her still further, and when she then encounters a knight, Philarchos, who assumes from her outlandish appearance that she is a madwoman and scorns her, she becomes almost wild with fury. This is presented as a highly comic scene: the more pompously Nereana, in her ridiculous costume, asserts her regal identity, the more Philarchos is convinced of her madness (pp. 164–8). Swift misses the comic tone of the episode:

Wroth recognizes that Nereana is mad mainly in the eyes of an unreasonable world. . . . In the story of Nereana, women are justly angry at being idolized as women and then rejected when they use the wisdom for which they are revered.[46]

But if the story is read in context and with attention to the narrator's tone, it is clear that Nereana is being satirized for her pride and lack of emotional control, and is shown as receiving poetic justice.

The latter reading is supported by the beginning of the episode, Pamphilia's reception of Nereana at her father's court. She tells her,

> in truth I am sorry, that such a Lady should take so great and painefull a voyage, to so fond an end, being the first that ever I heard of, who took so Knight-like a search in hand; men being us'd to follow scornefull Ladies, but you to wander after a passionate, or disdainefull Prince, it is great pitie for you. Yet *Madam*, so much I praise you for it, as I would incourage you to proceede. (p. 163)

She tells Nereana that since she has no use for Steriamus' love, Nereana is welcome to it. Pamphilia is subtly mocking Nereana for taking on the inappropriate role of a 'lady errant', like the chambermaid in the 1615 *Characters*. This is confirmed by Nereana's reaction:

> These words were spoken so, as, though proud *Nereana* were nettled with them, yet could she not in her judgement finde fault openly with them, but rather sufferd them with double force to bite, inwardly working upon her pride-fild heart, and that in her eyes she a little shewed, though she suffered her knees somewhat to bow in reverence to her. (p. 163)

Pamphilia's speech is later referred back to by the narrator, who describes Nereana as 'exercising the part of an adventurous lover, as *Pamphilia* in jest had call'd her' (p. 165).

The 'double force' felt by Nereana is irony: just as Pamphilia only expresses her feelings freely in private, so, in public, she discreetly conceals her true opinion behind a veil of irony, at once saying and not saying, using its double-edged sword in cutting fashion without breaching the social code of feminine decorum. Thus irony, like private versifying, is presented in the *Urania* as a legitimate though circumscribed means of female expression. Indeed, it is frequently employed by the narrator, especially at the expense of male inconstancy, and, in particular, Amphilanthus. When a lady named Luceania declares her love for him, we are told that he is 'rather sorrie, then [i.e. than] glad', being pledged to Pamphilia; but he acquiesces out of chivalry: 'considering gratefulnesse is required as a chiefe vertue in everie worthie man. . . . Hee kindly entertain'd her favours, and courteously requited them.' We are left in no doubt that he does not find this duty to the knightly code particularly onerous (p. 136). Later, the narrator exclaims, '*Amphilanthus* I pittie thee . . . for inconstancy, was, and is the onely touch [i.e. fault] thou hast, yet can I not say, but thou art constant to love; for never art thou out of love' (p. 312). Just as Pamphilia uses 'double force' against Nereana, so the narrator frequently uses the form of compliment for teasing criticism of her hero.

In the mockery of Nereana for adopting the role of 'lady errant', Wroth reinforces stereotypical notions of appropriate masculine and feminine roles. There are other points in the narrative where women who appropriate masculine public roles are viewed with unease; in Book III, for instance, we encounter: 'a brave Lady, more manly in her demeanour, and discourse, then the modestest of her sexe would venture to be, and so much that fashion affected her, as she was a little too unlike a well governed Lady' (p. 351). Yet Pamphilia is sometimes praised for her 'brave and manlike spirit' (p. 483), when masculinity is being equated simply with emotional strength. There are places where Wroth seems anxious to revise feminine stereotypes, especially in the way she holds up women's private strengths for admiration. A knight describes his encounter with a bride whose lover has been slain:

> You will say, she wept, tore her haire, rent her clothes, cri'd, sobd, groand; No, she did not thus, she onely imbraced him, kissed him, and with as deadly a palenesse, as death could with most cunning counterfeit, and not execute, She entreated me to conduct her to the next Religious house, where shee would remaine till she might follow him. I admird her patience, but since more wonder'd at her worth. (p. 36)

Yet strength continues to be equated with masculinity, and weakness with femininity, sometimes producing paradox: Urania – a woman – forcefully urges Perissus – a man – to action, saying, 'Leave these teares, and woman-like complaints' (p. 13).

Swift rightly advises that we should not 'be antagonized by a woman writer's acceptance of the word "masculine" as synonymous with "strong" and "feminine" with "weak"'.[47] We must acknowledge the ideological and generic constraints upon Wroth's discourse, some of which she strains against, others of which she reproduces. For a modern feminist reader, one of the most problematic ways in which Wroth appears merely to reproduce conventions constructed by male authors is in the operation of the gaze in the *Urania*. Laura Mulvey has shown how, in traditional narrative cinema, a 'scopophilic' gaze operates, a 'determining male gaze', shared between male characters, camera and audience, which subordinates female characters and reduces them to a state of *'to-be-looked-at-ness'*. At the same time, the objectified woman is threatening, connoting castration, so that the feminine image is either fetishized, or subjected to sadistic voyeurism.[48] Nancy Vickers and Patricia Parker have shown that this model of the male gaze can be illuminating when applied to Renaissance texts, particularly those which use the blazon. They argue that the blazon, in analogy to the objectification of woman in narrative cinema, has less to do with the representation of women than with discursive display by a male speaker to a male audience.[49]

This model of the 'male gaze' creates problems in reading work like Wroth's. Though she is a woman writer, working in a genre of which a significant proportion of the readership was female, she introduces blazons at several points in the *Urania*'s narrative. One example is the Forest Knight's vision of Melasinda, the distressed Queen of Hungary: it runs through the conventional catalogue of hair, face, eyes, lips, a neck like marble and breasts like snow (p. 64). It is difficult to reconcile this with a concept of the workings of the male gaze as an exchange between male describer and audience. This is illustrated even more vividly in the representation of Limena. Limena is in love with Perissus, but her husband, Philargus, discovers this fact, and determines to kill her. It is notable that in this episode, as in many others in the *Urania*'s sub-narratives, adulterous love is presented as entirely admirable; it is the cuckolded husband who is the villain of the piece. It is partly because of the frequency of such episodes that Quilligan reads the *Urania* as exposing the 'traffic in women', the injustice of patriarchally arranged marriages, a view possibly reinforced by Wroth's own life-history. Krontiris, however, suggests that sixteenth- and seventeenth-century romance in general presented arranged marriages as oppressive, as it assimilated a courtly love-code which accommodated adultery with a new idealization of marriage for love.[50]

Just as Philargus was about to kill Limena, Perissus burst in. He describes what happened next:

> then untying a daintie embrodered wastcoate; see here, said she, the breast, (and a most heavenly breast it was) which you so dearly loved, or made me thinke so, calling it purest warme snow . . . but now 'tis ready to receive that stroake, shall bring my heart blood, cherish'd by you once, to dye it. . . . Whether these words, or that sight (which not to be seene without adoring) wrought most I knowe not, but both together so well prevaile as hee stood in a strange kind of fashion. (p. 11)

This is a narrative act of voyeurism, which can be interpreted in terms of Mulvey's discussion of scopophilia as described above. The admiring focus on the breast is fetishization; while, at the same time, the imagined scene of the white breast stained with red blood invokes sadism. Both male responses to the threat of the female body seem to be in play here, although the physical outbreak of sadism is delayed by the paralysing and stupefying sight of the breast. This hiatus in the onslaught of male-inflicted violence ties in with Vickers's and Parker's discussions of the erotic display of the female body as creating a stasis which is disempowering for the male onlooker, and which he defensively shatters by turning violence against the female body, such as in Petrarch's conversion of the destruction of Actaeon into the descriptive dismemberment of Diana, and the destruction of Acrasia and the Bower of Bliss in *The Faerie Queene*.[51]

When Limena's story is picked up again later, the narrator describes the spectacle of a woman, as yet unnamed, whom a man has stripped to the waist and tied to a pillar by her hair to whip her (p. 68). These figures are identified as Limena and Philargus; Limena is rescued, then continues the narrative herself:

> When I had put of all my apparell but one little Petticote, he opened my breast, and gave me many wounds, the markes you may here yet discerne, (letting the Mantle fall againe a little lower, to shew the cruell remembrance of his crueltie). (p. 71)

Here we have the figure of a woman, in a woman-authored text, who tantalizingly invites our gaze upon her body, marked by male sadism, as an erotic object. The male gaze is supposed to operate by the collusion of a male audience in the erotic objectification of the female body by male characters in a male-authored text; but, here, such a gaze is shown to operate when a female character in a female-authored text describes herself to a largely female readership. E. Ann Kaplan has asked whether, in film, the gaze as an instrument of power might be by its very nature inherently and inevitably male, and her questions and conclusions seem relevant here:

> Perhaps we can . . . say that in locating herself in fantasy in the erotic, the woman places herself as either passive recipient of male desire, or, at one remove, positions herself as *watching* a woman who is passive recipient of male desires and sexual actions. . . . The gaze is not necessarily male (literally), but to own and activate the gaze, given our language and the structure of the unconscious, is to be in the male position.[52]

These examples of the male gaze in the *Urania* illustrate the internalization by a female author of ways of seeing and representing which are associated with masculine sexuality. Here is another limitation upon the 'female consciousness' to be found in Wroth's romance.

However, alongside these instances where Wroth writes 'as a man', deploying a male or masculine gaze in ways which are oppressive to her own sex, there are other ways in which the gaze operates in the *Urania*. There are numerous episodes where an exchange of gazes, especially between female characters, marks an epiphanic moment of revelation and mutual affirmation. In Book II, Mellissea, a benign sorceress, prophesies their future fate to Pamphilia and her closest friend, Urania. Afterwards, 'they both stood gazing in each others face, as if the shining day Starre had stood still to looke her in a glasse'. Amphilanthus, who is with them, is excluded from this moment of revelation and mutual female reflection: in characteristically cavalier fashion, he forestalls Mellissea's attempt to prophesy to him: 'Nay, say no more, cry'd he, this is enough, and let me this enjoy, Ile feare no ills that Prophesies can tell' (p. 160). In a later episode, the shepherdess Veralinda is wandering, lamenting the loss of her love when she encounters a nymph of Diana, Leonia, who is also bemoaning her lost love. Again, a bond of similitude and empathy between them is sealed by a gaze. Veralinda has eyes 'so full of love, as all loving creatures found a power in them to draw them to her call'. Leonia's eyes 'full of teares were seeing themselves in the streame, shewing their watry pictures to each other'. But her gaze is drawn by Veralinda's, and the quest for solace in a reflection is redirected to her. They resolve to live together and return to Veralinda's home, 'the Shepheard[es]s passionately beholding *Leonia* in memory of her love, and the Nimph amorously gazing on her in her owne passions' (pp. 369–72).

In these examples, the exchange of gazes between women provides emotional solace and affirms their sense of self. It is analogous to another sort of visual pleasure identified by Mulvey, drawing on Lacan's description of the 'mirror stage' in infant development: that of identification with the image seen, which operates as a superior, perfected mirror-image, an ideal ego.[53] There is a further example in Pamphilia's encounter with another nymph of Diana, Allarina. Pamphilia and her ladies are hunting when they come across Allarina bathing in a stream, with her quiver and bow on the bank. Allarina tries to hide herself, but Pamphilia reassures her that she is no Actaeon: 'Sweete Nimph bee not thus dismaid, wee are none such as will give cause of any harme to you; wee are your friends, and following the sport which you oft do.' In an all-female company, the gaze does not intrude or engender violence; instead, it engenders empathy and communion. Like the confrontation between the male gaze and the female body, this encounter creates stasis, and Allarina is momentarily dumbstruck: 'when I did see you first I was amas'd'. But this is the stasis not of a disempowerment of the intratextual viewer which provokes defensive violence, but of wonder and revelation; as for Lacan's infant, visual recognition is the moment preceding language. Pamphilia, in drawing attention to the fact that she is hunting, indicates her likeness to the nymph; Allarina in turn confides that she has often secretly watched Pamphilia when she was hunting. Their mutual gaze encapsulates a mutual fascination and identification. The obvious echo of the myth of Diana and Actaeon makes this episode a direct all-female revision of the operation of the male gaze, converting its dominance and violence to peaceful reciprocity.

Allarina explains to Pamphilia that, having been abandoned by a faithless lover, she has 'wedded my selfe to chast *Dianas* life', changed her name to Silviana, and embraced solitude and self-reliance: 'I love my selfe, my selfe now loveth me.' The parallels between her and Pamphilia are evident, but she has gone further in achieving a complete renunciation of love, for which Pamphilia admires her. Her story presents a striking and positive example of total female autonomy (pp. 181 [numbered 281]–8). However, Wroth does not leave the story here. Over two hundred pages later, Pamphilia returns to Silviana's country, eager to see her again, only to find to her dismay that Silviana has reverted to her persona of Allarina and is getting married. Her explanation is simply that her old lover returned to her, which reduces her earlier dedication to chastity to mere hypocrisy or expediency (pp. 409–11). Likewise, the story of Veralinda and Leonia, apparently a celebration of passionate affection between women, is revised by the later course of the narrative: it turns out that all along Leonia was actually Leonius, Veralinda's male lover, in disguise (p. 389).[54] In these sub-plots, potentially radical models of female community or autonomy are asserted, but are ultimately reversed or contained.

It is necessary to stress the plurality of romance, and especially Wroth's romance. As I have said, Wroth's narrative voice differs from that of male-authored romance in that it is not explicitly gendered. In fact, Wroth's narrator is often in the shadows, on the sidelines, as narratives are framed within narratives. Whenever two characters meet, they tell each other their stories, or those of others, and such recessed narratives make up the bulk of the text. This means that there is a plethora of narrative voices, of both genders; and the multiplicity of voices and points of view render it an inaccuracy to assert that the story is simply about the constancy of women and inconstancy of men; rather, constancy is a theme which is explored dialectically. The character of Urania and her story propose an alternative to Pamphilia's fixed constancy as a response to the changefulness of men and of the world in general. Urania changes lovers, with no slur on her virtue, and is identified with variety, flexibility and common sense. She debates the value of constancy with Pamphilia, and exposes the sterility and excessiveness of Pamphilia's creed: love 'is not such a Deity, as your Idolatry makes him', and 'Tis pittie said *Urania*, that ever that fruitlesse thing Constancy was taught you as a vertue' (pp. 399–400).[55] Furthermore, in the many sub-narratives, women are as often inconstant as men.[56] There are many debates between characters on the themes of love and constancy: the Prince of Thiques reports of his encounter with the Lady of Rhodes, 'shee could say nothing against men, that I had not as much, or more to speak against women'. She 'at last agree'd with mee, that Man was the constanter of the two uncertainties' (p. 464). Earlier,

Dolorindus and Steriamus engage in 'deep, and almost collerick dispute, against, and for the worth of women kinde'. Dolorindus has been deserted by his mistress, and Steriamus accuses him of bias: 'Love in aboundance made you too farre crost, blame Love then, not her scorne' (p. 159). This suggests that we should regard all the various voices in the *Urania* as subjective and relative.

However, despite these many counterpoints to the central narrative of Pamphilia and Amphilanthus, constant woman and inconstant man, it remains central, and the narrator seems to have a particular sympathy with her heroine. Indeed, many of Wroth's contemporaries assumed that she was representing herself in Pamphilia. This reading is sustained by the fact that Pamphilia is herself a writer, and the representation of women's reading and writing within a piece of women's writing sets up a complex sequence of narrative frames. For instance, at one point we see Pamphilia, characteristically, sitting alone in a thick wood reading a romance:

> the subject was Love, and the story she then was reading, the affection of a Lady to a brave Gentleman, who equally loved, but being a man, it was necessary for him to exceede a woman in all things, so much as inconstancie was found fit for him to excell her in, hee left her for a new. (p. 264)

This sounds uncannily like a description of the *Urania* itself: Pamphilia is reading her own story. Ironically, she doesn't enjoy the book, and throws it away. Later, Pamphilia tells Dorolina the story of Lindamira, 'faigning it to be written in a French Story'. In fact, the events of Lindamira's life bear a striking resemblance to Wroth's own; for instance, she abruptly falls from her Queen's favour, 'remaining like one in a gay Masque, the night pass'd, they are in their old clothes againe, and no appearance of what was' (pp. 423–4). Dorolina admires the story, 'which shee thought was some thing more exactly related then a fixion' (p. 429). So, here, Lady Mary tells the story of Pamphilia who in turn tells the story of Lady Mary/Lindamira.

In this story of Lindamira, and in the whole *Urania* as a *roman-à-clef*, Wroth attempts to use fiction as a veil, a coded means of telling 'real-life' stories, at once revealing and concealing them. Intensifying the effect of Chinese boxes, her heroine does the same. In Book I, Antissia finds some of Pamphilia's verses carved on a tree; she triumphantly confronts Pamphilia with the information that she has discovered her secret love: 'You cannot thus dissemble (replied *Antissia*), your owne hand in yonder faire Ash will witnes against you. Not so (said *Pamphilia*) for many Poets write aswell by imitation, as by sence of passion' (p. 77 [numbered 67]). This sounds very like Wroth defending the *Urania* against Denny's charge of libel. Both the author and her heroine disclaim a connection between life and art in order to protect themselves. Fiction, like irony, has a 'double force', at once saying and not saying; and, like irony or private versifying, Wroth seeks to appropriate fiction as a means of 'safe' female expression. Both she and her female characters attempt to use fiction as an outlet for personal grievances and a means of achieving desired ends, without risking the breach of social codes of courtesy and femininity. In Book IV, Elyna gets rid of an unwanted suitor by telling him: 'a tale before him of himselfe, his wooing so dully, her scorne, and affection to another, all in the third parsons, but so plainely and finely, as he left her to her pleasures' (p. 508).

Unfortunately, for Wroth, fiction was not so efficacious. It seems clear that she drew upon people in her social circle as material for her romance, while refuting such interpretation of it as 'strang constructions which are made of my booke contrary to my imagination, and as farr from my meaning as is possible for truth to bee from conjecture'.[57] Her dilemma as author of a *roman-à-clef* was that she must at once use and disclaim reality; her further predicament was that she must rely on her reader's recognition of the real correlatives of her fictions, while also relying on such recognition as being tacit and acquiescent, as in the case of Elyna's suitor, who took the hint without objection. On page 416 of the *Urania*, Perissus is walking with Limena and the Queens of Naples and Sicily in a grove, where:

> Going along the Spring they found many knots, & names ingraven upon the trees, which they understood not perfectly, because when they had decipher'd some of them, they then found they were names fained and so knew them not. But *Perissus* remembred one of the Ciphers, yet because it was *Pamphilias* hee would not knowe it.

He does not mention it to his companions; and this was exactly the type of discreet deciphering, of courteous though knowing collusion in her act of veiling, which Wroth required of her readers.

The fact that they did not oblige seems to have been partly

because her allusions to factual events were too obvious, partly because some of the events which she chose to depict were too sensitive, and partly because she was deemed to have acted in a manner improper for a woman. John Chamberlain's letter to Sir Dudley Carleton at the height of the *Urania* scandal said that Wroth 'takes great libertie or rather licence to traduce whom she please, and thincks she daunces in a net'.[58] The expression 'to dance in a net' seems to have been proverbial, with the primary sense that the dancer exposes her/himself while thinking s/he is concealed.[59] It may therefore have the sense here that Wroth, by straying too far into the recognizably real and personal, had exposed herself improperly, in a manner analogous to physical self-exposure. The veil of fiction behind which she presumed to hide was deemed too thin for decency.[60]

Zurcher has eloquently shown how aptly the phrase 'dancing in a net' describes Wroth's predicament, on many grounds:

> As an author who relies on her own position inside society at the same time she pitches herself outside it, Wroth is thus bound by the same ambivalence that liberates her, dancing a teetering dance on the lines of a net. . . . In a precarious and not-quite-definable position socially, financially, literarily because of both her gender and her family, the author was caught between past and present, action and inaction, meaning and non-meaning, and her romance is the reflection both of the power and the paralysis this predicament brought her as a writer.[61]

From this unstable position, Wroth engages ambivalently with the conventions of male-authored romance. Sometimes she merely reproduces masculine conventions, even when they are oppressive to women. Sometimes she overturns them only to reinstate them at later stages of the narrative, enacting a form of contained transgression. But she performed an act of outright radicalism in her very authorship of a romance; and in her bold and repeated assertion throughout her book that literary activity, whether the writing of poetry or the reading of romances, is appropriate, indeed, invaluable for women. In debate with Urania, Pamphilia declares,

> yet I must say some thing in loves defence . . . that I have read in all stories, and at all times, that the wisest, bravest,

and most excellent men have been lovers, and are subject to this passion. (p. 399)

Her reading of romances provides her with an authorization of her way of life; and, in particular, it authorizes the primacy of the private, emotional and personal, the 'feminine' domain. Just as the reciprocal gaze between women can be a source of support and self-affirmation, so fiction is also a kind of mirror in which the female reader can see her experiences duplicated and thereby, paradoxically, made more real.[62] Elsewhere, Pamphilia asks Limena to tell her a story, hoping that, by measuring her experiences against those of the characters, she will be able to raise herself from a despairing mood:

> let me but understand the choice varieties of Love, and the mistakings, the changes, the crosses; if none of these you know, yet tell me some such fiction. (p. 188)

Fiction is at once a guide to life, consolation for heartache, and a private pleasure.

In this Pamphilia resembles the modern women readers of romantic fiction studied by Janice Radway, and some of the questions raised by Radway become relevant. Could Renaissance romance subvert the patriarchal order in its demarcation of private, autonomous, imaginative, female space? Or, by enabling women to escape from their daily lives, and by its presentation of iniquitous relations between the sexes as timeless and 'natural', did it distract them from protest or resistance and reinforce the status quo? Pamphilia finds solace and self-reliance in her reading and writing, but they perpetuate her passive resignation to Amphilanthus' mistreatment. Wroth's negotiations of the conventions of romance illustrate how the supposed 'femininity' of the genre held both positive and negative aspects for female writers and readers.

NOTES

(Place of publication for works printed before 1800 is London unless otherwise stated. Original spellings have been retained, apart from u/v and i/j, and book titles, which have been modernized, and quotations from modernized sources.)

I am indebted to Clare Brant, Katherine Duncan-Jones, Dennis Kay, Diane Purkiss, Josephine Roberts and Sophie Tomlinson for their extremely helpful comments on this piece.

1 See Louis B. Wright, *Middle-Class Culture in Elizabethan England*, Chapel Hill, University of North Carolina Press, 1935, pp. 111–17; Tina Krontiris, 'Breaking the Barriers of Genre and Gender: Margaret Tyler's Translation of *The Mirrour of Knighthood*', in *English Literary Renaissance*, 1988, vol. 18, no. 1, pp. 24–5.

2 For a definition of romance, see Gillian Beer, *The Romance*, London, Methuen, 1970, pp. 1–12. Lennard J. Davis, *Factual Fictions: The Origins of the English Novel*, New York, Columbia University Press, 1983, p. 40, lists characteristic differences between the novel and the romance.

3 On the class and gender of the readership of Renaissance romances, see Wright, pp. 111–17; Margaret Spufford, *Small Books and Pleasant Histories: Popular Fiction and its Readership in Seventeenth-Century England*, Cambridge, Cambridge University Press, 1985, pp. 34–6, 50–1, 233–4; Caroline Lucas, *Writing for Women: The Example of Woman as Reader in Elizabethan Romance*, Milton Keynes, Open University Press, 1989, pp. 8–18.

4 Barnaby Rich, *Rich's Farewell to Military Profession*, 1581, ed. Thomas M. Cranfill, Austin, University of Texas Press, 1959, pp. 3–19; John Lyly, *Euphues: The Anatomy of Wit, Euphues and his England*, ed. M.W. Croll and H. Clemons, London, Routledge, 1916, pp. 191–204.

5 Lyly, p. 201; Sir Philip Sidney, *The Countess of Pembroke's Arcadia (The Old Arcadia)*, ed. Katherine Duncan-Jones, Oxford, Oxford University Press, 1985, p. 3.

6 Paul Salzman, *English Prose Fiction 1558–1700: A Critical History*, Oxford, Clarendon, 1985, p. 17.

7 Robert Greene, *Penelope's Web*, 1587, in Alexander B. Grosart (ed.), *The Life and Complete Works of Robert Greene*, 15 vols, N.p. Huth Library, 1881–6, vol. V, pp. 144–5.

8 Lucas, pp. 18–26.

9 Wright, p. 110.

10 Janice A. Radway, *Reading the Romance: Women, Patriarchy and Popular Literature*, Chapel Hill and London, University of North Carolina Press, 1984, pp. 86–118, 209–22; and see also Lucas, pp. 22–6; Tania Modleski, *Loving with a Vengeance: Mass-produced Fantasies for Women*, New York, Methuen, 1984; Jean Radford, 'Introduction', in *The Progress of Romance: The Politics of Popular Fiction*, London, Routledge Kegan Paul, 1986, pp. 1–20.

11 Sir Thomas Overbury, *New and Choise Characters of Severall Authors*, 6th edn, 1615, sigs G4V-5R. For discussion of the phrase 'lady errant', see Hero Chalmers's chapter in this volume.

12 Thomas Powell, *Tom of All Trades. Or the Plaine Path-Way To Preferment*, 1631, p. 47.

13 'Poetresse' is simply an obsolete term for 'poetess'; see the *Oxford English Dictionary*, 2nd edn, Oxford, Clarendon, 1989.

14 Patricia Parker, *Literary Fat Ladies: Rhetoric, Gender, Property*, London, Methuen, 1987, pp. 8–35, especially pp. 10–11.
15 Roger Ascham, *The Schoolmaster*, 1570, ed. Lawrence V. Ryan, Ithaca, NY, Cornell University Press, 1967, p. 67.
16 Sidney, p. 25.
17 George Gascoigne, *The Adventures of Master F.J.*, 1573, in Paul Salzman (ed.), *An Anthology of Elizabethan Prose Fiction*, Oxford, Oxford University Press, 1987, pp. 54–8, 67–73.
18 Greene, pp. 194, 233, 154–5, 162.
19 Spufford, pp. 4–6, 12–13, 59, 62, 79–80, 172.
20 e.g. George Peele's play, *The Old Wives' Tale*, 1595.
21 See also Philip Massinger, *The Guardian*, in Philip Edwards and Colin Gibson (eds), *The Plays and Poems of Philip Massinger*, vol. IV, Oxford, Oxford University Press, 1976, I. ii. 66–71.
22 Margaret Tyler, 'To the Reader', in Diego Ortuñez de Calahorra, *The Mirrour of Princely Deedes and Knighthood*, trans. M[argaret] T[yler], Thomas East, 1578, sigs A3R-4V. Subsequent quotations from Tyler are taken from her epistle to the reader.
23 See Margaret Patterson Hannay (ed.), *Silent But for the Word: Tudor Women as Patrons, Translators, and Writers of Religious Works*, Kent, Ohio, Kent State University Press, 1985, especially 'Introduction', pp. 1–14.
24 For further biographical detail, see Lady Mary Wroth, *The Poems of Lady Mary Wroth*, ed. Josephine A. Roberts, Baton Rouge and London, Louisiana State University Press, 1983, pp. 3–40.
25 Lady Mary Wroth, *The Countesse of Mountgomeries Urania*, 1621, p. 250. All further references to this work will be referred to by page number in the text. Josephine A. Roberts is preparing a new edition of the *Urania* which she hopes to complete in 1992.
26 Wroth, *Poems*, p. 70, n. 15. Dale Spender thinks that Wroth wrote the *Urania* in order to rescue herself from debt, and may therefore have been the first woman to write for money (Dale Spender, *Mothers of the Novel: 100 Good Women Writers before Jane Austen*, London, Pandora, 1986, pp. 11–22).
27 I am grateful to Josephine A. Roberts for this information.
28 The manuscript is in the Newberry Library, Chicago, call no. Case MS f.Y1565.W95.
29 Wroth, *Poems*, pp. 31–5, 238–9.
30 See Elaine V. Beilin, *Redeeming Eve: Women Writers of the English Renaissance*, Princeton, Princeton University Press, 1987, p. 212.
31 Wroth, *Poems*, quotes Chamberlain on p. 36 and Manners's letter on pp. 29, 244–5. Other analogies are discussed on pp. 29–31. Margaret Hannay also discusses possible family references in the *Urania* in '"Your vertuous and learned Aunt": the Countess of Pembroke as a Mentor to Lady Wroth', to appear in a forthcoming collection of essays on Wroth, ed. Gary Waller and Naomi Miller. I am grateful to Professor Hannay for allowing me to read this piece prior to publication.
32 Salzman, *Anthology*, p. xiii.
33 Wroth, *Poems*, p. 28.

34 Davis, pp. 11–24, 35–6, 212.

35 Other details of the *Arcadia* which suggested 'real-life' referents included the story of Argalus and Parthenia, perhaps drawing on Sidney's mother's disfigurement by smallpox; and the description of Queen Helen of Corinth, who resembles Queen Elizabeth.

36 Amelia Zurcher, '"Dauncing in a Net": Representation in Lady Mary Wroth's *Urania*', unpublished M.Phil. thesis, Oxford University, 1989, p. 7. I am very grateful to the author for permission to quote from this thesis.

37 Zurcher lists echoes of the *Arcadia* in the *Urania*, p. 8. Beilin, p. 215, points out that the name Pamphilia is an amalgam of Pamela and Philoclea. In Wroth, *Poems*, Roberts's notes on Wroth's poems point out numerous correspondences between her work and that of Philip and other Sidneys.

38 See Elaine V. Beilin, '"The Onely Perfect Vertue": Constancy in Mary Wroth's *Pamphilia to Amphilanthus*', *Spenser Studies*, 1981, vol. 2, pp. 229–45; Beilin, *Redeeming Eve*, pp. 232–43.

39 The Countess of Montgomery was Susan Vere, a close neighbour and friend of Wroth's; she was married to Wroth's cousin, Sir Philip Herbert, brother of William Herbert. See Wroth, *Poems*, p. 27.

40 See Maureen Quilligan, 'Lady Mary Wroth: Female Authority and the Family Romance', in George M. Logan and Gordon Teskey (eds), *Unfolded Tales: Essays on Renaissance Romance*, Ithaca, NY, Cornell University Press, 1989, pp. 257–80, for discussion of specific incidents in the *Urania* which rewrite episodes from the *Arcadia* and *The Faerie Queene*.

41 Carolyn Ruth Swift, 'Female Identity in Lady Mary Wroth's Romance *Urania*', *English Literary Renaissance*, 1984, vol. 14, no. 3, pp. 330, 331. See also Carolyn Ruth Swift, 'Feminine Self-definition in Lady Mary Wroth's *Love's Victorie (c.* 1621)', *English Literary Renaissance*, 1989, vol. 19, no. 2, pp. 171–88.

42 Quilligan, p. 261 and *passim*.

43 This description does not quite fit Pamphilia's strategies in the manuscript continuation, but for brevity's sake this discussion is confined to the published 1621 *Urania*.

44 For a fuller discussion of the importance of secrets and their selective disclosure as a source of female strength and identity in the *Urania*, see Zurcher, pp. 17–26.

45 Wroth, Newberry MS, ff. 11R–12R, 15V–16V.

46 Swift, 'Female Identity', p. 345.

47 ibid., p. 346.

48 Laura Mulvey, 'Visual Pleasure and Narrative Cinema', *Screen*, 1975, vol. 16, no. 3, pp. 6–18.

49 Nancy J. Vickers, '"The blazon of sweet beauty's best": Shakespeare's *Lucrece*', in Patricia Parker and Geoffrey Hartman (eds), *Shakespeare and the Question of Theory*, New York and London, Methuen, 1985, pp. 95–115; Nancy J. Vickers, 'Diana Described: Scattered Woman and Scattered Rhyme', in Elizabeth Abel (ed.), *Writing and Sexual Difference*, Brighton, Harvester, 1982, pp. 265–79; Parker, pp. 65–6, 126–54.

50 Quilligan, *passim*; Krontiris, pp. 25–36. See also Josephine Roberts, '"The Knott Never to Bee Untide": The Controversy Regarding Marriage in Lady Mary Wroth's *Urania*', in Waller and Miller, forthcoming (see n. 31 above).

51 Vickers, 'Diana Described'; Edmund Spenser, *The Faerie Queene*, ed. A.C. Hamilton, London, Longman, 1977, II. xii; Parker, pp. 65–6.

52 E. Ann Kaplan, 'Is the Gaze Male?', in Ann Snitow, Christine Stansell and Sharon Thompson (eds), *Desire: The Politics of Sexuality*, London, Virago, 1984, pp. 328, 331.

53 Jacques Lacan, 'The Mirror Stage as Formative of the Function of the I', in *Ecrits: A Selection*, trans. Alan Sheridan, London, Tavistock, 1977, pp. 1–7; Mulvey, pp. 9–10, 12.

54 Indeed, the first encounter between Veralinda and 'Leonia' and their mutual gaze strongly resembles the meeting between Philoclea and 'Cleophila' in the *Old Arcadia* which culminates in an embrace and Pyrocles' revelation of his identity (Sidney, pp. 104–5).

55 For further discussion of Urania as representing a positive alternative to Pamphilia's constancy, see Zurcher, pp. 57–9, 67–80. Zurcher also suggests that Urania is identified with the plurality and prose of romance narrative, while Pamphilia is identified with the emotional directness of lyric poetry.

56 See, for example, the Lady-of-May-type figure who is satirized for her inability to choose between two lovers (pp. 382–6); and Lady Fancy in the manuscript continuation (Wroth, Newberry MS, ff. 12R–V).

57 Wroth, *Poems*, p. 236.

58 Wroth, *Poems*, p. 36.

59 See Zurcher, pp. 2–3, 81–2, n. 4.

60 See Rosalind Ballaster's chapter in this volume on Delarivier Manley, a later woman writer who caused scandal through her use of the *roman-à-clef*.

61 Zurcher, pp. 9–13.

62 See Hero Chalmers's chapter in this volume on Mary Carleton, a woman of the later seventeenth century who used the discursive models of romance in 'real life' for both the authorization of female subjectivity and the disruption of masculine definitions of identity.

3

MATERIAL GIRLS: THE SEVENTEENTH-CENTURY WOMAN DEBATE

Diane Purkiss

The kind of attention paid collectively to the texts of the late Elizabethan and Jacobean 'woman debate' signed with female names suggests that many critics understand feminism to be a relatively recognizable political and literary category which, though historically variable, is also visible across historical boundaries.[1] This chapter explores the possibility that the identification of oppositional resistance as expressed by a single author may be a difficult matter historically; texts we recognize as feminist in our present circumstances might in their historical context represent not feminist univocality, but an awkward combination of contradictory speaking-positions such as the assumption of a negotiating stance on the terrain of politics, a subversive play with the question of gender in terms unfamiliar to modern feminism, and the production of femininity as a saleable commodity in the literary market. What we recognize in these texts may be the processing of woman as a theatrical role or masquerade which can never be equated with an essential woman or audible authorial voice but which, rather, troubles the very existence of such a self-identical figure. These are texts which cannot be put easily into categories of metaphor alone or categories of authentic voicing; instead, they are texts where the metaphors used to naturalize the gender systems of early modern England are both assaulted and upheld. I shall explore these speculations, and the anxieties that attend them, through a reading of the late Elizabethan and Jacobean texts signed by women. These include *Jane Anger her Protection for Women* (1589), *A Mouzell for Melastomus*, by Rachel Speght (1617), *Ester hath Hang'd Haman*, by Ester Sowernam (1617), *The Worming of A Mad Dogge*, by

Constantia Munda (1617), and *The Women's Sharp Revenge*, by Mary Tattle-well and Joan Hit–Him–Home (1640), but I shall be focusing particularly on the responses to Joseph Swetnam's *The Arraignment of Lewd, Idle, Froward and Unconstant Woman* (1615), which include Speght, 'Sowernam' and 'Munda'.[2] These texts, I shall argue, pose a series of challenges to feminist reading practices which have never been fully addressed. Because they purport to be by women, they seem to offer a visible female self-consciousness about gender, a site upon which female agency is fully and openly displayed in a manner recognizable or nameable as feminism. In other words, they excite the desire to recognize the present in the past, to name what we can term our *own* history. But because what is at stake in these texts seems at first glance so familiar and understandable, it is possible that their estranging or culturally autonomous aspects may not be fully noticed; moreover, because they can so readily be situated in the context of gender politics, they are never fully situated in the political and discursive specificities of the early modern period.

These texts have been read by feminists through a reductive and often unconsidered attribution to a single or unified female author. The kinds of investments made in the location of a protofeminist agency in these texts and, by extension, in early modern women synecdochally represented in them, can be glimpsed in the choice of epithets used to describe the pieces by feminist critics. These epithets all read the speaking voice of the pamphlets as a representation of a female figure whose tangibility can be established by recourse to the texts. Angeline Goreau, for example, argues that 'The repeated attacks on women . . . provided a great source of anger that pushed women to answer in print', while Joan Kelly writes that 'Constantia Munda and the circle of women with which she says she discussed the matter were clearly outraged by a mounting wave of misogyny'. Katherine Usher Henderson and Barbara McManus write of Munda's 'impassioned invective' and 'fervour'.[3] More recently, Betty Travitsky writes of women's 'anger' and 'powerful invective', while Elaine Beilin insists on the writers' 'anger on behalf of their whole sex'.[4] 'Anger', 'outrage', 'fervour', 'passion': these are recognizable keywords in the rhetoric of certain kinds of radical feminism which characteristically valorize the emotions of rebellion. Joan Kelly's title, 'Early Feminist Theory', makes explicit the desire to locate both academic and early modern text in a historical continuum of identity. Early feminism becomes an enabling pretext for the production of feminism now.

Such reading strategies necessarily lead to an assumption that texts signed by women are indeed the work of women; the language of criticism reveals a desire for material girls, women as real as ourselves. Having located the emotion-laden speaking voice of an author in the text, this voice must in turn be sited in a female agent; indeed the voice is prized less for itself than as a sign pointing towards such an authorial presence. A logocentric cycle is set up whereby a female signature prompts a reading strategy designed to uncover female consciousness in texts, and this consciousness in turn is held to manifest the presence of a female author.

But because four of the sixteenth- and seventeenth-century texts I am discussing here are pseudonymous, the gendering of their authors remains open to question. A reading strategy that would overlook these problems is problematic not only because it is troublingly logocentric, eliding the literary and textual aspects of the pamphlets in the interests of reconstructing a female speaking voice, but also because it is politically dangerous. The acceptance of internal evidence for the gendering of authorship – where that is in serious doubt – can often reinscribe singular notions of woman's essential character or voice, writing the female as something immediately visible or identifiable. It is not my aim in this chapter to try to establish the gender of the authors of these pamphlets: rather it is my purpose to try to *dis*establish what has been too easily assumed. I shall be arguing for a reading strategy which takes account of the function of the pseudonymous signatures as they can be read within the texts themselves, rather than as pointers to an originary author figure who stands outside the text. In order to determine the workings of the 'woman debate' genre, I shall begin with Swetnam's *Arraignment of Lewd, Idle, Froward and Unconstant Woman*, to try to locate some of the pleasures provided by Swetnam's play with the discourses of moral debate and suggest a way of reading the pseudonymous pamphlet replies to him.

In a sense Swetnam's text is the source of the patterns of (mis)reading which I have been discussing. Until very recently, Swetnam's arguments and his textual means of presenting them were assumed to be synecdochal of the views of an established patriarchy being challenged by the liberalization of puritanism on one hand and the women's defences on the other. But not only has the liberating effect of puritanism come into serious question in recent years, the notion of an established patriarchy has itself been subjected to critical scrutiny.[5] One of the literary causes for the instatement of an ahistorical patriarchy as a staple of women's history was the conflation of patriarchy with misogyny. Anthologies such as Julia O'Faolain's and Lauro Martines's *Not in God's Image* sought to show the continuity of woman-hatred from the ancient world to the present, and a strong strand of radical feminism also produced an ahistorical narrative of woman-hatred or gynocide and female opposition.[6] Because of the dominance of these stories, few attempts were made to relate misogyny to patriarchy, or to ask how discourses of woman-hatred acted upon other coercive or oppressive material and discursive practices which subordinate women.

Attempts to ask or answer this question are complicated by the very feature of misogynistic discourses which led to the construction of this ahistorical story in the first place. This feature is their frequent deployment of a rhetoric of citation.[7] From the beginning, misogyny does not purport to be originary or creative; instead, its characteristic move is to reiterate or re-cite stories or figures always already known. In this sense, misogyny is less a single unified voice than a collocation of stories and speeches that can be voiced at any time, and thus it is that some of the tropes of woman-hatred do appear to transcend cultural specificity.[8] The sixteenth- and seventeenth-century writers under discussion here are especially dependent on a rhetoric of citation, and Swetnam is a particularly egregious instance.[9] Repeatedly, critics stigmatize him for lack of originality: Simon Shepherd calls his work 'grossly derivative in its language and ideas' (p. 53), while Linda Woodbridge and Ann Rosalind Jones argue that Swetnam's weak argument, implicitly linked by both writers to his unoriginality, allowed women to respond to him.[10] This notion ignores both the remarkable popularity of Swetnam's pamphlet and its place within a genre of misogynistic writing which was constructed in and by its citational rhetoric. The place of citation in misogyny seems to go beyond what can be explained by a simple liking for the predictable, or at any rate critics have so far failed to ask why the predictable should be so desirable in this particular context.

Citation seems at once to act as an authenticating discourse which validates the misogynistic enterprise by aligning it with what is always already apparent, and a displacing move which is supposed to make it impossible to read an individual male writer as the author of misogyny. Just as the ambivalence of pseudonyms troubles our notion of authorship in the case of the pamphlets signed by women, so the genre of misogynistic invective refuses our desire to locate its texts in an originating author. In this way, the problematization of authorship is intrinsic to the woman–debate genre in both attack and defence.[11] Swetnam's citations make his text difficult to read because they trouble attempts to reduce the text to a particular point of view; the text is multivalent and self-contradictory not because Swetnam was somehow a terrible writer, but because the project of his work depends in the end less on coherence than on contradiction. In producing a reading of it, I will inevitably be eliding some of its twists and turns myself.

Swetnam's deployment of a rhetoric of citation goes beyond the mere reiteration of the familiar, creating at certain points an intertextual *bricolage* of considerable subversive power. It is important to distinguish his misogyny from the more general conception of patriarchy or a patriarchal social order because in *The Arraignment* misogyny is frequently opposed to the powerful and institutionalized discourses of patriarchy, particularly those emerging discourses of conduct and providence which sought to coerce both men and women into exceptionally well-marked social roles. These discourses, to be found in sermons and 'marriage manuals' which advocate the moral order of what may be recognizable as early capitalism, are characteristically exaggerated or comically inverted by Swetnam. For example, the Biblical notion that woman is a helpmeet to man was a staple text of these moral discourses, characteristically used to place the woman in an economically subordinate position; her husband was to obtain money or goods, and she was to care for them.[12] In Swetnam, this Biblical text is duly cited, but this traditional exegesis is reversed:

> Moses describeth a woman thus: 'At the first beginning' saith he, 'a woman was made to be a helper unto man'. And so they are indeed, for she helpeth to spend and consume that which man painfully getteth.[13]

Here woman is barred from occupying her appropriate place; Swetnam breaks down the polarity between the helpful woman who supports her husband's endeavour and the woman who enacts her own desires in defiance of his. But the joke on which the pleasure of the passage depends is not only on women, but on the morally earnest discourse which glosses helpmeet more diversely. To put this in more literary terms, it is a carnivalesque moment, in which the low inserts itself subversively into the high.

The discourses of morality and prudence become pretexts for a pleasurable carnivalesque play with their terms. Similarly, many 'marriage manuals' gave lengthy and earnest advice on the process of choosing a good wife. Swetnam tackles the problem by citing the advice of 'an ancient Father' who tells a young man that to choose a wife he must run blindfold into a group of young maidens and seize one of them, making her his wife (pp. 45–6). When the young man protests that he may be deceived, the old sage explains that this may happen even if he keeps his eyes open. The play on the unavoidability of women's deceit is less crucial here, perhaps, than the way in which an earnest and careful economic decision is transmuted by Swetnam into a holiday game of Blind Man's Buff, a festive pastime.

Thus woman is less an object of interest in herself than a site of conflict between classes and discourses. Swetnam's pamphlet is obsessed with money, social hierarchy and money as a solvent of social hierarchy. Again and again he refers to women's capacity to spend money,[14] and he also describes women as commodities: 'a beautiful woman is for the most part costly', women are 'jewels', 'all precious, yet they are not all of one price' (p. 7, sig. A2V). Repeating the proverb that 'there is more to housekeeping than fower bare legs in a bed', he writes:

> there are many who think when they are married that they may live by love, but if wealth be wanting, hot love will soon be cold. . . . For all thy money wastes in toys and is spent in banqueting. . . . For commonly women are proud without profit, and that is a good purgation for thy purse, and when thy purse is light, then will thy heart be heavy. (pp. 6, 23–4).

What is at stake here is the place of woman in the economy of the household, a topic central to the moral discourses Swetnam satirizes. Woman is anomalous in the household economy because she can spend money but cannot produce it. But whereas in the writings of moralists woman's place is normalized as the keeper or retainer of goods, in Swetnam woman signifies the leakage into the market of goods that ought to be stored. She is a signifier of wastage, not merely the absence of productivity but a prodigal consumption of resources. The point, however, is that woman spends money on her *own* desires, 'toys', 'banqueting' and female pride.

As Lorna Hutson has shown, the notion of 'profitable' learning circulated an economic conception of the process of acquiring knowledge. Knowledge was stored up as the profit to be gained from reading, often in the form of *exempla*. Hutson contrasts this notion of profitability with the textual play of Nashe, who squanders the resources of learning in a figuration of the writer as spendthrift which engages subversively with the costive discourse of humanist morality.[15] Given this model, what is curious or anomalous about Swetnam's place within it is that his anxieties about female prodigality and his retention and re-citation of traditional stories are placed in a text which self-consciously allies its own speaking voice with a Nashean prodigality rather than a moral providentiality, both in terms of content and in terms of its figuration of its own production. The idle pastimes ceaselessly inveighed against by moralists as forms of consumptive waste are the very ones through which Swetnam tropes his own activity. In his epistle to male readers, for example, Swetnam writes:

> If thou meanst to see the Bearbaiting of women, then trudge to this beargarden apace and get in betimes. And view every room wh[e]re thou mayest best sit for thine owne pleasure. ('Epistle to Men', sig. A3V.)

Bearbaiting was frequently represented as an idle pastime by puritan moralists like Philip Stubbes.[16] Swetnam figures his text and its production as a vulgar, unprofitable pleasure for those who buy it – though profitable for himself, the showman. Similarly, he makes frequent mention of alehouses and taverns. Repeatedly, he describes his book as the product of his own idleness: 'Musing with myself, being idle, and having little ease to pass the time withal' ('Epistle to women readers', sig. A2R), and he concludes by exhorting all his readers to 'take it merrily, and to esteme of this book onely as the toyes of an idle head' (p. 64). Swetnam thus figures his book as a pastime, the antithesis of the use of time advocated by the discourses of morality. He figures himself both as showman and as participant in a festive process, in which he both displays pleasures for his audience and joins them in seeking entertainment. In this way, Swetnam's text constitutes its relations with its audience as an exchange of pleasures.

As the writings of Lévi-Strauss and Irigaray might suggest, the structural basis for this discursive exchange is perhaps the exchange of women themselves as commodities through marriage; in this way, women can be made to seem productive or economically viable.[17] It is thus not surprising to find that a central trope of Swetnam's text is the exchange of sexually open or available women, together with knowledge of how to gain access to them. Swetnam boastfully stresses the ease with which women can be obtained: 'women are easily wooed and soon won, got with an apple and lost with the paring . . . golden gifts easily overcome wanton's desires' (pp. 26–7, 33). Women are available because, like bearbaiting, they are pleasures which can be exchanged for money. This also aligns them with Swetnam's text itself, which enacts the circulation of pleasures it describes by circulating stories about pleasures to give pleasure. But Swetnam's picture of circulating wantons is the antithesis of the social stability supposedly produced by women's marketing in marriage. For him, women circulate *freely* among men; that is, the *men* are free to exchange them. Like pleasure, their circulation is not regulated by ownership; it is inherently transitory.

The exchange of women's bodies for money is troped not as a sign of male wealth, however, but as a sign of the dissolution of class and wealth boundaries. Swetnam dilates upon the proverb 'Jone is as good as my lady':

> Jone is as good as my lady; according to the Countery-mans Proverbe, who gave a great summe of money to lye with a Lady, and going homewards, he made a grievous mone for his money, and one being on the other side the hedge, heard him say, that his Jone at home was as good as the lady.[18] (p. 9)

The pure masculinity of the economy of pleasure transcends and dissolves class boundaries, but not in any idealistic manner. Rather, the point is that in terms of that pleasure economy, Jack enjoys exactly what his master enjoys. Troping the pleasure available from women as always the same regardless of wealth and rank is an obviously consolatory fantasy in the hierarchized society of Jacobean England, so that once again women are a mere site upon which male anxieties about other men can be allayed.

But this is another story about feminine deception and economic prodigality too. The lady appears more valuable than Jone, but the pleasure she provides, constructed here as the locus of her true value, does not justify her high price. The story reduces women's extravagance, inveighed against elsewhere, to a deceitful inflation of their market price. Once again this inverts the arguments of moralists like Stubbes, for whom female extravagance was problematic precisely because it *unsettled* the social order.[19]

The locus of all value for Swetnam is pleasure, not wealth or birth or social rank, and all women offer the same pleasure. Female extravagance is troped in a manner very different from the masculine pleasure in 'idle toyes', like the pamphlet itself; perhaps this is because it poses a threat to man's economic power. Swetnam repeatedly tropes female mastery or shrewishness as mastery over money. A rich widow, he explains, will curtail her husband's pleasures:

> If thou chance to dine at home, she will bid thee go sup with thy harlots abroad; if thou go abroad and spend anything before thou comest home, she will say 'A beggar I found thee, and a beggar thou meanest to leave me'.(p. 60)

Woman presents a threat to the masculine economy of pleasure; marriage is figured here, as in several ballads of the seventeenth century, as an end to the pure pleasures of bachelorhood.[20] Consequently, given the careful construction in Swetnam's text of a notion of masculinity predicated on this pleasurable economy and its power to control and exchange women, marriage comes to signify a kind of emasculation in itself.

Swetnam's speaking position thus closely resembles that of the youths' and men's clubs of the early modern period; it is grounded in a male-only world of licensed entertainment, pleasure and occasional violence. He addresses his epistle to male readers to 'the ordinary sort of giddy-headed young men'.[21] Swetnam himself kept a fencing school; after *The Arraignment* he published a guide to fencing, and thus he may actually have been part of a group of young blades; in any case he seems to adopt the speaking position of this kind of figure, though not without some irony.[22] Such groups, often represented satirically in drama as themselves a signifier of social disorder, occupied a liminal space in early modern society between childhood and full adulthood or household headship, and thus were unamenable to the discourses of social control which interpellated more clearly delineated groupings. Their self-constitution was dependent on their emergence into publicity from the household of childhood; in gender terms, their emergence from a feminized sphere into a masculine one.[23] In most cultures, moreover, male-dominated or male-only environments, particularly those festive or military, are often characterized by the near-ritual abuse of women, abuse which constitutes the group's masculinity by symbolically expelling the feminine from it. In a significant passage, Swetnam delineates sexual difference through men's delight in arms and women's pleasure in luxuries:

> Is it not strange that men should be so foolish to doat on women who differ so farre in nature from men? for a man delights in armes & in hearing the rattling drums, but a woman loves to heare sweet musicke on the lute . . . a man rejoices to march among the murthered carkasses, but a woman to dance on a silken carpet. (p. 38)

Clearly femininity represents a dilution – literally a *softening* – of masculinity here. Women and other pollutants can mark out the boundaries of the group, constituting it as such; Swetnam, characteristically, valorizes the pleasure offered by women as their only possible value, but also tropes that pleasure as polluting disease or waste. We might read Swetnam's text as a literary embodiment of this social process, more characteristically associated with the alehouse and the bearbaiting themselves, a process of constituting a male group (Swetnam and his readers) by the self-conscious voiding of femininity. However, it is important to note that Swetnam seems to anticipate both male and female readers for his texts; one might conjecture that the pleasure offered to women by misogynistic discourses of this kind was partly voyeuristic – a glimpse of the self-consciously men-only world from which they were debarred by the very discourses which delineated it. Possibly, however, the satiric deflation of swashbuckling masculinity familiar from stage representations of such figures offered a space for a more sceptical reading.[24]

I spoke earlier about the dependence of misogyny upon a rhetoric of citation; it now seems possible to argue that citation is a crucial part of the function of misogyny as a means for constituting masculinity and a male group.[25] In texts, women themselves cannot be the medium of exchange; instead what is shared is stories about women, or stories about sharing women.[26] This reading has the advantage of tying the popular cultural tropes Swetnam deploys with the tradition of rhetorical and moral debates about women on which he also draws. In both medieval schools of scholastic logic and Renaissance schools of rhetoric, the nature or virtue of woman were popular debating subjects. One might read this too as a literary ritual, marking the absence of women or of femininity from the institutions of higher education,[27] but it had another function: to place debaters in a tradition of writing and speaking about woman which went back to the classics. Because misogyny involved an extensive rhetoric of citation, to speak misogyny attached the speaker to the voicing of the words of others.

Among Swetnam's generic origins is another popular genre also concerned with the exchange of woman: the ballad genre, and specifically ballads about unruly women. Because these ballads are less complex textually than Swetnam's pamphlet, and because their connection with social codes and behaviours is easier to establish, an examination of their workings may help to lay bare what was at stake in the more complex prose debate. 'The Cruell Shrew, or the Patient Man's Woe', published in James I's reign, has close affinities with Swetnam's discourse and concerns.[28] The wife's shrewishness is first defined in terms of her speech; she 'never linnes [ceases] her bauling/Her tongue it is so loud'. But through a series of metonymies, this distinctive aspect of shrewishness is linked with the economic unruliness central to Swetnam's text. The wife remains 'snorting' in bed until eight o'clock; while the husband is out labouring in the fields 'in dust and mire', she puts on 'her brave attire/That fine and costly be'. She is unduly sociable, gossiping and attending alehouses; as in Swetnam, she denies her husband pleasures, accusing him of going out to meet his whore if he leaves the house and cursing him for entertaining his friends with a pot of beer.

There are links of similitude as well as association between the wife's expenditure of words and her expenditure of money; she is not virtuously 'closed'. This troubling openness is also signified by the unruly publicity of the wife; she circulates among her friends, instead of remaining stored up at home to signify her husband's ownership of her. This public life or circulation is translated into a worldliness or knowingness which finds its outlet in her abuse of her husband: that abuse is itself knowledgeable in a manner which is understood to be both improper and threatening. What is threatened is the man's power to pursue pleasure, and ultimately shrewishness and female knowledge are figured as the marks of the failure of masculinity. In *The Scolding Wife's Vindication*, a reply voiced by a female speaker to an earlier ballad complaining of a scolding wife, the wife explains her unruliness as the result of her husband's copulatory impotence. One kind of softness is equated with another:

I am a young buxom Dame, and fain would my joys renew,
But my poor cuckold is to blame, he nothing at all will do . . .
He lyes like a lump of clay, such Husbands there is but few,
'Twould make a woman run astray, he nothing at all will do.[29]

Masculinity is signified in pamphlets like Swetnam's as the power
to exchange women, or the power to exchange them symbolically
through storytelling. But in the case of the husband in this ballad,
its absence is signified by the husband's failure to keep his wife *out* of
circulation; to possess her and to remove her from the marketplace
is the mark of masculinity. Thus anxieties about masculine identity
are mapped onto the woman, whose knowing speech constitutes a
threat to the public masculine identity.

This connects with the publication/publicity of the ballads
themselves. The ballads, like the women they voice and stigmatize, are public; both are improper, revealing what might be
kept hidden in the household to the community, and doing so in
indecorous language. Both can be found in alehouses;[30] both are
noisy; their power depends on the voice. The ballads duplicate the
disorder of woman: they publicize woman already public, display a
display, make visible what is already only too apparent. Swetnam's
pamphlet too is notorious, 'low', available and at the same time
already known.

How might this excess of publicity, this duplication of the story
in the genre, work as part of that story? One clue might lie in
the ballads' reproduction of ritual public punishments for female
unruliness. In *Have Among You! Good Women*, the cucking-stool
and other punishments are relishingly applied to the appropriate
female crimes:

What thinke you of Alice that sells butter?
Her neighbour's headcloths off she pluckt
And she scolded from dinner to supper
'Oh! Such a scold would be cuckt!'[31]

The ballad's representation of the punishments acts as a display
which resembles their own operation. The punishment depends
entirely upon its visibility, and the visibility of the criminal. A
clearer instance of the replication of such punishments in ballad
form is the woodcut illustrating the ballad *The Patient Husband to
the Scolding Wife*. On the left a man sits backwards on a horse,
grasping its tail with both hands: a riding is illustrated, which

often took the form of seating the victim backwards on a horse or on a cowlstaff or stang representing a horse.[32] On the right a separate picture shows a man seated in a chair, being beaten by one woman while another pours the contents of a chamberpot over his head. Ridings were used when a wife beat her husband, or was thought insubordinate in some other clear way. It was the husband or a surrogate, not the wife, who received the punishment, so that again the social problem of female unruliness is figured as a defect in man. Like the cucking–stool, such punishments depended on publicity for their effect; they exert control over behaviour by bringing individual activities under the gaze of the public. The arrangement of the pictures in the ballad woodcut suggests not a narrative of cause and effect or crime and punishment, but a kind of symbolic equivalence.

Ritual punishments depend on the replication of a source of social disorder in a symbol of disorder.[33] As the woodcut shows, a perceived inversion of the social order is both represented and corrected by another, different inversion. The husband riding backwards on a horse and the woman beating or abusing her husband both represent disorder, but the former also represents the latter in a manner which works to neutralize its effect. Because the early modern semiotic system continued to operate through similitude, the operation of disorder in one area was thought to imply disorder elsewhere, so that synecdochal representation could quickly be elided with what it represented. Crucial to this process was the way the symbolic inversion acted to name and publicize disorder, making it visible through similitude. Showing disorder in public helped to control it.

The ballads I have been discussing may have performed a similar social function. Ballads sometimes become part of rituals and punishments. Martin Ingram has documented the use of what he terms 'mocking rhymes' and lampoons either in conjunction with ridings or as separate forms of public punishment; some cases he cites imply that well-known ballads were simply recited or disseminated to the persons seen as disorderly.[34] Like ridings, ballads name and thus define acts of disorder, and their public or published display of that disorder operates to neutralize its threat. The pleasure they provide is anticipated by the speakers in *Have Among You! Good Women*: the pleasure of locating disorder in femininity and expelling both from man. They constitute the male group and the male subject as those from which femininity has been excluded and who are thus in a position to possess women.

The misogynistic 'woman debate' pamphlets operate in a similar fashion, especially those like Swetnam's which seek to define a youthful and essentially plebeian masculinity over and against the coercive discourses of morality as well as over and against femininity. The subversive operation of Swetnam's text on the authoritative discourses of morality may thus be linked with its ritualistic misogyny. There are many well-documented cases of the signifiers of domestic disorder being used by early modern people to legitimate or define acts of carnival, riot or rebellion. Accusations of effeminacy or cuckoldry and the figure of the husband unable to control the unruly wife were staples of every kind of political satire and lampoon from attacks on the monarch to attacks on the local landlord or magistrate.[35] This domestic rhetoric did not merely reflect the early modern troping of the state or rule as a household; it also allowed criticism of the government or local landlord to take place under the putatively festive licence of the figure of the disorderly woman. In this sense, the figure of the woman on top could signify and enable direct assaults on individuals and institutions which were otherwise unassailable. Swetnam's subject-matter allows him his licence to assail the provident rhetoric of middle-class morality, as well as operating to contain the threat of emasculation posed by it by localizing disorder in woman.

I want to try to use this reading of Swetnam and the figure of disorderly woman to read the replies to Swetnam with female signatures, beginning with the question of authorship. I want to turn authorship from the always already assumed basis for reading these texts into a question they pose; it is not my project to counter previous claims for authorship with others. Rather, I shall suggest that the gender of these authors is not fully accessible to us, and that this reflects upon some early modern reading practices while unsettling our own. I want to take this up through the question of festive licence and disorder, for it seems that figures symbolic of disorder are often of indeterminate gender or represent it through cross-dressing. In the case of the Maldon food riots, the leader was not a woman but a man, 'Captain' Alice Clark, acting out the part of a disorderly woman.[36] Because of this tradition, seventeenth-century men were prone to dismiss the political activities of women as theatrical stagings of femininity by men. When women demonstrated outside the House of Commons on 9 August 1643 it was thought that 'some Men of the Rabble in Womens Clothes mixing among 'em had set them on'.[37] This way of reading female activity sought to limit its disorderly consequences, but also to understand it in terms of the festive licence and ritual significance attached to the symbol of disorderly femininity produced by a man. There is ample evidence that the political ferment of the Civil War period saw repeated uses of this means of troping disorder in a manner which sought to make male agency visible and render female engagement in politics a male masquerade, while exploiting the subversive significance of the disorderly female figure. One of the characteristic forms taken by this double manoeuvre was the production of political texts and satires purporting to be by women, but signed with clearly pseudonymous names. *The Good Womans Cryes* (1650), for example, purports to be by 'Mary Stiff', while *The Ladies Remonstrance* (1659) is said to be printed for 'Virgin Want' and to be sold by 'John Satisfie'. Other satires, such as the *Parliament of Ladies* series of the 1640s, invoke well-known female figures of the stage, such as Moll Cutpurse, as their spokespeople; mock-petitions such as *The Widowes Lamentation* (1643) and *The Midwives Just Complaint* (1643) parody female grievances by connecting them all with insatiable female sexual desire in a manner very reminiscent of Swetnam and the ballads discussed here.[38] These theatrical stagings of the unruly female empowered criticism of regimes and governments even as they delineated the acceptable place women could occupy in the state.

These texts recycle a satiric formula implicit in the ballad genre with its voicing of female replies to complaints about scolding and inconstancy, and explicit in the sixteenth-century 'woman debate' pamphlets, taking the disorderly woman as a pretext for political opposition.[39] A lost text called *A Mery Metynge of Maydens in London* (1567) was replied to by *A Letter Sent by the Maydens of London* (1567), a text which Fehrenbach has argued is probably not by a woman.[40] Like the Civil War satires, *A Letter Sent by the Maydens* deploys the figure of the disorderly woman and the rhetoric of the woman debate for a more broadly political purpose: it ironically attacks the idleness of the upper classes and their dependence on their servants, foregrounding the kind of putatively traditional contractual relation between master and servant which was to become a matter for serious political debate in the seventeenth century. This is not to argue that the tract has nothing to say about gender – the whole notion of what constitutes idleness and suitable labour is filtered through a configuration of gender in relation to class – but it cannot be read as a piece of forensic rhetoric on the nature of woman. The Jacobean *Hic Mulier* controversy, almost contemporary with the tracts under discussion here, ostensibly debates the problem of the unfixing of gender through dress, but all three pamphlets are also concerned with the place of the court in setting fashions, and with covert criticism of the effeminization of courtly men.[41]

The theatrical figure of the unruly woman thus signified and to some extent legitimated social and political criticism. I would like to consider the function of female pseudonyms in the context of a popular culture which sometimes placed gender indeterminacy in its festive repertoire, and to suggest that the pamphlets provide several clues to the kind of female voice figured in them. Read beside names like 'Mary Stiff' and 'Virgin Want', names like 'Jane Anger' and 'Ester Sowernam' seem to point less towards a substantive female author too modest to put her name in print than into the texts themselves, placing them not as the product of particular people but as operative parts of a particular strand of symbolism which had become a textual genre. Often read by feminist critics as tropes of modesty, the specificity of these pseudonyms rather foregrounds feminine unruliness.[42] The pseudonyms create a speaking position for the respondents not outside but at the centre of the woman debate because the names are exemplary, taken from the terms of the debate's citations, from allegories ('Constantia' and 'Prudentia') to Biblical heroines ('Ester') and scolds and unruly women of the lower orders ('Jane Anger', 'Joan Sharp', 'Mary Tattle-well'). These names are themselves part of a rhetoric of citation, indicating not individuality but the circulation of names in culture, not proper names but improper stories. Products of the woman-debate genre, the names also attach the speaking voices of the pamphlets firmly to particular debating roles, often the role of respondent. 'Sowernam', for example, is simply the opposite of Swe(e)tnam, sour (like scolds and shrews) where he is sweet. All of this is quite alien to our own post-Enlightenment way of understanding signatures as proper names abstracted from the texts in which they appear because they represent the point of origin of those texts; the names under which the pamphlets appear mean that though they purport to be by women, the reader is invited to see this as a penetrable screen identity, a theatrical performance of femininity which indicates a joke at women's expense. The names do not clearly illustrate female agency; rather, they illustrate the taking-up of the position of a disorderly woman for the purpose of signifying disorder of some kind, domestic or political.

None of this by any means rules out the possibility that the authors of the pamphlets may be women, but if so they are women acting women, staging disorderly femininity in a manner which refuses the elision of the symbolic and personal realms sought by modern critics. Such stagings cannot signify an expressive logic of deep feeling unlocked, but a highly unstable enactment of the signifiers of femininity that could perhaps be likened to Irigarayan mimicry, that mimicry in which femininity is seen to become not natural or biological but theatrical.[43]

A festive licence of some sort may be engaged as cover for a political critique in 'Sowernam's' extravagant praise of Elizabeth I; the praise may reflect upon the perceived dissolution of moral and sexual boundaries at the court of James I, since Elizabeth is praised for an assumption of public virtues as part of an argument for women's superiority to men: 'Elizabeth our late sovreign: not only the glory of our sex but a pattern for the best men to imitate, of whom I will say no more but that while she lived she was the mirror of the world.'[44] But it is impossible to make such brief and elliptical references to politics the sole motivation of 'Sowernam's' text. Another form of transgression under a kind of festive licence may be involved, one that hovers uncertainly between the seriousness of defence and the carnivalesque play of the marketplace. Like Swetnam's text, 'Sowernam's' speaks from the ambivalent position of female knowledge, putting into circulation the figure of a woman who knows the masculine world delineated by Swetnam. Regardless of the question of authorship, such a representation of femininity carries its own peculiar subversive charge.

Ironically, 'Sowernam's' equivalence to Swetnam is produced not just in her text but in his. Several passages in *The Arraignment* seem to anticipate a reply, and they construct a reply of a certain kind: 'I know I shall be bitten because I touch many, but . . . whatsoever you think privately, I wish you to conceal it with silence, lest in starting up to find fault you prove yourselves guilty of these monstrous accusations' ('To Women Readers', sig. A2R). In his address to male readers Swetnam anticipates a scolding or unruly response: 'I know women will bite the lip at me, and censure of me hardly.'[45] Critics have read these remarks as attempts to forestall a reply, but they can also be read as advertisements for a debate which Swetnam knew or hoped would occur. An audience primed by the reading of ballads on women would have anticipated a reply, possibly one voiced by an unruly woman, whether or not they were familiar with the humanist terms of debate. And they would also have anticipated the kind of female voice expected by Swetnam; the voice of the unruly woman herself.

There are many clues to 'Sowernam's' participation in the fantasy of female disorder established in Swetnam's attack. 'Sowernam' defines herself in a manner which alludes to Swetnam's description of unmarried wantons as 'neither maidens, widows or wives'; on the title page she calls herself, 'neither maid, wife nor widow, yet really all, and therefore *experienced* to defend all' (emphasis mine). 'Sowernam's' experience in this context is telling; she is the voice of social and sexual experience, the voice of that knowingness which in Swetnam both provides and threatens male pleasures. This speaking position is further established by 'Sowernam's' references to what is probably Rachel Speght's work: 'Sowernam' describes Speght twice as 'the maid' and stresses that she is 'a Minister's daughter', in a manner which seems to criticize Speght's lack of the experience which 'Sowernam' by contrast seems to possess. The name 'Ester' appears ambiguous in this context, since Esther as well as being the saviour of her people was also supposed to be dangerously beautiful and seductive. Other clues include the many references to legal processes and the extensive use of legal terminology in *Ester hath Hang'd Haman*, and a reference to her return to London at the beginning of 'Michaelmas term'.[46] This language, taken together with this statement, suggests a link with the Inns of Court in particular, which reflects on 'Sowernam's' reputation, since several contemporary works refer to the Inns and their students as the especial prey both of prostitutes and of rapacious serving women. This link with law and legal discourse also manifests itself in 'Sowernam's' arraignment of Swetnam; it is even more apparent in 'Munda's' text, which offers to arraign Swetnam and all his kind both through the law courts and through recourse to the duel for which they substituted: 'we will cancell your accusations, trauvers your bills, and come upon you for a false indictment' and 'if your currish disposition had dealt with men, you were afraid that *Lex talionis* would meet with you'. 'Sowernam' and

'Munda's' arraignment of Swetnam seems to suggest a litigious-ness characteristically associated also with female financial or sexual greed, and in drama associated with the lower orders and again with prostitutes.[47] 'Sowernam's' problematic 'experience' may be hinted at too in her address to 'the best disposed and worthiest Apprentices of London'; this seems to reflect upon Swetnam's reiteration of the rapacity of widows expressing itself in the desire for young men, and the unruliness of the apprentices themselves, who were caught up in various forms of civil disorder, reinforces the impression that 'Sowernam' is not speaking with propriety.[48] Then, the 'supper among friends' at which the number of the sexes was equal where 'Sowernam' hears of Swetnam's tract suggests the kind of public existence feared by both Swetnam and the moralists; one might compare 'Sowernam's' admission with the virtuous protest of Sir Thomas Elyot's Zenobia, who explains that she does not go out in the evenings for fear of her reputation.[49]

The second authorial signature of the pamphlet, that of Joan Sharp, is appended to a poem which summarizes the main prose argument with fair accuracy and would thus seem to form part of the same work. Joan Sharp is also a scolding or unruly name, and the existence of *two* pseudonyms troubles the attribution of the work to a single and serious author, if not to a single general speaking position. Finally, the title-page makes available two suggestive quotations. One derives from Ovid's *Ars Amatoria*, which, though not necessarily an impossible text for a woman to know, was notorious for its representation of female sexual wiles and its tutelage in improper knowledge.[50] The biblical motto is taken from the story of the woman taken in adultery, conflated by the Renaissance with the prostitute Mary Magdalene: 'He that is without sin among you, let him first cast a stone at her.'[51]

Taken together, these clues suggest that 'Sowernam's' speaking-voice and position, like her signature, are products of the debate genre as written by Swetnam. 'Sowernam' speaks to and from Swetnam's textual delineation of a sexually experienced and 'know-ing' woman who provides male pleasure and also threatens it; unsurprisingly, she also speaks from the position of the scold occasionally, while disavowing that position at other times. Yet 'Sowernam's' arguments and citations are by no means all com-pletely in line with this speaking position; her pre-texts in the woman-debate genre are more diverse even than Swetnam's and the result is an unsettling mixture of popular and high culture which repeats the kind of carnivalesque engagements which characterize Swetnam's discourse. The text of *Ester hath Hang'd Haman* is divided into two main sections: a defence of women which deploys the rhetoric of citation I have been discussing, and an attack on Swetnam as a representative of male sexual exploitation of women. The former appears to be a dignified assertion of women's virtue consisting primarily of the familiar historical evidence rehearsed and put into circulation, but there are a few discordant notes even in this apparent innocence. 'Sowernam' cites particularly freely from the defence rhetoric first established by Cornelius Agrippa's *A Treatise of the Nobilitie and Excellencye of Womankynde* (1542), a text which Linda Woodbridge calls 'suspiciously rhetorical' in its defence of woman, largely because it argues not for equality but for female superiority.[52] In a sense, Woodbridge's remark is misleading, because the move made repeatedly by Agrippa in this work is to put the Erasmean rhetorical doctrines of ingenuity, pleasure and strikingness into a subversive play which undermines their power to produce truth. By deploying the power of rhetoric to prove the palpably absurd case that women are superior to men, Agrippa subtly undermines its forensic claims.[53] As with other woman-debate texts, Agrippa is less concerned to regulate women than to regulate or control masculine questions by staging a debate on the terrain of woman. Because gender relations appear to be a given, they can be exploited for such polemical purposes. Thus it is odd that 'Sowernam' faithfully reproduces many of Agrippa's arguments, notably the ingenious assertion that whereas Adam was made of clay, Eve was made of the purer substance of Adam's flesh, and hence was his superior.[54] 'Sowernam' inverts many texts used to prove women's subordination in a manner which might be called playful rather than earnest: 'it is said (*Eccl* xxv) "Sin had his beginnings in woman"; *ergo*, his fullness in man.'[55] If 'Sowernam's' speaking position is figured as a signifier of disorder, her words too signal their inversion of the positions taken by orthodox moralists. But in taking this line, 'Sowernam' does not repudiate Swetnam, but replicates his approach.

I suggested that the discourse of legality might be a suspect representation of female unruliness earlier; at the same time, 'Sowernam's' figuration of herself as a lawyer or advocate suggests the kind of festive mock-trial or hierarchical reversal exploited by Shakespeare in the figure of Portia in *The Merchant of Venice* and by Webster in Vittoria's defence of herself in *The White Devil*.

Both Portia and Vittoria, in very different ways, suggest the incompatibility of femininity and advocacy while staging their combination as a metaphor for the unhinging of the social order and its ultimate restoration through subsequent inversion. Here 'Sowernam's' arraignment of Swetnam becomes a means of putting disorder to rights while symbolizing its effects. Moreover, her arguments speak from the same position of problematic knowledge of masculinity which both Portia and Vittoria differently exploit. 'Sowernam' is able to denounce male location of sexuality in women by writing from the place of one who knows male sexuality:

> How rare a thing is it for woman to prostitute and offer themselves? How common a practice is it for men to seek and solicit women to lewdness? What charge do they spare? . . . They hire panders, they write letters, they seal them with damnations and execrations to assure them of love where the end proves lust. (p. 113)

Here 'Sowernam' figures herself as the knowledgeable guide to the economic and textual tricks of seducers; she echoes the speeches of those sexually experienced women on the Jacobean stage who theatrically displayed the voice of sexuality in order to rebuke seduction from a moral position. But on stage that moral position was always outside the woman herself, who remained a locus of sexual corruption even as she voiced a repudiation of it. Here too 'Sowernam's' experience is foregrounded in a manner which allows her to voice morality but not to embody it.

'Munda's' moves on the same terrain are even more strikingly in step with the terms of Swetnam's attack. She figures his knowledge of female sexuality as proof of his own immorality, problematizing his awareness of the tricks of whores by asking how he came to know of them:

> how you happened in some stews or brothel houses to be acquainted with their cheats and evasions; how you came to be so expert in their subtle qualities; how politicly you caught the daughter in the oven, but never were in there yourself.[56]

Both 'Sowernam' and 'Munda' sporadically speak from precisely the place Swetnam speaks against, naming themselves as his targets and as the products of his discourse. These representations of women on top offer a figure for women to read with pleasure even as they also represent that figure as an outsider. Natalie Zemon

Davis has argued that the spectacle of women on top may have shaken social certainties about gender and provided a story for female rebellion to tell even though it could also sustain gender hierarchy. Similarly, the placing of a discourse of invective and experience in the mouth of a woman, however fictional, creates a spectacle of female power which displays precisely what Swetnam fears: the strength of knowledge as a means to curtail pleasure.

Ironically, many feminist critics have as much difficulty with the contradictions written into these speaking positions as Swetnam. One particular problem is their participation in a level of print culture governed by the marketplace and by commerce. Ann Rosalind Jones has suggested that 'Munda's' work is a satire on the woman debate as a whole, and adds that she suspects male authorship because the text is concerned with literary competition in the marketplace as its *raison d'être*, rather than with the defence of women. The suspicion of male authorship seems here to arise out of the notion of commercial motives; the linkage between perceived commerce and perceived insincerity or duplicity is also clear in Simon Shepherd's edition of the pamphlets, where the suggestion that replies may have been part of a debate staged by printers provokes speculations about male authors working behind the screen of a pseudonym.[57] Modern critics appear to feel that if women wrote these texts, then they must or ought to have done so from pure political motives; that if women are to be material then they cannot be materialist.[58] 'Munda's' concern with competition and placement in the literary marketplace is actually no more egregious than that demonstrated by 'Sowernam' and (more significantly) by Rachel Speght in her later *Mortalities Memorandum* (1621), which comments upon the events of the Swetnam controversy. 'Munda's' project is to define Swetnam's place in the emergent print culture as 'low':

> the Itching desire of oppressing the press with many sottish and illiterate libels stuffed with all manner of ribaldry and sordid inventions – when every foul-mouthed malcontent may disgorge his Licambian poison in the face of all the world – hath broken out into such a dismal contagion in these our days, that every scandalous tongue and opprobrious wit . . . will advance their peddling wares of detracting virulence in the public piazza of every stationers' shop.[59]

'Munda' contrasts Swetnam's 'dissolute pamphlet' with the 'storehouse' and 'treasure' that print was intended to be; a familiar argument from moralists, but one which could also be deployed as part of print invectives which participated in the very culture they stigmatized. Scandal sheets and prodigy tales often distinguish their own provident or improving or truthful tales from those purveyed by rival writers, so that protestations of veracity and high-minded disassociation from the 'low' could paradoxically affirm participation in its competitive commercial economy.[60] 'Munda' also carefully detaches her writing from the 'public theatre' in which 'unseemly figments' of femininity are represented in order to teach 'the worser sort . . . a compendious way to learn to be sinful' while she repeatedly makes use of 'low' sexual and scatological discourse, soliciting at least a voyeuristic gaze at the low life represented there.[61]

The invective is motivated by precisely the kind of literary competitiveness from which Speght in turn seeks to disassociate herself in *Mortalities Memorandum*, but which she also very plainly displays. At once apologetic and defiant, Speght's second work uneasily glosses the commercial imperatives of the woman debate, linking her new text with her previous publication even as she struggles to write from a different and more elevated position. In the dedication to her godmother, Speght seeks to apologize for intervening in a controversy governed by the marketplace, echoing 'Munda's' terms:

> I know these populous times afoord plentie of forward Writers, and critical Readers; My selfe hath made the number of the one too many by one, and having bin toucht by the censures of the other, by occasion of my mouzeling *melastomus*, I am now, as by a strong motive induced (for my rights sake) to produce and divulge this of spring of my indeavour.[62]

'Populous times' reflects 'Munda's' linkage of Swetnam with the popular press; in *A Mouzell for Melastomus* too, Swetnam's class position and readership become the basis for stigmatizing him as 'seducer of the vulgar sort of men' and terming his pamphlet 'illiterate'.[63] 'Forward' however appears to comment upon Speght's own intrusion into the public space as a writer: 'my experience confirm[s] that apothegeme which doth affirme Censure to be inevitable to a publique act.' The publicity of Speght's act makes her a scandal and opens her to the criticism she fears; at the same time she attempts to dismiss it as the lower reaches of print culture, and to distance herself from the realm into which she once ventured.

She likens her critical readers to the illiterate; 'Readers too common, and plentifull be/For readers there are that can read a, b, c,/And utter their verdict on what they doe view',[64] and advises herself to ignore them as 'ignorant dunces'. In her often ironic dream vision of the controversy, Speght identifies these ignorant dunces and uneducated readers with 'Sowernam' and 'Munda', explaining that 'Sowernam' 'past her censure on my weake exploite' and calling her 'a selfe-conceited creature'.[65]

Speght addresses 'Sowernam' as critically as she addressed Swetnam, having no sense of political solidarity in the face of more immediate imperatives such as literary competition and the defence of reputation. Speght also gestures satirically at the commercial imperatives which she takes to cause 'Munda's' intervention. Ridiculing the notion that a creature already hanged must have his mouth stopped to prevent him biting, she writes: 'And yet her enterprise had some defect/ the Monster surely was not hanged quite.'[66] By stigmatizing her competitors in *Mortalities Memorandum*, Speght makes apparent the economic stakes in the production of responses to Swetnam; the debate was a game with two sides, and the female signatories jostle for position, explaining away their own apparent superfluity by criticizing each other. Speght figures this jostling as the outcome of participation in a literary marketplace dominated by the vulgar and the illiterate, much as 'Munda' does. But in doing this she has to make clear her own previous text's participation in that commercial economy. Having done this, she produces *Mortalities Memorandum* as a supplement to it, a supplement which will show its defects and also cure them.

Yet *A Mouzell for Melastomus* has a great deal in common with *Mortalities Memorandum*; central to both is a defence of the hierarchies of religion and discourse which are the object of carnivalesque laughter in Swetnam and 'Munda', and in parts of 'Sowernam' too. Feminist critics have tended to prefer this subversion to the discourses Speght defends, and to dismiss her text in a proscriptive fashion as ideologically unacceptable. For Henderson and McManus, Speght's defences are 'rather weak, possibly because of her especially religious orientation'; for Linda Woodbridge, 'Speght's feminism is hobbled by her faith'; for Angeline Goreau, Speght's defence is 'an unfortunately inept jumble of quoted Scripture, practically unintelligible for a modern reader'.[67] Woodbridge illustrates the prevailing impression that Speght's feminism is primary and her religion somehow secondary, an unnecessary or added element which impedes the path to political correctness. What seems more probable, reading Speght's tract, is that what Woodbridge terms feminism was a by-product of an uneasy combination of religious and social disapproval and commercial motivation. Speght is reacting complexly to the pressure to defend her sex and her social class; her father was a London clergyman, one of the authoritative perpetrators of the discourses Swetnam disrupts. Her class and gender positions were under simultaneous assault, since gendering was class-specific; the two are not separable in her tract, and neither can be dissociated from the overriding question of religion. Speght's concern to defend the place assigned to women by puritan moralists may seem to us a case of thorough self-oppression, since this position turned out to be women's constrained future in early and middle capitalism; it is therefore *our* immediate past, and we necessarily read it as unacceptably conservative. But in Speght's case, it offers the only possible position from which to confront Swetnam's misogyny within the terms of the woman debate without exposing herself to placement within Swetnam's misogynistic figurations of unruly womanhood.

Speght's tactic is to negotiate a position for woman to speak, write and defend herself from within the discourses of morality which insisted on her silence, to oppose Swetnam by abducting authority from the very discourse he disrupts. The bulk of her tract is directed against what she reads as Swetnam's blasphemy, a reading also taken up at some points by 'Sowernam',[68] but in far less detail. Linking Swetnam with the devil in her preface she suggests that 'fear of God' should have 'restrained' his 'raving quill', and she calls his pamphlet 'an unlearned religious provocation'.[69] The first part of her argument is entirely devoted to defending woman's creation, in other words, to defending God from the charge of error. The rhetoric of blasphemy Speght deploys is mixed with a rhetoric of defamation (blasphemy being defamation of God). Unlike 'Sowernam', who prosecutes Swetnam and all mankind personally, Speght prosecutes her defamation case by conflating female honour and reputation with divine honour and reputation, and by appealing to biblical authority. It thus becomes clear that it is not merely strategically but structurally necessary that Speght should defend God; the whole point is that God does not really need defending, so that Speght as a woman can take up a legal discourse without incurring the shame of publicity that might accrue to a defence of herself, or the shame of too-knowing abuse that might flow from the arraignment of Swetnam. It also means that she can insistently draw attention to those aspects of Swetnam's discourse which do *not* represent authoritative social norms but instead pose a threat to them.

Speght's underwriting of these norms means that she repeatedly places herself as subordinate, figuring herself as the obedient and educable wife of a husband-teacher who will enlighten her frequently mentioned ignorance. She allows herself to be placed by the discourses of morality Swetnam tries to undo because his tract illustrates rather precisely that these discourses offered women some kind of social function and protection, some kind of clear and recognizable starting-point from which to speak as woman without attracting instant condemnation. Swetnam's carnivalesque dispersal of hierarchy and authority occurs at women's expense; carnival might attract modern readers, but has its risks for women. Like Katharina in *Taming of the Shrew*, Speght is voicing patriarchy, but at least she is speaking at length, beginning the long task of speaking for women by speaking from precisely the place assigned to them.

In *Mortalities Memorandum* Speght is particularly keen to address the attribution of her *Mouzell for Melastomus* to her father; her father, she writes, is the author of her, but she is the author of her book. The trope of authorship for creation of persons and books allows Speght to suggest the problematic overlap between fatherhood, authorship and authority in seventeenth-century theories of literary production. Speght tries to sketch a position as female author while demonstrating the basis for incredulity about such a being. Her voicing of authority becomes a means by which her own voice becomes inaudible for contemporaries, fathering her pamphlet upon her father. Her irony reflects on my own project perhaps, in that it illustrates just what a major rethink was necessary for the seventeenth century to believe in women as authors. Speght's authorship derives its authority from discourses we would describe as patriarchal; its obverse is the replies to Swetnam which voice from a place proscribed by authority and always open to censure. Neither group marks a clean or revolutionary break with patriarchal figurations of femininity, representing equivocally and sometimes simultaneously the bifurcated figures of female virtue and vice on which the woman debate always depended. At the end of this momentous period for women's writing, Speght's strategy was adopted and adapted by defenders of women like Mary Astell and her circle, the first to create the self-conscious feminist counterpublic sphere to which Speght herself could not appeal. But the alternative strategy returned uncannily too in the troping of the woman on the literary marketplace as whore described recently by Catherine Gallagher in the writings of Aphra Behn.[70] These figurations of femininity cannot be equated with Astell and Behn, any more than their representation in the woman–debate texts can be dissolved into the real presence of a woman author. We cannot locate the single and effective voice of female agency we seek in the two positions on display in the replies to Swetnam, or in any conflictual or negotiable play between them, but we might want to read both as part of the risky, contradictory and processual production of the subject positions which were to become, far in the historical distance, the voices of feminism.

NOTES

(Place of publication for works printed before 1800 is London unless otherwise stated.)

Note on the title: 'Material girls' refers to the song performed by Madonna on her album 'Like a Virgin'. Although the song, with its subversive emphasis on female bodily and sexual identity and on woman's power to 'market' these and to consume (or even exhaust) the resources of 'boys', is strongly associated with Madonna's unsettling and theatrical representations of femininity, it was in fact written by two *male* songwriters, and arguably enacts as well a patriarchal and fearful fantasy about female sexuality, ultimately voiced by a woman. In this way, the voice of the song is not the 'real' voice of a 'material' girl but the voicing of a materialist girl.

I am deeply grateful to Clare Brant, Julia Briggs, David Norbrook and Ivan Dowling for their sensitive and careful readings of earlier versions of this chapter.

1 This despite the recent concern about the univocal claims of feminism to speak for all women, and the category of 'women' itself; see Teresa de Lauretis, 'The Technology of Gender', in *Technologies of Gender: Essays on Theory, Film, and Fiction*, Bloomington and Indianapolis, Indiana University Press, 1987, pp. 1–30; Denise Riley, '*Am I That Name?' Feminism and the Category of 'Women' in History*, London, Macmillan, 1988; Diana Fuss, *Essentially Speaking*, London, Routledge, 1990.

2 Simon Shepherd (ed.), *The Women's Sharp Revenge: Five Women's Pamphlets from the Renaissance*, London, Fourth Estate, 1985. Despite

the disadvantages of Shepherd's edition (modernized spellings and punctuation) I have chosen to quote from it because the texts I discuss are not widely available in any other form. Very small excerpts of the texts signed by women are reprinted in Betty Travitsky, *The Paradise of Women: Writings by Englishwomen of the Renaissance*, New York, Columbia University Press, 1989, and in Katherine Usher Henderson and Barbara McManus, *Half Humankind: Contexts and Texts of the Controversy about Women in England 1540–1640*, Urbana, University of Chicago Press, 1985, which likewise reprints selections from Swetnam. I have also chosen (somewhat uneasily) to continue to refer to the authors as 'she' and 'her', but to enclose their names in quotation marks.

3 Angeline Goreau, *The Whole Duty of A Woman: Female Writers in Seventeenth-Century England*, New York, Dial, 1985, p. 67. Joan Kelly, 'Early Feminist Theory and the *querelle des femmes*', in *Women, History and Theory: The Essays of Joan Kelly*, Chicago, University of Chicago Press, 1984, p. 76; Henderson and McManus, pp. 17, 28.

4 Betty Travitsky, 'The Lady Doth Protest: Protest in the Popular Writings of Renaissance Englishwomen', *English Literary Renaissance*, 1984, vol. 14, p. 285; Elaine V. Beilin, *Redeeming Eve: Women Writers of the English Renaissance*, Princeton, Princeton University Press, 1987, p. 250. Beilin recognizes that these voices may be personae (p. 249), but does not draw out the implications of this idea. Doubts about female authorship of the texts are expressed by Germaine Greer, Jeslyn Medoff, Melinda Sansone and Susan Hastings (eds) in *Kissing the Rod: An Anthology of Seventeenth-Century Women's Verse*, London, Virago, 1988, p. 78, n. 255; Catherine Belsey, *The Subject of Tragedy*, London, Methuen, 1985, p. 219, and Shepherd on 'Munda' and especially 'Tattle-well', which he attributes to John Taylor, the author of the text to which *The Womens Sharpe Revenge* responds. Ann Rosalind Jones excludes Tattle-well and argues that 'Munda' was authored by a man in 'Counterattacks on "the Bayter of Women": Three Pamphleteers of the Early Seventeenth Century', in Anne M. Haselkorn and Betty S. Travitsky (eds), *The Renaissance Englishwoman in Print: Counterbalancing the Canon*, Amherst, Massachusetts University Press, 1990, pp. 45–62; I had not seen her stimulating article until after the first draft of this chapter was complete.

5 For the notion that Protestantism was beneficial to women in connection with the woman debate, see Louis B. Wright, *Middle-Class Culture in Elizabethan England*, Chapel Hill, University of North Carolina Press, 1935; for a refutation of the notion that Protestantism benefited women, see Lyndal Roper, *The Holy Household*, Oxford, Oxford University Press, 1990. On an ahistorical patriarchy see Joan Wallach Scott, 'Gender: A Useful Category of Historical Analysis', in *Gender and the Politics of History*, New York, Columbia University Press, 1988.

6 Julia O'Faolain and Lauro Martines (eds), *Not in God's Image*, London, Women's Press, 1973; Mary Daly (*Gyn/Ecology*, London, Women's

Press, 1978) discusses such diverse cultural practices as Chinese footbinding and witchcraft persecutions as aspects of woman hatred. I do not differ from this obvious conclusion; I suggest that misogyny, like other forms of oppression, has its own cultural specificity, and opposition to it will be more effective if this specificity is recognized.

7 R. Howard Bloch, 'Medieval Misogyny', *Representations*, 1987, vol. 20, pp. 1–24.

8 The horrifyingly misogynistic, violent and racist USAF *Gambler's Song Book* (n.d.) locates itself as 'a collection of 75 years of tradition', suggesting that misogyny still finds this trope workable. Cited by Joan Smith, *Misogynies*, London, Faber, 1989, pp. 99ff.

9 Pamphleteers routinely accuse their opponents of lacking originality while citing extensively themselves. Accusations of plagiarism are themselves citational, part of the genre of debate and invective.

10 Linda Woodbridge, *Women in the English Renaissance*, Brighton, Harvester, 1984, p. 85, and see Jones, p. 45.

11 Like 'Sowernam' and 'Munda', Swetnam writes under a pseudonym, 'Thomas Tel-troth'.

12 For an example, see John Dod and Richard Cleaver, *A Godly Forme of Householde Governmente*, 1614, especially sigs L4–5. For feminist readings of these moral discourses, see Linda Fitz, '"What Says the Married Woman?" Marriage Theory and Feminism in the English Renaissance', *Mosaic*, 1980, vol. 13, pp. 1–22; Susan Dwyer Amussen, *An Ordered Society: Gender and Class in Early Modern England*, Oxford, Blackwell, 1988.

13 Swetnam, p. 1. All quotations from Swetnam are taken from the 1615 edition of *The Arraignment of Lewd, Idle, Froward and Unconstant Woman*, and cited by page number in the text.

14 This is a particular concern in the section on widows. Widows are repeatedly figured as knowing about male pleasure: 'what I hide secretly he privily stealeth away, and playeth away all my money at dice' (p. 61).

15 Lorna Hutson, *Thomas Nashe in Context*, Oxford, Clarendon, 1989.

16 Philip Stubbes, *The Anatomy of Abuses*, 1583.

17 Claude Lévi-Strauss, *The Elementary Structures of Kinship*, Boston, Massachusetts University Press, 1969, p. 36; Luce Irigaray, 'Women on the Market', in *This Sex Which Is Not One*, trans. Catherine Porter with Carolyn Burke, Ithaca, NY, Cornell University Press, 1985, pp. 170–97. This system, as Irigaray points out (and Lévi-Strauss emphatically does not), is inherently oppressive because it figures women as objects.

18 Ann Rosalind Jones in 'Counterattacks' also points to Swetnam's concern with wealth and class, but does not develop the question of how class antagonism interacts with misogyny (p. 48). This is not Swetnam's only levelling story; he also asserts that his book is like a horse, adding 'the Collier calls his Horse a Horse, and the King's great steed is but a horse' (sig. A4R).

19 For a reading of Stubbes which takes into account the connections

between female extravagance and theatricality, see Jean E. Howard, 'Renaissance Antitheatricality and the Politics of Gender and Rank in *Much Ado About Nothing*' in Jean E. Howard and Marion F. O'Connor (eds), *Shakespeare Reproduced*, London, Methuen, 1987, pp. 163–87.

20 For a similar set of figures, see *The Patient Husband to the Scolding Wife*, in *The Roxburghe Ballads*, ed. William Chappell and Joseph Woodfall Ebsworth, 9 vols, Hertford, Austin, 1871–99, vol. VII, pp. 182–4: 'When I was as single as some of you be,/I was beloved like other young men;/I lived at my ease and did what I please;/. . . I could sing and be merry, drink white wine and sherry'. Like Swetnam's stories, this ballad depicts male violence and a masculine search for pleasure as reasonable.

21 On young men's clubs, see Natalie Zemon Davis, 'The Reasons of Misrule', *Society and Culture in Early Modern France*, Cambridge, Polity, 1987 (first pub. 1965), pp. 98–123. See also Emmanuel Le Roy Ladurie's comments on the labouring poor's characteristic misogyny in *Carnival at Romans*, Harmondsworth, Penguin, 1979, p. 212.

22 Joseph Swetnam, *The Schoole of the Noble and Worthie Art of Fencing*, 1617. Like *The Arraignment*, this text contains a number of debunking remarks about class, but it is dedicated to the Prince of Wales.

23 Thomas Laqueur, 'Orgasm, Generation, and the Politics of Reproductive Biology', *Representations*, 1986, vol. 14, pp. 1–41.

24 It is difficult to assess the readership of texts like Swetnam's with precision, but the respondents to Swetnam were at pains to locate his work at the lowest possible level of print culture.

25 My discussion of the genesis of misogyny is indebted to Klaus Theweleit's study of the German *Freikorps*: *Male Fantasies: Volume I: Women, Floods, Bodies, History*, trans. Stephen Conway, Cambridge, Polity, 1987 (first pub. in German 1977).

26 A similar move from ritual to text is enacted in the popular autobiography discussed by Robert Darnton in 'Don Juanism from Below', in Jonathan Miller (ed.), *The Don Giovanni Book: Myths of Seduction and Betrayal*, London, Faber, 1990, pp. 20–35. Oddly, and perhaps defensively, Darnton stresses throughout the estranging effect of this text's focus on the sexual commodification of women.

27 See Walter Ong's similar argument in 'Latin Language Study as a Renaissance Puberty Rite', *Studies in Philology*, 1959, vol. 56, pp. 103–24.

28 'The Cruell Shrew, or the Patient Man's Woe', c. 1610, *Roxburghe Ballads*, vol. I, pp. 94–8. For a different reading of ballads about shrews and scolds, see J.A. Sharpe, 'Plebeian Marriage in Stuart England; Some Evidence from Popular Literature', *Transactions of the Royal Historical Society*, 1986, vol. 36, pp. 69–90.

29 *Roxburghe Ballads*, vol. VII, p. 197.

30 Bernard Capp, 'Popular Literature', in Barry Reay (ed.), *Popular Culture in Seventeenth-Century England*, London, Routledge, 1985, pp. 198–243; Leslie Shepard, *The Broadside Ballad: A Study in Origins and Meaning*, London, Jenkins, 1962.

31 *Roxburghe Ballads*, vol. I, pp. 435–7.

32 Martin Ingram, 'Ridings, Rough Music and Mocking Rhymes in Early Modern England', in Reay, pp. 166–97.

33 For the argument about carnival as a social practice and differing points of view on it, see Victor Turner, *The Ritual Process: Structure and Antistructure*, Chicago, University of Chicago Press, 1965, chs 3–5; Natalie Zemon Davis, 'Women on Top', in *Society and Culture, in Early Modern France*, Cambridge, Polity, 1987, especially p. 131; Mikhail Bakhtin, *Rabelais and his World*, trans. Helene Iswolsky, Bloomington, Indiana University Press, 1984 (1st pub. 1968); Peter Stallybrass and Allon White, *The Politics and Poetics of Transgression*, London and New York, Methuen, 1986; Peter Stallybrass, '"Drunk With The Cup Of Liberty": Robin Hood, the Carnivalesque and the Rhetoric of Violence in Early Modern England', in Nancy Armstrong and Leonard Tennenhouse (eds), *The Violence of Representation: Literature and the History of Violence*, London and New York, Routledge, 1990, pp. 45–76; Sharpe, pp. 88–90; Ingram, pp. 167–9.

34 Ingram, pp. 179–80.

35 For the disorderly woman as a signifier of riot, see Davis, 'Women on Top'; David Underdown, *Revel, Riot and Rebellion: Popular Politics and Culture in England 1603–1660*, Oxford, Oxford University Press, 1985. See, for example, *Craftie Crumwell*, 1649, which tells of the sexual rapacity and adultery of Elizabeth Cromwell (!).

36 For the Maldon food riots, see Davis, 'Women on Top'.

37 J. Rushworth, *Historical Collections*, 1708, vol. V, p. 143, cited by Patricia Higgins, 'The Reactions of Women, with Special Reference to Women Petitioners', in Brian Manning (ed.), *Politics, Religion and the English Civil War*, London, Arnold, 1973, p. 197.

38 The 'women' want peace because war takes all the young and virile men from London. See *The Virgins Complaint*, 1643; *The Widowes Lamentation*, 1643; *The Parliament of Women . . . with the Merry Laws*, 1646; *Hey Hoe for a Husband, or, the Parliament of Maides*, 1647; Henry Neville, *The Parliament of Ladies*, 1647; *An Exact Diurnall of the Parliament of Ladyes*, 1647.

39 Gender ventriloquism was characteristic of the woman debate. Elyot presents both sides of the argument about female virtue in his *Defence of Good Women*, 1542, and, like the Civil War pamphlets, this too may have been produced in political debate rather than gender debate; Constance Jordan, 'Feminism and the Humanists: The Case of Sir Thomas Elyot's *Defence of Good Women*', in Margaret W. Ferguson, Maureen Quilligan and Nancy J. Vickers (eds), *Rewriting the Renaissance: The Discourses of Sexual Difference in Early Modern Europe*, Chicago, University of Chicago Press, 1986, pp. 242–58. Edward Gosynhill staged both sides of the debate in writing first the invective *Scolehouse of Women* and then a defence replying to it, *Mulierum Paen*, both 1542.

40 R.J. Fehrenbach, 'A Letter Sent by the Maydens of London (1567)', *English Literary Renaissance*, 1984, vol. 14, pp. 285–304.

41 See *Hic Mulier, or the Man-Woman*, 1620; *Haec Vir, or the Womanish Man*, 1620; *Mulde Sacke, or the Apology of Hic Mulier*, 1620; texts

which gloss the ungendering of woman as the consequence of the emasculation of men at court in a manner which recalls both anxieties about James I and homosexuality and the ballads containing shrews' replies to their critics. The latter two pamphlets are partly voiced by a female speaker. See Dianne Dugaw, *Warrior Women and Popular Balladry 1650–1850*, Cambridge, Cambridge University Press, 1990, ch. 7. For anxiety about courtiers under James I, see Alan Bray, *Homosexuality in Renaissance England*, London, Gay Men's Press, 1982, pp. 55, 70.

42 Speght uses the trope of modesty most often, and her text is the only reply to Swetnam not signed with a pseudonym. Swetnam also uses this trope; his epistle to men is signed 'thy friend nameles to keepe my self blameles' (sig. A2V).

43 Luce Irigaray, 'La Mysterique', in *Speculum of the Other Woman*, trans. Catherine Porter, Ithaca, NY, Cornell University Press, 1985, pp. 191–202. I owe this suggestion to Clare Brant. Hero Chalmers's chapter in this volume canvasses what may be a similar case in her discussion of Mary Carleton's assumption of the position of rogue and sexual spectacle. Sophie Tomlinson's chapter in this volume engages much more closely than there is space for here with the question of female theatricality.

44 'Sowernam', in Shepherd, p. 101.

45 Swetnam also anticipates a response from himself, describing his assault on women as a two-stage military campaign ('Epistle to Men', A2V).

46 'Sowernam', in Shepherd, p. 87.

47 For the fear of widows' financial power and litigiousness, which troubled Swetnam so particularly, see Barbara J. Todd, 'The Remarrying Widow: A Stereotype Reconsidered', in Mary Prior (ed.), *Women in English Society 1500–1800*, London, Methuen, 1985, pp. 54–92. For the litigiousness of prostitutes, see G.R. Quaife, *Wanton Wenches and Wayward Wives*, London, Croom Helm, 1979.

48 For the apprentices' rebellions, see Buchanan Sharp, 'Popular Protest in Seventeenth-Century England', in Reay, p. 286.

49 Elyot, sig. D1; see also Philip Stubbes, *A Christall Glass for Christen Women*, 1591, in which Katherine Stubbes's virtue is epitomized by her refusal to go to dinner parties.

50 '*Neque anim lex iusticior ulla/Quam necis Artificem arte parire sua*' (for there is no law more just than that the creator of a piece of violence should perish by his own art); 'Sowernam', title-page.

51 For the significance of title-pages and prefatory matter in shaping ways of reading texts in this period, see Annabel Patterson, *Censorship and Interpretation: The Conditions of Writing and Reading in Early Modern England*, Madison, University of Wisconsin Press, 1984, pp. 47–8.

52 Woodbridge, p. 38.

53 Cornelius Agrippa, *A Treatise of the Nobilitie and Excellencye of Womankynde*, trans. David Clapham, 1542. Agrippa also wrote an attack on humanist learning, *Of the Vanitie and Uncertaintie of the Arts and Sciences*, trans. Ja. San., 1569 (first pub. in Latin 1531).

54 'Sowernam', p. 91.
55 ibid., p. 94.
56 'Munda', p. 135.
57 Jones, p. 58; Shepherd, p. 86. See Shepherd for the connections between the replies and Swetnam through printers; Speght's text was published first and its printer was Nicholas Okes, who was not one of Swetnam's original printers, though he did print Swetnam's later treatise on fencing. However, *A Mouzell* was printed to be sold by Thomas Archer, Swetnam's bookseller.
58 For an example of a woman's writing which explicitly locates itself in a commercial discourse, see Isabella Whitney's 'Wyll and Testament', ed. Betty Travitsky, in *English Literary Renaissance*, 1980, vol. 10, pp. 76–94.
59 'Munda', p. 130.
60 Michael McKeon, *The Origins of the English Novel*, London, Hutchinson, and Baltimore, Johns Hopkins University Press, 1987; Stallybrass and White, ch. 1.
61 'Munda', p. 131.
62 Rachel Speght, *Mortalities Memorandum*, 1621, sig. A2V.
63 Speght, *Mouzell*, p. 61.
64 Speght, *Mortalities*, 'To the reader'.
65 The term 'selfe-conceited' may gesture at the theatricality of 'Sowernam's' enterprise, and at her gender. 'Conceit' might carry the meaning 'trope' or 'figure' as well as the more usual sense.
66 Speght, *Mortalities*, p. 9.
67 Henderson and McManus, pp. 16–17; Woodbridge, p. 90; Goreau, p. 67. Compare the rehabilitation of women's religious writings in works like Margaret Patterson Hannay, *Silent But For the Word: Tudor Women as Patrons, Translators and Writers of Religious Works*, Kent, OH, Kent State University Press, 1985, and in Beilin.
68 See, for example, 'Sowernam', p. 91.
69 Speght, *Mouzell*, pp. 61, 74.
70 Catherine Gallagher, 'Who was that Masked Woman? The Prostitute and the Playwright in the Comedies of Aphra Behn', *Women's Studies*, 1988, vol. 15, pp. 23–42. For the figure of the whore as a site of conflict see Bridget Orr's chapter in this volume.

4

BLAZING WORLDS: SEVENTEENTH-CENTURY WOMEN'S UTOPIAN WRITING

Kate Lilley

Utopian writing has become a privileged formal and theoretical domain for feminist women, in ways that explore and frequently erode the distinctions between 'primary' and 'secondary', 'creative' and 'critical', 'theory' and 'practice'. Such writing shares an experimental and analytic drive; a desire to subvert those categories and boundaries which guarantee disciplinary, discursive and sexual hygiene, by licensing exchange between the arts and sciences, the 'irrational' and the 'rational', the fantastic/abnormal and the natural/normal. Different agents have different stakes, and certainly this is true within the field of contemporary feminisms, but it is instructive to step back from the specific goals and products of such encounters momentarily, to mark the proliferation of contemporary utopian writings by women, and their corollary: the emergent construction of a history of utopian writing by women, and a metadiscourse about utopian writing by women.

Of the latter, contemporary writing has commanded most attention, with notable patches of interest in a disparate collection of earlier fictional utopias, which chiefly have in common the fact that they have been reprinted: Charlotte Perkins Gilman's *Herland*; Sarah Scott's *Millenium Hall*; Christine de Pisan's *City of Ladies*. To this we might add a non-fiction text, Mary Astell's two-volume *A Serious Proposal to the Ladies*, a blueprint for a kind of secular nunnery, which is now attracting attention in the wake of Bridget Hill's edition and Ruth Perry's critical biography, which also includes Astell's manuscript poetry and a selection of her letters.[1]

Women's contributions to utopian discourse have manifold claims on feminist attention – political, philosophical, historical, generic, rhetorical. The recent concentration on twentieth-century texts springs not only from a response to a thriving collocation of gender and genre, but from their inherent topicality.[2] All utopias are necessarily works of theory, of criticism, and of speculative fiction. If the division between fiction and non-fiction, as well as 'high' and 'low' genres, has been consciously eroded and problematized in contemporary feminist discourses, that is partly because of, and enabled by, the privileging of utopian formal strategies, and a pan-feminist commitment to the 're-vision' of 'knowledges, discourses, and practices'.[3]

From the side of genre criticism there has also been a great deal of work on utopian writing, much of it unusually (though not surprisingly) theoretically sophisticated, with notable contributions by Louis Marin, Paul Ricoeur, Fredric Jameson, Raymond Williams and Michèle Le Doeuff.[4] Utopian writing is always of particular interest for genre theory, since any utopian speculation brings with it a meta-concern with systematicity and taxonomy itself; with interpretative categories and the elaboration of, and motivation of, imagined spaces. Both discourses share a repertoire of tropes of exploration, demarcation, mapping and listing. But in this dialogue between utopian writing and genre theory, only Le Doeuff attends to questions of gender and sexual difference: the explicit focus is politics, more or less untroubled by sexual politics, and women writers rarely feature, despite the fact that they are now prolific and experimental producers of utopian discourse. Academic feminist theory and women's fiction for the popular science fiction/fantasy market respectively identify the self-consciously 'high' and 'low' poles of this continuum, but there is by no means always a sharp distinction between them, and much cross-fertilization. Donna Haraway's 'A Manifesto for Cyborgs', for instance, seeks a productive cross-talk between the putatively discrete fields of the humanities and sciences, and between fictional and non-fictional texts, citing fiction and poetry by contemporary feminist women (among them Joanna Russ, Octavia Butler, Monique Wittig, Audre Lorde, Cherrie Moraga, Vonda McIntyre) as 'theorists for cyborgs'.[5]

Both the writing and reading of utopias has until recently been thought of as the province of well-educated men, exploring and debating the possibilities for systematizing happiness – their happiness – within an 'enlightened' public sphere which, in part, defined itself through the exclusion of women as agents, and by contrast with a feminized private sphere. Only the figure of woman has currency for this public sphere, as a muse/scribe for the lettered male imagination.[6] The contemporary efflorescence of women's utopian writing, and writing about that writing, is a conscious intervention in this masculine tradition of pedagogy and debate, masquerading as gender and class-neutral universalism. It may be that an implicitly masculine history of male-centred and authored utopias is giving way to an explicitly feminist analysis of woman-centred or separatist utopian writing. At the same time, gender has become an increasingly crucial category of analysis for diverse theoretical and disciplinary discourses, one of the hopeful signs of which is the unsettling of the divisions between 'male theory' and 'feminist theory', and of the unproblematic gendering of public and private spheres, in a new rhetoric of enlightenment founded on difference and dialogue rather than universalism/separatism.

What is perhaps surprising, and depressing, is the lack of intellectual contact so far between (masculine) genre studies of (male) utopias (which would include the gender-blind work of women) and feminist studies of women's utopian writing, emerging under the (inter)disciplinary rubric of 'women's studies' – a lack of contact which institutionalizes the notion of 'separate spheres' and parallel genealogies. If my own discussion of seventeenth-century women's utopian writing replicates, in part, this separation of texts on lines of sexual difference, that is a function of pragmatics rather than theory. My intentions are three-fold in this context: to offer proof of the agency of women as writers of utopian texts of various kinds in the seventeenth century in a way that challenges a gender-blind generic history; to offer readings which focus figurations and inflections of gender in those texts; and to show that each of these women uses utopian writing to participate in a metadiscourse on the relations of gender and genre, public and private. It is by no means my intention to show the coherence of a 'separate sphere' or alternative genealogy of utopian writing by women, except in so far as the texts I discuss differently enact, and explicitly theorize, the particular attractions of utopian discourse for women.

Seventeenth-century women's utopian writing focuses questions of control, knowledge, opportunity and freedom, through an attention to sociality and culture rather than the political and juridical, narrowly conceived. In the discussion that follows I prefer the greater flexibility of the category 'utopian writing' over the notoriously unstable notion of a utopia proper, particularly since the generic propriety or classifiability of women's writing in the seventeenth century is always problematic. In putting together these two unstable terms, 'women's writing' and 'utopian writing', I hope to partly discover, and partly produce, some fruitful dialogue between them, as well as between feminist theory and genre theory. The texts on which I will concentrate span the second half of the seventeenth century: the Fifth Monarchist Mary Cary's *A New and More Exact Mappe of New Jerusalems Glory when Jesus Christ and his Saints with him shall reign on earth a Thousand years, and possess all Kingdoms* (1651), Margaret Cavendish's *The Description of a New World, called the Blazing-World* (1666), Aphra Behn's 'The Golden Age' (1684) and Mary Astell's *A Serious Proposal to the Ladies* (1694–7).[7]

What, then, of utopian writing by seventeenth-century women, and of its invisibility as an object of critical enquiry? Lyman Tower Sargent's specialized checklist includes two titles by Margaret Cavendish, Duchess of Newcastle: *The Inventory of Judgement's Commonwealth, the Author cares not in what World it is established* (the final part of *The World's Olio*, 1655), and her much longer work, *The Description of a New World, called the Blazing-World*, a companion piece to Cavendish's *Observations Upon Experimental Philosophy* in the same volume (1666).[8] Sargent also lists Aphra Behn's *Oroonoko* as a 'borderline' case – an instance of the uneasy conflation of new-world narrative with utopian writing.[9] I would call Behn's anti-slavery, pro-Royalist colonial narrative a dystopia – one that shifts strangely between 'eye-witness' account of the 'other world'[10] and topical political allegory of the world to which it is addressed.[11] Certainly *Oroonoko* begins with a utopian scenario of civilized contact, but this 'perfect tranquility, and good understanding'[12] between the 'free' natives and colonists of Surinam is only used to frame a narrative of the tragic and barbaric effects of slavery. Its dystopian climax is the shockingly detailed description of the dismemberment of Oroonoko/Caesar, the martyred 'Royal Slave', with Behn as the chief mourner and witness of the 'frightful spectacle of a mangled King'.[13]

Another specialist list by R.W. Gibson and J. Max Patrick, 'Utopias and Dystopias 1500–1750', which offers itself as generically strict, also includes *The Blazing-World*, and two different Behn texts: the farce, *The Emperor of the Moon* (1687), and her translation of Bernard Le Bovier de Fontenelle's *A Discovery of*

New Worlds (1688), a guide to astronomy and physics in the form of a dialogue between a Marchioness and a male philosopher, specifically addressed to women.[14] Both lists agree that Cavendish's *Blazing-World* is the only utopia-proper by a woman in the seventeenth century, and that Behn is the only other woman working in this territory, engaged in utopian writing through translation, farce and new-world narrative. Other relevant texts by Cavendish are her closet dramas, *The Female Academy* (1662) and *The Convent of Pleasure* (1668), both centring on the promotion of women's intellectual development in a separatist environment; while some of Behn's poetry, notably 'The Golden Age', and *The Voyage to the Island of Love* can also usefully be considered under the rubric of utopian writing.[15]

The fact that neither Sargent's nor Gibson and Patrick's lists mention Mary Astell's *Serious Proposal* is a curious lacuna, and points to feminism's separate genealogy. The entry under 'utopias, female' in the new *Feminist Companion to Literature in English* mentions Cavendish and Katherine Philips but takes Astell's *Proposal* (1694) as its chief starting point.[16] Often women's utopian writing is conflated with one of its major instantiations, representations of separatist female communities, for which Astell's polemic is a convenient origin. But Astell's is not the only separatist text by a seventeenth-century woman, and separatism is not the only form which utopian writing by seventeenth-century women takes.

We know that women wrote far more religious material than anything else in the seventeenth century, including both a great deal of radical sectarian tracts and broadsides, and a conservative high culture literature of piety and feminine virtue. The Fifth Monarchist, Mary Cary, and the Anglican Tory, Mary Astell, can be taken to represent these two strands of women's participation in utopian writing through religious discourse. Much of the prophetic writing by women is almost purely apocalyptic and dystopian, consisting of warnings and lamentations like Hester Biddle's even-handed *Wo to Thee, City of Oxford* (1655) and *Wo to Thee, Town of Cambridge* (1655). Some of it, though, addresses itself directly to the figuring of the next world, sometimes mapped onto or prefigured in this world – as in the writing of Fifth Monarchist women like Cary and Anna Trapnel. When Gibson and Patrick include only William Aspinwall's *A Brief Description of the Fifth Monarchy* (1653) in their utopian checklist, with the dismissive note, 'typical of hundreds of works expressive of chiliastic utopianism published in the seventeenth century but unlisted here', they relegate one of the most prolific and politically volatile areas of literary production in mid-century to the margins of generic interest. In doing so, they also effectively dispose of a territory in which women found an unprecedented access, not only to print, but also to a public, male politico-religious discursive arena, partly governed by the conventions and motivations of utopian and dystopian writing, with direct tropological ambitions in the real world.[17]

As Mary Cary writes in her *Twelve Humble Proposals To the Supreme Governours of the three Nations now assembled at Westminster* (1653):

> the time of the reign of Christ is at hand . . . either immedi-
> ately in his own person, or mediately by his Saints . . . do as
> much as in you liethe to set up the Kingdom of Jesus Christ
> on earth, and to hasten the glorious time . . . I say be speedy
> (though not without seriousness and consideration) for hope
> deferred maketh the heart sick, and the tedious delays of your
> predecessors in authority, made the common-wealth sick and
> weary . . . as if there was nothing now to be done, but to spin
> out the time of a perpetuall Parliament from age to age.[18]

She follows with a number of proposals for reform concerning taxa-tion, public and unrestricted preaching, rationalization of parishes, public responsibility for the universities and redistribution of uni-versity wealth, direct and indirect relief for the poor, appointment of local commissioners to hear grievances, simplification of the law, public ownership of lands, and 'moderate and reasonable stipends' for public officers.

Two years earlier Cary published *A New and More Exact Mappe of New Jerusalems Glory*.[19] This text comes framed by testimonies from several men attesting to its method and authenticity as 'a Gentlewomans thoughts put into form and order by herself' (sig. A7); 'Scriptures clearly opened, and properly applied; yea, so well, that you might easily think she plow'd with anothers Heifer, were not the contrary well known' (sig. A2). One of the testimonies stresses the text's particular exemplarity for women, citing Proverbs 31: 31, 'let her own works praise her in the gates': 'She hath taught her sexe that there are more ways than one to avoid idleness. . . . They that will not use the Distaff, may improve a Pen' (sig. A2). There is also a dedication to women and an epistle to the reader by Cary herself, full of the authorizing rhetoric of female instrumentality and tropes of automatic writing: 'I could do no more herein . . . of my self, then a pensill, or pen can do, when no hand guides it . . . *my sufficiency is of God*' (sig. A8).

A New and More Exact Mappe addresses itself to the time when 'the confusions, and combustions, and oppressions, and troubles that were in the old frame of the world shall be forgotten' (p. 71), when the Saints 'shall build houses and inhabit them, and plant vineyards and eat the fruit of them. They shall not build and another inhabit; they shall not plant, and another eate' (p. 69). In this new world of georgic self-sufficiency and unalienated labour, Cary imagines a 'state of freedome and liberty' for all individuals (p. 89), aligning her own prophetic, utopian voice with 'great voices in heaven':

> they are not the whimsicall notions of unsound and rotten men . . . not some poore weak suppositions, or maybe's: Nor secondly, are they some weake faint sayings; but they are great, that is, effectuall, convincing, and unquestionable speakings. (p. 95)

This utopian 'effectual' voice is figured as speaking to 'all people, and nations, and languages' (p. 97), for the New Jerusalem will supersede all previous divisions, gathering the 'Nations them-selves', 'not their wealthe, but their weale; not their treasure, but their safety; not their riches but their happinesse; not their outward things, but the salvation of their souls', into a single empire which, as it 'shall minister joy and gladnesse to the saints', 'speakes and works their ruine' who do not believe (p. 56). Cary's utopian writing relies on a principle of election to the company of 'saints', but makes no *a priori* exclusions on the basis of sexual difference or social rank. Its apparent elitism is radically tempered by the insistence that election is available to all true initiates. Although the pedagogical work of conversion maintains a distinction between those who know and those who do not yet know, in its fully utopian and perfected realization, pedagogy itself would be abolished.

In Anna Trapnel's *The Cry of a Stone* the very act of speaking is made proleptic of utopian fulfilment:

> They that would not any bawlk here,
> But openly declare,
> Oh it is they shall come to him,
> Whom nothing can compare.

> For they that Zealous have been for
> A Christ as Lord and King:
> He will himself open their mouth,
> And make them for to sing.[20]

Salvation is figured as the inauguration of full and sweet voice, almost always activated by a trope of incorporation in which the material body is lost in pure vocality. As Trapnel writes: 'Vision! the body crumbles before it, and becomes weak.' Equally, those who are literally cursed are damned to exile, material affliction and stuttering: 'He will trample you under foot/Who is my joy and Song.'[21]

Utopian writing offers a critique of the world as it is, and also of representation as it is. At the level of narrative, Mary Cary prophesies the reversal of fortune in the triumph of the saints, focusing the active possibilities, including discursive freedom, for women in the New Jerusalem.[22] At the level of representation and textual authority, Cary's Christian utopia, like other millenarian commentaries, is always written as if in the margins of nominated and carefully chosen sacred texts, particularly the Book of Daniel, and is aligned with a specific and collective exegetical practice.[23] It offers itself as a reading, as always secondary but in an active sense of exegetical responsibility. Its own textual presence is diffuse and displaced, with Cary's authorial voice always figured as subsumed in the voices of Heaven, and the voices of other saints, in a pre-emptive fantasy of collective, effectual voice.

Since, for Cary, experience itself is providential, allegorical and textual, utopian writing becomes a direct mode of truth-telling and correct interpretation. Cary's prophetic agency is located in her linked, gender-inflected roles of true witness and right reader. A feminized posture of listening, waiting and watching the signs enables her to be a transcriber or conduit for the revelation of a text that, in a mystical and allegorical sense, always pre-exists any reading or writing in its inexorable unfolding. The significance of a feminized line of transmission is made explicit in Cary's dedication to Elizabeth Cromwell, Bridget Ireton and Margaret Role:

> I have therefore chosen, (being of your own sex) to dedicate these Treatises to your Ladiships, (whom I honour because God hath honoured) and under your favourable aspects, to publish them in the world . . . knowing that every thing of this nature, from how weak an instrument soever it be, (so it bee with the plaine, and cleer demonstrations of the holy

Scripture, and the holy Spirit) is very acceptable unto you, who are in that waiting and expecting posture. (sig. A5)

Cary offers her own authorship in *Twelve Humble Proposals* as almost incidental:

> as for me, I could not chuse but communicate those few things, that were upon my heart . . . though I should have been glad if others had been more forward, and prevented me herein: for so it had been done, I should have been satisfied.[24]

Implicitly, writing is troped as a feminized bodily process or labour, which brings forth a revelation of the concealed truth: a labour which is both necessary and inevitable because 'Scripture is so pregnant'.[25]

This sense of inevitability leads to a disavowal of the possessive ideology of authorship, of textual ownership and invention, which is consonant with the importance of collectivity in Cary's New Jerusalem. In its place is a rhetoric of active reciprocity, reinforcement and coalition. In *The Little Horns Doom and Downfall* (which Cary prints with *A New and More Exact Mappe*, but claims to have written 'above seven yeares since' and withheld 'because that men would then generally have been more incapable of receiving of such things, then now they are, because now these things are fulfilled; and prophecies are then best understood, when they are fulfilled', sig. A7), Cary includes among the saints 'even such as were most faithfull, and most circumspect in their way, and who most desired to worship God in his Ordinances in their purity, such as they termed Roundheads, Puritans, Independents, Presbyterians, Anabaptists, Sectaries, Precisians, and what not' (p. 22). She writes militantly of God's army: they are 'his instruments: so that he does it, and they do it . . . ten thousand times ten thousand standing before him, ready to execute his will, and do his pleasure . . . multitudes, both of Celestiall, and terrestrial creatures to attend him' (pp. 30–1). Equally, her own disseminating and instrumental discursive roles are figured as the revelation and indirect representation of the agency of the Word itself, cognate with the justified 'use of the materiall Sword in the ruining of the enemies of Christ' (sig. A2): 'Now they shall have together with the high praises of God in their mouth, a two-edged sword in their hands, to execute vengeance' (p. 62).

Just as Cary makes no distinction between one saint's voice and another's, she recognizes no gap between here and there, now and then, terrestrial and celestial. In the space of her writing, utopia is figured as present possibility and collective identity, which also brings with it a dismantling of social hierarchy and gender inequality which is particularly enabling for women:

> The truth is, that which is given to the Husband, the wife must partake of: for there is nothing that he possesses that she hath not a right unto. And the Saints of Christ are the members of Christ, they are the Lambs wife: and having given himself unto them, he will not with-hold anything that is his from them; but when all the Kingdomes and Dominions under the whole heaven are given to him, they shall possesse them with him. (p. 54)

Redemption means, for Cary, that the feminine or wifely position with respect to a masculine Godhead will become universally acknowledged and available to both male and female saints. The utopian prophetic discourse of women like Cary and Trapnel positively revalues and privileges the 'feminine', altering its place within patriarchal coding with radical consequences for the imagined and actual agency of women. It is ironically *as a woman*, privileged by her access to the feminine, that Cary offers to extend the benefits of her own position to men, so that they too may become brides of Christ. It should be noted, however, that the georgically inflected trope of mystical marriage as mutual receipt and mutual possession, is kept in place in *A New and More Exact Mappe* by an equally powerful anti-masculine rhetoric of vengeance and dispossession, directed against the 'ripe harvest of wicked men' (p. 77); those who 'doe covet to treasure up most riches for themselves, and to poll, and rob, and cheat the people, to . . . make themselves great in the world' (p. 56). But neither gender nor wealth nor social rank will be an insuperable barrier to the New Jerusalem: 'not onely the poore, and the mean among the Gentiles; but some of their Kings, and great ones shall be converted, and imbrace the light, and come to the brightnesse of the saints rising' (p. 66). For one of the promises of redemption and the inauguration of the time of the saints in 'new heaven and a new earth' is a prophylactic obliteration and forgetting: 'the former shall not be remembered' (pp. 68–9).

Sectarian women were often literally imprisoned for their transgressive apocalyptic and utopian writing; in Astell's unpublished poetry, written before she was 22, it is the bondage of sexual ideology against which she writes.[26] Heaven is figured as her soul's 'native place': she writes not as a stranger but an exile, her utopian project the reclaiming of a rightful place:

> Help me my Muse, thou who are unconfin'd,
> And with no luggage of a body joyn'd,
>   Untie those chains that hold
>   My heav'n born Soul imprison'd here,
>   Raise it above the seventh Sphere;
> Thou who dost Natures secret mysteries unfold,
>   A second nature art,
> And from wild fancies Chaos can'st impart
>   New creatures of thine own,
>   To natures self unknown. ('Heaven', p. 431)

Astell's unconfined immaterial muse combines the freedom of the soul with the liberating possibilities of virtuous, contemplative, disciplined writing: 'Heav'n alone must exercise my mind and quill', specifically rejecting the debased feminine arena of the theatre and 'Pleasures golden dreams' (p. 430). Like Cary, Astell meditates on the promise of the place where language is perfected as both praise and blame, and the desire to be a present conduit, an 'Angels tongue' (p. 435), for that fully expressive but unrepresentable word/Word: 'For what large word can we invent,/T'express that glory, which can never be/So much as comprehended by mortalitie.' She conducts a running satire on inauthentic utopian quests motivated by material ambition and covetousness, 'Those which make dareing men out brave the Sea' (p. 431), troping female poetic flight as the true adventure:

> What bold Pindarique strains can further go?
>   What Metaphors suffice to shew?
>   That unexpressible delight,
>   Flows from the beatifick sight,
>   Enough, enough and come not ne're
> This abyss, only say the GOD is there;
> This said all other words are dull and flat,
> For ev'ry joy thou comprehends in that.
> Here JESUS lives, and here the rapt'rous sight,
> Of him who dwells in unapproached light

> Shall be unveil'd, here we shall see, and be,
> I know not what——
> O alsufficient GOD we shall be full of Thee. (p. 435)

Language's 'abyss', like the abyss of female sexuality, is filled with the 'alsufficient' word, 'GOD', which engulfs all other words and identities via a trope of mutual unveiling. The unveiling of divine mystery, 'the beatifick sight', is figured as simultaneous with the unveiling of the speaker's virgin soul. As 'I' shifts to 'we', the speaker's material body becomes part of the blazing Word. This pure presence and radiance, outside human language, time and gender, is made discursively available through a deictic reversal. No longer addressed from 'here' to 'there' – 'only say that GOD is there' – a grammatical manipulation coincident with the mutual unveiling at the poem's climax seems to permit speaker and reader to overgo that earlier interdiction, 'come not near'. In the final lines of 'Heaven' we seem to be transported to utopia itself: 'Here JESUS lives, and here the rapt'rous sight'; 'here we shall see, and be'. The utopian moment shimmers before us, and only the triple reiteration of 'shall' conserves the gap between language and what it speaks.

Comparatives, negatives and superlatives are the mainstay of utopian description:

> The pain of asking shall have here no place,
> No fear of disappointment or disgrace,
> No stormy passion can approach thy gate,
> O most refin'd and happy state! (p. 433)

But such strategies are founded in a recognition of a shortfall or incapacity which, by the 'prudent management' of 'Providence', is perversely pleasurable: 'Shew us sweet fruit reer'd from a bitter ground' (p. 433). The enquiring female mind and unencumbered soul in Astell's 'Heaven' ranges widely, though the body remains at home. The sedentary model of a woman's life is recuperated in terms of the authentic discoveries of active contemplation, humility and the pleasurable accommodation of, and capitalization on, structures of deferral and displacement. Self-government is a particularly rich trope for women, who are unlikely to govern anything else. Where Cavendish, in *The Blazing-World*, regretfully abandons her desire to be Empress of a material world as impractical, Astell repudiates masculine ambition and feminine vanity, renouncing all but the desire to be 'Great in Humilitie':

> Vile Greatness! I disdain to bow to thee,
>   Thou art below ev'n lowly me,
>   I wou'd no Fame, no Titles have,
> And no more Land than what will make a grave.
> I scorn to weep for Worlds, may I but reign
>   And Empire o're my self obtain,
>   In Caesars throne I'de not sit down,
> Nor would I stoop for Alexanders Crown. ('Ambition', p. 405)

Mary Astell's most fully utopian text is *A Serious Proposal to the Ladies For the Advancement of their True and Greatest Interest* (1694), and its 1697 sequel, 'Wherein a Method is offer'd for the Improvement of their Minds' (1697).[27] The *Proposal* evinces a separatism that is necessarily compromised in various ways. First, by its dialogic status as a polemical intervention in an already existing debate on both women and education, and women and marriage. Second, the status of the retreat in Astell's text is open: it may be a permanent withdrawal or a temporary respite from, and preparation for, the world of men. Certainly, the female students who are essential to Astell's scheme for pedagogical improvement and good works are not envisaged as themselves withdrawn. Astell's vision is not of a closed order, but a flexible separatist retreat, which acknowledges, and makes integral, responsibilities in the world at large. Third, the failure of the *Proposal* to garner the support required for its implementation led Astell to offer a Part II, 'Wherein a Method is offer'd for the Improvement of [Women's] Minds' (1697). In this sequel the benefits for women of education and the cultivation of innate rationality are recycled in a form which is, if anything, anti-separatist – even if that is only a compensatory mechanism.

Astell's 'Method' stresses the general social benefits of the women, like herself, 'who aspire no further than to be intimately acquainted with our own hearts', and 'to be absolute Monarchs in our own Bosoms': 'it is fit we Retire a little, to furnish our Understandings with useful Principles, to set our inclinations right, and to manage our Passions, and when this is well done, but not till then, we may safely venture out' (II, p. 179). Here, through the double strategy of the language of (female) domestic economy applied to mental furnishings, and the appropriation for women of the privileges and prerogatives of the (male) individual subject, the need for a literally separate and separatist building is obviated. Separatist retirement is retroped as temporarily and freely available to the inwardness of self-knowledge, a self-regulated and self-regulating oscillation between active contemplation and contemplative action which offers equilibrium and improvement:

> Knowledge makes a better mother – 'Nor will Knowledge lie dead upon their hands who have no Children to Instruct; the whole World is a single Lady's Family, her opportunities of doing good are not lessen'd but encreas'd by her being unconfin'd. (p. 178)

What Astell does reject violently, in her critique of 'Custom, that merciless torrent that carries all before it' (I, p. 147), is the co-optation and complicity of women in patriarchal representations and scenarios of the figure of woman, and in the logic of the male gaze: 'How can you be content to be in the World like Tulips in a Garden, to make a fine *shew* and be good for nothing.' Female overvaluation of the body, and of ornament is offered as an irrational commitment to materiality and mortality, 'a garnish'd Sepulchre, which for all its glittering, has nothing within but emptiness or putrefaction!' (p. 141). In Astell's terms, the cultivation of outward beauty is a false profit which sacrifices substance for shadow, reality for appearance, the 'more glorious and durable Mansion' of the soul for the 'Tenement' of the body (p. 147), 'instructive discourses' for 'idle tales' (p. 150). To abandon the false flattery of men and listen to Astell's pleadings is the necessary first step in re-education for the pursuit of 'Heroick Vertue':

> Hither, Ladies, I desire you wou'd aspire, 'tis a noble and becoming Ambition, and to remove such Obstacles as lie in your way is the design of this Paper. We will therefore enquire what it is that stops your flight, that keeps you groveling here below, like *Domitian* catching Flies when you should be busied in obtaining Empires. (p. 143)

In the first part of the *Serious Proposal*, Astell's separatist retreat promises a prefiguration of heavenly reward:

> Happy Retreat! which will be the introducing you into such a *Paradise* as your Mother *Eve* forfeited, where you shall feast on Pleasures, that do not like those of the World, disappoint your expectations . . . but such as will make you *truly* happy

now, and prepare you to be *perfectly* so hereafter. Here are no Serpents to deceive you, whilst you entertain your selves in these delicious Gardens. . . . In fine, the place to which you are invited is a Type and Antepast of Heav'n. . . . (p. 151)

The immaterial but profoundly gratifying spiritual, social and intellectual pleasures promised to the inhabitants of Astell's seminary as a second Eden are also offered as partly reproducible outside the walls of the retreat. The 'second Nature' of perfected discipline allows the autoerotic enjoyment of the enclosed garden of the withdrawn mind, as well as the returns of pedagogy. In Astell's georgic rhetoric of self-management and improvement, those women who have been transplanted ('there are *tender* Vertues who need to be screened from the ill Airs of the World . . . such tender *Cyons* shou'd be transplanted', p. 166) will re-emerge as angels of husbandry. They, 'having long since laid the Ax to the root of sin, and destroy'd the whole body of it' (p. 156), will 'root and establish' virtuous knowledge wherever they go:

> Religion will become a second Nature, and we must do strange violences to our selves, if after that we dare venture to oppose it. . . . And then what a blessed World shou'd we have, shining with so many stars of *Vertue*. . . . Having gain'd an entrance into Paradise themselves, they wou'd both shew the way, and invite others to partake of their felicity. (p. 164)

The women for whom Astell chiefly writes are women of her own kind, and her pedagogical programme carries with it a vocational sense of class responsibility: 'she who does not thus improve her Talent, is more vile and despicable than the meanest Creature that attends her' (p. 165). Astell's punitive rhetoric is not reserved for men alone; some of it is reserved for women who turn their backs on a pious life to pursue a corrupt and corrupting worldliness: 'There is a sort of Learning indeed which is worse than the greatest Ignorance: A Woman may study Plays and Romances all her days, and be a great deal more knowing but never a jot the wiser' (p. 154). 'Wisdom' is opposed to 'knowing' as the inwardly blazing 'stars of *Vertue*', aligned with 'the glorious Lights of Heaven', are opposed to the vulgarly glittering spectacle of women as public or private actresses for the male gaze.

Part II substitutes individual contemplation and metaphorical withdrawal for collective retreat. If it is a 'method' born of the failure of the 'proposal', it is also more egalitarian. The seminary envisaged in the *Proposal* is for women 'whose Dispositions as well as their Births are to be Generous' (p. 157): 'Who will think 500 pounds too much to lay out for the purchase of so much Wisdom and Happiness?' (p. 168). Astell's sequel stresses, instead, the tropological responsibility and potential of each woman towards herself and other women:

> An Ingenious Woman is no Prodigy to be star'd on, for you have it in your power to inform the World, that you can every one of you be so, if you please yourselves. It is not enough to wish and to would it, or t'afford a faint Encomium upon what you pretend is beyond your Power; Imitation is the heartiest Praise you can give, and is a Debt which Justice requires to be paid to every worthy Action. . . . If you *approve*, why don't you *follow*? (II, pp. 173–4)

Even more than in the original *Proposal*, Astell's 'method' locates the possibility of female liberty, 'a natural Liberty within us', in a changed understanding and self-valuation (p. 177). She stresses what can be done alone, and without special circumstances or privileges: 'All have not leisure to Learn Languages and pore on Books, nor Opportunity to converse with the Learned; but all may *Think*, may use their own Faculties rightly, and consult the Master who is within them' (p. 176). The 'Master within' is implicitly contrasted with the masters without, whose 'Prerogatives' and 'Lawful Privileges' Astell equally reaffirms and repudiates, along with 'the Knowledge of the World, and all the Pleasures and Follies of it' (p. 179). In Part II, an individual commitment to cultivate contemplation, reading and virtuous imitation is represented as the means by which women can transform themselves from passive objects 'to be star'd on', or 'little useless and impertinent animals' (I, p. 152), into self-governing, rational subjects whose 'only endeavour shall be to be absolute Monarchs in our own Bosoms' (II, p. 179). Astell claims to leave existing patriarchal power relations intact, not out of respect but out of scorn:

> The Men therefore may still enjoy their Prerogatives for us, we mean not to intrench on any of their Lawful Privileges . . . nor can they who are so well assur'd of their own Merit entertain the least Suspicion that we shall overtop them. (ibid.)

Her mock-feminine disavowals of 'encroachment' come loaded with contempt, while her passionate, direct appeals to women readers advocate both passive and active resistance to that which 'has nothing but Authority to back it' (p. 177), as well as the reciprocal rewards of pedagogy: 'For an Active Life consists not barely in *Being in the World*, but in *doing much good in it*' (p. 178).

Men's utopias have focused on political systems and laws; utopian writing by women has tended to focus strategically on the possibilities and problems of gendered social life and the weight of custom – micropolitical questions of sexuality, maternity, education, domesticity and self-government – while declining the burden of representing a fully articulated model of a new political order. Even Astell's *Serious Proposal* distances itself, in its title and within the text, from the finality of complete detail: 'To enter into the detail of the particulars concerning the Government of the *Religious*, their Offices of Devotion, Employments, Work, etc. is not now necessary' (I, pp. 155–6). Deferral is crucial to the utopian rhetorical structure of the *Proposal*, as prefiguration and cumulative pedagogical effect are crucial to its utopian progressive narrative of perfectibility. Astell positions her own text as a double prefiguration. It is a self-consciously incomplete act of speculative imagination and resistance, which proposes a seminary for women – a literal building. Addressed chiefly to women, the *Proposal* is also a work of pedagogy, which makes incompletion the necessary precondition for its own success in originating a chain of further speculation and resistance. Characteristically, Astell presents herself as both student and teacher, improver and improved, in a guarded strategy which seems to adopt a rhetoric of feminine modesty but conspicuously declines to gender the 'better Pen' or 'wiser heads' who would continue her labour:

> To close all, if this *Proposal* which is but a rough draught and rude Essay, and which might be made more beautiful by a bet-ter Pen, give occasion to wiser heads to improve and perfect it, I have my end. For imperfect as it is, it seems so desirable, that she who drew the Scheme is full of hopes, it will not want kind hands to perform and compleat it. But if it miss of that, it is but a few hours thrown away, and a little labour in vain, which yet will not be lost, if what is here offer'd may serve to express her hearty Good-will, and how much she desires your Improve-ment, who is Ladies, *Your very humble Servant*. (p. 172)

The utopian writing of Margaret Cavendish and Aphra Behn is, by contrast with Cary and Astell, secular and materialist. What Astell desires for herself and other women is a diamond soul, 'Polish'd by that w[hi]ch breaks the counterfeiting Glass': 'Poverty, pain, disgrace and all/What you mistaken men afflictions call' ('Judgement', p. 419). Margaret Cavendish's *The Blazing-World* is propelled by an opposite fantasy of a blazing name and a blazing person. Her female imperialism requires the subjection and the admiration of men, including the Emperor (who becomes a wifely consort), and her hydridized male-animal courtiers:

> No sooner was the Lady brought before the Emperor, but he conceived her to be some Goddess, and offered to worship her; which she refused, telling him, (for by that time she had pretty well learned their Language) that although she came out of another world, yet was she but a mortal. At which the Emperor rejoycing, made her his Wife, and gave her an absolute power to rule and govern all that World as she pleased. But her subjects, who could hardly be perswaded to believe her mortal, tender'd her all the Veneration and Worship due to a Deity.
>
> Her Accoutrement after she was made Empress, was as followeth: On her head she wore a Cap of Pearl, and a Half-moon of Diamonds just before it; on the top of her Crown came spreading over a broad Carbuncle, cut in the form of the Sun; her Coat was of Pearl, mixt with blew Diamonds, and frindged with red ones; her Buskins and Sandals were of green Diamonds: In her left hand she held a Buckler, to signifie the Defence of her Dominions; which Buckler was made of that sort of Diamond as has several different Colours; and being cut and made in the form of an Arch, shewed like a Rain-bow; In her right hand she carried a Spear made of white Diamond, cut like the tail of a Blazing-Star, which signified that she was ready to assault those that proved her Enemies.[28]

Building on a consciously anachronistic Petrarchism, and the rhetorical centrality of the blazon in her *Blazing-World*, Cavendish's Empress is a kind of warrior queen, Elizabeth *redivivas* (who in the course of the narrative succeeds in putting down rebellion both at home and abroad), for whom marriage is not a problem. (In the preface to *The Blazing-World*, Cavendish also crowns herself

'Margaret the First'.) *The Blazing-World* figures marriage and friendship as complementary ideals. At different times the Duchess (in her astral body) literally inhabits both the Empress's soul, and her husband's; and on one occasion the souls of the Duchess and the Empress enter the Duke of Newcastle's soul together, where they are entertained with 'all kinds of harmless sports' (p. 111).

Until very recently *The Blazing-World* has elicited only passing and derisive attention as a curious example of a fantastic kingdom with an absolute monarchy. Noting that a woman as utopian heroine is 'a variation . . . I have not seen before', Marjorie Hope Nicolson goes on:

> If you wish to journey to the celestial worlds of Margaret of Newcastle, you must go alone with her in the pages of her ponderous tome. I have made these journeys once, and my head – not too good for heights, in spite of my long training – still spins.[29]

Manuel and Manuel, in their *Utopian Thought in the Western World*, go further:

> There are utopias so private that they border on schizophrenia. *The Description of a New World, called the Blazing-World* (1666) . . . has much in common with the delusions of Dr Schreber analyzed by Sigmund Freud. . . . Uncounted utopian worlds of this stripe . . . are being conjured up every day, in and out of hospitals, though few of them are ever set in print.[30]

Recently, however, there are signs that *The Blazing-World*, along with its much-abused author, is being rehabilitated.[31] What is most interesting, for my purposes, is its meta-concern with the relations between power, gender and discourse, and with the attractions of utopian writing for women as an arena of unrestricted fancy, through which perceived wants can be aesthetically supplied. It is a text which revels in design, ornament, rhetorical description and amplification, a material and linguistic opulence which is self-consciously extravagant and excessive, even parodic.

Cavendish is unusual in combining a narrative of the effortless rise of a woman to absolute power, with a narrative of the liberty of the female soul and the emancipatory possibilities of utopian writing for women. She introduces a simulacrum of herself as a valued character and recommended author into *The Blazing-World*: 'a plain and rational writer; for the principle of her Writings is sense and reason' (p. 89). Summoned to Paradise, the royal city at the centre of the Blazing-World, 'Margaret Cavendish' becomes the Empress's chief confidante, and an acerbic commentator on the world ('E') she has left, and the losses she and her husband have sustained there as a result of civil war ('above Half a Million of Pounds', p. 109).

Although 'Margaret Cavendish' is finally unable to devise a way to transport material wealth from the Blazing-World to 'E' as a literal compensation (giving rise to further lamentation), the material opulence of the text, and the lavish praise bestowed on both the Empress and the Duchess, is offered as a fantasized compensation. Through the example of the Empress, as well as the conversation between the two women, Cavendish offers a vindication of monarchy and hierarchy. *The Blazing-World* is colour-coded by degree and has only one language, and 'but one Religion in all that World, nor no diversity of opinions in that same Religion' (pp. 16–17). After early consultation, however, the Empress decides to found 'a Congregation of Women, whereof she intended to be the head her self, and to instruct them in the several points of her Religion' (p. 60); before long she has converted the entire Blazing-World. Initially, *The Blazing-World* also has only one Emperor, but the unnamed captive virgin daughter who escapes death and dishonour 'by the light of her Beauty, the heat of her Youth, and Protection of the Gods', so captivates the Blazing-World that the Emperor instantly stands aside (p. 2). The Empress with her invisible but devoted Emperor, and 'Margaret Cavendish' with her equally devoted and absent Duke, are the text's complementary realizations of female power enabled by marriage.

However, the text also offers an ambivalently negative realization of wifely influence in plebeian marriage, in the voice of the Empress's advisers:

> although [women] are not admitted to publick Employments,
> yet are they so prevalent with their Husbands and Parents,
> that many times by their importunate perswasions, they cause
> as much, nay, more mischief secretly, then if they had the
> management of publick affairs. (p. 18)

This remark passes without comment, but in view of the Empress's scant regard for the opinions of her male courtiers, and her confidence in her own, and those of her confidante, 'Margaret Cavendish', it would seem to be silently ironized. Irony notwithstanding, though, the Empress's failure to respond also preserves a sharp class distinction between plebeian and aristocratic women as daughters and wives (and potential rulers) which is entirely characteristic of Cavendish's insistence on the authenticity of hierarchy.

We should not forget that the entire narrative has its genesis in the transgressive desire of a foreign merchant for 'a young Lady': 'being beneath her, both in Birth and Wealth', he abducts her in a Packet-boat, but rapidly loses control of the boat's direction. As they pass from 'the very end point of the Pole of that World, but even to another Pole of another World', experiencing extremes of cold and heat, the merchant and his accomplices first freeze to death and then 'thaw, and corrupt'. The merchant's initial crime against rank and property/propriety is appropriately punished by a fatal crossing between worlds, while the 'distressed Lady' not only providentially makes this transition unscathed, but profits greatly by it. For this new world, into which she comes as a foreigner, receives her not only with 'all civility and kindness imaginable', but with spontaneous praise and the highest recognition of her innate merit and nobility (pp. 3–5).

Married and crowned Empress, the Blazing-World is the site of, and the occasion for, the young lady's secular apotheosis and perpetual blazoning. It is not surprising, then, that the relation between the Empress and the Duchess emerges as the text's strongest form of fantasized utopian doubling: 'the Empress's Soul embrac'd and kiss'd the Duchess's Soul with an Immaterial Kiss, and shed Immaterial Tears . . . finding her not a flattering Parasite, but a true Friend' (p. 123). As an abduction narrative which shifts quickly into a romance plot of deserved but providential female advancement, *The Blazing-World* has embedded within it a mirror-narrative of fortunate female:female abduction, of which the 'Duchess of Newcastle' is the deserving beneficiary:

> That Lady, then, said the Empress, will I chuse for my Scribe, neither will the Emperor have reason to be jealous, she being one of my own sex. In truth, said the Spirit, Husbands have reason to be jealous of *Platonick* Lovers, for they are very dangerous, as being not onely very intimate and close, but subtil and insinuating. You say well, replied the Empress; wherefore I pray send me the *Duchess of Newcastle*'s Soul; which the Spirit did. (p. 89)

Through the introduction of her double, 'Margaret Cavendish', the Empress's scribe, Margaret Cavendish as author-scribe of *The Blazing-World* stages a self-confirming dialogue on the production of fictional worlds as a beneficial and pleasurable activity for women:

> The Duchess of Newcastle was most earnest and industrious to make her World, because she had none at present. . . . At last, when the Duchess saw that no patterns would do her any good in the framing of her World; she was resolved to make a World of her own Invention . . . which World, after it was made, appear'd so curious and full of variety; so well order'd and wisely govern'd, that it cannot possibly be expressed by words, nor the delight and pleasure which the Duchess took in making this World-of-her-own. (pp. 98–101)

The Duchess's world is finally figured as irreducibly speculative and secret, while the text focuses on the pleasure of its construction and its uniqueness. Equally, *The Blazing-World* provides a space in which the historical Duchess, 'Margaret the First', can vindicate and demonstrate her infamous 'singularity' through her scribe, 'Margaret Cavendish':

> After several questions which the Empress's soul asked the Duchess, she desired to know the reason why she did take such delight when she was joyned to her Body, in being singular both in Accoutrements, Behaviour and Discourse? The Duchess's soul answered, she confessed that it was extravagant, and beyond what was usual and ordinary; but yet her ambition being such, that she would not be like others in any thing, if it were possible, I endeavour, said she, to be as singular as I can; for it argues but a mean Nature to imitate others; and though I do not love to be imitated, if I can possibly avoid it, yet rather than imitate others, I should chuse to be imitated by others; for my nature is such, that I had rather appear worse in singularity, than better in the Mode. (p. 149)

For both Astell and Cavendish, the extreme practice of living singularly, rather than 'in the Mode' or according to 'custom', is troped as cognate with the singular practice of (utopian) writing – despite the fact that their projects are antithetical. Where Cavendish's only models for imitation and worthy companionship are the Empress and 'Margaret Cavendish', Astell's *Proposal* insists on the imitability and iterability of her own example, and the transformative possibilities of 'Vertuous and Disinteress'd Friendship' between women – a model of female friendship and pedagogy which tentatively extends its gendered solidarity across class lines (p. 155).

Behn's 198-line 'The Golden Age. A Paraphrase on a Translation out of French' is loosely based on the first chorus from Tasso's *Aminta*, but twice as long and quite different in the range and kind of its sexual and social critique.[32] Most particularly, Behn makes women, as subjects and objects of desire, crucial to her expansion and rewriting of Tasso, uneasily balancing a permissive, atemporal libertinism against a cynical recognition of the difference, in patriarchal coding, between an unchangingly desirable figure of Woman, and women of flesh and blood.[33]

'The Golden Age' is a nostalgic utopian poem which looks to the prehistory of pastoral, 'When no scorn'd Shepherds on your Banks were seen,/Tortur'd by Love, by Jealousie, or Fear' (ll. 3–4), where a feminized nature offers the model of autoerotic generativity and inclusivity, 'As if within her Teeming Womb,/All Nature, and all Sexes lay' (ll. 35–6):

> The groves appeared all drest with Wreaths of Flowers,
> And from their Leaves dropt Aromatick Showers,
> Whose fragrant Heads in Mystick Twines above,
> Exchang'd their Sweets, and mixed with thousand Kisses.
> (ll. 9–12)

In this atemporal eutopia there is no contamination or disease, and no impediment to pleasure. The garden has no secret menace; there snakes are without 'spiteful venom' (l. 47), 'Ambition was not known,/That Poyson to Content, Bane to Repose' (ll. 55–6), and power's 'Poyson was not mixt with our unbounded Joyes' (l. 79):

> Then it was glory to pursue delight,
> And that was lawful all, that Pleasure did invite,
> Then 'twas the amorous world enjoy'd its Reign;
> And Tyrant Honour strove t'usurp in Vain. (ll. 80–3)

Through this Edenic bower of bliss where lovers 'uncontroul'd did meet' (l. 105), Behn offers a powerful critique of women's internalization of repressive sexual codes, and the patriarchal fetishization of women's bodies – bound, veiled, netted, stinted, and starved in the name of honour:

Honour! who first taught lovely Eyes the art,
　　To wound, and not to cure the heart:
With Love to invite, but to forbid with Awe,
And to themselves prescribe a Cruel Law;
　　　To Veil 'em from the Lookers on,
　　　When they are sure the slave's undone,
And all the charmingst part of Beauty hid;
Soft Looks, consenting Wishes, all deny'd.
　　　It gathers up the flowing Hair,
　　　That loosely plaid with wanton Air.
The Envious Net, and stinted order hold,
The lovely Curls of Jet and shining Gold;
No more neglected on the Shoulders hurl'd:
Now drest to Tempt, not gratify the World,
Thou Miser Honour, hord'st the sacred store,
And starv'st thyself to keep thy Votaries poor. (ll. 122–36)

In the economy of female chastity, seduction promises no 'cure', and women are the subjects of an accounting which hoards to starve. The logic of deferral is shown to be especially disabling for women, leaving them in time bankrupt of pleasure and without the equity of their beauty. The poem's closing lines advise Sylvia, one such 'Ruin'd Shrine', in a spirit of *carpe diem* libertinism: 'the Gay, hasty minutes prize.' The speaking subject is not strictly gender-specific, identifying both with the votaries of chastity and the virile swains. It is part of the poem's permissiveness that the conclusion can be read in various ways: as the swain's warning and injunction to Sylvia not to be coy; or as another young woman's advice to her friend to take pleasure while she is desired; or even as lesbian invitation.[34]

There is a decorous reading which recuperates the poem's critique as masculine wish-fulfilment, its praise of unfettered eroticism as the circumventing of female refusal:

And she in vain denies, whilst we can guess,
She only shows the Jilt to teach man how,
To turn the false Artillery on the Cunning Foe. (ll. 171–3)

But we might also read a valorization of female cunning and female licence in the openness of identifications and interpretations permitted. Female sexual resistance is troped as either mere teasing and time-wasting or misguided self-censorship, and the threat of temporality returns with a vengeance as a warning specifically to women that, for them, there can be no 'eternal Spring'.[35] But the poem does gesture towards the value of female pleasure and women's sexual self-determination, as well as an anti-courtly, unambitious space where nature's generalized (auto)eroticism and productivity, troped as feminine, does not require either masculine sanction or participation:

> The stubborn Plough had then
> Made no rude Rapes upon the Virgin Earth;
> Who yielded of her own accord her plentious Birth,
> Without the Aids of men. (ll. 31–4)

Away from 'the Trading Court,/That busie Market for Phantastick Things' (ll. 154–5), the poem posits an escape from temporality, and the threat of decay which haunts women. The critique is cunningly turned to promote masculine satisfaction: 'But let the humble honest Swain go on,/In the blest Paths of the first rate of man' (ll. 162–3). But this pastoral (or pre-pastoral) location is also troped as a space of mutual desire. Naturally reciprocal, it flourishes outside the marketplace and the seats of power, where the 'young wishing Maid' and 'the peaceful *Swain* love on'.

'The Golden Age' fantasizes a eutopian space outside of or prior to the commodification, regulation and sanitization of 'natural' female sexuality. But even as the poem seeks to unveil authentic female desire, it reinscribes a gap between an idealized, infantilized figure of woman and the mutable flesh of women. The address to 'Sylvia' signifies both the utopian movement out of the marketplace and behind the fetishizing veil, and the irony that attends such an appeal. For this anti-courtly, pastoral fantasy is proffered from within, and contained by, the courtly market in women's 'honour' which the poem discredits. As she strategically manoeuvres between text and intertext, Behn stages an uneasy rapprochement between a woman's strategic entrepreneurial self-marketing in the world of men, and a dream of original, atemporal, polymorphous but feminized pleasure and self-sufficiency.

With the exception of the Fifth Monarchist, Mary Cary, the political conservatism of the women I am concerned with (Margaret Cavendish, Aphra Behn and Mary Astell) is striking. Though I do not want to argue that it is a commitment to absolutism that *enables* their utopian project of the self as its own monarch,[36] Cavendish, Behn and Astell are able to mask and contain the transgressive potential of their sexual politics, and their own anxiety over hierarchy, by a contradictory reversion to, and accommodation of, the legitimacy of monarchy as the model and guarantee of order. In this, only Cavendish, the aristocratic Duchess of Newcastle, is directly protecting her own class privilege, in a political context in which it is threatened. Behn, as an independent, middle-class, professional woman writer, is a mobile client both for royal patronage, and the patronage of a public audience and public readership. Astell, the unusually well-educated daughter of a merchant, stakes a claim for the insertion of herself as professional female intellectual in a bourgeois, male public sphere, positioning herself as both reader and writer, student and teacher. She too is a client: for male respect, recognition and intellectual patronage; as well as for female students and followers.

In different ways, then, the radical sexual politics of Cavendish, Behn and Astell grows out of a sense of their exclusion as women from the privileges, possibilities and affiliations which are the unproblematic right of men of their social position. Their desires *as individuals* are notionally consonant with their class position, but not with their sexual subjection, and it is this sense of incongruity and injustice which motivates their critique of a bogus universalism which shores up patriarchal intellectual and sexual prerogatives. In negotiating this tricky balance, the rational basis of the female critique of male superiority, and the claims for the inherent rational capacity of women, become crucial.[37] In her dedicatory epistle, 'To the Two Most Famous Universities', for instance, Cavendish describes her book as a work for

> the good Encouragement of our Sex, lest in time we should grow Irrational as Idiots, by the Dejectedness of our Spirits, through the Careless Neglects and Despisements of the Masculine Sex to the Female, . . . for we are Kept like Birds in Cages to Hop up and down in our Houses, not Suffer'd to Fly abroad. . . . Shut out of all Power and Authority, by reason we are never Imployed either in Civil or Martial Affairs.[38]

In different ways both Astell and Cavendish privilege the benefits of women's lack of education (while railing against it) – Astell by claiming the 'natural' virtue of women; Cavendish by stressing their uncorrupted empirical abilities. Natural philosophy, she argues, is especially hospitable to the woman without formal education, among whom she includes herself: 'since, especially in Natural

Philosophy, Opinions have Freedome, I hope these my Opinions may also Injoy the same Liberty and Privilege that others have.'[39]

I want to suggest that the privileging of sexual, social and educational over legal and/or political reform in utopian writing by politically conservative seventeenth-century women is not a mark of generic failure or incapacity, but of specifically gendered insight into the diffuse, informal, ideological mechanisms by which women are controlled. If marriage is the institution of which these women most frequently write, in both positive and negative terms, that is because it is central to any analysis of the interactive, mutually constitutive relationship of the public and the private; and to any analysis of the political, legal, economic and sexual positioning of women according to marital status (married, unmarried, widowed). That none of them had children is also significant, giving them an actual and conceptual distance from the patriarchal confinement of female productivity within the maternal.

Behn's libertine sexual ethic and Astell's militant chastity have in common a feminist repudiation of the patriarchal marriage contract, and both locate authentic female desire outside it – the widow Behn in celebrating promiscuous circulation and sexual cross-dressing; the unmarried Astell in privileging female pedagogy and virtuous friendship, and in her reliance on the Christian trope of deferred marriage. For both, the pleasures of self-determination and of writing are linked to the interdicted autoerotic. Cavendish, on the other hand, consistently represents her own marriage as prestigious, enabling and protective, but stresses her independence in it – a freedom that is clearly dependent on the aristocratic wife's leisure, means and relative autonomy.

The semi-autonomy of the aristocratic wife is not, however, unproblematic. In the dedication to her husband in *Philosophical and Physical Opinions*, Cavendish confesses: 'the truth is, I have somewhat Err'd from good Huswifery, to write Nature's Philosophy, where, had I been prudent, I should have Translated Natural Philosophy into Good Huswifery.' She admits a potential breach between her wifely, domestic role and the writing of books which is healed by her husband's 'Leave to Publish them, which is a Favour, few Husbands would grant their Wives; but Your Lordship is an Extraordinary Husband.' The prefatory letter to the Duke of Newcastle in *Observations Upon Experimental Philosophy* (published together with *The Blazing-World*) constructs him as her ideal reader: 'if your Grace do but approve of it, I care not if all the World condemn it.'[40]

Cavendish tropes texts as children, claiming that 'as there is Procreation of Thoughts, so there is Procreation of Words'.[41] For her, each book brought out with the endorsement and collaboration of her husband is a living proof of the inherent capacity of women: 'if a Man can draw the Picture of a Man, or any thing else, although he never draws it, yet the Art is inherent in the Man, and the Picture in the Art, as long as the Man lives';[42] but if a woman does not demonstrate what she can do, the world accounts her of no capacity.

In *The Blazing-World*, Cavendish not only demonstrates her own imaginative, literary and conceptual capacities but, within the narrative, represents a woman ascending by 'natural' merit to a position of supreme power, with another woman (none other than 'Margaret Cavendish') as her scribe and confidante. That she remains technically married to the Emperor is a mere alibi – while 'Margaret Cavendish' as astral traveller makes occasional fond forays from the Blazing-World to her marital home. Cavendish consistently recuperates marriage and makes use of the trope of husbandly permission to authorize the radical potential of her own thoughts and productions.

I have tried to show the significance of utopian strategies, figures and models in some secular and religious, fictional and non-fictional writings by English women in the latter half of the seventeenth century, and the ways in which these writings engage the often contradictory or ambivalent relations between politics and sexual politics, public and private. In each case these utopian writings involve a commentary on gender and genre; and on the possibilities and limitations of utopian discourse for women. Each is partly motivated by the always unrealizable desire for efficacious voice and language – a goal that is especially interdicted for the seventeenth-century woman writer in every setting. Nevertheless, for a woman 'willing to follow the thread of her own Thoughts',[43] the perverse pleasures and transformations of utopian writing must have been particularly keen; for, as Astell cautioned, the 'course of the World does not often lodge Power and Authority in Women's hands'.[44]

NOTES

(Places of publication for works printed before 1800 is London unless otherwise stated.)

1 Charlotte Perkins Gilman, *Herland*, 1915, reissued by the Women's Press, 1979; Sarah Scott, *Millenium Hall*, 1762, reissued by Virago, 1986; Christine de Pizan, *The Book of the City of Ladies*, 1405, first translated into English in 1521, reissued by Picador (London) in 1983; Bridget Hill, *The First English Feminist: Reflections Upon Marriage and other Writings by Mary Astell*, London, Gower/Temple Smith, 1986; Ruth Perry, *The Celebrated Mary Astell: An Early English Feminist*, Chicago, University of Chicago Press, 1986.

2 See, for instance, Frances Bartkowski, *Feminist Utopias*, Lincoln, University of Nebraska Press, 1989; Nan Bowman Albinski, *Women's Utopias in British and American Fiction*, London, Routledge, 1988; Marleen S. Barr (ed.), *Future Females: A Critical Anthology*, Bowling Green, OH, Bowling Green State University Press, 1981; Marleen S. Barr and Nicholas D. Smith (eds), *Women and Utopia: Critical Interpretations*, Landham, MD, University Press of America, 1983; Natalie M. Rosinsky, *Feminist Futures: Contemporary Women's Speculative Fiction*, Ann Arbor, UMI Research Press, 1984; Sarah Lefanu, *In the Chinks of the World Machine. Feminism and Science Fiction*, London, Women's Press, 1988; Rosemary Jackson, *Fantasy: The Literature of Subversion*, London, Methuen, 1981.

3 Teresa de Lauretis, 'The essence of the triangle or, taking the risk of essentialism seriously: feminist theory in Italy, the U.S., and Britain', *differences*, 1989, vol. 1, no. 2, pp. 4–5. See also Donna Haraway, 'A Manifesto for Cyborgs: Science, Technology, and Socialist Feminism in the 1980s', in Elizabeth Weed (ed.), *Coming to Terms: Feminism, Theory, Politics*, London, Routledge, 1989 (first pub. 1985); Hélène Cixous and Catherine Clément, *The Newly Born Woman*, trans. Betsy Wing, Minneapolis, University of Minnesota Press, 1986 (first pub. 1975), and the sections on utopias in Elaine Marks and Isabelle de Courtivron (eds), *New French Feminisms*, Amherst, University of Massachusetts Press, 1980, and Toril Moi, *Sexual/Textual Politics*, London, Methuen, 1985.

4 Louis Marin, *Utopics: Spatial Play*, trans. Robert A. Vollrath, London, Macmillan, 1984; Paul Ricoeur, *Lectures on Ideology and Utopia*, ed. George H. Taylor, New York, Columbia University Press, 1986; Fredric Jameson, 'Of islands and trenches: naturalizations and the production of utopian discourse', *diacritics*, 1977, vol. 7, no. 2, pp. 2–21; Raymond Williams, 'Utopia and Science Fiction', *Science Fiction Studies*, 1978, vol. 5, no. 3, pp. 203–14; Michèle Le Doeuff, *The Philosophical Imaginary*, trans. Colin Gordon, London, Athlone Press, 1989.

5 Haraway, pp. 197–203.

6 See Nancy Fraser, *Unruly Practices: Power, Discourse and Gender in Contemporary Social Theory*, Minneapolis, University of Minnesota Press, 1989, ch. 6, for an outline of Habermas's theory of the public sphere, 'the space of political participation, debate, and opinion formation' (p. 119), and a sympathetic critique of its 'unthematized gender subtext' (p. 123). For another feminist critique of the gender-blind 'universality' of the public sphere see Le Doeuff.

7 In the first half of the seventeenth century there are utopian elements at least in the two romances by women which actively engage the allegorical model of Sidney's *Arcadia*. Lady Mary Wroth's incomplete *roman-à-clef*, *The Countesse of Montgomeries Urania*, 1621, is close kin to her uncle's monumental, incomplete romance, and Anna Weamys's *A Continuation of Sir Philip Sidney's Arcadia*, 1651, is, as its title implies, a self-elected act of homage and filiation, which aligns her not only with Philip Sidney, but also with the supplementary editorial and textual labour of his sister, the Countess of Pembroke. This strain of allegorical romance, with its utopian and anti-utopian features, resurfaces in parodic form in popular early eighteenth-century texts like Delarivier Manley's scandalous *roman-à-clef*, *Secret Memoirs of the New Atalantis*, 1709, and Eliza Haywood's dystopian *Memoirs of a Certain Island Adjacent to the Kingdom of Utopia*, 1725. See also Helen Hackett's and Rosalind Ballaster's chapters in this volume.

8 Lyman Tower Sargent, *British and American Utopian Literature 1516–1985: An Annotated, Chronological Bibliography*, New York, Garland, 1988.

9 Aphra Behn, *Oroonoko and Other Stories*, ed. Maureen Duffy, London, Methuen, 1986 (first pub. 1688).

10 Behn, p. 25.

11 For different interpretations of the political allegory see Laura Brown, 'The Romance of Empire: Oroonoko and the Trade in Slaves', in Laura Brown and Felicity A. Nussbaum (eds), *The New Eighteenth Century*, New York, Methuen, 1987, pp. 41–61; and Duffy, 'Introduction' to Behn, pp. 10–12.

12 Behn, p. 30.

13 ibid., p. 32.

14 R.W. Gibson and J. Max Patrick, 'Utopias and Dystopias 1500–1750', in *St. Thomas More: A Preliminary Bibliography of his Works and of Moreana to the Year 1750*, New Haven, Yale University Press, 1961, p. ix.

15 For Cavendish's *Convent of Pleasure*, see Sophie Tomlinson's chapter in this volume; for 'The Golden Age' and *The Voyage to the Island of Love*, see *Poems Upon Several Occasions*, 1684. Behn also wrote a prefatory poem for the first edition of Edward Howard's play, *The Six Days Adventure or the New Utopia* (1671) – a comedy in which female rule is renounced when men threaten to withdraw their love, ending in multiple marriages.

16 Virginia Blain, Patricia Clements and Isobel Grundy (eds), *The Feminist Companion to Literature in English: Women Writers from the Middle Ages to the Present*, London, Batsford, 1990, pp. 1107–8.

17 On the connections between utopia and the millenarian predictions of the Fifth Monarchists see Frank E. Manuel and Fritzie P. Manuel, *Utopian Thought in the Western World*, Oxford, Blackwell, 1979, pp. 358–61; and especially James Holstun, *A Rational Millennium: Puritan Utopias of Seventeenth-Century England and America*, New York and Oxford, Oxford University Press, 1987. J.C. Davis, *Utopia and the Ideal Society. A Study of English Utopian Writing 1516–1700*,

Cambridge, Cambridge University Press, 1981, pp. 31–7, identifies Fifth Monarchist writing as one of four early modern discourses of the ideal society which are not properly utopian, along with the perfect moral commonwealth, the Land of Cockaygne, and Arcadia. His typology stresses the centrality of order and institutional detail to the utopia-proper, arguing that Fifth Monarchist millenarianism 'does not have the "blueprint" quality of the utopia' (p. 36). On Cary, Trapnel and other prophetic women during the Interregnum, see Nigel Smith, *Perfection Proclaimed*, Oxford, Clarendon, 1989; Phyllis Mack, 'Women as Prophets during the English Civil War', *Feminist Studies*, 1982, vol. 8, no. 1, pp. 18–45; Elaine Hobby, *Virtue of Necessity. English Women's Writing 1649–88*, London, Virago, 1988; Alfred Cohen, 'The Fifth Monarchy Mind: Mary Cary and the Origins of Totalitarianism', *Social Research*, 1964, vol. 31, pp. 195–213; Keith Thomas, 'Women and the Civil War Sects', *Past and Present*, 1955, vol. 13, pp. 42–64; Christine Berg and Philippa Berry, 'Spiritual Whoredom: An Essay on Female Prophets in the Seventeenth Century', in Francis Barker *et al.* (eds), *1642: Literature and Power in the Seventeenth Century*, Colchester, University of Essex, 1981, pp. 37–54.

18 M.R. [Mary Cary], *Twelve Humble Proposals To the Supreme Governours of the three Nations now assembled at Westminster*, 1653, pp. 3–4.

19 Mary Rande [Cary], *The Little Horns Doom and Downfall*, followed by *A New and More Exact Mappe of New Jerusalems Glory when Jesus Christ and his Saints with him shall Reign on Earth a Thousand Years, and Possess all Kingdoms*, 1651. All subsequent citations of this work will be from this edition by signature or page number in the text.

20 Anna Trapnel, *The Cry of A Stone: or a Relation of Something Spoken in Whitehall, by Anna Trapnel, being in the Visions of God*, 1654, p. 72.

21 ibid., p. 73.

22 Hobby, p. 31.

23 See Holstun, pp. 49–50.

24 Cary, *Proposals*, p. 2.

25 ibid., p. 57.

26 In the following discussion, Astell's poems are cited from Appendix D of Perry, pp. 400–54, by page number in the text.

27 All citations of Astell's prose are from Hill's edition, by part and page number in the text.

28 Margaret Cavendish, *Observations upon Experimental Philosophy* followed by *The Description of a New World, called the Blazing-World*, 1668 (first pub. 1666), pp. 13–14. All citations from *The Blazing-World* are from this edition, by page number in the text.

29 Marjorie Hope Nicolson, *Voyages to the Moon*, New York, Macmillan, 1948, p. 224.

30 Manuel and Manuel, p. 7.

31 See Janet Todd, *The Sign of Angellica: Women, Writing, and Fiction 1660–1800*, London, Virago, 1989, pp. 67–8; Lisa T. Sarashon, 'A Science Turned Upside Down: Feminism and the Natural Philosophy of Margaret Cavendish', *Huntington Library Quarterly* 1984, vol. 47,

pp. 299–307; Catherine Gallagher, 'Embracing the Absolute: The Politics of the Female Subject in Seventeenth-century England', *Genders*, 1988, vol. 1, no. 1, pp. 24–39; and Paul Salzman, *English Prose Fiction 1558–1700: A Critical History*, Oxford, Clarendon, 1985, pp. 292–9.

32 Behn, *Poems*, pp. 1–12. Subsequent citations of this poem are by line number in the text.

33 See Henry Reynolds's 1628 translation of Tasso's 'Golden Age' chorus (69 lines), which his modern editor, Clifford Davidson, describes as 'relatively faithful', if slightly weakening the licence of the Italian original: Clifford Davidson (ed.), *Torquato Tasso's Aminta Englisht. The Henry Reynolds Translation*, Fennimore, WN, Westburg, 1972, p. xvi. Reynolds omits 'S'ei piace, ei lice', i.e. 'that which pleases is permitted'. Behn writes: 'that was lawful all, that Pleasure did invite' (l. 81). A literal translation of the Chorus is available in E. Lord, *Translation of the Orpheus of Angelo Politian and the Aminta of Torquato Tasso*, 1931. For a valuable discussion of 'The Golden Age' and other Behn poems in the context of epicureanism, see Sara Heller Mendelson, *The Mental World of Stuart Women: Three Case Studies*, Brighton, Harvester, 1987, pp. 162–72. Behn's 'Golden Age' has been reprinted in semi-modernized form in Katharine M. Rogers and William McCarthy, *The Meridian Anthology of Early Women Writers: British Literary Women from Aphra Behn to Maria Edgeworth 1660–1800*, New York, Meridian, 1987, pp. 8–14.

34 In Reynolds's translation the speaker is male ('let us meaner men alone', l. 61), while Behn's redaction resists any clear ascription of gender.

35 This is perhaps the most revisionary of Behn's revisionary genderings; see Reynolds: 'Live we in love, for our lives houres/ Hast on to death, that all at length devoures', in Davidson, p. 21.

36 See Gallagher, p. 25.

37 See Hilda Smith, *Reason's Disciples: Seventeenth-Century English Feminists*, Urbana, University of Illinois Press, 1982; and Gallagher, p. 35.

38 Margaret Cavendish, *Philosophical and Physical Opinions*, 1663, 'Epistle to the . . . Universities'.

39 Cavendish, *Opinions*, third 'Epistle to the Reader'.

40 Cavendish, *Observations*, sig. A3.

41 ibid., pp. 71–2.

42 ibid., p. 94.

43 Astell, *The Christian Religion*, 1705, in Hill, p. 202.

44 ibid.

5

'MY BRAIN THE STAGE': MARGARET CAVENDISH AND THE FANTASY OF FEMALE PERFORMANCE

Sophie Tomlinson

In one of her *Sociable Letters* (1664) written during her exile from the English Protectorate with her husband, the then Marquis of Newcastle, Margaret Cavendish describes to a female correspondent some of the 'several Sights and Shews' to be purchased at 'Carneval Time' in the city of Antwerp. From a medley of human and animal performers she singles out a female freak, half woman, half animal:

> amongst the rest there was a Woman brought to me, who was like a Shagg-dog, not in Shape, but Hair, as Grown all over her Body, which Sight stay'd in my Memory, not for the Pleasantness, but Strangeness, as she troubled my Mind a Long time, but at last my Mind kick'd her Figure out, bidding it to be gone, as a Doglike Creature.[1]

Repressing in this way the psychological disturbance caused by this figure Cavendish recounts how she was further fascinated by an Italian mountebank, who had with him a man who 'did Act the part of a Fool', together with 'two Handsom Women Actors, both Sisters . . . one of [whom] was the Mountebank's, th'other the Fool's Wife'. The second of these women, in Cavendish's estimate, far outshone the other, both for her beauty and her skill in acting and dancing. 'Indeed', she writes,

> she was the Best Female Actor that ever I saw; and for Acting a Man's Part, she did it so Naturally as if she had been of that Sex, and yet she was of a Neat, Slender Shape; but being in her

Dublet and Breeches, and a Sword hanging by her side, one would have believed she had never worn a Petticoat, and had been more used to Handle a Sword than a Distaff; and when she Danced in a Masculine Habit, she would Caper Higher, and Oftener than any of the Men, although they were great Masters in the Art of Dancing, and when she Danced after the Fashion of her own Sex, she Danced Justly, Evenly, Smoothly, and Gracefully. (pp. 406–7)

In the rest of the letter Cavendish explains how she took such delight in seeing 'this Woman, and the Fool her Husband' act, that she hired a room in the house next to the stage and went daily to watch them. However, in what seemed a short time, and 'to [her] great Grief', the itinerant troupe was commanded out of town by the local magistrate. To compensate for her loss Cavendish effected a characteristic gesture of interior withdrawal, in which

to please me, my Fancy set up a Stage in my Brain . . . and the Incorporeal Thoughts were the several Actors, and my Wit play'd the Jack Fool, which Pleased me so much, as to make me Laugh Loud at the Actions in my Mind . . . but after my Thoughts had Acted, Danced, and Played the Fool, some several times of Contemplating, my Philosophical and Physical Opinions, which are as the Doctors of, and in the Mind, went to the Judgement, Reason, Discretion, Consideration, and the like, as to the Magistrates, and told them, it was very Unprofitable to let such Idle Company be in the Mind . . . whereupon the Magistrates of the Mind Commanded the Fancy-Stage to be taken down, and the Thought-Actors to go out, and would not suffer them to Cheat, or Fool any longer. (p. 408)

Subscribing herself, 'And so leaving my Mind Free of such Strangers', Cavendish brings her letter to a close.

Cavendish's writing is acutely conscious of 'Fancy's' power to substitute the scene of the mind for the theatre of the world. In this letter, however, it is a real theatre which is so transposed, and transposed twice over, from open-air stage to private room, from private room to a closet theatre of the mind. While the first of these retreats is occasioned by the joint constraints of Cavendish's class and gender, she is compelled to the second only by the magistrate's order to the players to leave. In another of the *Sociable Letters*, in which she defends her 'Retired Life', Cavendish claims that she prefers her fantasy stage to worldly recreations:

> and though I do not go Personally to Masks, Balls, and Playes, yet my Thoughts entertain my Mind with such Pleasures, for some of my Thoughts make Playes, and others Act those Playes on the Stage of Imagination, where my Mind sits as a Spectator.[2]

But Cavendish's rapt viewing of the woman–actor undermines the integrity of this disavowal. 'Troubled for the Loss of that Pastime', she rehearses the scene in her head until her own regulatory controls intervene, suppressing the 'Fancy-Stage' and its cheating, fooling 'Strangers'. In a similar way her mind had earlier rid itself of the strange, amphibious 'Doglike Creature'. I want to suggest that the acts of suppression are linked, and that Cavendish, in a manner appropriate to fantasy, was simultaneously enthralled and disturbed by the actress's ambidextrous shifting between sexes.[3]

One reason why the cross-dressing actress might be a disturbing as well as pleasurable figure is that her performance seals the argument which Cavendish's texts constantly broach as to whether gender difference is natural or constructed.[4] Not only does the actress play a man 'so Naturally as if she had been of that Sex', she excels her male colleagues in the frequency and height of her capers. For Margaret, Duchess of Newcastle, at once pampered and constrained, wanting 'the Agility, Art, Courage [and] Liberty' to slide on the ice,[5] the female actor embodies a potent fantasy – not just of freedom from a natural femininity – but of litheness, aptitude, art and aspiration.

In the dedication to the first of her two books of plays, published respectively in 1662 and 1668, Cavendish traces her pleasure in 'making' plays to the imagined performance which accompanies their conception. She dedicates her book chiefly

> to my own Delight, for I did take
> Much pleasure and delight these Playes to make;
> For all the time my Playes a making were,
> My brain the Stage, my thoughts were acting there.[6]

The last line is redolent of Cavendish's creative resource, the power of her imagination to usurp the real. It gestures at the same time to the absence of a material stage, for as she goes on to indicate in one of her prefatory addresses, Cavendish wrote the plays which were published in her first volume during the Interregnum when public theatre performance was officially banned. One of the most striking features of Cavendish's plays is their use of performance as a metaphor of possibility for women. This embracing of the idea of acting as a means of becoming or self-realization is coupled in the first volume with a disparaging view of professional players, who counterfeit identities not truly their own.

As this attitude suggests, there are other contexts for Cavendish's engagement with female performance than the professional actress on the continent, or subsequently in Restoration England. In 1653, in the euphoria of her first publication, she proclaimed that 'this Age hath produced many effeminate Writers, as well as Preachers, and many effeminate Rulers, as well as Actors'.[7] One woman who belonged to the denomination of 'Royal Actors' was Charles I's French consort, Queen Henrietta Maria. Her practice of her native custom of performing, not just in masques, but in spoken drama at the Caroline court turned female acting into a fashionable and controversial issue in the period and inspired a growth in women's participation in private theatricals which continued into the Interregnum years. Acting formed part of the spectrum of the queen's social and religious interests, chief among which was a cult of platonic love, mediated through French romance and pastoral drama, which projected women centre-stage as the embodiment of ideal beauty.[8] The unprecedented feminine focus of court culture produced a division between an attitude which countenances the notion of women as theatrical, and one which stigmatizes female theatricality as sexually transgressive. The latter response is exemplified by the Puritan William Prynne's attack on women-actors as 'notorious whores' in his *Histrio-Mastix* (1633): the anti-theatrical tract which was construed as aiming at Henrietta Maria, and at the panoply of court culture and religion. The political furore caused by Prynne's book added fuel to a growing literary debate over the issue of women's cultural visibility and agency.[9]

One index of this debate is the new model of the court lady stereotype in Caroline drama, who is distinguished by her passion for acting and theatre. This figure is characterized by unruly behaviour, rising in degree from the frisky ladies-in-waiting who amuse themselves by acting Jupiter and Danae in James Shirley's *The Bird in a Cage* (1633), to the woman-antic as homicide in John

Ford's *Love's Sacrifice* (1633) to the actress as political subversive in William Cartwright's *The Lady-Errant* (1628–43?).

One can see a different kind of rapprochement with the notion of women as theatrical in the dramatic figure of the platonic mistress, whose role is essentially one of 'setting herselfe at gaze', playing prima donna to an audience of spectator servants whom she keeps at a distance through her artful language and wit. The discourse of acting and counterfeit attached to women within the platonic cult is clearly established in Jonson's *The New Inn* (1629) in the scenes in which Lady Frampul performs and so acts herself into her feeling for Lovel. This portrayal of the witty mistress as an actress persists in the series of capricious women in Shirley's comedies. In his play *The Ball* (1632) the demand for women-actors in England forms a fashionable talking point, while theatricality furnishes a standard for the behaviour of Lucilla, a rich young widow, who, entertaining three suitors in a row, jokes with her maid, 'Away, Scutilla, and/Laugh not [too] loud between our acts'.[10] A concept of theatricality as a necessary feminine ruse informs the household drama *The Concealed Fansyes*, written and perhaps performed in the mid-1640s by the sisters Lady Jane Cavendish and Lady Elizabeth Brackley. In their play the language of disguise and concealment expressed in the title is used consistently to characterize the two sisters' strategic obstruction of their lovers' address; their tormenting them, Beatrice-like, on the rack of their language: 'Sister pray tell mee in what humour thou wert wth thy servant yesterday, prethee tell mee how you acted yo^e Sceane.'[11]

When they wrote their play the Cavendish sisters were about to become stepdaughters to Margaret Lucas, who married their father, William Cavendish, in Paris in 1645. The fact that the sisters also authored a pastoral suggests that their dramatic writing, like that of their stepmother, was in part an effect of the culture set in motion by Henrietta Maria.[12]

Despite her disclaimers, the details of Cavendish's life support the more than passing acquaintance with theatre which is reflected in her work. In her autobiography she describes her family's manner of spending half of each year in London where they engaged in a typical range of 'town' recreations, one of which was 'in winter time to go sometimes to plays'.[13] Of crucial importance is Cavendish's volunteering as a maid of honour to Henrietta Maria in Oxford in 1643; a gesture which demonstrates her royalism, her social ambition and her identification with the queen's feminocentric culture.[14] At Oxford she would have witnessed the plays and other entertainments which continued to be staged in modified form.[15] The masque appears in her early work such as her prose fiction 'The Contract', in which two lovers are smitten during the dancing of the revels. The details of the occasion are carefully sketched, notably in the description of the tumult encountered by the heroine and her uncle as they attempt to gain access:

> and when they came to enter through the Door to the Masquing Room, there was such a Croud, and such a Noyse, the Officers beating the People back, the Women squeaking, and the Men cursing, the Officers threatening and the Enterers praying, which Confusion made her afraid.[16]

There is more evidence of Cavendish's colloquy with the culture surrounding the queen. The exiling of Henrietta's court to her native Paris supplied further contexts in which Cavendish could witness amateur and professional women actors, respectively in the distinctive French spectacle of the '*ballet de cour*', and in performances by local and visiting theatre companies.[17] Her play *The Presence* (1668), which dramatizes this period of her life, ends with '*a Ball after the* French fashion', followed by '*an Anti-Mask*',[18] and in another play, *The Female Academy* (1662), a woman delivers an oration on the theme of 'a Theatre' in which she criticizes the 'feign'd and constrain'd' acting of French and Italian players (p. 671). It was in Paris too, while in the service of the queen, that Margaret met and married William Cavendish, Marquis of Newcastle, a man who brought with him a host of theatrical connections. One of the new breed of courtier dramatists encouraged by Charles and Henrietta Maria's theatrical interests, he patronized and received professional assistance from a number of playwrights spanning the Caroline and Restoration periods, including Jonson, Shirley, Flecknoe, Shadwell and Dryden. In the dedicatory epistle to her first volume of plays Cavendish states that it was his reading his plays to her which made her take up the form (sig. A3R). The Marquis's dramatic leanings, moreover, were more than academic, as he was also involved in theatrical production. His plays *The Country Captain* and *The Varietie* had professional performances at the beginning of the 1640s. While he was in Paris he wrote 'several things' for the company of English players maintained by Prince Charles, and in 1658 the Newcastles gave a ball for Charles and his entourage in Antwerp involving four hours of dancing, speeches of

welcome and farewell penned by Newcastle and delivered by the
English actor Michael Mohun, and one of his songs, performed
by 'Lady Moore, dressed in feathers'.[19] Finally, as we have seen, it
was in Antwerp that Cavendish encountered women acting in street
theatre, women for whom performance was a profession as opposed
to a pastime. And once back in England this was the dispensation of
the Restoration theatre, in which women-actors were a vital new
force.[20]

In the rest of this chapter I show how Cavendish's dramatic
writing draws on this changing cultural and discursive status of
female performance to enable fantasies of female self-representation.
It is not my intention to suggest that Cavendish's plays were written
for women actors. Rather I want to show that because of her
particular historical position, performance - simulated in the mind
of her reader - is a bookish but catalysing fantasy in her plays.

Cavendish's first book of plays contains a total of eleven prefatory
addresses ranging from a justification of their deliberate structural
disunity to a prescription for how they are to be read aloud. In two
of these addresses she constantly raises and displaces the possibility
of her plays being performed. They are, she tells her 'Lordship' in
the dedicatory epistle,

> like dull dead statues, which is the reason I send them forth to
> be printed, rather than keep them concealed in hopes to have
> them first Acted; and this advantage I have, that is, I am out of
> the fear of having them hissed off from the Stage, for they are
> not like to come thereon; but were they such as might deserve
> applause, yet if Envy did make a faction against them, they
> would have had a publick Condemnation . . . [and] it would
> have made me a little Melancholy to have my harmless and
> innocent Playes go weeping from the Stage, and whipt by
> malicious and hard-hearted censurers; but the truth is, I am
> careless, for so I have your applause I desire no more.(sigs
> A3R–V)

In dialogue with her 'Noble Readers', however, the reason Cavendish prints her plays,

> before they are Acted, is, first, that I know not when they will
> be Acted, by reason they are in English, and England doth
> not permit . . . of Playes . . . but the printing of my Playes

spoils them for ever to be Acted (because what takes with the spectators is novelty) so that my Playes would seem lame or tired in action, and dull to hearing on the Stage, for which reason, I shall never desire they should be Acted. (sig. X1V)

At the end of this address Cavendish's 'reason' has come full circle and the reason she puts her plays out in print is because they will not be acted because she puts them out in print. As if to confirm this failure to squash the genie of performance Cavendish returns to the issue of acting in a further address. Here she refutes 'an erronious opinion got into this our Modern time and men . . . that it should be thought a crime or debasement for the nobler sort to Act Playes, especially on publick Theatres' (sig. X2R). Retaining the masculine bias of her previous address she argues for the edifying function of acting for 'the noblest youths':

> for it learns them gracefull behaviours and demeanors, it puts Spirit and Life into them, it teaches them Wit, and makes their Speech both voluble and tunable, besides it gives them Confidence, all which ought every man to have, that is of quality. (sig. X2R)

Cavendish contrasts this mode of acting, that is 'for Honour, and becoming' with the 'mercenary Players' who act solely for financial profit.

These passages are important because together they reveal that Cavendish did fantasize her plays as being performed, outside the theatre of her mind. Moreover they show that this fantasy remains couched within a masculine discourse. Even though her reference to the 'erronious opinion got into this our Modern time and men' might be construed as alluding to Prynne's attack on Henrietta Maria, the terms Cavendish uses, 'noblest youths', 'every man . . . of quality', indicate that she is speaking here of male-actors.

What apology for actors does Cavendish give? The concept of acting which she articulates in her address is scholastic and aristocratic. It views theatrical performance as a mode of self-enhancement, of becoming one's best self, stressing the reciprocity between actor and part. We can see this theory of acting applied to female performance in a letter from Richard Flecknoe's *A Relation of Ten Years Travells* (1654). Flecknoe describes to a female correspondent the play he is writing, a tragicomedy called *The Temple of Frendship*. The play deals with 'a Commonwealth of Amazons' who are clearly bound by ties of platonic love. The letter is worth quoting at length, both as an illustration of the aristocratic theory of *female* performance and for the light it sheds on the relation between this theory and the neo-platonic idealization of women:

> Frendship being our second Religion, and so main a part of our first, I have design'd to present it so beautiful to the Eye, as all should be ravisht with its Love and Admiration. To that end I have personated it in the loveliest Sex, and that betwixt persons of the same sex too, for avoiding all suspect; *Frendship being nothing but Love stript of suspition of Harm*. For representing it by Ladies, after the like example of the Queen and her Ladies here formerly, & of the greatest Ladies & Princesses in *Spain, France Flandres*, and elsewhere, I thought none reasonably could take exceptions, nor think me too ambitious in't, especially I having been long Time train'd up & conversant in the Courts of the greatest Queens and Princesses in *Europe*, and consequently not altogether ignorant of personating and presenting them according to their dignity and quality.[21]

Consistent with his allusion to Henrietta Maria ('the Queen and her Ladies here formerly') Flecknoe's emphasis is on the presentational nature of aristocratic performance, the aptness or accord between the part and the person who plays it and the need for the dramatist to be schooled in noble society. This theory of performance depends on a rigid ideology of social order; the corollary is Cavendish's contempt for 'mercenary Players', who not only make 'a work of labour' that which should remain an exercise of 'honour' or 'delight' (sig. X2R), but who disrupt the social order by imitating noble status. Rather than viewing acting as an extension of the self, professional players engage in a form of *anti*-self-fashioning, or self-subversion: a deliberate fashioning of the self as other. We can see how Cavendish distrusts this protean theatricality and the social mobility it simulates by looking briefly at her play *The Apocriphal Ladies* (1662).

In this play, one of those which takes the form of a series of dialogues, the 'Unfortunate Dutchess' has been dispossessed of the right of her kingdom by her husband, the Duke Inconstancy. Living in exile, her woman brings her news of her husband's remarriage to the 'Apocriphal Dutchess', who is elsewhere termed the 'Comical

Dutchess' (p. 649). The ensuing dialogue between the true Duchess and her woman elaborates the theatrical metaphor:

(Woman) – She will be as a Dutchess in a Play, she will only act the part of greatness.
(Unfortunate Dutchess) – Indeed most Stage-Players are Curtizans.
(W) – And most Curtizans are good Actors.
(UD) – I make no question but she will now have enough Spectators.
(W) – But I hope they will hiss her off from the Stage. (p. 641)

The passage uses the trope of female acting, or strictly, stage-playing, to signify social and sexual inauthenticity. Its obvious point of reference is Prynne's index entry, 'women-actors, notorious whores'. This critique of social imposture conducted through the metaphor of female acting or make-believe is repeated several times in the text: through the Creating Princess who marries beneath her, so 'creat[ing] [her] Husband to Honour', and the Imaginary Queen, who steps into a vacant throne but 'cannot act the part, for she appears like a good Country Housewife' (p. 646). It is further reinforced by a long oration delivered by the Lady True-Honour, who asks resoundingly 'shall Princes in Royal Courts, give place to Princes in Playes?' (p. 647).

The anti-feminist, anti-theatrical discourse articulated in *The Apocriphal Ladies* raises the question of why Cavendish couches her prefatory defence of noble performance in exclusively masculine terms. The explanation may lie in the passage from her dedicatory address to Newcastle quoted above (p. 140), in which she fantasizes, not simply her plays' performance, but their 'publick Condemnation'. The passage elaborates the fear from which Cavendish states she is saved by printing her plays, namely, 'the fear of having them hissed off from the Stage'. Her language personifies the plays as feminine, putting the case in which her 'harmless and innocent Plays' would be 'hissed' and 'whipt', and would exit 'weeping from the Stage'. As her echo of the last line in the dialogue from *The Apocriphal Ladies* confirms, Cavendish imagines her plays receiving the punitive treatment of a prostitute or public woman.[22] Her address aligns the female dramatist whose plays are performed with the actress–whore, each notorious by reason of her self-promotion.[23]

This dangerous proximity of the roles of public female dramatist and actress accounts for the divorce between the mooting of the issue of male performance in Cavendish's prefaces, and the feminine theatrical discourse of her plays. If we look at the place of this discourse in her 1662 volume we can see the positive constructions of female performance feasible within the enclosure of her 'Fancy-Stage'.

The use of theatrical metaphor to enable the performance of female identity is developed in *Youths Glory and Deaths Banquet*. Its protagonist, Lady Sanspareille, is blessed with a father who not only provides her with a rigorously learned, masculine education but is willing to forgo his posterity in order to abet his daughter's quest for fame. Early in the play Cavendish characterizes Lady Sanspareille's unusual expressiveness in terms of a theatrical trope. As her daughter wafts in 'repeating some verses of her own making' Lady Sanspareille's mother accuses her, 'I am sure you are transformed from what you should be, from a sober young maid, to a Stage-player, as to act Parts, speak Speeches, rehearse Verses, sing Sonets, and the like' (p. 126). Lady Sanspareille replies with a speech which reiterates Cavendish's prefatory address, defending theatre as a means for 'the education of noble youth'. She rejects her mother's use of the term 'stage-player', drawing the same distinction we saw Cavendish make between noble amateurs and mercenary professionals: 'shall Kings, Princes or noble Persons, that dances, sings, or playes on Musick, or presents themselves in Masks, be thought, or called Dancers, or Fidlers, Morris-dancers, Stage-players, or the like, as in their masking attire?' (p. 127). In view of her subsequent career as a woman-orator, Lady Sanspareille's omission of spoken acting from her defence of courtly performance can only be construed as a strategic display of daughterly tact. For later we learn that acting does indeed form part of her vocation, which involves the pervasive exercise of public speech. As a gentleman remarks,

> this Lady Sanspareile hath a strange spreading wit, for she can plead causes at the Bar, decide causes in the court of Judicature, make Orations on publick Theatres, act parts, and speak speeches on the Stage, argue in the Schooles, preach in the Pulpits, either in Theology, Philosophy, moral and natural, and also phisick and Metaphysick. (p. 158)

Here Cavendish uses 'acting' simply as a metonym for female public utterance. Specifically, she affirms as a female trait the boldness or confidence that one of her Lady Speakers in *The Female Academy* describes as belonging to 'Preachers, Pleaders, and Players, that can present themselves, speak and act freely, in a publick Assembly' (p. 674).

Although stage acting is subsumed as one facet of Lady Sanspareille's verbal prowess the play leaves no doubt of the showiness of her orations. She speaks from a rostrum described as 'a place raised and railed with guilt rayles', and of which a philosopher remarks to her father, 'Sir, you have adorned her Theater to inthrone her wit' (p. 136). Apart from the attendance of Queen Attention at her oration on government Lady Sanspareille's audience is wholly male. Moreover the text emphatically marks the scopic nature of the event. For her first oration she appears *'drest all in black'*; upon her entrance the spectators are *'struck with amaze of her beauty'*, one of them remarking to her father, 'Sir, we perceive now, you have invited us to feast our eyes, not our eares' (p. 136). For her final oration in which she justifies her vow never to marry, Lady Sanspareille enters *'all in white Satin, like as a Bride, and her Father and her audience, which are all Lovers; these stand gazing upon her'* (p. 158). At the end the lovers exit silently in various states of transport, *'some lifting up their eyes, others their hands, some striking their hands on their breast, and the like'* (p. 161). Susan Wiseman has commented on Cavendish's presentation of women who display themselves both educationally and erotically within a masculine preserve.[24] The erotic spectacle of Lady Sanspareille's final address echoes the role of women in the platonic theatre of cruelty in Caroline drama, in which, as I have indicated, the position of the platonic mistress is that of an actress. The platonic lady's power lies in her deployment of what *The Concealed Fansyes* calls her 'sceane self'. Lady Sanspareille's performance – dressed in white bridal satin before an audience of lovers, delivering an oration denouncing marriage as an impediment to the contemplative life – is the acme of sexual provocation and the platonic woman's 'will to power'.[25]

One may speculate about the topicality of Cavendish's fantasies of women's public speaking. Lois Potter cites as a precedent for her 'obsession with public orations' the academies offering public lectures which had existed for some time on the continent. In 1649 a similar institution had been opened in London by the royalist Sir Balthazar Gerbier, at which, 'by special request', a lecture was given for ladies, 'concerning the *Art of Well Speaking*'.[26] A remark by Francis Osborne in his *Historical memoires on the reigns of Queen Elizabeth, and King James* (1658) suggests a shift in attitude towards the kind of theatricality which Cavendish makes typical of Lady Sanspareille:

> Her Sex did beare out many impertinences in her words and actions, as *her making Latin speeches in the Universities*, and professing her selfe in publique *a Muse, then thought something too Theatrical for a virgine Prince*. (final italics mine)[27]

It is instructive to compare Cavendish's fantasy of public discoursing with her account of one of the few occasions in her life when she had the chance to make effective use of public speech. In her autobiography she describes her trip into England with her brother-in-law Sir Charles Cavendish in order to petition the parliamentary committee for compounding for a wife's share in Newcastle's sequestered estates. She received 'an absolute refusal' of her claim, being told in no uncertain terms that she had no entitlement to Newcastle's estate since she had married him after his delinquency, and moreover that she deserved nothing, her husband 'being the greatest traitor to the State'. Far from producing a show-stopping display of eloquence Cavendish

> whisperingly spoke to my brother to conduct me out of that ungentlemanly place, so without speaking to them one word good or bad, I returned to my lodgings, and as that committee was the first, so was it the last, I ever was at as a petitioner.[28]

In contrast to Dr Denton's commendation of the political usefulness of women's histrionic powers in a letter to Sir Ralph Verney, Cavendish patently failed, in his words, 'to act it with committees'.[29] In the self-defence which follows she ascribes her failure partly to bashfulness, but she precedes this by criticizing the contemporary state of affairs in England where 'women become pleaders, attorneys, petitioners, and the like', an activity which she sees as a form of indecorous self-aggrandizement, 'nothing but jostl[ing] for the pre-eminence of words'.[30]

In considering this passage we should recall the type of bashfulness described by one of the Lady Speakers in *The Female Academy* as proceeding from the desire 'to out-act all others in Excellencies'

(p. 674). Cavendish's stressing of her shyness is undoubtedly a symptom of what Elaine Hobby calls her 'highly repressive image of her own femininity',[31] but her attack on women who spoke in public could equally well be motivated by the bashfulness produced by 'aspiring Ambition'. As the correspondence between Lady Sanspareille's behaviour and Osborne's observation on Queen Elizabeth suggests, Cavendish's fantasies of action and expression are based on the figure of the female monarch. In his funeral oration for his daughter the first two things to which Sir Thomas Father Love compares her life are a masque and a monarchy. In the final play I wish to discuss from this volume, *Bell in Campo*, we can see Cavendish's identification with Queen Henrietta Maria as an actor in 'the Theatre of Warr' (p. 669).

In the play Lady Victoria persuades her husband the Lord General to allow her to accompany him to war, inspiring five or six thousand women to follow suit. When the men refuse to grant the women an active role Lady Victoria addresses the 'number of women of all sorts' who have imitated her example, and marshalling a panoply of rousing feminist arguments convinces them to form their own army, of which they elect her the 'Generaless'. Determined to prove themselves equal to men in constancy and valour the women 'surprize, seise and plunder' the garrison town, recruit its female population, and entrench themselves to practise their military manoeuvres. The chance arises to rescue their flagging male counterparts: the 'Amazonian Army' moves in, vanquishes the enemy forces and performs further military feats. When the men capitulate by sending the women 'a complemental letter' the female army delivers up its gains, happy with the honour of victory and passes the rest of the time in heroic sports on the frontiers while their husbands get on with conquering the 'Kingdom of Faction'. At the end of the play Lady Victoria is brought into the city in a military triumph and is greeted by the king. Several acts are then read: one grants all women in the kingdom precedence in the home; another ensures that Lady Victoria will be memorialized in history.

Bell in Campo gives full rein to Cavendish's fantasy of entering the male world of heroic action and honour. In constructing this fantasy she drew on a contemporary lexicon of female heroism, a lexicon expressed both in visual iconography and in a literature valorizing the heroic deeds of illustrious women. This cultural movement had an efflorescence in France in the 1640s, partly as a response to the participation in government and war of women like Anne of Austria, Queen Regent of France from 1643 to 1652, and her niece Anne Marie d'Orléans, the 'Grande Mademoiselle', who fought in the French civil wars known as the Fronde. As Ian Maclean has demonstrated, this movement was accompanied by an upsurge of feminist debate in France – a feminism he defines as 'a reassessment in women's favour of the relative capacities of the sexes'.[32]

While the image of the heroic woman flourished most visibly in France, it was also embodied in displaced form in England by Henrietta Maria. Decorous figures of female valour began to appear in Caroline masques and drama from the mid-1630s and with the onset of civil war Henrietta Maria embraced the chance to act out her role as a 'martial lady'. In her letters to Charles she draws amused attention to this role, dubbing herself 'her she-majesty, generalissima', while in Madame de Motteville's romantic transcription of the queen's account of 'the Troubles in England' she is compared to no less a figure than Alexander.[33] As Cavendish's two favourite heroes were Alexander and Caesar it is unsurprising that she should identify with this aspect of Henrietta Maria's persona.[34] It was Newcastle himself, as commander of the loyalist forces in the north, who met the queen on her landing from Holland and conducted her to York, from where she journeyed to Oxford with part of his army as escort. Cavendish was in Oxford with her family when the queen made what was reported as 'a most triumphant and magnificent entry' into the city and it was there that she conceived what she describes as 'a great desire to be one of her maids of honour'.[35] Rather than following the romantic model of the lone Lady Errant, or the solitary heroic endeavour of the 'femme forte', Lady Victoria's desire to participate in her husband's actions seems more likely to be modelled on the conjugal team of Henrietta Maria and Charles. At one point Cavendish even makes fun of the queen's foibles. Early in the play a gentleman complains of the encumbrance of a woman in war, saying, 'and if her Dog should be left in any place, as being forgotten, all the whole Army must make a halt whilst the Dog is fetcht, and Trooper after Trooper must be sent to bring intelligence of the Dogs coming' (p. 583), a detail which rather dresses down the story of Henrietta Maria's heroic rescue of her lapdog during the bombardment of her dwelling at Bridlington Bay. As Madame de Motteville embroiders:

> She had an ugly Lap-Dog, nam'd *Mitte*, which she was very fond of; and remembering in the Middle of the Village, that she had left *Mitte* asleep in her Bed, she returned the Way she Came, and not fearing her Pursuers, she brought away her Favourite, and then retired as fast as she could from Cannon-Shot.[36]

The inflationary gesture of Lady Victoria's triumph can also be compared to the actual state entries in Europe of women like Queen Christina of Sweden, of which Henrietta Maria's Oxford entry may have been a modified version.[37]

Bell in Campo thus gives ample witness of Cavendish's imaginative investment in an ethic of female heroism, in the ostentation and bravura of a monarchist culture, and in the concept of individual sovereignty pertaining to it. While the play leaves us in no doubt of the apotheosis of its female hero, the nature of the gains won for women through her endeavours are rather more fragile. In the laws which are passed at the end of the play the changes affecting women's status are limited to the domestic sphere, where women are to be 'Mistris in their own Houses and Families', to sit above their husbands at the table, to keep the purse, to appoint the servants, to have ownership and management of the household goods, and lastly, to 'be of their Husband's Counsel' (p. 631).

These reforms first invert the structure of the patriarchal family, then backtrack pathetically to a provision for partnership in marriage. Their narrowing of scope in relation to the preceding action is echoed in the second plot, where in opposition to Lady Victoria's acting in the world and entering history, Madam Jantil, after the death of her husband, withdraws into his mausoleum and stages her own prolonged self-extinction, having first carefully arranged for the writing of her husband's *Life*. This division between the two plots, between Lady Victoria's public triumph and the rewards offered women in general is echoed by a division within the women's Act itself. There are four further clauses which unleash all the feminine frivolity which defies attempts to regulate and control women's existence:

Seventhly,   They shall wear what fashioned Clothes they will.
Eightly,   They shall go abroad when they will, without controul, or giving of any account thereof.
Ninthly,   They shall eat when they will, and of what they will, and as much as they will, and as often as they will.

Tenthly,   They shall go to Playes, Masks, Balls, Churchings,
             Christenings, Preachings, whensoever they will, and
             as fine and bravely attired as they will. (p. 631)

These clauses show a glimpse of a Land of Cockayne, a world
of inversion in which feminine folly and freedom have reign. In
contrast to the inflationary fantasy of the foregoing play this vision
of licence is disarmingly local and domestic. The freedom to eat,
to roam, to indulge in the pleasures of self-display and theatrical, sociable pastimes forms a nucleus of resistance to women's
entrenchment in the family. In the context of the play this fantasy
is both deflationary and recuperative; in the context of the Act it is
a relic of female survival.

Thus far I have been discussing Cavendish's use of a theatrical
discourse to represent a particular kind of female identity. Cavendish uses theatrical tropes in her first volume of plays to legitimize
a self which is envisaged not merely as authentic, but as fantastically
inflated and absolute. This use of theatricality to supplement the
self produces a subjectivity at once singular and sovereign because
its boundaries are perceived as all-extensive. It would perhaps be
useful to distinguish this fantasized subjectivity from the model of
the female subject obtaining in Cavendish's non-dramatic writing.

Catherine Gallagher reads Cavendish as installing herself as
absolute monarch of a fantasy microcosm, producing a self which
is private, interior and infinitely recessive.[38] In Cavendish's plays,
however, performance means crossing the boundary between inside
and outside, animating the self in front of the gaze of others.
This fantasy depends on self-projection, not self-withdrawal; even
though the self is part of the audience. In her closet theatre of the
mind Cavendish can marry the contrary impulses to solitude and
sociability, bashfulness and exhibitionism, which inform the text
of her life.

Cavendish's second volume of plays (1668) marks a shift from a
fantasy of identity as static and sovereign to a fantasy of identity
as dynamic and provisional. The single preface 'To the Readers' is a
defiant rejoinder to the criticism which she implies had been heaped
on her first volume. Cavendish makes no pretence that her plays
conform either to the 'ancient Rules' or 'the modern Humor', but
simply 'having pleased my Fancy in writing many Dialogues upon
several Subjects, and having afterwards order'd them into Acts and
Scenes, I will venture, in spight of the Criticks, to call them Plays'
(sig. A2V).[39]

Ironically, despite this claim, the plays in this volume do conform more both to dramatic and theatrical conventions: in the orthodox numbering of scenes within acts, in the restricted number of plots, in the use of dance and song, and in the more interactive nature of the writing.[40] The influence of Restoration drama is especially apparent in the first play in the volume, *The Sociable Companions; or, the Female Wits*, with its double-barrelled title and its use of personal first names like 'Peg Valorosa' for the female protagonists. The influence is most marked in the play's heightened awareness of a theatrical culture. At one point Will Fullwit is reported to have gone to the playhouse, or 'the Acting-house' as one character calls it (p. 15); when he returns he fools his friend into believing him first dead, then mad. Reverting to sanity he explains that he has 'only acted an Intrigue', a humour he got 'With seeing a new Play' (p. 18).

In keeping with this newly localized sense of theatre the play is constructed around a series of female-inspired intrigues in which dissembling and disguise are made concrete devices. Cavendish creates an unusually precise scenario showing a group of disbanded cavalier soldiers who, resentful of the poor reward of their loyalty, are squandering all the money they have in taverns. Frustrated by their brothers' lethargy in seeking 'some good Offices and Employments' that would 'maintain us according to our births and breedings' (p. 30), the sisters of the soldiers resolve to use their 'Wits and Honesty' to get rich husbands (p. 48). One of their designs involves Peg Valorosa testifying in a counterfeit spiritual court with the help of a fraudulent midwife that she has become platonically pregnant, the 'Idea of a Man' having created a child by conceit. In a parallel intrigue Jane Fullwit dresses as 'Jack Clerk' and enters the service of Lawyer Plead-all, whom she tricks into laying a charge against her brother. By counter-accusing Plead-all of keeping a gentlewoman in man's clothes sister and brother cozen the lawyer into marriage.

The Sociable Companions represents a major alteration in the status of acting and theatricality in Cavendish's texts. Whereas in her previous volume acting or disguise is used either metaphorically or as part of Cavendish's reworking of the codes of romance, this play inscribes theatricality as a distinctive practice, vindicating the resourceful use – by indigent cavaliers – of female counterfeit or intrigue. Though the nature of the women's necessitous marriages is never queried, their tactical use of intrigue and disguise is contrasted with the character Prudence, whose father Save-all abstained from fighting in the war and is therefore able to provide his daughter with a portion. In the manner of a similarly named character in the earlier play *The Publick Wooing* (1662), Prudence, granted her own choice by her father, hears the suits of potential lovers herself. The final scene of the play takes the form of a public assembly in which she delivers a speech to her suitors, simultaneously justifying her choice of an 'ancient man' for a husband and her act of exercising that choice:

> Concerning the Church and State, since they do allow of buying and selling young Maids to Men to be their Wives, they cannot condemn those Maids that make their bargains to their own advantage, and chuse rather to be bought then sold. (p. 95)

The discourse of authenticity which accrues to Prudence in the play, who is able through her father's dishonour to conduct her wooing in the open and to her own advantage, co-exists with, rather than undermines, the other women's paradoxically 'honest' (because politically honourable) deployment of female deceit and disguise.

All of the four complete plays in Cavendish's 1668 volume make similarly concrete use of theatricality, in particular the device of cross-dressing for both sexes.[41] One might attribute the emphasis on female cross-dressing to the situation on the Restoration stage, where in contrast to the ornamental 'masculine' costuming adopted in female performances at the Caroline court, transvestite parts did involve the assumption of full masculine dress, including wearing breeches. The device of cross-dressing appears at its most complex in the final play in the book, *The Convent of Pleasure*, where it functions simultaneously as a form of male sexual expediency and as part of a feminine fantasy world. For this play Cavendish drew on an established romantic/comic plot in which a man enters a convent in female disguise.[42] What is appealing about her use of this plot is the way in which the male voyeurism made possible through the cross-dressing device is subordinated to the romantic perspective of Lady Happy, the founder of the convent, who fully believes that she has fallen in love with a woman.

In the play the heiress Lady Happy decides to 'incloister [her]self from the World', both to avoid the company of men, 'who make the Female Sex their slaves', and to enjoy the pleasures she can afford with her father's fortune (pp. 6, 7). She defines her action in chaste and pragmatic opposition to orthodox sexual choice, for as she remarks, 'Marriage to those that are virtuous is a greater restraint than a Monastery' and 'should I quit Reputation and turn Courtizan, there would be more lost in my Health, then gained by my Lovers' (p. 3). Accordingly Lady Happy sets up cloister with 'a number of noble women, of greater birth than fortune', all of whom have vowed virginity, and together they embark on a life in which each sense is supplied, and as Madam Mediator remarks, 'every Lady . . . enjoyeth as much Pleasure as any absolute Monarch can do, without the Troubles and Cares, that wait on Royalty' (p. 17). In a lavish inventory, reminiscent of poetic invitations to the pastoral realm, Lady Happy describes to the women 'how I have order'd this our *Convent of Pleasure*'. The vision she creates is one of a domesticated golden world in which changes of season will merely bring increased sensual delights and in which luxury will extend to the smallest detail. Significantly, men are wholly excluded from this world: in contrast to the voyeuristic access granted men to the earlier Female Academy, Lady Happy's convent 'will admit none of the Masculine Sex, not so much as to a Grate' (p. 11).

In one scene however Cavendish portrays the comic eagerness of a group of gallants to invade and disrupt this community of women. Their designs include 'smoak[ing] them out, as they do a Swarm of Bees' (p. 18) and entering the convent 'in Womens apparel' (p. 20). This last idea is discounted by one of the gallants who argues that they would discover themselves by their masculine voices and behaviour, 'for we are as untoward to make Curtsies in Petticoats, as Women are to make Legs in Breeches' (p. 20). This assertion of sexual determinism goes hand in hand with the men's facile desire to create sexual havoc in the convent. Having raised this possibility the play then shifts into a romantic register which accommodates sexual ambiguity within a make-believe, theatrical world.

Shortly after the convent is established Lady Happy admits as a novice to her female community 'a great Foreign Princess', described as 'a Princely brave Woman truly, of a Masculine Presence' (p. 16), who hearing of the convent's fame has decided to 'quit a court of trouble for a *Convent of Pleasure*' (p. 22). The Princess tells Lady Happy that 'the greatest pleasure I could receive, were to have your Friendship', and desiring that Lady Happy 'would be my Mistress, and I your Servant' she makes one particular request:

> I observing in your several Recreations, some of your Ladies do accoustre [sic] Themselves in Masculine-Habits, and act Lovers-parts; I desire you will give me leave to be sometimes so accoustred and act the part of your loving Servant. (p. 22)

Lady Happy is delighted with the innocence of this request and sits down with the Princess to watch a play performed by the other women.[43] Rather than a gentle and decorous feminine pastoral, the play is a grim sequence of episodes depicting the miseries of marriage and the female condition, from the negligence and promiscuity of husbands, perpetual pregnancy, infant mortality, wife-abuse, the pains of childbirth, the irresponsibility of children, and death in childbirth to the sexual predatoriness of Lords. The epilogue hammers home the socially inclusive message of this feminist drama: 'Marriage is a Curse we find, / Especially to Womenkind: / From the Cobler's Wife we see, / To Ladies, they unhappie be' (p. 30). This theatrical elaboration of the grotesqueness of the female condition in the workaday world functions as anti-masque to the recreative theatrical wooing of the Princess and Lady Happy. Just prior to their scene together Lady Happy enters 'drest as a Shepherdess', and debates with herself:

> My name is Happy, and so was my Condition, before I saw this Princess, but now I am like to be the most unhappy Maid alive: But why may I not love a Woman with the same affection I could a Man? (p. 32)

Lady Happy dissuades herself of this possibility by averring the unchanging laws of nature, after which the Princess enters 'in Masculine Shepherd's Clothes'. She responds to Lady Happy's doubts by asserting the virtuous, innocent and harmless nature of their love, in a discourse which draws on the tenets of platonic friendship: 'Let us please ourselves, as harmless Lovers use to do . . . as, to discourse, imbrace and kiss, so mingle souls together' (pp. 32–3). In answer to Lady Happy's objection, 'But innocent Lovers do not use to kiss', the Princess replies 'Not any act more frequent among us Women-kind; nay, it were a sin in friendship, should we not kiss', after which there is the stage description 'They imbrace and kiss, and hold each other in their Arms', followed by the Princess's at once transgressive and salacious couplet: 'These my imbraces

though of Femal kind,/ May be as fervent as a Masculine mind.'
Her couplet is followed by the extraordinary stage description:

> The Scene is open'd, the Princess and L. Happy go in
>   A Pastoral within the Scene.
> The Scene is chang'd to a Green, or Plain, where Sheep
>   are feeding, and a May-Pole in the middle.
> L. Happy as a Shepherdess, and the Princess as a Shepherd
>   are sitting there. (p. 33)

In this transformation Cavendish shows us the moment of entry
into the fictive theatrical world. In the ensuing scene the Princess
and Lady Happy praise one another's wit and poetic genius,
distinguishing their wooing from the 'amorous . . . Verse' of
'other Pastoral Lovers' (p. 37). The 'amorous' dimension of their
courtship conveyed by Lady Happy's profession, 'I can neither
deny you my Love nor Person' is channelled into the 'Rural Sports'
which follow, at the end of which the Princess and Lady Happy are
crowned 'King and Queen of the Shepherds' (p. 38). In a subsequent
marine masque the Princess and Lady Happy appear as Neptune and
a Sea-Goddess, surrounded by 'the rest of the Ladies . . . drest like
Water-Nymphs' (p. 41).

At these points Cavendish's play takes on the infinitely recessive
quality which Gallagher notes[44] as peculiar to her writing. Within
her closet theatre of the mind she imagines a female convent
within which there is a theatre in which women act out fantasy
selves. Their acting, moreover, is freed from necessity, for within
their self-enclosed female environment they mimic heterosexual
conventions for pleasure. Though the Princess defines their love as
harmless, Lady Happy has graver misgivings and bursts out shortly
after the rural scene:

> O Nature, O you Gods above,
> Suffer me not to fall in Love;
> O Strike me dead here in this place
> Rather than fall into disgrace. (p. 40)

Because Lady Happy has already queried the legitimacy of her love
for a woman, this last line must be read as referring to the disgrace,
not simply of falling in love, but of falling in love with a woman.
Cavendish seems to have married the cross-dressing convention of

a female theatre with the chastity of platonic friendship derived from Henrietta Maria's feminized culture to allow a fleeting fantasy of what we would call lesbian love.[45] It is fleeting because the hints of the Princess's self-division which have already been laid are borne out immediately after the pastoral in a soliloquy:

> What have I on a petticoat, *Oh Mars*! thou God of War, pardon my sloth . . . But what is a Kingdom in comparison of a Beautiful Mistress? (p. 39)

Yet with wonderful tenacity Cavendish will not abandon her view of the Princess's sex, for the stage description above the soliloquy reads 'Enter *the Princess Sola*, and walks a turn or two in a Musing posture, then views *her* Self and speaks' (p. 39, italics mine). Contrary to her earlier practice in *Loves Adventures* (1662) where the descriptions of the disguised Affectionata's soliloquies and asides revealing her true identity use feminine pronouns, Cavendish introduces a discrepancy between the prose description and the dramatic situation, in which the 'Princess' reveals himself as a man in disguise. The Princess is subsequently described as again 'in a Man's Apparel' (p. 44), producing the effect of an endlessly inhabitable series of sexual selves. This absolute uncertainty of the Princess's gender is sustained at the moment of catastrophe in which Madam Mediator interrupts the Princess and Lady Happy dancing. At this point the text moves into an extended passage of description:

> *And after they have Danced a little while, in comes Madam Mediator wringing her hands, and spreading her arms; and full of Passion cries out.*
>
> O Ladies Ladies! you're all betrayed, undone, undone; for there is a man in the Convent, search and you'l find it.
>
> *They all skip from each other, as afraid of each other; only the Princess and the Lady Happy stand still together.* (pp. 44-5)

Madam Mediator's use of the indefinite pronoun, 'search and you'l find it', registers at the climax of the play a moment of aporia, in which it is impossible to know whether the Princess is, as we are directed to believe, 'a Princely brave Woman, *truly* of a Masculine presence', or as Cavendish's comma has it, 'a Princely brave *Woman truly*, of a Masculine presence' (p. 16). In the dénouement the entrance of an 'embassador to the Prince' simultaneously forces the dissolution of the convent's fantasy feminine world and marks the decisive entry of a masculinist discourse into the play, as the 'Prince' declares that if his counsellors of state refuse him leave to marry Lady Happy he will 'have her by force of Arms' (p. 47).

Clearly *The Convent of Pleasure* offers different kinds of textual pleasure to different readers. The reader engaged in one way by Lady Happy's feminine world may share her credulity as to the Princess's gender and enjoy the suggestion of an erotic relationship between women. For other readers the story of a Prince who infiltrates a convent disguised as a woman who then acts as a man offers fantasies of voyeuristic access to a woman-centred world, and of the suspension of an essential masculine identity. We could see the play itself as caught in a conflict between these different, sexually determined modes of reading. For there is some doubt as to whether Cavendish's disposal of her female freak at the end of the play is a gesture motivated solely by her own reason. Rather than the infiltration of a man into the convent there is evidence that a man may have penetrated Cavendish's text. In some copies of the 1668 *Plays*[46] the final two scenes after the revelation of the Princess as a man are headed with a pasted-in slip reading 'Written by my Lord Duke' (p. 47), but with no indication, as with similar instances elsewhere in Cavendish's texts, of where 'my Lord Duke's' ends. There are two ways of construing this textual anomaly: either Cavendish lost interest after the disclosure of the Princess as a man and left the writing of the rest of her play to her husband, or she did write the final two scenes, which poke fun at Puritan prurience and older women's sexual desires, but suspected they would be thought unseemly coming from a woman. Whoever wrote the final two scenes, it is Cavendish who has the last word on the Princess's gender, for in one of her breaks with tradition in this volume she prints the 'dramatis personae', or 'the Actors Names', at the end rather than at the beginning of the play, and if we look at the final page of the text of *The Convent of Pleasure* we will see that, contrary to the fool's assertion that 'the Prince has imitated a woman' (p. 51), in Cavendish's mind 'the Princess' was not an actor but an actress. We might speculate on Cavendish's placing of 'the Actors Names' at the end of three of the plays in this volume, as a means of deliberately enhancing the suspense enjoyed by the reader with respect to the gender of the characters. Certainly *The Convent of Pleasure* takes her experimentation with the closet drama form to the most sophisticated degree of the page becoming stage, producing the ultimate textual fantasy of female performance.

There is evidence that Cavendish herself in her rhetoric of dress and behaviour aimed at a blurring of the boundaries between genders similar to that produced by *The Convent of Pleasure*. Charles Lyttleton wrote of his meeting with the Newcastles on the way to York in 1665 that Margaret was 'dressed in a vest, and, instead of courtsies, made legs and bows to the ground with her hand and head'.[47] His description of her masculine dress and gestures echoes Bulstrode Whitelocke's account of the clothing and behaviour of Queen Christina of Sweden on his first reception at her court as Cromwell's ambassador. According to Whitelocke, Christina appeared soberly dressed in grey, with 'a jackett such as men weare' over her habit, and 'a black velvet cappe . . . which she used to put off and on as men doe their hattes'.[48] Whitelocke's representation of Christina's attitude suggests a social fantasy of her behaviour as sexually provocative and intimidating:

> The queen was very attentive whilst he spake, and comming up close to him, by her looks and gestures (as was supposed) would have daunted him; butt those who have bin conversant in the late great affayres in England, are not so soon as others appaled, with the presence of a young lady and her servants.[49]

Whitelocke both evokes, and distances himself from, a form of seductiveness able to be manipulated by women in positions of power; an example of which is the overt sexual display characteristic of aristocratic female performance. Whitelocke saw Christina act 'a moorish lady' and 'a citizen's wife' in a court masque.[50] He also witnessed her abdication, after which she set off on an extravagant tour of Europe where her flamboyant conduct, particularly her masculine dress and behaviour, caused much amazed comment.[51] This contextualizes Samuel Pepys's remark that there was as much expectation of Cavendish's coming to court in London in 1667, 'that so [many] people may come to see her, as if it were the Queen of Sweden.'[52] Many details in Pepys's diary concur with Whitelocke's image of Queen Christina, which suggests that Cavendish may also have been trying to create an image of herself as 'a Princely brave Woman truly, of a Masculine Presence'. Pepys refers to Cavendish's 'velvet-cap', her 'many black patches', her décolletage, and her 'black juste-au-corps', a garment similar to a masculine riding coat, made popular as a fashion for women by Queen Catherine of Braganza. He also refers twice to her 'antic' dress and appearance.[53] Mary Evelyn's account of Cavendish as a spectacle viewed at close quarters confirms the hint that her presentation as a self-fashioned artifact using the discourse of dress should be seen as forming a continuum with her creation of fantasy selves in her writing:

> I was surprised to find so much extravagancy and vanity in any person not confined within four walls. Her habit particular, fantastical . . . . Her mien surpasses the imagination of poets, or the descriptions of a romance heroine's greatness: her gracious bows, seasonable nods, courteous stretching out of her hands, twinkling of her eyes, and various gestures of approbation, show what may be expected from her discourse, which is as airy, empty, whimsical and rambling as her books.[54]

This image of excess, of Cavendish bursting out of confinement, chimes with Colley Cibber's description of the actress Susannah Mountfort's performance as Melantha in Dryden's *Marriage à la Mode* (1673), as seeming 'to contain the most compleat System of Female Foppery that could possibly be crowded into the tortur'd form of a fine Lady'.[55] The comparison is enhanced by the fact that, with her gentry origins, Cavendish was herself an apocryphal lady.[56] Evelyn indicates that 'the theatre of Margaret' was the ultimate monologic performance: 'My part was not yet to speak, but to admire.'[57] Only at one point in her London visit did Cavendish engage in a performative act which had a semblance of the dialogic, during her visit with the Duke of Newcastle to the Lincoln's Inn Theatre for a performance of Newcastle's play *The Humourous Lovers* (1667). Pepys assumed that the play was by Cavendish and recorded how 'she at the end made her respect to the players from her box and did give them thanks.'[58] A contemporary letter alluding to this event describes the Duchess as 'all yᵉ pageant now discoursed on: Her brests all laid out to view in a play house with scarlett trimd nipples.'[59] Cavendish's acting out the fantasy of having her plays performed was itself a piece of theatre. It seems appropriate that her acknowledgement of the art of female performance should have taken the form of such an outrageous upstaging.

NOTES

(Place of publication for works printed before 1800 is London unless otherwise stated.)

I am very grateful to Clare Brant, Diane Purkiss and Ruth Little for their scrupulous reading and editing of this chapter.

1 Margaret Cavendish, *CCXI Sociable Letters*, 1664, no. CXCV, p. 405. The reference to 'Carneval Time' is from the preceding letter (no. CXCIV, p. 402), which is related in content to no. CXCV. Further references to letter no. CXCV are given in the text.
2 Cavendish, *Letters*, no. XXIX, p. 57.
3 I use the word 'fantasy' here in the modern sense of the imaginary fulfilment of conscious or unconscious wishes (*OED*, 3b). In seventeenth-century usage the words 'fantasy' and 'fancy' were used interchangeably to signify the imaginative faculty or process. However the *OED* also gives as a possible meaning of 'fantasy' from the fourteenth century onwards, 'the fact or habit of deluding oneself by imaginary perceptions or reminiscences' (3a), which indicates an earlier form of the modern usage. Cavendish's letter, and the rest of her writing, testify to the fluidity between her concept of 'fancy', and 'fantasy' in its modern form.
4 A pertinent example is the series of 'Femal Orations' in Margaret Cavendish, *Orations of Divers Sorts, Accommodated to Divers Places*, 1662, pp. 225–32, especially p. 229.
5 Cavendish, *Letters*, no. CXCII, p. 400.
6 Margaret Cavendish, *Playes Written by the Thrice Noble, Illustrious and Excellent Princess, the Lady Marchioness of Newcastle*, 1662, sig. A2R. Further references to this volume are given in the text.
7 Margaret Cavendish, 'To all Writing Ladies', *Poems and Fancies*, 1653, sig. A1V [p. 161] (unnumbered page following p. 160). This epistle is omitted from the second impression of *Poems and Phancies*, 1664.
8 For a study of the queen's social fashions of platonic love and *préciosité*, which reads them in the context of her Catholic interests, see E. Veevers, *Images of Love and Religion: Queen Henrietta Maria and Court Entertainments*, Cambridge, Cambridge University Press, 1988.
9 I discuss the material summarized in the next two paragraphs in my chapter, 'She that Plays the King: Henrietta Maria and the Threat of the Actress in Caroline Culture' in G. McMullan and J. Hope (eds), *The Politics of Tragicomedy: Shakespeare and After*, Routledge, 1991.
10 Ben Jonson, *The New Inn*, ed. M. Hattaway, *The Revels Plays*, Manchester, Manchester University Press, 1984, III.ii; IV.iv; James Shirley, *The Dramatic Works and Poems of James Shirley*, ed. W. Gifford and A. Dyce, 6 vols, London, 1833, vol. III, pp. 79, 27.
11 N.C. Starr (ed.), '*The Concealed Fansyes*: A Play by Lady Jane Cavendish and Lady Elizabeth Brackley', *PMLA*, 1931, vol. 46, p. 809.
12 Excerpts from *A Pastorall* are printed in Germaine Greer, Jeslyn Medoff, Melinda Sansone and Susan Hastings (eds), *Kissing the Rod:*

   An Anthology of Seventeenth-Century Women's Verse, London, Virago, 1988, pp. 109–15.

13 Margaret Cavendish, *The Life of William Cavendish, Duke of Newcastle, to Which is Added the True Relation of my Birth, Breeding and Life*, ed. C. H. Firth, 2nd edn, London, Routledge, 1906, p. 160.

14 Cavendish, *Life*, pp. 161–2; Kathleen Jones, *A Glorious Fame: The Life of Margaret Cavendish, Duchess of Newcastle, 1623–1673*, London, Bloomsbury, 1988, pp. 22–7; N. Cotton, *Women Playwrights in England c. 1363–1750*, London and Toronto, Associated University Presses, 1980, pp. 42–3; Sarah Heller Mendelson, *The Mental World of Stuart Women: Three Case Studies*, Brighton, Harvester, 1987, pp. 16–18.

15 C. Oman, *Henrietta Maria*, London, Hodder and Stoughton, 1936, p. 151; L. Hotson, *The Commonwealth and Restoration Stage*, Cambridge, MA, Harvard University Press, 1928, pp. 8–9.

16 Margaret Cavendish, *Natures Pictures drawn by Fancies Pencil to the Life*, 1656, p. 190.

17 On the entertainments of royalists in Paris and Holland see Hotson, pp. 21–3 and A. Harbage, *Cavalier Drama*, New York, Russell, 1964 (first pub. 1936), pp. 207–8.

18 Margaret Cavendish, *Plays, Never Before Printed*, 1668, p. 92.

19 P. Edwards *et al.*, *The Revels History of Drama in English: Volume IV 1613–1660*, London and New York, Methuen, 1981, pp. 24, 278; Hotson, pp. 20–2; D. Grant, *Margaret the First: A Biography of Margaret Cavendish, Duchess of Newcastle*, London, Rupert Hart-Daries, 1957, pp. 173–4; *Calendar of State Papers Domestic*, 1657–8, pp. 296, 311.

20 See E. Howe, *Women and Drama: The First English Actresses*, Cambridge, Cambridge University Press, forthcoming.

21 Richard Flecknoe, *A Relation of Ten Years Travells in Europe, Asia, Affrique, and America*, 1654, p. 147; for details of Flecknoe's activity in Holland during the Interregnum and the suggestion that the Duchess acted as his patron see Harbage, p. 207.

22 This was the treatment given to actresses belonging to the French troupe which visited London in 1629, who were 'hissed, hooted, and pippin-pelted from the stage' in one of their three performances; G. E. Bentley, *The Jacobean and Caroline Stage*, 7 vols, Oxford, Clarendon, 1941–68, vol. I, p. 25.

23 In an important essay Catherine Gallagher discusses Aphra Behn's very different self-alignment with the figure of the prostitute: see 'Who was that Masked Woman? The Prostitute and the Playwright in the Comedies of Aphra Behn', *Women's Studies*, 1988, vol. 15, pp. 23–42.

24 Susan J. Wiseman, 'Gender and Status in Dramatic Discourse: Margaret Cavendish, Duchess of Newcastle', in Isobel Grundy and Susan J. Wiseman (eds), *Women/Writing/History 1640–1740*, London, Batsford, forthcoming. I have benefited much from Susan Wiseman's work on Cavendish.

25 Cf. Mendelson's observation that in Cavendish's fiction 'the focus is not on love *per se* but on a woman's "will to power", expressed as the chronicle of her extraordinary ambitions, or as her psychological

conquest of a male protagonist', p. 22.

26 Edwards *et al.*, p. 278; Hotson, p. 136. See also Mendelson, p. 45.

27 Francis Osborne, *Historical Memoires on the Reigns of Queen Elizabeth, and King James*, 1658, p. 60. After one of Sanspareille's orations a poet declares that 'the Lady Muses are deposed' (p. 152), and she herself asks to be remembered among the Muses in her dying speech. After her death her statue is to be set up 'in every College, and in most publick places in the City' (p. 173).

28 Cavendish, *Life*, pp. 166–7.

29 Quoted in A. Clark, *Working Life of Women in the Seventeenth Century*, London, Routledge & Kegan Paul, 1982 (first pub. 1919), p. 20.

30 Cavendish, *Life*, pp. 167–8.

31 Elaine Hobby, *Virtue of Necessity: English Women's Writing 1649–88*, London, Virago, 1988, p. 83; on Cavendish's bashfulness see also J. Pearson, *The Prostituted Muse: Images of Women and Women Dramatists 1642–1737*, Brighton, Harvester, 1988, pp. 128–9; Mendelson, pp. 17–18.

32 Ian Maclean, *Woman Triumphant: Feminism in French Literature 1610–1652*, Oxford, Oxford University Press, 1977, p. viii; Jones, pp. 56–7.

33 M.A.E. Green, *Letters of Queen Henrietta Maria*, London, 1857, p. 222; Françoise Bertaud de Motteville, 'A Short History of the Troubles in England', in *Memoirs for the History of Anne of Austria*, translated from the French, 5 vols, 1725–6, vol. I, p. 220.

34 See Cavendish, *Life*, p. 178, *Letters*, no. XXVII, pp. 52–3, 'To All Noble and Worthy Ladies', *The Description of a New World called the Blazing-World*, in *Observations upon Experimental Philosophy*, 1668, sig. A4V.

35 Cavendish, *Life*, pp. 18–19, 23, 161; Jones, pp. 22–3.

36 Motteville, vol. I, p. 220.

37 Following her abdication in 1654 and her conversion to Catholicism Christina embarked on a triumphal tour of Europe, beginning with the Italian papal states; see G. Masson, *Queen Christina*, London, Secker & Warburg, 1968, chs 7 and 8, *passim*.

38 Catherine Gallagher, 'Embracing the Absolute: The Politics of the Female Subject in Seventeenth-Century England', *Genders*, 1988, vol. 1, no. 1, pp. 25–33.

39 Cavendish, *Plays, Never Before Printed*, sig. A2V. Further references to this volume are given in the text. The plays in this volume are paginated individually.

40 Cf. Hobby, pp. 106–7.

41 See Pearson, pp. 140–2, and D. Paloma, 'Margaret Cavendish: Defining the Female Self', *Women's Studies*, 1980, vol. 7, pp. 63–4.

42 Cavendish could have found this plot either in Fletcher's play *Monsieur Thomas* (performed 1610–16, published 1639) or in Fletcher's source, the French pastoral romance *L'Astrée* by Honoré d'Urfé, 1607–27, trans. 1620. I am grateful to Hester Jones for suggesting *Monsieur Thomas* as a source.

43 This play within a play evokes a medieval and Renaissance tradition

of convent theatre and drama; see Cotton, pp. 27–8, 213, n. 2, and Elissa Weaver, 'Spiritual Fun: A Study of Sixteenth-Century Tuscan Convent Theatre', in Mary Beth Rose (ed.), *Women in the Middle Ages and the Renaissance: Literary and Historical Perspectives*, Syracuse, NY, Syracuse University Press, 1986, pp. 173–205.

44 Gallagher, 'Embracing the Absolute', pp. 30–3.

45 Cf. the use of a platonic discourse in *The Blazing-World*, pp. 89–92, 110. In making this statement I am trying to provide a historical explanation for what Moira Ferguson problematically describes as the play's 'sympathetic, tender, and natural portrayal of lesbian love', in *First Feminists: British Women Writers 1578–1799*, Bloomington, Indiana University Press, 1985, p. 12. A context for the idea of love between women modelled on female friendship is Katherine Philips's poetry; see Hobby, pp. 128, 134–41.

46 The three copies of the 1668 *Plays* in the British Library, and the copy in the Cambridge University Library, all contain the pasted-in slip. It does not appear in the copy of the 1668 *Plays* in the Bodleian Library.

47 Cited in Grant, p. 184.

48 Bulstrode Whitelocke, *A Journal of the Swedish Embassy in the Years 1653 and 1654*, 2 vols, London, 1772, vol. I, p. 234. I am grateful to Susan Wiseman for alerting me to this text.

49 ibid., vol. I, pp. 235–6.

50 ibid., vol. II, pp. 52–3.

51 See the accounts by Madame de Motteville and Anne Marie d'Orléans of Christina at the French court in 1656 in Masson, pp. 274–7.

52 Samuel Pepys, *The Diary of Samuel Pepys*, ed. Robert Latham and William Matthews, London, Bell, 11 vols, 1970–83, vol. VII, pp. 163–4. According to Kathleen Jones, p. 102, the Newcastles met Queen Christina briefly on her visit to Antwerp in 1654.

53 Pepys, vol. VII, pp. 186–7, 163, 243. Hero Chalmers shows that Cavendish's contemporary, Mary Carleton, invokes Queen Christina as a model for her self-portrayal as a romance heroine; see her chapter in this volume.

54 Quoted in Myra Reynolds, *The Learned Lady in England from 1650 to 1760*, Gloucester, MA, Peter Smith, 1964 [1920], p. 51. Cf. Pepys's remark, 'The whole story of this Lady is a romance, and all she doth is romantic', vol. VII, p. 163.

55 B.R. Fone (ed.), *An Apology for the Life of Colley Cibber, With an Historical View of the Stage during his own Times*, Ann Arbor, University of Michigan Press, 1968, p. 96.

56 See Mendelson, pp. 12, 22.

57 Quoted in Mendelson, p. 53. I owe the aperçu 'the theatre of Margaret' to Susan Wiseman.

58 Pepys, vol. VII, p. 163; Cotton, pp. 48–9.

59 Letter from Charles North to his father, 13 April 1667, Bodleian MS. North. c. 4., fol. 146. I am grateful to Robert Jordan for this reference.

6

'THE PERSON I AM, OR WHAT THEY MADE ME TO BE': THE CONSTRUCTION OF THE FEMININE SUBJECT IN THE AUTOBIOGRAPHIES OF MARY CARLETON

Hero Chalmers

Mary Moders seems to have been born into the lower ranks of society in Canterbury some time during the mid-1630s. In 1660 she was tried for bigamy but acquitted with a reprimand, since she alleged that she had heard that her first husband had been killed on active service abroad before she married again. Undeterred, however, she married a third time. The family of her third and last husband, John Carleton, a law student, was made aware of her maritally dubious past shortly after the wedding. In June 1663 they brought her to trial at the Old Bailey.[1]

Though the jury acquitted her on the charge of bigamy, owing to insufficient evidence for the prosecution, the case immediately became notorious. Its scandal potential was greatly enhanced by John Carleton's allegations that his wife had impersonated a 'German Princess' in order to entrap him. While she claimed that it was the Carletons who had mistakenly believed her to be a Princess, her autobiographical account maintained that she was at least of noble – if not royal – birth, being the daughter of a German diplomat.[2] Not surprisingly, the story spawned a considerable number of pamphlets, of which John and Mary Carleton were among the authors. Carleton left the public eye for ten years after the trial, but her hanging at Tyburn in London for petty larceny in January 1673 provided sensational material for a further crop of texts. Some ventured to account for her activities during the previous decade by suggesting that she had been transported to Jamaica for theft.[3]

The marketability of Carleton's life-story has encouraged assertions that a 'hack' journalist or 'press-agent' wrote her autobiographies for personal gain.[4] Such allegations remain unsubstantiated. The twentieth-century critic Ernest Bernbaum, alluding in particular to her citation of classical authorities, asserts that the texts show 'signs of an education superior to her own'.[5] The details of her upbringing are so elusive as to render it impossible to make assumptions about her education. The author of *Memories of the Life of the Famous Madam Charlton* (1673) relates that the youthful Carleton (then Moders) achieved social elevation by ingratiating herself with 'the best Children in the City'.[6] Despite the fictional flavour of this claim, familiar to many modern readers through the early life of Defoe's *Moll Flanders*, the story is not so very unlikely when one considers Carleton's accomplished social mobility as an adult.[7] A variety of people of 'the Nobler sort' visited her in prison and were convinced, as the Carleton family had formerly been, by her professions of noble birth. Pepys, who had also visited 'the Germane Princess' in the Gatehouse, was pleased to hear that she had been acquitted, and spoke 'in the defence of her wit and spirit'.[8] Even if he was simply relishing the practical joke, he evidently credited her with the skill to maintain the imposture successfully. Even as he denounces her, her dupe, John, marvels of Carleton that, 'so Noble a Mind should descend of such an Ignoble Race'.[9] It seems not only possible, then, but likely, that Carleton was indeed the author of the texts which bear her name.

A number of recent studies of women's autobiographical writing have taken as one theoretical starting-point notions of subject-formation through entry into the linguistic structures established by the dominant culture.[10] As Felicity Nussbaum puts it, 'Individuals construct themselves as subjects through language, but individual subjects – rather than being the source of their own self-generated and self-expressive meaning – adopt positions available within language at a given moment'.[11] In the light of such a model, Nussbaum and others have investigated possible ways in which women writing in patriarchal culture might 'produce', 'disrupt or transform', as well as reflecting, 'historicized concepts of self and gender'.[12] In this study of the autobiographical writings of Mary Carleton I hope to show how both reflection and disruption participate in a historically specific process of gendered subject–construction.

In describing Carleton's use of romance conventions, other commentators have already begun to notice one way in which she uses the reflection of existing models of feminine identity in creating a self.[13] Building on their insights, I shall begin by reviewing and further developing an analysis which shows how Carleton exploited contemporary perceptions of the romance genre in order to construct a feminine identity which was both credible and attractive in her particular cultural and historical setting.

However, I shall go on to suggest that the romance persona in Carleton's texts is combined with a conflicting self-image that may be traced to the opposing but equally current generic model exploited by her biographers. In this way, I shall locate more specifically Janet Todd's claim that Carleton's texts offer a mixed self-projection, 'in keeping with other Restoration images created by women, with men in mind'.[14] I shall also argue that Carleton's texts present not one dual-faceted image but a mutually destabilizing conjunction of distinct personae. The resulting generic mixture is, I shall argue, intimately linked with the mechanics of Carleton's social transgressions.

While the success of her imposture depends on maintaining the illusion that the models of identity she adopts voice an unmediated feminine subjectivity, she resists the determination of her identity within these models by highlighting the very processes of its mediation or construction.

The transgressive approach to identity embodied in Carleton's texts engages contemporary epistemological anxieties which may be linked to the perception of a specifically feminine-gendered threat to the stability of patriarchal authority. Carleton's writings, however, explore the notion that patriarchal authority itself has created the possibility for the feminine transgressiveness which she comes to represent.

Even before she began to write a narrative of her life, Carleton started to construct a subjectivity using the conventions of romance, the contemporary discourse which most credibly authenticated her claim to be an aristocratic foreign woman. *The Lawyers Clarke*

Trappan'd by the Crafty Whore of Canterbury (1663) – the first pamphlet to publish details of the Carleton case before Carleton's trial – suggests the kind of motifs which Carleton borrowed from romance in creating the oral narrative of her life. John Carleton, in his *Ultimum Vale* (1663), later corroborates the account of Carleton's story offered by *The Lawyers Clarke*. Carleton claims that she is:

> Daughter to a Great Prince in Germany, and that when she was Two years old, she was put in a Nunnery. . . . Thence she came to her own Country in Germany, and some of the Princes there would have perswaded her to marry an Old Man.[15]

In the true spirit of the high-minded aristocratic heroine, Carleton cannot tolerate the prospect of contamination by an odious arranged marriage, and is forced to flee to England.

Though the first and shorter of Carleton's two autobiographies, *An Historicall Narrative of the German Princess* (1663), omits any narrative of her life previous to arriving in England, it constructs a persona of heroic ladyhood entirely consistent with that of the romance protagonist of the alleged oral narrative of her life. Her citation of classical authorities in *An Historicall Narrative* testifies to the wit and erudition which her later *Case of Madam Mary Carleton* (1663) reveals that she has acquired under the tutelage of an English governess.[16] In this respect, *An Historicall Narrative* develops qualities in Carleton already familiar to her readership through *A Vindication of a Distressed Lady* (1663) and another largely sympathetic pamphlet entitled *The Great Tryall and Arraignment of the Late Distressed Lady* (1663).[17] In addition, *An Historicall Narrative* stresses Carleton's superior honesty and moral probity, opening with an abstract discussion of 'that Virtue called *Truth*'. Appended to the text is 'An Encomiastick POEM UPON *The* German Princess' which praises not only her 'INNOCENCE and Exc'lent WIT', but her 'Brave and Noble Vertues', thereby substantiating the persona she has been at pains to manufacture.[18]

In *The Case of Madam Mary Carleton*, Carleton reproduces the oral narrative of her early life but embellishes and expands it with added romance touches. The orphaned 'Maria' is placed in a nunnery, but yearns to escape. On doing so, she is beset by two unwelcome suitors, a 'young and pale Student', and an old

'*Soldado*'. Extricating herself from their clutches, she ultimately makes for England, 'incognito', to escape 'an unliked and unsutable match'. Once in England, she meets Carleton and marries him, only to discover that he was only after her wealth. When he finds that she is poorer than he thought, he fabricates the accusation of bigamy in order to be rid of her. Writing to defend 'the injured innocence of a Forain & desolate woman', she plays on the romantic appeal of the helpless foreign damsel invoked by an earlier apologist in the title, *A Vindication of A Distressed Lady*.[19] The author of *The Memoires of Mary Carleton* (1673) confirms the topical attraction of such a persona when he states that Englishmen were particularly susceptible to Carleton's ruse, being 'so debonair and affable to Forrainers (especially Females)'.[20]

In portraying herself as a heroine of romance, Carleton exploits the popularity of a fashionable literary genre. The newer French heroic romance, detailing the passions and adventures of the continental aristocracy, had been pioneered in France during the 1640s, by writers like Madeleine de Scudéry and Gaultier de Coste de la Calprenède. However, prompt translation soon ensured its infiltration of an English readership, and both cavalier noblewomen and their exiled husbands became particularly avid readers.[21]

The receptivity of Carleton's readers to romance convention as a credible articulation of a feminine subjectivity may also be accounted for by the developing notional conflation of women readers, writers and heroines, of romance.[22] For some time, male authors had been dedicating romances to a female readership who were thus already constructed as being more disposed than male readers towards this genre.[23] First-person feminine narration helped to cement the idea of romance heroine as author.[24] Janet Todd writes of the French heroic romance that it 'was primarily concerned with love and with women as writers and readers. It was connected with the salons of the précieuses.'[25] Women writers of romance in the latter part of the seventeenth century exploited and thereby reinforced the idea that the amatory preoccupations of the romance genre were the natural feminine sphere of interest.[26]

Husband John's comments demonstrate that Carleton's employment of the discursive models of romance served to guarantee the authenticity of the feminine subjectivity which she projected, rather than exposing its fictionality. For, though he claims that, the 'story . . . of her great Adventure . . . seemed to me to be a pretty Romance', he goes on to state that:

> You may imagine . . . that she haveing begun such a designe, and pretending to be such a person, how cunningly she glossed over her Romantick storyes and pretences with great zeal as comeing from a Nunnery, a handsome and noble deportment as a person of quality, and good languages as being well breed; all which are but suitable, and to be expected to make her self out, had she been what she pretended and represented her self to be, which seeming reality did in a growing familiarity and acquaintance encrease mine and many wise persons beleife.[27]

In Carleton's texts, as in the oral narrative of her life which she apparently delivered to John and his family, she allows her identity to be determined by a cultural discourse of femininity which supplies what is 'to be expected' from an aristocratic foreign lady. Nevertheless, her subtextual inscription of an alternative persona undermines the superficial illusion that her subjectivity may be encompassed by the romantic model of femininity through which she finds it expedient to speak.

The pragmatic justification for an ambiguous self-projection seems evident if we examine Carleton's circumstances at the time of writing. She was faced with financial difficulties. Her 'Fortune', she claimed, had *'frowardly shrunk into nothing'*.[28] Though she had already been cleared of the charge of bigamy in court, a significant portion of her potential readership was entrenched in the belief that she was an impostor. *The Lawyers Clarke* had branded her as a cunning and bigamous fraud, the 'Fidlers Daughter . . . of CANTERBURY'.[29] Despite the subsequent publication (apparently on Carleton's behalf) of the brief defence contained in *A Vindication of a Distressed Lady*, the image of her as 'the Crafty Whore' remained strong in the popular imagination. It was reinforced by John Carleton who, in his reply to *A Vindication*, entitled, *The Replication, Or Certain Vindicatory Depositions* (1663), insisted that his wife had indeed wilfully deceived him.[30] Though *The Arraignment, Tryal and Examination of Mary Moders* (1663) recorded the court proceedings and verdict of 'Not guilty', it still erred on the side of portraying Carleton as a gloating trickster.[31] *A True Account of the Tryal of Mrs Mary Carlton* (1663), which reprinted *The Arraignment* with subtle modifications in her favour, did not serve to clear her name, despite

169

its claim to be, 'Published for Her Vindication, at Her own Request'.[32]

A catch-all strategy, designed to appeal to detractors as well as believers, might solve her financial predicament by ensuring maximum returns on the sale of her texts, while also attempting to attract benefactors from among those who took her self-vindication in good faith.

While Carleton's ostensible self-vindications exploited the weight of cultural expectation shaped by romance representations of feminine identity, the literature of her detractors drew on and reinforced contrasting expectations fashioned by the popular tradition of criminal rogue biography. The completeness with which she had been subsumed into the rogue type by the time of her execution in 1673 is suggested by the author of *The Memoires of Mary Carleton*, one of the group of works published in the year of her death. 'Let the proud *Don* boast no more', he exclaims, 'of his *Guzman*, *Quixot*, or *Lazarillo*, nor the aery *Monsieur* of his *Francion*, or *Du Vall*, since here is a poor *Kentish* Girl . . . a frisking fidling *Canterbury* Lass that hath out-done them all.'[33] Here, Carleton's antecedents are seen to be the archetypal Spanish picaresque heroes, Guzman and Lazarillo, and the real and imaginary French rogues, Du Vall and Francion.[34]

Fewer potential female rogue ancestors exist for Carleton than male ones. Though some criminal biographies did have female protagonists, those in the earlier part of the seventeenth century appear to have been chiefly murderers and thus hardly material for a rogue treatment.[35] The two roaring girls, Long Meg of Westminster, and Mary Frith (alias Moll Cutpurse), along with the brothel owner Dona Britanica Hollandia, are the chief surviving examples of female roguery before Carleton.[36] The *Life and Death of Mrs Mary Frith. Commonly Called Mal Cutpurse* (1662) and its abridgment, *The Womans Champion* (1662), had been published in the year before the Carleton trial. The stock rogue vocabulary which lists the 'Mad Merry Prankes' of Long Meg, or the 'mad Pranks, merry Conceits . . . and most unheard of Stratagems' of the 'crafty' Moll Cutpurse, is echoed in the '*Pranks, witty Exploits and unheard of Stratagems*' perpetrated by the 'Crafty Whore', Mary Carleton.[37] However, the masculine attire and irreproachable sexual morality of Mary Frith and Long Meg, like the 'Masculine . . . disposition' of Dona Britanica Hollandia, set them apart from the bigamous Carleton whose roguishness is associated with sexual promiscuity.[38] This contrast between Carleton and her predecessors illustrates Roger Thompson's contention that the depiction of female rogues became highly sexualized from the time of the Restoration.[39]

The sexual element in the early portrayal of Carleton seems to associate her with the contemporary literature of prostitution. The title, *The Lawyers Clarke Trappan'd by the Crafty Whore of Canterbury*, echoes that of a pornographic dialogue between two bawds, entitled *The Crafty Whore* (1658). The pseudo–diary of Mary Frith, extracted in *The Life and Death*, appears to define 'that abominable Villany, called *Trapanning*', as a prostitute's trick for blackmailing clients with the threat of disclosure to their wives.[40] 'Trappanners' also appear among the 'Bawds . . . Whores . . . Pimps' and other disreputables listed at the end of *The Fifth . . . Part of the Wandring Whore* (1661), a dialogue between a prostitute and her allies.[41]

A survey of the network of booksellers involved in distributing the Carleton pamphlets offers further evidence that a potentially lucrative connection was made between the Carleton story and the industry of prostitutional or sexually titillating literature. *The Lawyers Clarke* was printed for John Johnson for whom the sixth part of *The Wandring Whore* was printed in the same year. Roger Thompson has suggested that John Johnson may have been related to Thomas and Marmaduke Johnson who were connected with the 'group responsible for many of the dirty books published in London around the period of the Restoration'. Certainly, the three other key members of this 'group', Nathaniel Brooke, Francis Kirkman and Henry Marsh, all published Carleton material.[42]

When she came to write her autobiographies, Carleton herself was certainly alive to the currency in the popular imagination of the roguish whore image which her biographers had already begun to propagate. She archly complains of the pressures on her to produce herself in this popular image, claiming that the 'world doth . . . prefer my Wit and Artful Carriage to my Honesty, and take this untoward passage of my life for some festivous and merry accident of the times, and look upon me as a notorious . . . person'.[43]

In her most direct attempt to satisfy the readers' desire for a 'festivous and merry' narrative of her 'Artful Carriage', Carleton appends to her account of the trial the story of Billing the bricklayer who comes to Newgate after her acquittal claiming to be her husband. The prison warders present him with another woman convict, Grizel Hudson, whom he claims is Carleton. Billing's

prurient and deluded imposition of the persona of 'rogue' onto
Grizel Hudson parodies the popular desire to fashion Carleton
as the protagonist of a titillating rogue narrative. Billing refers
to Grizel Hudson by the nickname of 'Moll', with its sexually
disreputable and criminal associations.[44] He asks why she remains
in Newgate among '*Rogues and Whores*' and tells her she is 'a wicked
Rogue' and '*a cunning Rogue*', accusing her of having cheated him
of forty pounds and stolen goods from his daughter. He 'merrily'
adds that, '*he never lay with her, but he had kist her, and felt her a hundred
times*'.[45]

While the Billing episode seems to mock the wilful miscasting
of Carleton in the role of female rogue, she nevertheless allows
this image to break the surface of her dignified self-vindications
by means of allusion and innuendo, for the benefit of the readers
who are disposed to see it emerge. Her summary of the subsidiary
charges against her, for cheating a vintner and a French merchant,
and for picking a Kentish lord's pocket, repeat the roguish 'Pranks'
listed on the title-page of *The Lawyers Clarke*.[46] She echoes the
prurient slant of that pamphlet by exploiting her sexuality to titillate
the reader.[47] An incident briefly discussed in *The Lawyers Clarke*, in
which Mary is stripped of her clothes and jewels, is expanded in her
own accounts and transplanted in time such that the Carleton family
and their allies become the aggressors on discovering her supposed
imposture. Though her earlier apologist had included this story in
his *Vindication*, Carleton's versions of the incident are certainly more
florid.[48] Borrowing again from *The Lawyers Clarke*, she elsewhere
protests that she should have been accused of pronouncing her
German name 'de Wolway' as 'De Vulva'.[49] *The Case* quotes a
letter to the Carletons, claiming that she is a bigamist and stating
that one of her distinguishing features is that she '*hath very high
Breasts, &c.*'. She reiterates this comment in quoting her defence
at the trial.[50] An engraving facing the title-page of *An Historicall
Narrative*, follows *The Arraignment* in presenting an alluring view
of her *en décolleté*.

Throughout her texts the puns, double-meanings and occasional
cheap laughs introduce shades of 'the crafty whore' into the solemn
complaint of 'the distressed lady'. Asked by the judge if she has two
husbands, Carleton relates that she replied: 'if I had, He was one of
them, which I believe incensed Him . . . but I did not know the
Authority and dignity of his place, so much am I a stranger to this
Kingdom.' Entering the tavern where she is lodging with Carleton's

sister and brother-in-law, she finds John Carleton, 'standing at the Bar', but adds cheekily, '(not the Bar his Lordship was afterwards pleased to be one of the Instruments to make me stand at)'. She describes herself in prison as being left with no 'remembrance of my beloved Lord . . . a sacred relique of a person dear to me', wryly adding, '(I think indeed the dearest that ever woman had)'.[51]

Her pleas of apparent naïve innocence become rich with satirical potential for the reader who believes her to be a fraud. Ironically, in view of her probable former marriage to a shoemaker, she swears to John that she *will never be a Mistris to the greatest of Princes*', but, '*rather chuse to be a Wife to the meanest of men*'.[52] With seeming ingenuousness, she records the unheeding warning of John Carleton's brother-in-law that, '*the Town was full of wickedness, and that I might have some trick put upon me*'.[53]

Slippages of identity between the elevated romance heroine and the mischievous low-life trickster are paralleled by literary allusions whose dignity collapses into farce or bawdy by virtue of their secondary associations. In comparing '*these Novels of my Life*' to '*those of* Boccace, *but that they are more serious and tragical*', Carleton may perhaps invoke the irreverent fabliaux of the *Decameron*, while appearing to claim romance gentility.[54] An allusion to the cousin of the *Canterbury Tales* would have particular aptness in view of the readiness of her satirists to spot Chaucerian links with Carleton's Kentish origins. A ribald ballad, *The Westminster Wedding* (1663) refers to her story as a '*Canterbury*-Tale', as do the *Memoires of Mary Carleton*.[55] Carleton's praise of 'the onely Lady Errant in the World', and her promise to give 'some account of this my (Errant-like) Adventure', may recall the well-circulated whore-story, *La Putana Errante*, from which *The Wandring Whore* borrowed its title and characters. Certainly, later Carleton biographers appreciated the seamier implications of the term 'errant', describing Carleton as, so 'errant a Baggage', or as one who will 'Whore-*Errant-at* a while'.[56]

While cultural expectation dictates that Carleton should voice herself through the discourses of romance and rogue literature, her combination of the mutually deconstructive models of her identity supplied by these genres satirizes cultural limitations imposed on female subjectivity. In addition to suggesting that neither myth of feminine identity can succeed in containing her, the split magnifies the absurd paradox attendant upon women writing in the seventeenth century. Since the act of female authorship, let alone publication, was seen to jeopardize the cardinal feminine virtues of silence, modesty and even chastity, the respectable lady writing in defence of her innocence risked losing her respectability in the very act of taking up the pen.[57] In propagating conflicting myths of herself as virtuous romance heroine and fraudulent rogue, Carleton merely amplifies divisions inherent in the attempt to speak as a female subject in her culture. Nevertheless, she exploits the association between publication and unchastity to enhance the titillatory appeal of her texts, as another of her doubles entendres suggests. Her 'bare-faced appearance to all-comers', she complains, has set her apart from respectable womanhood, 'so that, That which other Women hide and Mask for Modesty I must shew and set to public view for my Justification'. Proclaiming that her *fame shall speedily rise in its due lusture*', she once again highlights her equivocal status as a woman writing in her own defence.[58] For, while 'fame' may mean simply honourable reputation, or chastity, it also suggests widespread public familiarity, or the notoriety of rumour.[59] Her refusal to 'prostitute' her 'fame' to her detractors ironically encapsulates precisely her strategy in capitalizing on the notoriety afforded by self-publicization.[60]

By juxtaposing her competing feminine personae, Carleton questions the assumed stability of gendered identity which guarantees patriarchal social relations. In this respect, her textual strategy embodies the essence of her social transgressions. Through repeated bigamy, she refuses the fixed or monogamous feminine identity which sustains the system of patriarchal ownership and control. Similarly, she challenges the illusion of a stable or organic social hierarchy by swapping class identities. Carleton's destabilization of hierarchy is borne out in her texts by the mingling of 'high' and 'low' genres.

Graham, Hinds, Hobby and Wilcox have sounded a warning note against the total conflation of the textual and material spheres, rightly reminding us that, 'there are hazards in collapsing our categories of life and text too far', and that Carleton was eventually hanged.[61] Nevertheless, the materiality of texts and discourses in the Carleton case is clearly manifest in the way both Carleton's self-representations and the biographical representations of her shaped the perceived identities and therefore the material social circumstances open to her. Ultimately, it was the textual might of her detractors which overwhelmed the official innocence accorded her by her legal acquittal. The material obstacle of financial impoverishment need not in itself have destroyed the image of the romance heroine, and might have been overcome had the romance image not been overwhelmed by its more marketable roguish counterpart. As Graham *et al.* point out, 'a struggle over meaning can be part of an actual, material struggle'.[62] Carleton takes the 'struggle over meaning' between texts and subtly locates it within her own text. As her social transgressions are enabled by a refusal to be fixed by the class and gender meanings which her society attaches to individuals, so the text – as a site on which meanings are contested – may be seen as, in some sense, materially transgressive.

Carleton underlines the provisional and constructed character of the feminine subjectivities available to her, not only by juxtaposing competing meanings but by drawing attention to the manner in which subjectivity is fashioned through the discursive medium.

Her construction of herself through romance is clearly signalled in the request that her readers 'cast a favourable eye upon *these Novels of my Life*, not much unlike *those of* Boccace, *but that they are more serious and tragical*'. Her claim to have read 'Romances and other Heroical Ablandiments . . . written for the most and best part in *French*', again highlights the fictional sources of the narrative scheme which fashions her autobiography. She glances ironically at the manner in which, as John Carleton's response demonstrates, her very reproduction of the textual patterns of romance ensures her historical credibility. 'I am not', she insists,

> the first woman, that hath put her self upon such hazards, or pilgrimages, the stories of all times abound with such Examples, enough to make up a volume. I might as well have given lustre to a Romance as any any any of those supposed *Heroina's*.[63]

She goes on to indicate, however, that while the generic conventions of texts may produce history by shaping perceptions of identity which influence social relations, her exploitation of romance has a limited capacity to map its easy closures onto her lived experience. She wryly speculates of romances that:

> since it is the method of those peices to perplex and intricate the commencement and progress of such adventures, with unexpected and various difficulties . . . and at last bring them to the long desired fruition of their dear bought content, I am not altogether out of heart, but that Providence may have some tender and more Courteous consideration of me.[64]

Carleton's foregrounding of the discursive mediation of her subjectivity is complemented by a focus on her legally mediated status as a woman. In accounts of her trial in both *The Case* and *An Historicall Narrative*, she alleges that the Carletons have jewels and clothes belonging to her, and is told by the judge that, since she is John Carleton's wife, they are his property and *'he must sue for them'*. *The Case* recounts how John threatens to kill himself if his wife tries to bring a criminal prosecution against his father for the return of her jewels. Devoid of her husband's support in the matter, she finally visits Carleton senior in person, only to be told by him that John Carleton has the jewels. Though she claims that her 'Lawyers' have advised her to 'prosecute my adversaries in the same manner, and at the same Bar where they arraigned me . . . for that riot against the publick peace committed upon my person', her legal predicament with regard to her property leads her to criticize 'the Laws of this Kingdom made against *Femes Covert*' in her prefatory appeal to Prince Rupert.[65]

The term *'feme covert'* expresses the married woman's lack of autonomous legal subjectivity through a metaphor of literal mediation. In his *Lawes Resolution of Womens Rights* (1632), T.E. states that all women 'are understood either married or to bee married', and later that, 'A woman as soone as she is married is called covert, in Latine *nupta*, that is, vailed, as it were, clouded and over-shadowed'.[66] Carleton experiences the ramifications of being legally 'veiled' or mediated by her husband at first hand, with John Carleton becoming the rightful owner of all her property.[67]

Bemoaning the status of a wife in English law, she expresses her doubtful response to the proverb which told her, 'England *was a Heaven for women*', since 'It is to be enjoyed but at second hand, and all by the husbands title.' In an even more bitter attack on feminine dependency in marriage, she complains that the *'mistaken advantages'* of the matrimonial state *'have turned to my real damage: so that when I might have bin happy in myself, I must needs transplant my content into a sterile ungrateful soil, and be miserable by another'*.[68]

While Carleton's specific circumstances are the immediate catalyst for her critique of women's legal subordination, we may also regard her as building on a generally heightened consciousness of this issue in the latter part of the seventeenth century. Women's awareness of their legal position had been increased throughout the period of the Civil War and Interregnum. During this time they had come to speak and write as petitioners to parliament, both singly on matters of their own or their husbands' property, and in groups protesting about political matters.[69] On 7 May 1647, for example, 10,000 Leveller women signed a petition protesting that women deserved equal property rights with men since all were equal in the sight of God.[70] Women's petitioning activities offset their statutory lack of legal autonomy. Unease at this unfamiliar dimension to feminine conduct is reflected in the rash of mock-petitions printed, ridiculing women's speaking up for their legal and political rights, usually by alleging that they were merely concerned to secure their conjugal rights.[71]

More sympathetic were the portrayals in Restoration drama of women's greater awareness of the trammels of their legal status. In Dryden's *The Wild Gallant* (1663), Isabelle insists that she will make her 'own conditions' for a prospective marriage to Sir Timorous. The last of these conditions is 'to have all the money in my disposing'. Having stated her terms, she asserts: 'I have led all women the way, if they dare but follow me.' Similarly, Widow Rich, in Etherege's *The Comical Revenge* (1664) refuses to marry Sir Frederick Frollick until she has secured equal property rights. The play's epilogue presents the newly married widow triumphant, having '*couzen'd*' Sir Frederick by making over her wealth to her trustees. In Wycherley's *The Plain Dealer* (1676), the highly litigious Widow Blackacre eloquently sums up: 'Matrimony, to a woman, worse than Excommunication, in depriving her of the benefit of the Law.'[72]

The critique of women's inferior position in law provided another opportunity to lift the *querelle des femmes* (or literary battle of the sexes) out of its perennial enumeration of supposedly intrinsic feminine virtues and vices.[73] The facts concerning women's legal status substantiated the claim, made in relation to their education, in *The Women's Sharpe Revenge* (1640) that: 'if we [women] be weak by nature, they [men] strive to make us more weak by our nurture, and if in degree of place low, they strive by their policy to keep us more under.'[74] Attacks on women's legal inferiority as the product of 'nurture' unjustified by 'nature' could serve as a potential reminder that feminine identity was extrinsic and socially constructed.

In Mary Carleton's texts, the critique of a legal construction of feminine identity in which the wife attains subjectivity only through the medium of the husband may be seen to elucidate the discursive construction of feminine identity through the medium of patriarchal representation. Graham, Hinds, Hobby and Wilcox have suggested that 'the non-recognition of women as full legal subjects in the seventeenth century perhaps gives a particular significance to women writing the self and being recognized'.[75] However, for Carleton, the legal 'non-recognition' of her subjectivity may also be seen to illuminate precisely the representational masking with which female subjects must contend in the very act of 'writing the self'.

Highlighting the anomaly by which her husband takes on the privileges but not the responsibilities of his dominant legal position, she states that:

> I may in some sort complain of my Husband, who wore a Sword by his side, and yet could suffer me to be stript of my necessary Rayment. But instead of that Civil Defence, the least of Kindnesses he might have afforded me, that had enjoyed all *Hymen's* Rites with me so lately before that Tragick-Part, he encountreth me with a Volume of one Sheet in Quarto.[76]

Carleton's complaint against John links her lack of marital autonomy to her lack of autonomy in representing a subjectivity. The protection or veiling of a 'Civil Defence' with which her husband should provide her as a *'feme covert'*, is replaced by an equivalent representational 'veiling' or mediation of her identity in the text he produces. The connection between legal and representational mediations of women in patriarchy is further suggested by Carleton's contention that:

> all Nations do observe it as a Law, That a Dissolute Life in Men, is not held to be such a Vice as in Women. That let a Report passe of a Woman, True or False, Irreparably she lyeth under Infamy.[77]

In this metaphor, the representation of feminine identity assumes the status of a 'Law'. Like the *'feme covert'*, the slandered woman finds herself passively 'covered' or mediated by the infamous 'Report'.

Nevertheless, as Carleton exposes the provisional and constructed status of the representations which mediate her subjectivity, so she underscores the culturally relative basis of her mediation in law. Her juxtaposition of contradictory representations of feminine identity is paralleled by her exposition of conflicting definitions of women's legal status in different countries. Of England, she remarks that:

> The fashions and customs here are much different from those of our Country [Germany], where the wife shares an equal portion with her husband in all things of weal and woe, and can *liber intentare*, begin and commence, and finish a suit in her own name.

Continuing her comparison, she claims that 'I could instance in many other customes of nearer Nations, in respect to female right and propriety in their own Dowers, as well in their husbands estates'.[78]

The notion that social identity is not intrinsic to the individual – to which Carleton's texts point, and which enables her socially transgressive behaviour – may be seen as having been fostered by, and to play on, topical epistemological anxieties. In exposing the relative character of feminine identity as constructed in English law, Carleton engages a contemporary spirit of scepticism concerning the traditional assumption that the local laws of society were underwritten by an absolute and universal natural law.[79] Her method is akin to that of seventeenth-century literary excursions to foreign settings, in which the novel culture and customs of real or imaginary discovered lands could function as a challenge to the correctness of more familiar social mores.[80] Incarcerated in the nunnery, she experiences:

> strong impulses and natural instincts to be ranging abroad . . . as the first finders of Terra Incognita were urged with, to the discovery of those Regions, of whose Existence they had no further assurance than their own hopeful bodings and divinations.[81]

Though her youthful urge to explore unknown lands may ironically reflect the picaresque 'analogy between physical and social mobility', noted by McKeon, it also acts as a metaphor for her exploration of alternative subjectivities.[82] This is facilitated by her refusal to accept as absolute the familiar social laws which dictate that she should remain at home within the precincts of her given class and gender identity.

A desire to test or confirm natural law as an anchor for social order relates to other topical destabilizing factors. The empirical science nurtured by the newly established Royal Society developed philosophical speculations concerning the separation of appearance and nature already articulated in the sensory scepticism of Descartes and Hobbes, and later of Locke.[83] If the human perception of objects did not correspond exactly to the empirical nature of those objects, then the human perception of people might also be deluded as to their inner nature by their outward appearance. Thus contemporary philosophical thought may be seen to have reinforced the apparent potential for the usurpation of social rank foregrounded by the events of the Civil War and Interregnum. It is perhaps this combination of scientific and political climates which led Francis Kirkman to describe Mary Carleton as '*a Looking-glass wherein we may see the Vices of this Age Epitomized*'. Both he and the author of *Vercingetorixa* (1663) – an irreverent verse account of the Carleton case – compare Mary Carleton to the grand usurper, Perkin Warbeck.[84] She herself revels in the Carletons' inability to tell a '*Princess*' from a '*Prentice*'.[85]

Exposing the indeterminacy of the boundaries separating history and fiction, Carleton once again touches on the potential deceptiveness of appearance, as emphasized by the contemporary fluidity of the generic categories of 'true history', romance and novel.[86] Her *Historicall Narrative*, described as 'a History of part of my Life', pleads veracity but also evokes the 'histories' which constituted self-sufficient life-stories within long heroic romances.[87] It is with ironic precision (given the nature of her autobiography) that she divides her youthful reading matter into 'History', 'literature' and 'Romances'. Meanwhile, the phrase '*Novels of my Life*' oscillates between the senses of news and fiction.[88]

Though Carleton reduces the difference between her underlying and perceived identities merely to that which separates a Princess from a diplomat's daughter, she audaciously suggests that consistency of outward appearance or disguise is the only tangible means of gauging identity. 'Grant the Question', she writes,

> that I am not so honourably descended as I insinuated to the Catchdolt my Father in Law, (which yet by their favour they shall first better and more evidently disprove . . . before I relinquish my just claym to my Honour) . . . if the best *things are to be imitated*, I had a good precept and warrant for my assumption of such a personage as they were willing to believe me to be; If . . . by any misbecoming act . . . unbefitting such a person, I had prophaned that quality . . . and discovered any inconsistent meanness therewith (as it was very difficult to personate greatness for so long a time without slips or mistakes) I had deserved to be severely punished.[89]

In this analysis, appearance and nature become synonymous, effectively demolishing the concept of an inner core of identity (in this case nobility) which can ultimately stabilize the position of individuals within society. The collapsing of difference between identity and disguise may also be the butt of a double entendre in the caption which accompanies Carleton's portrait opposite the title-page of *An Historicall Narrative*. There we find a potential pun on the word 'counterfeit' in its dual senses of 'image' and 'imitation'. The lines read 'Hence-forth there needs no mark of me be kno[wn]/ For the right Counterfeit is herein shown.' Highlighting the ambiguity, John Carleton, in his *Ultimum Vale*, marvels at the 'unparalell'd confidence' with which Carleton 'permitted the Counterfeit Effigies of her ill-shapen painted face to be inserted as a Prologue' to her text.[90]

Carleton's most overt statement and manipulation of the concept of identity as disguise came in April 1664 at the Lincoln's Inn Fields theatre when she starred as herself in Thomas Porter's play *A Witty Combat: or, The German Princess* (1663) which exposed her as a thorough, if witty, fraud.[91] The idea for this publicity stunt may have been spawned by associations of Carleton with Moll Cutpurse who had appeared on stage to entertain the audience with songs and lascivious speeches at a performance of Middleton and Dekker's play about her, *The Roaring Girl* (1611).[92] Though Carleton's stage appearance does represent a capitulation to the rogue image, whose currency in the popular imagination evidently held the financial rewards, it nevertheless emphasizes that identity for her is simply a matter of opportunistic role-play. By acting herself in the theatre she renders the truth of her entry into the rogue persona as questionable as that of her previous self-projections, and makes explicit the technique she has exploited all along.

Though her practical implementation of it is far more radical, Carleton apparently shared with her aristocratic contemporary Margaret Cavendish a notion of female performance, as (in Sophie Tomlinson's words) a 'metaphor of possibility for women'. However, Cavendish's first contact with female actors came through the court theatricals of Queen Henrietta Maria, and Tomlinson has identified in her work a marked difference in response to aristocratic and professional actors. Thus, despite their analogous use of female performance as an escape from deterministic notions of feminine identity, Carleton may be seen to materialize the very threat of social mobility which Cavendish perceived in professional actors and criticized through the language of theatrical imposture.[93]

Yet some of the responses to Carleton suggest that her self-creating social mobility was perceived as a specifically feminine social threat. While Kirkman sees in Carleton, 'the Vices of this Age', John Carleton, who likens himself to the '*beguiled*' Adam, resorts to a familiar anti-feminist, oxymoronic, rhetoric in calling Mary 'this Saint-like Divel', and '*Saint in thy Face, but Sathan in thy mind*'. Her transgressive powers of disguise become exaggerated in his claim that she is '*Only in shape a Woman, nay scarce so,/For* Proteus *like she can in all shapes go*'.[94]

Nevertheless, however Protean Carleton is made to seem by her rogue biographers, her disguises are consistently penetrated to reveal a true identity beneath. *The Lawyers Clarke* concludes with the evidence of a colleague of one of her earlier husbands who claims 'she was a Whore, and hee'd prov'd her a Whore'.[95] In a number of accounts published on the occasion of her execution in 1673, Carleton ultimately lays aside her artifice in favour of simple Christian penitence.[96] Like Francis Kirkman, in his title *The Counterfeit Lady Unveiled* (1673), John Carleton parries his wife's proliferation of identities by promising to '*un-dress all these prodigious shapes, and set them out singly in the naked truth*'. These metaphors of the quest for definitive identity materialize in recurrent stories of her having been stripped.[97] In *The Female-Hector* (1663) her alleged impersonation of a 'Distressed Lady' in Amsterdam is requited, on discovery, by a stripping (at the governor's command) which reduces her to 'her own old Weeds'. Meanwhile John Carleton claims that 'many others that knew her . . . were ready to tear the Cloaths off from her back'.[98]

By drawing an analogy with 'a story I have lately heard of the six woman shavers in *Drury Lane*', Carleton suggests that the stripping of her in her own accounts manifests a stock response to the perennial assumption of feminine duplicity.[99] Though she does not enlarge on the story of the shavers, its presence in *The Life and Death of Mrs Mary Frith* indicates that it was probably familiar to a London audience of the time.[100] Though the aggressors are women in the story of the shavers, their stripping and shaving of their female victim who, like Carleton, is believed to have behaved adulterously, represents the same removal of a notional disguise.

In Carleton's *Historicall Narrative*, her own attackers call her 'Cheat' and 'Harlot' while they strip her, as if this incantation of names can somehow fix a stable identity on the body devoid of its material disguise.[101] John Carleton propagates the idea that she has already been contained in this way when he states that *'they that would endeavour to defame her,/Need use no other words, but only name her'*. Nevertheless, he later provides a more radical statement of the urge to forestall any further ambiguities by indelibly imprinting identity or meaning on her body itself. In a startling metaphor, he conjures up an image of literal body-writing, as he plans 'to whet my Pen, and send a Satyr to her to scratch and lash her till the blood comes for her just deserts'.[102] This wielding the pen in an attack on the female body, like the images of stripping, links the desire to know and fix Carleton's identity with the exercise of quasi-sexual masculine aggression, emphasizing that her transgressive instability is perceived as a feminine threat to patriarchal control. With the phallic authority of his pen John aims to quell the self-generating multiplicity of the bigamous Protean woman which has led to his own emasculation as the cuckolded husband of pamphlets like *The Lawyers Clarke*. The aggressive physicality of John's language also suggests the legal reassertion of marital authority, since he has the right in law to subject his wife to 'bodily damage' in so far as it 'appertaines to the office of a Husband for lawfull and reasonable correction'.[103]

Carleton's perceived feminine threat and the nature of John's masculine response to it echo the symbolic logic of contemporary anti-feminist satires. As Felicity Nussbaum has shown, 'the myth of satires against women includes the myth that women create chaos, and the imposition of form (satire) on formlessness provides meaning and rationality when the fear of meaninglessness and insanity arises'.[104]

However, in taking up the pen herself, Carleton resists the external imposition of stable gendered meaning by continuing her proliferation of identities and celebrating precisely the feminine transgressiveness which disturbs her husband. She piously laments that her stripping deprived her of 'the female Arts of bravery and gallantry', which previously *'embelished,* and adorned' her, leaving her 'disrobed and disfigured . . . and almost left naked'.[105] Yet, given the subsequent continued success of her imposture in court, this statement seems to parody the notion that the assumed facility for feminine disguise can be controlled by a simple act of unveiling.

Though expediency forbids that she should enlarge fully on her impersonatory skills, other women in her texts feature as surrogates in the business of feminine disguise. Highlighting her own bold challenge to social hierarchy, she describes how her maid successfully assumes the identity of her mistress in order to decoy a mob of pursuers. Two other women in Carleton's accounts, Grizel Hudson and Elizabeth Collier, take on her identity in prison in order to deceive men who arrive claiming to be her husband.[106] In referring to these episodes, *The Arraignment* merely suggests that the women were passively mistaken for Carleton, rather than actively choosing to exploit a capacity for disguise.[107]

Though biographical allegations that Carleton even disguised herself as a man might appear to exaggerate the transgressive potential of her capacity for disguise, they tend ultimately to reassert masculine control over the Protean female. While accusations of cross-dressing against Carleton may hope to exploit the female rogue precedent set by Moll Cutpurse, we might also link them to the titillating spectacle of Restoration actresses playing 'breeches' parts.[108] After all, the prospect of the 'crafty whore' in male costume offers a sexual frisson which is far less apparent in the depiction of the transvestite antics of the ugly, celibate and masculine Moll Cutpurse in *The Life and Death of Mrs Mary Frith*. There, the author indicates that male attire seemed the natural clothing for one of Moll's disposition: 'For never was any . . . woman so like her in her cloaths.' Moll's clothes merely serve as a corrective to the exceptional accident by which she has been born into a female body. This portrayal, enhanced by her masculine condemnations of unchaste female conduct, attempts to recuperate any general threat to the conventional order of gender relations posed by her cross-dressing.[109] In the Restoration theatre, however, a recuperation of the transgressive potential of female transvestism may be seen to take place by means of the objectifying male gaze which relishes the unequivocally female body displayed more evidently in male attire. It is this undeceived male knowledge of the true sex of the female transvestite which informs accounts of Carleton's supposed impersonation of a man.

Describing how she 'went to the Right Honourable the Lord Mayor in mans Apparel', John Carleton reminds us of her feminine charms by referring to her as 'this pretty Fidlers brat'. The event is described towards the end of a text which repeatedly offers a highly sexualized portrayal of Carleton, soliciting the aggressively desiring responses of a putative masculine readership.[110] Though the author of *The Female-Hector, or, the Germane Lady Turn'd Mounsieur* praises Carleton for her convincing portrayal of 'some Mounsieur of great rank', the reader's perception of this successful imposture is filtered through an established vision of her as the female rogue. The incident occurs at the end of a catalogue of her other exploits as an audacious woman and begins by describing her as 'this new vampt *Canterbury* Lady'. Her impersonation is short-lived, as she soon reveals herself to her friends in the Smithfield Tavern where it takes place. The author concludes by remarking that 'she would make a stout General at the head of an Army of *Amazonian* Ladies'.[111] If this is an unambiguous compliment, then the author is inserting Carleton into the mythical model of the ideally chaste and virtuous classical Amazon whose apparent distance from actual gender transgression permits a safe aesthetic appreciation of women adopting a masculine role.[112] However, it seems likely that the author is appealing to the equally recuperative portrayal supplied by the jovially prurient approach to female transvestism with which the Amazon becomes associated in contemporary ballads. In *The Female Warrior* (*c.* 1680), for example, the '*valiant* Amazon' disguises herself as an ensign in order to follow her beloved into the army. With heavy innuendo, the ballad informs us that she was 'at push of Pike some say, as good as ever struck'. Sure enough, her '*courage*' is soon undermined by pregnancy, and her feminine gender reasserts itself: '*She fell a pieces and was made a Mother.*'[113]

Like the mythical or ballad Amazons and the cross-dressing actress, Carleton herself offers an entertaining glimpse of female transvestism while delimiting its tangible transgressive potential. Though she reiterates allegations of cross-dressing made against her, she hotly denies them. Her 'Amazonian' fantasy of what McKeon calls 'some radical internalization of neochivalric force and freedom' is set firmly within the pragmatics of contemporary ideologies of feminine conduct.[114] Of her father-in-law, she states that she 'would Require the Combate of him to appear in the Field', but 'the Modesty of . . . [her] Sex' does not permit her to do so.[115] She is careful to confine her stated desires for masculine agency to the praiseworthy realm of unfulfilled longings which acknowledge feminine insufficiency. Though her 'masculine conceptions' prompt her to escape from the nunnery, she reveals that 'I blindly wished I were . . . a man, and exempt from that tedious life'.[116]

Nevertheless, she once again turns to stories of other women as a means of suggesting the subversive possibilities for women appropriating masculine roles. Continuing her comparison between herself and the 'Heroina's' of romance, she asserts:

> Nor do the Modern and very late Times want Examples of the like adventures. I could mention a Princess, and great Personage out of the North, who not long since came into my Country [i.e. Germany], and hath passed two or three times between Italy and France, and keeps her design yet undiscovered, and is the onely Lady Errant in the World. I could mention another . . . in this Country, a She-General, who followed the Camp to the other World in America. . . . Mine compared with those are meer puny stories.[117]

Michael McKeon regards this passage as an unconvincing attempt by Carleton to specify a romance motif to her modern setting.[118] However, in Queen Christina of Sweden we find a likely candidate for the 'Princess . . . out of the North' to whom Carleton refers.[119] *A Relation of the Life of Christina Queen of Sweden* (1656) describes Christina's abdication in favour of a 'vagabond and wandering life' which takes her through Europe and ultimately to Rome to pay homage to the father of the Catholic faith which she has embraced on the way. Christina is said to travel for the most part, 'in mens apparel', and to spend her time '*seeking Adventures in strange Lands*'.[120] Though the identity of the 'She-General' remains unclear, it is possible that she too represents a genuine figure of the times. As Sophie Tomlinson has pointed out, Henrietta Maria and certain French royal women had adopted martial roles earlier in the century.[121] On a less elevated social level, instances of women dressing up as male soldiers either to act as prostitutes in army-camps, to follow loved ones, or simply for patriotic reasons, were by no means unheard of at this time.[122]

Carleton's two 'Modern . . . Examples' demonstrate that the safely fictional assumption of a masculine role in romance may become realized in the exploits of actual women, enabling them to subvert the tangible gender limitations placed on them. Her use of the term 'Lady Errant' foregrounds anxieties concerning the misappropriation of the role of female knight, since it appears to have been adopted frequently for the parody of improper feminine pretensions in this direction. Queen Christina herself is described in *A Relation* as having '*become a Lady Errant*', a transformation which the author associates with a general decline into obscenities of speech and action.[123] The 'errant' mobility achieved by Carleton's two modern heroines in emulating what she portrays as a romance model of feminine conduct ciphers her own acquisition of class and gender mobility in the assumption of another of the feminine disguises provided by the romance tradition.

However, it is not a woman, but a man, John Carleton, onto whom Carleton most directly transfers her impersonatory activities. Alleging that John pretended to be a lord in order to win her favours, she deflects suspicions concerning her own misconduct with the proverbial retort that, 'to deceive the deceiver, is no deceit'.[124] Taken in its broader context, this statement draws attention to the fact that feminine duplicity is not, as patriarchal culture suggests, innate, but rather, that it is the inevitable result of the imposition on women of androcentric versions of truth. Since men set the terms of feminine identity, women may be seen to be in a perennial state of enforced disguise inside the costumes with which patriarchy has fitted them out. To deceive the deceiver, as Carleton demonstrates, means that, while the dominant male culture may fashion the disguises of feminine identity, women may actively select and swap those disguises, thereby intervening in the process of their subject construction.

The life and writings of Mary Carleton illustrate both the predicaments and possibilities surrounding women attempting to represent themselves in her historical setting. The exigencies of her situation and the highly public arena in which her self-presentation takes place magnify the pressures to voice a female subjectivity through the discourses of femininity sanctioned by the patriarchal culture of Restoration England. Nevertheless, her example indicates that an awareness of the extrinsic or provisional character of the subjectivities produced in this way can enable women actively to construct identities which, while culturally viable, allow a negotiation of more advantageous social spaces. The possibilities for women to approach identity in this way may be seen to be intensified at this moment in history by the scientific and socio-political climates; by the appearance of professional actresses; and by a heightened perception of women's status in law. A notion of feminine identity as disguise liberates the potential for an exchange of disguises. This not only offers social mobility, but persistently ironizes or foregrounds the illusory nature of supposedly intrinsic or essential feminine identities.

Carleton's eventual hanging must necessarily qualify any notion of the materially transgressive power of her writings. Nevertheless, her textual strategies offer an important resistance to the gambits of her male biographers which make a manifest contribution to her material fate by writing her into the rogue life of which the inevitable closure is death on the scaffold. In writing her autobiographies, she not only exploits, but begins to expose, the perennial elision in feminine subject-construction, aptly referring to herself as 'the person I am, or what they made me to be'.[125]

NOTES

(Place of publication for works printed before 1800 is London unless otherwise stated.)

1 John Carleton, *The Ultimum Vale of John Carleton*, 1663, pp. 1, 3, 14, 27, 36; *The Arraignment, Tryal and Examination of Mary Moders*, 1663, pp. 6, 14.
2 John Carleton, *Ultimum Vale*, pp. 2–3; Mary Carleton, *The Case of Madam Mary Carleton*, 1663, pp. 9–10, 43, 64–5, 136, 137–8; Mary Carleton, *An Historicall Narrative of the German Princess*, 1663, p. 8.
3 *News from Jamaica*, 1671; *The Memoires of Mary Carleton*, 1673, p. 53; Francis Kirkman, *The Counterfeit Lady Unveiled*, 1673, p. 170; *The Life and Character of Mrs Mary Moders*, 2nd edn, 1732, p. 75. So far, no copies of the first edition of *The Life and Character* have been traced and its date remains uncertain, though 1673 seems a plausible suggestion as it deals with her entire life story up to and including her execution in that year.
4 C.F. Main, 'The German Princess; or, Mary Carleton in Fact and Fiction', *Harvard Library Bulletin*, 1956, vol. 10, pp. 173, 175; see also John Carleton, *Ultimum Vale*, pp. 12, 140; Ernest Bernbaum, *The Mary Carleton Narratives 1663–1673*, Cambridge, MA, Harvard University Press, 1914, pp. 20–4, 25.
5 Bernbaum, p. 24.
6 *Memories of the Life of the Famous Madam Charlton*, 1673, p. 4.
7 Daniel Defoe, *Moll Flanders*, ed. David Blewett, London, Penguin, 1989, pp. 52–3, 55–6. Although they range beyond the scope of the present investigation, I plan to consider elsewhere possible links between the Carleton narratives and Defoe's *Moll Flanders* and *Roxana*.
8 Samuel Pepys, *The Diary of Samuel Pepys*, ed. Robert Latham and William Matthews, London, Bell, 11 vols, 1970–83, vol. IV, pp. 163, 177, 29 May and 7 June 1663.
9 John Carleton, *The Replication, or Certain Vindicatory Depositions*, 1663, p. 6.
10 Linda Anderson, 'At the Threshold of the Self: Women and Autobiography', in Moira Monteith (ed.), *Women's Writing: A Challenge to Theory*, Brighton, Harvester, 1986, p. 59; Susan Stanford Friedman, 'Women's Autobiographical Selves', in Shari Benstock (ed.), *The Private Self: Theory and Practice of Women's Autobiographical Writings*,

London and New York, Routledge, 1988, pp. 38–9; Elspeth Graham, Hilary Hinds, Elaine Hobby, and Helen Wilcox (eds), *Her Own Life: Autobiographical Writings by Seventeenth-Century Englishwomen*, London and New York, Routledge, 1989, p. 19; Felicity A. Nussbaum, 'Eighteenth-Century Women's Autobiographical Commonplaces', in Benstock, pp. 148–50; Felicity A. Nussbaum, 'Heteroclites: The Gender of Character in the Scandalous Memoirs', in Laura Brown and Felicity A. Nussbaum (eds), *The New Eighteenth Century*, London, Methuen, 1987, p. 145; Mary Beth Rose, 'Gender, Genre, and History: Seventeenth-Century English Women and the Art of Autobiography', in *Women in the Middle Ages and the Renaissance: Literary and Historical Perspectives*, Syracuse, NY, Syracuse University Press, 1986, p. 249.

11 Nussbaum, 'Autobiographical Commonplaces', p. 149. Nussbaum ascribes this model to 'post-Lacanian and post-Althusserian theorists'. Friedman, p. 37, and Graham *et al.*, p. 19, specifically cite Lacan. Friedman, p. 34, also cites George Gusdorf's theories of the construction of the subject in autobiography, as does Anderson, p. 56.

12 Nussbaum, 'Autobiographical Commonplaces', p. 149. See also Anderson, p. 59; Friedman, pp. 40–1; Graham *et al.*, p. 19; Nussbaum, 'Heteroclites', p. 146; Rose, p. 249.

13 See Graham *et al.*, pp. 5, 18, 24, 133; Elaine Hobby, *Virtue of Necessity: English Women's Writing 1649–88*, London, Virago, 1988, pp. 88, 92–6; Michael McKeon, *The Origins of the English Novel 1600–1740*, Baltimore and London, Johns Hopkins University Press, 1987, pp. 100, 241–4.

14 Janet Todd, *The Sign of Angellica: Women, Writing and Fiction, 1660–1880*, London, Virago, 1989, p. 53.

15 *The Lawyers Clarke Trappan'd by the Crafty Whore of Canterbury*, 1663, p. 4; John Carleton, *Ultimum Vale*, pp. 2–3.

16 Mary Carleton, *Narrative*, p. 6; *The Case*, pp. 19–22.

17 *A Vindication of a Distressed Lady*, 1663, pp. 3–4; *The Great Tryall and Arraignment of the Late Distressed Lady*, 1663, pp. 6.

18 Mary Carleton, *Narrative*, pp. 6, 22.

19 Mary Carleton, *The Case*, pp. 13–19, 26–8, 32, sig. A1R.

20 *The Memoires*, p. 2.

21 Paul Salzman, *English Prose Fiction 1558–1700: A Critical History*, Oxford, Clarendon, 1985, pp. 177–8; Todd, p. 48.

22 Jane Spencer, *The Rise of the Woman Novelist from Aphra Behn to Jane Austen*, Oxford, Blackwell, 1986, pp. 23, 41.

23 Salzman, pp. 6, 41, 50–1, 111; Todd, p. 46; Louis B. Wright, *Middle-Class Culture in Elizabethan England*, Chapel Hill, University of North Carolina Press, 1935, pp. 114–17. See Helen Hackett's chapter in this volume.

24 Spencer, p. 23.

25 Todd, p. 48. See also Salzman, p. 181; Spencer, p. 23.

26 Spencer, p. 23. For an assessment of the response of an earlier woman writer to the romance genre, see Helen Hackett's chapter in this volume.

27 John Carleton, *Ultimum Vale*, pp. 7, 18.
28 Mary Carleton, *The Case*, sig. A6V. Todd, p. 53, considers the relationship between Carleton's financial predicament and the nature of her self-projection.
29 *The Lawyers Clarke*, p. 1.
30 John Carleton, *The Replication*, pp. 6–7.
31 *The Arraignment*, pp. 3, 4, 16.
32 *A True Account of the Tryal of Mrs Mary Moders*, 1663, sig. A1R.
33 *The Memoires*, p. 8.
34 See *La Vida de Lazarillo de Tormes*, 1554, translated into English by David Rowland in 1576; Mateo Aleman, *Guzman de Alfarache*, 1599, 1604, translated into English as *The Rogue* by James Mabbe in 1622; *Memoires of Monsieur Du Vall*, 1670; Charles Sorel, *L'Histoire Comique de Francion*, translated into English as *The Comical History of Francion*, 1623. Salzman, p. 207, discusses the importance of *Lazarillo* and *Guzman* in the picaresque tradition. McKeon, pp. 96–100, discusses the relationship between picaresque and criminal biography.
35 See the bibliography compiled by Lincoln B. Faller in his *Turned to Account: The Forms and Functions of Criminal Biography in Late Seventeenth- and Early Eighteenth-Century England*, Cambridge, Cambridge University Press, 1987, pp. 286–96.
36 See *The Life of Long Meg of Westminster*, 1635, reprinted in *Miscellanea Antiqua Anglicana; or, a Select Collection of Curious Tracts*, vol. I, London, 1816; *The Life and Death of Mrs Mary Frith. Commonly Called Mal Cutpurse*, 1662; Nicholas Goodman, *Hollands Leaguer*, 1632.
37 *Long Meg*, sig. D3R; *The Womans Champion*, 1662, sigs A1R, A2R; *The Lawyers Clarke*, sig. A1R. See also, for example, the running titles of biographies of highwayman James Hind, including *The Trial of Captain James Hind*, 1651, describing his 'Merry Conceits and witty Pranks'; *The English Gusman*, 1652, featuring his 'Madd Pranks' and 'Handsom Jests'; *We Have Brought our Hogs to a Fair Market*, 1652, enumerating 'His Merry Pranks'.
38 Goodman, sig. B1R.
39 Roger Thompson, *Unfit for Modest Ears: A Study of Pornographic, Obscene and Bawdy Works Written or Published in England in the Second Half of the Seventeenth Century*, London, Macmillan, 1979, p. 73.
40 *Mary Frith*, pp. 161–2.
41 *The Fifth and Last Part of the Wandring Whore*, 1661, p. 16. See also *The Caterpillars of This Nation Anatomized . . . To which is added, the Manner of Hectoring and Trepanning, as It Is Acted in and about the City of London*, 1659; *The Trepan*, 1656, in which two sisters con a Southwark dyer out of his property.
42 Thompson, pp. 65, 71–2, 73–4; Strickland Gibson, 'A Bibliography of Francis Kirkman', *Oxford Bibliographical Society Publications*, 1947, new series, vol. 1, p. 52.
43 Mary Carleton, *The Case*, p. 2.
44 See Blewett, p. 3.
45 Mary Carleton, *Narrative*, pp. 20–1; *The Case*, pp. 109–13.
46 Mary Carleton, *The Case*, pp. 74–5.

47 Todd, pp. 54–5, comments on this feature of Carleton's texts.
48 *The Lawyers Clarke*, p. 3; *A Vindication*, p. 6; Mary Carleton, *Narrative*, p. 12; *The Case*, pp. 69, 71–2.
49 Mary Carleton, *The Case*, pp. 46–7 [mispaginated 38–9]. See *The Lawyers Clarke*, sig. A1R.
50 Mary Carleton, *The Case*, pp. 71, 93.
51 ibid., pp. 74, 121–2; Mary Carleton, *Narrative*, p. 9.
52 Mary Carleton, *Narrative*, p. 9.
53 ibid., p. 7.
54 Mary Carleton, *The Case*, sig. A4V.
55 *The Westminster Wedding*, 1663, stanza 5. *The Memoires*, p. 1.
56 Mary Carleton, *The Case*, pp. 34, 6; John Carleton, *Ultimum Vale*, p. 43; Kirkman, p. 197. See also below, p. 186.
57 See Angeline Goreau, *The Whole Duty of a Woman: Female Writers in Seventeenth Century England*, New York, Dial, 1985, pp. 13, 16; Patricia Crawford, 'Women's Published Writings 1600–1700', in Mary Prior (ed.), *Women in English Society 1500–1800*, London, Methuen, 1985, p. 216; Ann Rosalind Jones, 'Surprising Fame: Renaissance Gender Ideologies and Women's Lyric', in Nancy K. Miller (ed.), *The Poetics of Gender*, New York, Columbia University Press, 1986, pp. 76–7.
58 Mary Carleton, *The Case*, p. 107, sig. A6V.
59 See Goreau, p. 14; Jones, p. 93.
60 Mary Carleton, *The Case*, pp. 124–5.
61 Graham *et al.*, p. 18.
62 ibid.
63 Mary Carleton, *The Case*, sig. A4V, pp. 23, 33.
64 ibid., pp. 33–4.
65 Mary Carleton, *Narrative*, pp. 19–20; *The Case*, pp. 104, 116–17, 118–19, 125, sig. A3R. For other discussions of Carleton's legal predicament, see Graham *et al.*, pp. 7, 133–5; Hobby, p. 95; McKeon, p. 242; Todd, p. 54.
66 T.E., *The Lawes Resolution of Womens Rights*, 1632, pp. 6, 125. For a discussion of the law of coverture, see Roger Thompson, *Women in Stuart England and America: A Comparative Study*, London, Routledge & Kegan Paul, 1974, pp. 162–4. For discussions of women's position in law as part of the historical context of seventeenth-century women's autobiography, see Graham *et al.*, pp. 7–10, 19; Sandra Findley and Elaine Hobby, 'Seventeenth-Century Women's Autobiography', in Francis Barker *et al.* (eds), *1642: Literature and Power in the Seventeenth Century*, Colchester, University of Essex, 1981, p. 13.
67 See T.E., p. 129.
68 Mary Carleton, *The Case*, pp. 126–7, sigs A5V [misplaced as A5R], A6R.
69 Graham *et al.*, p. 10; Hobby, pp. 4–5, 13–17, 39; Thompson, *Women in Stuart England*, p. 162.
70 See Simon Shepherd (ed.), *The Women's Sharp Revenge: Five Women's Pamphlets from the Renaissance*, London, Fourth Estate, 1985, p. 197.
71 See, for instance, *The Mid-Wives Just Petition*, 1643; *The City-Dames*

Petition, 1647; Henry Neville, *Newes from the New Exchange, or The Common-wealth of Ladies*, 1650. See also Hobby, p. 85.

72 John Dryden, *The Wild Gallant*, 1669, p. 23 (first performed 15 February 1663, see William Van Lennep (ed.), *The London Stage 1660–1800*, Part I, 1660–1700, Carbondale, Southern Illinois University Press, 1965, p. 62); George Etherege, *The Comical Revenge; or, Love in a Tub*, 1664, sig. N3R; William Wycherley, *The Plain Dealer*, 1677, p. 91 (first performed 11 December 1676, see Van Lennep, p. 253).

73 See, for example, in Shepherd: Jane Anger, *Jane Anger her Protection for Women*, 1589, pp. 37, 39; Rachel Speght, *A Mouzell for Melastomus*, 1617, pp. 75–6; *The Womens Sharpe Revenge*, 1640, p. 185. For discussions of the *querelle*, see Shepherd; Thompson, *Unfit for Modest Ears*, pp. 111–12; Betty Travitsky, 'The Lady Doth Protest: Protest in the Popular Writings of Renaissance Englishwomen', *English Literary Renaissance*, 1984, vol. 14, no. 3, p. 258; Diane Purkiss's chapter in this volume.

74 *The Womens Sharpe Revenge*, p. 170. Shepherd, pp. 160–1, rehearses the arguments for the likelihood that *The Womens Sharpe Revenge* (allegedly '*Performed by Mary Tattle-well* and Joan *Hit-him-home, spinsters*') was probably written by John Taylor, in an attempt to cash in on the *querelle*.

75 Graham *et al.*, p. 19.

76 Mary Carleton, *Narrative*, pp. 4–5.

77 ibid., pp. 3–4.

78 Mary Carleton, *The Case*, pp. 126, 127.

79 Susan Staves, *Players' Scepters: Fictions of Authority in the Restoration*, Lincoln, NB, and London, University of Nebraska Press, 1979, pp. 253, 257, 260, 271, 272.

80 See Henry Neville, *The Isle of Pines*, 1668; Edward Howard, *The Six Days Adventure*, 1671; William Davenaut and John Dryden, *The Tempest*, 1670 (adapted from Shakespeare and first performed 7 November 1667, see Van Lennep, p. 123); Staves, pp. 293–4; McKeon, pp. 248–9.

81 Mary Carleton, *The Case*, pp. 14–15.

82 McKeon, p. 248.

83 See René Descartes, *Meditations on the First Philosophy*, Meditation VI, 'Of the Existence of Material Things', in *The Method, Meditations, and Selections from the Principles of Descartes*, trans. John Veitch, Edinburgh and London, Blackwood, 1925, p. 159; Thomas Hobbes, *Leviathan*, 1651, part I, ch. I; Hobbes, *Human Nature or the Fundamental Elements of Policy*, ch. 2, in *Hobbs's Tripos, in Three Discourses*, 3rd edn, 1684, pp. 4–10; John Locke, *An Essay Concerning Human Understanding*, 1690, Bk II, ch. VIII, pp. 56–60.

84 Kirkman, sig. A5V, pp. 6, 95; F.B., *Vercingetorixa: or, the Germane Princess Reduc'd to an English Habit*, 1663, p. 42.

85 Mary Carleton, *The Case*, p. 135.

86 McKeon, pp. 52–64.

87 See Salzman, pp. 186–9.

88 Mary Carleton, *Narrative*, p. 7; *The Case*, p. 23, sig. A4V.

89 ibid., pp. 37–8 [mispaginated 37–46].

90 John Carleton, *Ultimum Vale*, p. 41.

91 See Pepys, vol. V, p. 124, 15 April 1664.

92 Thomas Middleton and Thomas Dekker, *The Roaring Girl*, ed. Paul A. Mulholland, *The Revels Plays*, Manchester, Manchester University Press, 1987, pp. 12, 262.

93 See Sophie Tomlinson's chapter in this volume.

94 John Carleton, *The Replication*, p. 6; *Ultimum Vale*, pp. 19, 48, 15.

95 *The Lawyers Clarke*, p. 5.

96 See Kirkman, pp. 206–19; *The Memoires*, pp. 98–118; *The Life and Character*, p. 76; *The Deportment and Carriage of the German Princess*, 1673, pp. 2–5.

97 John Carleton, *The Replication*, sig. A1V; *The Lawyers Clarke*, p. 5.

98 *The Female-Hector, or, the Germane Lady Turn'd Mounsieur*, 1663, sig. A1R; John Carleton, *Ultimum Vale*, p. 31.

99 Mary Carleton, *The Case*, p. 72.

100 *Mary Frith*, p. 92. In this account there are only five 'shavers'.

101 Mary Carleton, *Narrative*, p. 12.

102 John Carleton, *Ultimum Vale*, pp. 13, 40.

103 T.E., p. 128.

104 Felicity A. Nussbaum, *The Brink of All We Hate: English Satires on Women, 1660–1750*, Lexington, University Press of Kentucky, 1984, p. 20.

105 Mary Carleton, *The Case*, p. 73.

106 ibid., pp. 128–9, 109–13; *Narrative*, pp. 18, 20–1.

107 *The Arraignment*, p. 13.

108 Marion Jones outlines the practice of female cross-dressing in the Restoration theatre, in John Loftis, Richard Southern, Marion Jones and A.H. Scouten, *The Revels History of Drama in English, Volume V, 1660–1750*, London, Methuen, 1976, pp. 148–9.

109 *Mary Frith*, pp. 17, 82, 85.

110 John Carleton, *Ultimum Vale*, p. 39. See also sig. A2R, pp. 12, 15, 24.

111 *The Female-Hector*, p. 8.

112 See Simon Shepherd, *Amazons and Warrior Women: Varieties of Feminism in Seventeenth-Century Drama*, Brighton, Harvester, 1981, p. 13.

113 *The Female Warrior* (Wing offers the dates 1681–93 for this ballad, while the Bodleian Library catalogue dates it *c.* 1680). See also *The Gallant She-Souldier*, 1655, pp. 728–9, which has the same denouement.

114 McKeon, p. 243.

115 Mary Carleton, *Narrative*, p. 3. See also Mary Carleton, *The Case*, p. 130.

116 Mary Carleton, *The Case*, pp. 19, 16.

117 ibid., pp. 34–5.

118 McKeon, p. 241.

119 Tomlinson suggests the potency of Queen Christina as a figure of female heroism for Margaret Cavendish – see chapter 5 in this volume.

120 *A Relation of the Life of Christina Queen of Sweden*, 1656, sig. A2V, pp. 35, 37. O.P. Gilbert, *Women in Men's Guise*, trans. J. Lewis May, London, Bodley Head, 1932, pp. 95–135, tells Christina's story.

121 Tomlinson, see chapter 5 in this volume.

122 Antonia Fraser, *The Weaker Vessel: Woman's Lot in Seventeenth-Century England*, London, Weidenfeld & Nicolson, 1984, pp. 220–6. Rudolf Dekker and Lotte Van de Pol, in *The Tradition of Female Transvestism in Early Modern Europe*, London, Macmillan, 1989, pp. 1, 6–8, concentrate on the Netherlands, but reveal that 'a far-from-exhaustive investigation' yielded 'fifty authentic examples of female transvestism in the seventeenth and eighteenth centuries in Great Britain'. This does not include temporary instances of cross-dressing in, say, carnival contexts. Gilbert, pp. 146–70, relates the history of Catalina De Eranso, a Spanish nun turned soldier and adventurer in the first half of the seventeenth century.

123 *A Relation*, sig. A2V, pp. 7, 18. See also Sir Thomas Overbury, *New and Choise Characters*, 1615, sigs g4V–g5R. Sophie Tomlinson has indicated to me similar uses of the term 'lady errant' in Thomas Fuller, *The Church-History of Britain*, 1655, VI, p. 364, and a newsbook description of petitioning women Levellers in 1649, quoted in Patricia Higgins, 'The Reactions of Women, with Special Reference to Women Petitioners', in Brian Manning (ed.), *Politics, Religion and the Civil War*, London, Arnold, 1973, p. 205. See also above, p. 173. For a detailed examination of both approving and disapproving literary portrayals of the figure of the female warrior, see Shepherd, *Amazons*, ch. 1, pp. 5–17. See also Helen Hackett's chapter, this volume, for a discussion of responses to Nereana's 'Knight like . . . search' in Wroth's *Urania*.

124 Mary Carleton, *The Case*, pp. 46 [mispaginated 38], 51.

125 ibid., p. 106.

7

WHORES' RHETORIC AND THE MAPS OF LOVE: CONSTRUCTING THE FEMININE IN RESTORATION EROTICA

Bridget Orr

Francis Barker begins his account of shifts in the constitution of subjectivity in the seventeenth century with the famous extract from Pepys's *Diary* in which the latter records his reading, masturbating over and burning *L'Escolle des Filles*. For Barker, Pepys's private consumption of a 'lewd book' marks a point at which the 'spectacular corporeality of the Jacobean plenum' can be seen to be giving way to a new regime in which the body is simultaneously reduced to a 'private residuality' and reproduced as a 'positive object of knowledge' in a process which displaces 'the charge of the sexed body onto the sexed text'.[1] This subject is gendered male, and women function in this order as the (necessary) object of a (frustrated) desire, as 'spoken absence' or 'speechless presence' but never as 'the human subject which is to be the key organising figure of bourgeois culture . . . the woman is an objectified body at which speech is aimed, . . . but whose being is, so to speak, sub-discursive: dumb, reduced, corporeal matter.'[2]

Barker's attempt to read Pepys's consumption of a pornographic text as exemplary of a new mode of subjectivity and new discursive and representational regimes seems to echo certain aspects of the claims made some twenty years ago by Stephen Marcus's classic study of the cultural functions of pornography in the nineteenth century, *The Other Victorians*. In *The History of Sexuality* Foucault argues that Marcus's construction of a 'repressive hypothesis', which links the origins of a modern age of sexual subjection

195

and censorship to the development of capitalism, blinds us to the massive production of transformative discourses of sexuality in this period by subordinating the 'chronicle of sex' to the history of the modes of production.[3] However, Marcus's argument that urbanization, privatization, reading and sexuality are intimately connected seems to put into play the same terms Barker uses:

> Like the novel, pornography is connected with the growth of cities – with an urban society – and with an audience of literate readers rather than listeners or spectators. These considerations are in turn involved with the development of new kinds of experience – sociologists call the process 'privatisation'. If the novel is both evidence of and a response to the needs created by the possibilities of private experience, then pornography is a mad parody of the same situation. No experience of reading is more private, more solitary in every way.[4]

Barker's account of the development of the subject in the Restoration is only one version of a number to have appeared recently: others include Catherine Belsey's *The Subject of Tragedy* and Thomas Docherty's *On Modern Authority*. While all these attempts agree in locating a radical shift in the construction of both male and female subjectivity in north-west Europe in this period, they characterize the process in rather different ways. Despite their common concern with the realignment of identity around a reinscription of sexual difference, only Barker focuses on the specifically sexualized discourse of pornography which emerges in Europe in the middle of the seventeenth century. Conduct books, feminist and anti-feminist tracts, philosophical, poetic and theatrical discourses are all invoked as evidence by the new literary historians but the critical gaze has been resolutely averted from the obscene writings and graphic representations which are produced, often as translations or adaptations of continental texts, for the first time in England in significant numbers from the 1650s on.

This modern lack of interest seems curious given the prominence that analysis of pornography has recently assumed in academic feminist discourse: studies such as Susanne Kappeler's *The Pornography of Representation*, Day and Bloom's *Perspectives on Pornography*, and Jane Gallop's *Intersections* all represent scholarly interventions into a debate which now seems central to the feminist movement outside the academy as well as within its walls. The theoretical perspectives brought to bear on the subjects are various but post-Lacanian analyses of a visual regime governed by the voyeuristic scopophilia of the male gaze tend to dominate. Viewing pornography as a mode of representation, attempting to locate 'pornographic elements of our culture' rather than 'isolating a specific set of representations and calling them "pornographic"', feminist critics often deconstruct the opposition between high and low cultural products in order to extend their critique to canonical texts, uncovering an exploitative scopophilic logic in 'The Rape of the Lock' or *The White Hotel*.[5] With the exception of de Sade's work, however, very little material which has been traditionally defined as obscene has been discussed by critics interested in the historical construction of gendered identities. The value of such attention should, I think, be clear: whether one adopts Marcus's 'repressive hypothesis' about the development of sexuality or accepts the claim made by Foucault in *The History of Sexuality*, whereby the modern period is marked by a massive transformative production of sexual discourses, those materials in which the sexual is most overtly textualized deserve examination. Pornographic writings are not only an index or symptom of significant shifts in the constitution of the self but also presumably contribute to that process of change. If sexuality has a history, these texts form a crucial part of its archive: and a feminist engagement with them seems particularly important given the extent to which the work of historians of erotica such as Peter Wagner and Peter Webb often seems to be informed by an unreconstructed notion of a normative sexuality.

The dependence of much feminist analysis of pornography on psychoanalytic models can produce transhistorical and universalizing accounts of its ideological functions: and a totalized conception of the hegemony of western patriarchy can be subject to the same limitations. Thus, even a critic like Susanne Kappeler, who stresses the importance of cultural, political and economic contexts in the production and reception of representations, opens her critique of pornography by reading the murder and photographic framing of a black Namibian farm worker called Thomas Kasire as a classic Sadean scenario. The farmer and his friends took photographs of their victim as he died and Kappeler reads this as a classic instance of sadism:

For 'Thomas' – the 'boy' – put 'Justine' or 'Emmanuelle' or 'O' – the victim already designated by reduced identity, no family name. For 'farm' put 'chateau', retain the aristocratic patronym of its owner and you have the perfect scenario of Sadean libertinism, the classic paradigm of the genre.[6]

The effect of all these substitutions is disturbing; while taking Kappeler's point that the photographic framing of Kasire's suffering by his torturers was a crucial aspect of the violence enacted against him, the circumstances of the murder of a black farm worker in contemporary southern Africa have a cultural logic specific to that situation, which is erased by its use as an exemplary instance of 'Sadean libertinism'. The fixing of the feminine in 'the classic paradigm of the genre' is also problematic: pornographic writing is historically constructed like any other text and cannot really be adequately figured by a single paradigmatic scene – no paradigm is likely to be doing identical cultural work across several centuries and societies. Both Thomas Kasire (who may have been a SWAPO fighter) and European women – some at least of whom have actively resisted their assigned subject-positions – are here reduced to helplessness, repressing the extent to which *resistance* may have produced the spectacular reinscription of domination represented in *Justine* and the photographs which record the murder.

The possibilities of locating resistance to the imposition of traditional gendered identities within pornography have been argued for in several ways. First, as Gary Day suggests in 'Looking at Women', the fragmentation of the body in pornographic representation, the reduction of sexual encounters to mechanical processes in which both sexes share, tends to break down notions of a unified, self-identical body endowed with a 'natural' sexuality.[7] Second, Maggie Humm has argued that the orientation of much critical analysis around the male gaze erases the extent to which women's voices function within pornographic texts to disrupt or problematize the logic of their scenic dimension.[8] The third point concerns older pornography especially: in the early modern period, licentious and libertine writing was frequently tied to attacks on traditionally constituted notions of political and religious hierarchy and contributed to developing new notions of the individual in ways women writers in particular appear to have exploited.

The latter point is the one with which I wish to return to Barker's reading of Pepys's text. Barker assumes that in *L'Escolle des Filles*, as n Marvell's poem 'To His Coy Mistress', the woman is allotted 'the place of the body outside discourse, and therefore also outside the pertinent domain of legitimate subjecthood'.[9] However, like most pornographic texts written before the middle of the eighteenth century (when they tend to be replaced by autobiographical narration), *L'Escolle des Filles* is a dialogue between women; as Foxon remarks in his account, obscene writing in this period generally depends on the use of a 'loose woman's' voice.[10] The identification between prostitution and female writing and speaking is a commonplace of the period: Felicity Nussbaum cites a variety of instances of the topos in satire in *The Brink of All We Hate*. The anxiety about regulating female discourse, evident in 'popular' practices such as bridling scolds, as well as in the prohibitions against providing women with access to rhetoric is, as Patricia Parker and others have demonstrated, connected to a traditional masculine fear of mobile and public femininity which would threaten order and property:

> It was the public nature of rhetoric – taking women outside their proper 'province' or place – which disqualified them, in a long tradition from as ancient an authority of Aristotle's strictures that women were to be not only silent but identified with the property of the home and with the private sphere; with a private rather than a common place.
> . . . The clear link that would keep women from learning rhetoric as specifically public speech is the long association in which a 'public woman', and especially one who spoke in public, could only be called a whore.[11]

The latter part of the seventeenth century is, however, the period in which women assume a new prominence as writers across a wide range of genres but most spectacularly as playwrights and authors of novels. Recent accounts of two of the most famous of the female wits, Behn and Manley, have tended to suggest that they deliberately exploited the fetishized commodity status of the female performer or writer, capitalizing on the supposed handicap of a whorish identity either by constructing an alternative version of the self (one 'completely dependent on the necessity of multiple exchanges') or by producing an implicit critique of the masculinist spectatorial economy of the Restoration stage.[12] This is the point at which the current feminist critique of pornographic representation intersects with recent literary historical accounts of the institutional and discursive origins of the scopic regimes of modernity.

In a recent article on Behn's *The Rover*, W. Elin Diamond argues that the introduction of movable painted scenery and mechanical devices on the Restoration stage produced a dream-like, seductive, and commodity-intensive theatre with a new scopic economy and a new 'spectator-fetishist'.[13] The privileged object of this Restoration male gaze is the other primary novelty of the late seventeenth-century theatre, the actress. This analysis of the Restoration theatrical apparatus suggests the beginnings of that voyeuristic and fetishistic scopic regime whose current apotheosis is Hollywood cinema; an account which seems all the more convincing when one bears in mind that this newly illusionistic theatrical space framed with increasing frequency the violation of specifically female bodies during this period – Hume cites the conclusion of Settle's *The Conquest of China* where the stage is strewn with heaps of women's raped and murdered bodies – but equally exemplary is the climactic scene of Mary Pix's *Ibrahim*, where Morena, the hapless Lucretian victim of the despotic Sultan, clutches the bare blade of her rapist's scimitar only to have it drawn through her bloodied fingers.[14] The spectacular scenic and narrative exploitation of vulnerable female bodies in the theatre coincides with the sudden expansion in the writing and publication of pornography and, notwithstanding the apparent contrast between the public and private contexts of consumption, these phenomena would appear to be governed by the same cultural logic. As the bawd Creswel will remind her initiate in *The Whores Rhetorick*:

> I am against your reading Romances, where constancy in love is cryed up as a vertue and dying Lovers make up a great part in the Pageantry. The Modern Comedies are a Lecture much more adapted to the interest of my Scholar, for there you will find fraud and dissimulation called discretion and prudence: cuckolding Husbands, cheating Lovers, prudently styled Address and Wit. And for obscenity I recommend those pieces to you where you may be supplyed with a better stock than I can in Conscience expose in this my Rhetorick.[15]

The contemporary stage provides illustrative examples of the 'Theory' outlined in the 'Rhetorick'.

The logic linking the two discourses is in the first instance an exploitative one but both Diamond and Gallagher have suggested ways in which forms of scandalous writing could question, even as they reproduce, the terms of proper identity. The subversive implications of libertine writing by figures like Rochester have long been recognized but critics often read through the obscenity to uncover a veiled political or religious attack: the sexual vehicle is seen to be in the service of more serious seditious or heretical aims. To the extent that there was very little provision for or interest in the censorship and prosecution of specifically obscene as opposed to political or religiously subversive material until 1725, this is perhaps understandable.[16] But such readings still beg the question of why sexuality suddenly provided the privileged terrain for transgressive speculation of all kinds, as well as failing to account for the production of texts like *The Whores Rhetorick*, which in its Englished form, is rather resistant to allegorical interpretation. The standard accounts of early libertine literature provided by David Foxon and Roger Thompson both agree in relating the 'birth' of pornography – which they believe can be dated with surprising exactitude from the Italian publication of *The Wandering Whore* in 1642 – to the Counter-Reformation in Europe and Puritanism in England.[17] (Their accounts thus both bear out Marcus's post-Freudian repressive hypothesis, whereby a newly introspective, self-disciplining subject sublimates his specifically sexual drives in the service of other labours.)

Much early modern pornographic writing shares the Lockean assumption that the body and sensate experience provide the fundamental grounds of identity: a connection underscored by the readiness with which contemporary medical, biological and even horticultural discourses were exploited by writers of erotica in the early eighteenth century.[18] While this exorbitation of the corporeal and a concomitantly sexualized notion of the self have been regarded as damaging to women's ability to be defined and to define themselves as rational social agents, it has also been argued that forms of identity produced 'experimentally', provisionally and contingently, found in femininity (the traditional site of bodily and personal instability) a privileged model for a newly mobile notion of the self.[19] The cultural significance of the prostitute, the 'movable harlot' of Proverbs 6, thus perhaps stems from the corporeal, self-divided subject. Behn and Manley may have deliberately and critically capitalized on this capacity in their own writing: *The Whores Rhetorick* and *Erotopolis* attempt pleasurably

and profitably to contain the threat to a unified masculine identity presented by transgressive feminine sexuality but are in fact
incapable of achieving these aims. By the time Stretzer publishes
A New Description of Merryland in 1740, however, the judiciary,
the new sciences and the Society for the Reformation of Manners
have all been active in policing the new sexualized subject and this
text's mapping of the female body is concomitantly closed and
constraining.

Originally published in Italy in 1642, *The Whores Rhetorick* was
translated into English and published in London in 1683. Along
with *L'Escolle des Filles, Venus in the Cloister*, and Chorier's *Satyra
sotadica* it circulated widely among affluent and literate Englishmen.
In Italian the text functioned as a satire on rhetoric, on the Jesuits and
on religion but in its much adapted English form, despite its lack
of bawdy or obscene material, it was regarded and consumed as an
erotic text and prosecuted as such in 1683, although it reappeared the
following year in the Term Catalogue and was not again censored.
Its consistent focus is precisely the delineation of the prostitute's
modus vivendi and *operandi*. An institutional dialogue for initiates
into the trade, it parodies the forms of the conduct book.

The Whores Rhetorick has two dedicatory epistles: the first,
addressed 'To the Most Famous University of London Courtezans',
adopts a tone of mock-chivalric irony, setting up and undercutting
the equivalence the writer establishes between himself as Author
and his 'Artist' subjects, and his function as advertiser of their
wares, and theirs as 'Trading Ladies'. Figuring himself as the
'meanest poetical Dawber' of the stage, he suggests an adequate
representation of his subjects would require more than accurate
imitation by the qualities 'borrowed' through bodily union with
them. The uneasy movements between authorial identity with
and separation from his subjects are barely managed by the ironic
posture, a mocking invocation of the familiar trope by which the
writer's skill is attributed to the innate brilliance of his topic and
suggests that even the ventriloquism of whorish speech disturbs
masculine self-possession.

The second, 'Epistle to the Reader', opens in a tone of serious
self-assurance and proceeds to justify the text (in terms Pepys
would have recognized) as a prophylactic, an exposure of 'all
the tricks, all the finesses' of those detestable 'Monsters, who
can destroy miserable man with a single embrace'. But the high
moral ground claimed here is undercut by the writer's return to

the same analogy he drew in the 'Dedication' between his project and that of the whore:

> Who ever then would pretend with his Pen, to gratifie all Mankind; whoever would aspire to compose a Regal, adapted to every Man's palate . . . must be sure to have at all times these patterns of perfection before his Eyes, his lines must be drawn to the same perfection those others are in the Ladies face. (p. 17)

The writer is figured here as one who, like the prostitute, desires the desire of 'all Mankind' and must, like a Lady, construct his comparisons accordingly. The later claims to moral purpose – 'you are at the same time instructed to detect and to avoid the cheat' – are justified by the invocation of parallels with potentially dangerous medical and pedagogical practices, but the initial familiar analogies between writing and dressing and writing and painting are most powerfully activated in the text which follows, where the processes by which feminine identity is constructed and sexual exchanges are managed provide the obsessive focus.

If the proper management of the woman's mouth, body, and household governed normative discourses of femininity in the seventeenth century, *The Whores Rhetorick* presents a nightmarish inversion of the values of silence, chastity and domesticity. The text consists of a series of exchanges between a well-known London bawd, Mother Creswel, now in an advanced and repulsive state of physical decay, and Dorothea, the daughter of a ruined royalist. Dorothea's poverty provides the occasion for her induction into the profession but she exhibits no doubt or ambivalence about her position, taking up the lessons with an alacrity her mentor finds slightly shocking. It all seems to come quite 'naturally' to the pupil. Mother Creswel teaches her pupil the importance of verbal dissembling, profitable 'corporeal eloquence' and the importance of maintaining a 'small convenient House of her own' with several small chambers where she might 'entertain at once several Lovers' – customers whom she should call 'Brother, another Unkle, a third Cousin' to create a feigned family. The purpose of Creswel's transgressive speech is to maximize Dorothea's capacity for misrepresentation as she commodifies her sole capital, her body. Arguing that Dorothea must avoid the essentially feminine capacity for love, a free giving of oneself into another's possession, Creswel emphasizes that 'The whore is not a woman', that she is 'a person dead in Law' and 'dead to all Laws' except those prescribed by her own interest. Freed from all passion and restriction except avarice, she will be able to maximize her powers of accumulation.

> M.C. For that, Daughter, I must tell you: a Whore is a Whore, but a Whore is not a Woman; as being obliged to relinquish all those frailties that render the Sex weak and contemptible. A Whore ought not to think of her own pleasure, but how to gratifie her Bedfellow in his sensitive desires: She must mind her interest not her sport; the Lovers sport, the ruine of his interest and the emptying of his Purse. The unthinking part of Women place off their worldly happiness in the centre of venereal Pastimes, and they are all Mahometans so far as to wish a continuance of them in the world to come; though all these things are enjoyed by Wolves, Bears, Cats, Dogs and Rats, in an equal, if not a larger measure than what we can pretend to. (pp. 144–5)

In accordance with this scheme, two sets of tropes govern the representation of the whore's activity: on the one hand she is figured as an orator (with subsidiary comparisons to lawyers, politicians, artists and players) and on the other as an economic agent, whether trader, shopkeeper, merchant – or, later, as a bawd, as an usurer or broker.

> With all Men without distinction of persons, you must study to be in your dissembling and cheating Talents crafty and cunning, in your delights graceful, and in your perswasions powerful: thus you will in some sort imitate the good Orator, and fulfil the practical Doctrines in your own Rhetorick. The memory which belongs properly to you, is not so much an immense capacity, qualified to receive and retain all objects represented to the exterior, and thence introduced to the general and interior sense; as an artificial ready remembrance of all points necessary in your own Trade, and the perswading power of your eloquence, which consists in timing your words and actions with a seasonable discretion, assigning every part of your art its proper place, and feeding your Lover with a real, or at least an imaginary pleasure. (pp. 164–5)

Both these sets of figures emphasize the manipulative power of the prostitute, participating in a myth of sexual self-control which Maggie Humm identifies as a means by which female sexuality can be restricted by being written as capital which can be measured and disposed of in a controlled fashion: an inversion of proper femininity, perhaps, but one which comfortably confirms another cultural imperative, that of capital accumulation.

While *The Whores Rhetorick* clearly participates in this myth, female sexuality and identity are very far from being contained completely by Creswel's emphatic insistence on the primary importance of 'interest'. It is not simply that the whore's repressed femininity is likely to return – as Creswel herself says, encapsulating a narrative amplified by Angellica's fate in *The Rover*:

> I was not then so wise as to contain myself within the bounds of a Rhetorick . . . I fell in love with a dissolute and faithless fellow (Ah Daughter! This is the accurst bane of our sex but especially of this vocation . . .). (p. 20)

The notion of a 'Rhetorick' which can bound or contain identity and action depends on an understanding of human nature as constructed and positional: the successful whore is not just a great merchant but an impersonator, one whose body is designed to be misread. The whore should not only 'Carry herself at all times with a superficial stateliness, to gain respect', 'in your Cloaths appear beyond all measure high and magnificent' but should disguise her face, her breath, and her body and find veils 'to cover every fault'. As Creswel sketches out a likely clientele from boys down from Oxbridge to the old and impotent romancers, different personae and lines of action are proposed. Unsurprisingly, Creswel dwells on the effects of veils and masquerade on the easily bemused and seduced male gaze:

> These obscene Images do produce marvellous effects towards the propagation of Love, they insinuate at every pore of the Eye an extravagant desire to gratifie the sensitive appetite. (p. 170)

> When she finds a Customer cool in his desires, and no great extravagance in the carnal appetite, she must raise his passion and warm his blood into a luxuriant heat by artificial incentives drawn in, all at the Window of a lascivious eye, and created by a gentler touch. (pp. 114–15)

Dissembling representations structure the scenes (sometimes involving third players) which the prostitute acts out in her own chambers:

M.C. She thought it expedient to carry the joque one story higher; ordering a flippant young Fellow of her acquaintance, to call at her Lodgings, when he knew the Heir was there, and to personate a Man of quality, and a passionate Servant of her Ladyship. Accordingly the Mock-Lover comes, and as he was mounting the Stairs, the Lady desired her Dear (who came a little before) to retire into the Closet, for that the Knight, who was coming up was a troublesome Servant of hers, whom for his sake, she was forced to hate. The Youth obeys, and the Lover enters. He was a person well qualified for such a piece of Service, being by name a Player, one that could not walk the Street, but in the same method he trod the Stage, and was still full of the Hero he there represented. (pp. 96–7)

The whore is not simply reducible to actor or playwright but instead seems an exemplary figure of a recently defined instability in a self understood not only as a property but as a sign. Creswel herself refers to one such theorist of self-division, Hobbes, who, as Christopher Pye and Diamond note, provided models of personhood which use theatrical metaphors to emphasize the split self: 'a person is the same that an *actor* is, both on stage and in common conversation.'[20] The prostitute is not just such an actor, however, but also, crucially, a reader:

Reading men is the great work of her life. As it is among Gentlemen, a main principle of policy and prudence, and even more necessary than understanding Books; so in a Whore it is not ornamental only but an essential part of her breeding and qualification. (p. 35)

This process of reading is defined as what

Mr Hobbs, Child, says well, that Wisdom is nothing but experience; so by consequence the Bawd must supplant all mankind in point of Wisdom, in as much as her experimental knowledge does exceed all others. She has read men more than any mortal has Books. (p. 85)

The prostitute's bodily learning, her experimental knowledge of men, provides the means by which as a social actor she can manage and profit from masculine desire. Though representing the whore's carnal knowledge, *The Whores Rhetorick* attempts to appropriate and demystify such learning, containing its presumed power by unveiling its mechanisms. But this textual pimping cannot finally bind the threats presented by such a constructed and theatrical mode of feminine identity, given its peculiarly suggestive relation to emerging terms of selfhood.

If *The Whores Rhetorick* plays out and tries to bind masculine anxieties over the development of newly mobile forms of identity strikingly figured in the person of the prostitute, erotic cartographies provide the most literal possible attempts to define and map female 'nature'. Denise Riley suggests the late seventeenth and eighteenth centuries saw an increasing sexualization of women's natures along with their 'deep implausibility as ethical and political actors'. In this scenario the soul of the woman shrinks and is made gender-specific, while vice swells in a body whose territorial powers are concurrently enlarged. For Riley,

> the particular vexation and spur of seventeenth-century feminism is the state of soul as it relates to the increasingly sexed self. If a woman – who is not known – becomes more and more assigned to the natural order, in which human custom merely follows instinct, then the indeterminant self which education might improve, suffers a trivialising contraction.[21]

Erotic cartographies appear to exemplify this process; in *Erotopolis* and in *A New Description of Merryland* women are not social actors but are reduced to their reproductive functions. The subject of these texts is woman *per se*, feminine nature identified with the sexed female body, represented in allegories which draw on developing topographical, medical and biological discourses. In contrast to earlier idealized cartographic identifications such as that established between Elizabeth I and her realm in the Ditchley portrait, where the privileged, unique body of the sovereign is elided with a specific territory, erotic cartographies construct an account of femininity as a unified natural phenomenon which negates cultural and social distinctions, differentiating solely on the basis of biological functions such as fertility. Construed as unknown territory, farm property and landscape, which require discovery, survey, enclosure, ownership, cultivation and representation, 'woman' does figure in these texts as Barker describes her – as a specifically sexed, emphatically natural 'sub-discursive, corporeal matter'.

The first erotic cartography was produced in 1684 and is generally attributed to Charles Cotton, a minor royalist poet best known for his part-authorship of *The Compleat Angler*. *Erotopolis* has a bifurcated structure: its first half consists of a parody of topographical accounts of exotic territory and the second, a narration of a nocturnal trip through London's stews. The first section figures Bettyland's physical peculiarities, using cartographic, geographical, agricultural, legal and aesthetic metaphors. The continent has no limits and this unsettling lack of boundaries is matched by other oddities, such as mountains which swell on an annual basis:

> It is of so large an Extent, that it spreads itself through all degrees whatsoever . . . The great river is overlook'd by a great mountain which (strange to tell at some season of the year) will swell at such a rate that it is admirable to behold it. . . .[22]

The soil is most peculiar and frightening of all:

> for if a man make a hole in some part of the mould, and put but an inch of his flesh in, it will raise such a flame in his body, as would make him think Hell to be upon Earth: to say truth, the nature of the Soyl is very strange, so that if a man but take a piece of it in his hand 'twill cause (as it were) an immediate Delirium and make a man fall flat upon his face upon the ground, if he have not a care, he may chance to lose a limb, swallowed up in the whirlpit, not without the Effusion of the choycest part of the blood. (p. 6)

The male as tiller of a female soil is an archaic trope, with the joke here turning on the literalization of the metaphor. However, the anxiety latent in masculine susceptibility to sexual desire is also readable in a depiction of Mother Earth as hellish, a 'whirlpit'.

There is scant description of Bettyland's religious and political institutions but the legal arrangements which govern property relations between her chief inhabitants, farmers or husbandmen, are dwelt on at length:

> Having this fair occasion it will not be amiss to take notice by what Tenures the husbandmen hold their Farms most usually in this Country, some therefore you must know hold in Tail special . . . All men must confess that a strict property in a Tail Special is a very good thing but considering the Inconveniences that do attend it, a general Tail may be esteem'd the better Tenure as being accompanied by greater Advantages, for it requires not half the fealty and homage which the other does. (pp. 19–21)

Tail-special is marriage; the tail-general refers to a woman who is common property.

> Others there are that hold by Knights Service in the Courtesy of Bettyland . . . and others there are that hold in Fee simple, a miserable sort of Swains . . . (pp. 22–3)

For all this plethora of regulation, however, ensuring exclusive enjoyment of one's farm is not easy:

> there is no farmer in Bettyland can enclose . . . his own ground all the year long by the custom of the Country. . . . there is hardly a Farm in Bettyland where there is not some ground that lies common all the year long. (pp. 28–9)

The geographical, agricultural and legal metaphors are supplemented by one other topos: that of landscape.

> The more delightful the more naked it lies, it makes the finest Landskip in the world . . . and many of your rich husbandmen will never be without them hanging at their bedsides, especially they that have no farms of their own, merely that they may seem to enjoy what they have not . . . I could wish these Customs were left off of hanging these Landskips by the husbandmen's bedsides, for the consequence thereof are very mischievous, seeing that it causes them to desire and covet one anothers Farms with that eagerness, as if they were in open hostility with the Tenth Commandment, so that where they cannot get the prospect itself, they will have a Landskip. (pp. 14–16)

In this passage woman figures as a frameable portion of territory (the 'prospect') whose representation (as 'landskip') is capable of arousing competitive and possessive masculine desire. This suggests the text participates in that process discussed by Carole Fabricant and Simon Pugh, where the gendering of the language of enclosure, improvements and display which governed the theory and practice of Augustan landscape gardening, suggests that the identification of an improved nature with femininity not only stems from a long georgic tradition but helped naturalize the process by which various elite groups consolidated their grasp on rural land through enclosure.[23] The manipulation of a feminized landscape for the pleasure of a specifically masculine owner/observer which Fabricant explores in the construction of gardens equipped with

Vales of Venus, Aegerian Grotts, Lady's Temples and Temples of Flora, and country house poems is exemplified by *Erotopolis*'s representation of Bettyland as a site to be painted, quarrelled over and legally divided.

It is suggestive that Cotton's other works include not just *The Compleat Angler* and *The Compleat Gamester* but *The Planters Manual*, a handbook of horticultural instruction and 'The Wonders of the Peak', a long poem whose half-horrified evocation of the monstrous mountains of the Peak District serves to highlight the beacon of civility provided by Chatsworth, the seat of the Duke of Devonshire. An impecunious and rusticated royalist, Cotton none the less participated in the tradition of an ideal of genteel rural retirement which increasingly valued the improvement of a 'Nature' which was frequently evoked in frightening feminine terms. The invocation of cartographic, legal and aesthetic discourses in *Erotopolis* suggests that feminine nature can be surveyed, commodified and quantified unproblematically, but in fact Bettyland proves somewhat recalcitrant. Not only are her borders indeterminable but the earth itself is unpredictable. 'The Wonders of the Peak', which participates in a late seventeenth-century tradition of hard pastoral, amplifies this negative identification between a repulsive landscape and repellent gender:

A Country so deform'd, the Traveller
Would swear those Parts Natures Pudenda were:
Like Warts and Wens, Hills on the one side swell
To all but Natives Inaccessible:
Th'other a blue scrofulous Scum defiles,
Flowing from th'Earth's impostumated Boyles.[24]

The narrator's horror rises to a climax when he encounters a landscape which is both vulvic and Medusan in its effects:

Betwixt a verdant Mountain's falling Flanks
And within bounds or easie swelling Banks
That hem the wonder in on either side
A formidable scrissure gapes so wide
Steep, black and full of horror, thost who dare
Looks down into the Chasm; and keeps his hair
From lifting off his head, either has none
Or form more modish curls cashiers his own. (ll. 496–503)

In contrast to this engulfing and potentially castrating landscape, Chatsworth, similarly feminized, is enclosed, presided over and ordered by masculine power:

> A Tower of Antick Model the Bridge-foot
> From the Peak-rabble does securely shut . . .
> Environed round with nature's shows, and ills,
> Black Heaths, wide Rocks, bleak Craggs and naked hills,
> And the whole prospect is so firm, and rude,
> Who is it, but must presently conclude
> That this is paradise which seated stands
> In midst of deserts and of barren sands. (ll. 1269–80)

The flattering account of Chatsworth closes with a final tribute to the source of its civility, its male owner. In both these texts it seems that an inherently feminine natural order requires a firm shaping masculine hand not only to be rendered attractive and productive but also tamed and healed. Woman, metonymically merged with nature, stands as a limitless, passive and potentially dangerous force, which can be controlled only through a battery of legal restrictions and cultivating arts. Her representation as a physical resource, whether debased or elevated, in turn requires and justifies the shaping and ordering activity of the masculine owner and cultivator.

Cotton's evocation of nature, whether in Derbyshire or Betty-land, as incipiently hellish and in need of restoration, stands in contrast to the celebration of the American Eden in the New World descriptions which serve as the primary source for *Erotopolis* and also for Stretzer's *A New Description of Merryland*, published by Curll in 1740. Accounts of the American colonies provide the basic structure for both the erotic cartographies, listing location, the nature of the climate, soil, commodities, cattle, towns, religion and form of government: generally written with propagandistic intentions, the tone is enthusiastic and the inventories of commodities long. As various commentators have noted, the sexualized nature of the narratives, which shape several of the descriptions, is also striking.[25] George Alsop in his *Character of the Province of Maryland* seeks to 'display her glory in such scenes of Wit/That those who read must fall in love with it',[26] thus acting as a kind of verbal pander for the colony, while John Hammond, author of *Leah and Rachel: or the Two Fruitful Sisters Virginia and Maryland*, casts himself in the role of lover even more explicitly. His account of Maryland opens as follows:

> Having for 19. yeare served *Virginia* the elder sister, I casting my eye on Mary-land the younger, grew in amoured of her beauty, resolving like Jacob when he had first served Leah, to begin a fresh service for Rachell . . .
>
> Twice hath she been deflowred by her own Inhabitants, stript, shorne and made deformed; yet such a naturall fertility and comeliness doth she retain that she cannot but be loved, but be pittied.[27]

The description of Maryland as an American Eden incestuously deformed stands in contrast to Cotton's nature, always already fallen, whether in Derbyshire or Bettyland, but the metaphorical structure of possessive display of a territorialized femininity is identical.

Stretzer's *Description of Merryland* achieved rapid popularity, going through at least ten editions and giving rise to various spinoffs; the text is more tightly organized than *Erotopolis* and much less anxious about its subject matter. In *Merryland* the uncertainty over the country's location and dimension simply gives rise to a boastful narratorial joking about the expansion of the female parts with age and the continuing 'great perfection' of his own 'proper instruments' of measurement: it is, he claims, undamaged by 'time and frequent use'. Although there is a chapter devoted to Merryland's 'Several Tenures', the topos is not nearly as dominant as in *Erotopolis*; instead, medical and biological discourses (signalled by the dedication to Cheyne, author of the recently published *Essay on Regimen* and theorist of sensibility) provide the primary vehicles of metaphor. Merryland's heat is not as terrible as Bettyland's because one can now wear protective clothing:

> of which they have a sort which is very commodious and, peculiarly adapted to this country: [being] made of an extraordinary fine thin substance, and contrived to be all of one piece, and without a seam.[28]

The description of Merryland works its conceit relentlessly, depicting the female reproductive system in detail, along with menstruation and pregnancy. As in *Erotopolis*, however, the material on the religion, customs and government of the country is sparse in comparison with the evocation of physical features: 'No part of Christendom may truly be said to be less religious than this' (p. 142). The language, 'very sweet and emphatick', is little needed due to the inhabitants' great art in 'communicating their sentiments very plainly by their Eyes and Actions': if not entirely 'sub-discursive', a society under 'Female Government' is none the less well served it seems by body language only.

The *Description of Merryland* culminates in a chapter purporting to describe its 'Harbours, Bays, Creeks, Sands, Rocks and Other Dangerous Places', and providing for the 'safe direction for Strangers steering into Merryland'. Although the reader has already taken imaginative possession of the interior of the territory, the text closes by describing a range of approaches and modes of entering (via 'that part of the continent called Lips; along shore to the Bubby-Mountains or . . . boldly up the Straights of Tibia'). The *Description of Merryland* concludes with a panegyric to the pleasures of masculine enjoyment in the female body, represented as an undefended territory, filled with pleasure-loving, irreligious inhabitants.

This conclusion stands in contrast to Cotton's: in the latter part of *Erotopolis*, the farmers of Bettyland are abruptly joined by a welter of shepherdesses, sirens and decoy ducks as the narrative switches to focus on a tour through London's stews. The primary pleasures of this section of the text are overtly voyeuristic: the most striking scene places the narrator and his companion peeping behind a door and watching an old farmer of Bettyland now 'unfit for action' watch a 'young syren':

In a short while betaking herself to the Chimny, she stood bolt upright, and having the signal given (as they draw the Curtain up from before the Scenes of a Theatre) she drew the Curtain gently up that was before it and showed the Prospect of a very fair Garden-plot of Maiden-hair . . . The Fields about were imbroidered over with white Daisies and yellow pissabeds; but the old Farmer, who neither cared for Innocency, and had been sufficiently plagued with Jealousie, and consequently could endure neither of these colours, caused her to daub her hand with the Soot of the Chimny, to disfigure the whole prospect of those more pleasant colours, not permitting her to leave anything but what was black within the horizon of his View. Then he pleased his aged Eyes with beholding the whole, commending what he thought fit to be commended, and reading a lecture of Bettyland Husbandry, over every part, till satiated with the Prospect and his Discourse, the Curtain was again let down and the Syren sent away. (pp. 98–100)

The theatrical nature of the scene, in which, for a fee, the framed but naked female body is painted to become a dusky statue and hence a pleasing prospect for the viewer and reader, stands in contrast to but renders transparent the logic of masculine desire which governs the rest of the text. Here the voyeuristic sexual exchange – which involves the re-presentation of the female body to produce a purely scopic and perverse masculine pleasure is not naturalized in any way – it is cash for an image. The process by which the natural woman is transformed into a fetish reveals her as a social actor in a relation of exchange – she receives payment for painting and displaying herself. The latter half of *Erotopolis* is full of such designing sirens, who, like the subjects of Pope's *Epistle to a Lady*, 'appear in all colours like chameleons, in all shapes like She-Proteus'; called 'Besmeared ones, Varnish-daubers, Plaisteres and Red-painters, with whom when a man converses, he talks to that which is not', they draw themselves and become 'statues of their own making'. The revulsion from women whose unnaturalness is marked by their attempt actively to control their own self-representation – a process conventionally figured by the use of 'paint' – is commonplace: what is interesting is its eruption in a text whose primary conceit works precisely to deny the possibility of female agency in the construction of gendered identities and the processes of sexual exchange.

Erotopolis's failure to restrict the definitions of female nature to the grounds of bodily identity as the extended allegorical structure gives way to narrative may signal that modes of feminine subjectivity, hardening around new, more domestic and maternal ideals in the mid-eighteenth century, were rather more fluid in the late Restoration. Stretzer's *Merryland* is a much more closed text than Cotton's: the reader's progress depends upon his or her ability to read the Latinate anagrams which teasingly signal his location. Unveiling each female part confirms a masculine position of mastery and possession, not just as a voyaging voyeur but as a reader, possessed of a variety of knowledges and power. There is no shift into a narrative where, within a specific time and place, women must be confronted as social actors: the allegorical structure which, in addition to the voyaging tropes, mobilizes these developing physiological discourses which ground identity in biology, remains closed and intact. Constructed across a plethora of rhetorics, 'woman' here figures penetrable and contained, no longer *terra incognita* but mapped, measured and known. Only the elaboration of the figurative structure necessary to perform this work of containment, which must continually draw attention to its own constructedness, the artificiality of its central device, perhaps casts doubt on the transparency of that natural ordering of sexuality which is its project to confirm.

NOTES

(Place of publication for works printed before 1800 is London unless otherwise stated.)

1 Francis Barker, *The Tremulous Private Body*, London and New York, Methuen, 1984, p. 3.

2 ibid., p. 93.

3 Michel Foucault, *The History of Sexuality Volume 1: An Introduction*, trans. Robert Hurley, Harmondsworth, Penguin, 1984, p. 5.

4 Steven Marcus, *The Other Victorians: A Study of Sexuality and Pornography in Mid-Nineteenth-Century England*, New York, Median, 1964, p. 282.

5 Cf. especially Susanne Kappeler, *The Pornography of Representation*, Cambridge, Polity, 1986.

6 ibid., p. 7.

7 Gary Day, 'Looking at Women: Notes Towards a Theory of Porn', in Gary Day and Clive Bloom (eds), *Perspectives on Pornography: Sexuality in Film and Literature*, London, Macmillan, 1988, pp. 83–100.

8 Maggie Humm, 'Is the Gaze Feminist? Pornography, Film and Feminism', in Day and Bloom, pp. 69–82.

9 Barker, p. 100.

10 David Foxon, *Libertine Literature in England 1660–1745*, New York, University Books, 1965, p. 49.

11 Patricia Parker, *Literary Fat Ladies: Rhetoric, Gender, Property*, London, Methuen, 1987, p. 104. For another instance of the interactions between rhetoric and gender, see Lorna Hutson's chapter in this volume.

12 Cf. especially Catherine Gallagher, 'Who was that Masked Woman? The Prostitute and the Playwright in the Comedies of Aphra Behn', *Women's Studies*, 1988, vol. 15, pp. 23–42, and Elin Diamond, '*Gestus* and Signature in Aphra Behn's *The Rover*', *English Literary History*, 1989, vol. 56, pp. 519–41.

13 Diamond, pp. 521–3. Diamond points to the crucial work done by feminist film theorists such as Laura Mulvey in developing an analysis of the male gaze in the context of narrative cinema. Another useful, more historicist, perspective is provided by the essays edited by Hal Foster, *Vision and Visuality*, Seattle, Bay Press, 1988.

14 R.D. Hume, *The Development of English Drama in the Late Seventeenth Century*, Oxford, Clarendon, 1976, pp. 201–2.

15 F. Pallavicino, *The Whores Rhetorick Calculated to the Meridian of London and Conformed to the Rules of Art in Two Dialogues*, 1683, pp. 50–1. Further citations are from this edition by page number in the text.

16 The fullest discussion of the process by which censorship was extended to obscenity can be found in Donald Thomas, *A Long Time Burning: The History of Literary Censorship in England*, London, Routledge & Kegan Paul, 1969; see also Foxon.

17 Foxon, pp. 48–51; and Roger Thompson, *Unfit for Modest Ears: A Study of Pornographic, Obscene and Bawdy Works Written or Published in England in the Second Half of the Seventeenth Century*, London, Macmillan, 1979.

18 Peter Wagner, *Eros Revived: Erotica of the Enlightenment in England and America*, London, Secker and Warburg, 1988, provides a fairly full descriptive account of such texts.

19 Cf. Gallagher, pp. 28–9. Gallagher suggests that Behn sacrifices the ideal of a totalized woman in order to create a different idea of identity, 'one complexly dependent on the necessity of multiple exchanges. She who is able to repeat the action of self-alienation an unlimited number of times is she who is there to regenerate, possess and sell a series of provisional, constructed identities.' My reading of *The Whores Rhetorick* is much indebted to this account.

20 Thomas Hobbes, *Leviathan*, ed. Michael Oakeshott, New York, Collins, 1968, p. 125, cited by Diamond.

21 Denise Riley, *'Am I That Name?': Feminism and the Category of 'Women' in History*, London, Macmillan, 1988, p. 41.

22 Charles Cotton, *Erotopolis: or the Present State of Bettyland*, 1684, p. 14; further citations are by page number in the text.

23 See Simon Pugh, *Garden-Nature-Language*, Manchester, Manchester University Press, 1988, and Carole Fabricant, 'Binding and Dressing Nature's Loose Tresses: The Ideology of Augustan Landscape Design', *Studies in Eighteenth Century Culture*, 1979, vol. 8, pp. 109–35. My discussion is also dependent upon Parker, ch. 7, pp. 126–54.

24 Charles Cotton, 'The Wonders of the Peak', in J. Buxton (ed.), *The Poems of Charles Cotton*, London, Routledge & Kegan Paul, 1958, 11. 8–13; further citations are by line number in the text.

25 See Annette Kolodny, *The Lay of the Land: Metaphor as Experience and History in American Life and Letters*, Chapel Hill, University of North Carolina Press, 1975, and W. Franklin, *Discoverers, Explorers, Settlers: The Diligent Writers of Early America*, Chicago and London, Chicago University Press, 1979.

26 G. Alsop, *A Character of the Province of Maryland*, 1666, pp. 14–15.

27 John Hammond, *Leah and Rachel: or the Two Fruitful Sisters Virginia and Maryland*, in C.C. Hall (ed.), *Narratives of Early Maryland 1633–1684*, New York, Scribner's, 1910, pp. 281–304.

28 T. Stretzer, *A New Description of Merryland. Containing a Topographical, Geographical and Natural History of that Country*, 1740.

8

MANL(E)Y FORMS: SEX AND THE FEMALE SATIRIST

Rosalind Ballaster

In an autobiographical fiction published in 1714 and entitled *The Adventures of Rivella* the Tory propagandist, Delarivier Manley, provides her readers with a significant interchange on the subject of the propriety of women taking up the satiric pen. The fictional narrator of Rivella/Delarivier's life, one Sir Charles Lovemore, who claims to have been a close friend of his subject throughout her career, attempts to persuade her against indulging in 'party' fiction, capitalizing on her fears following the experience of imprisonment and trial for the publication of an incendiary work.[1] Lovemore reports that:

> when I would argue with her the Folly of a Woman's disobliging any one Party, by a Pen equally qualified to divert all, she agreed my Reflection was just, and promis'd not to repeat her Fault, provided the World wou'd have the Goodness to forget those she had already committed, and that henceforward her Business should be to write of Pleasure and Entertainment only, wherein Party should no longer mingle. . . . She now agrees with me, that Politicks is not the Business of a Woman, especially of one that can so well delight and entertain her Readers with more gentle pleasing Theams.[2]

By 1714, with Queen Anne dead and Whig hegemony virtually inevitable upon Hanoverian succession, Manley may have felt it necessary to abjure her history of enthusiastic propagandistic activity on the part of the Tory Party. In fact, her claim to have turned to writing only of 'Pleasure and Entertainment' following her imprisonment and trial is itself a piece of faction-making, since she went on to produce a sequel to the *New Atalantis* under the title of *Memoirs of Europe* (volumes one and two published in 1710), as well as a series of political pamphlets in collaboration with Robert Harley's leading Tory propagandist of the period, Jonathan Swift.

In *Rivella*, Manley consistently parodies the prejudice of the masculinist critic (Lovemore) that 'Politicks is not the Business of a Woman' and his attempts to 'sell' the woman writer to her readers as an erotic connoisseur rather than a political commentator. Lovemore's blindness lies in his inability to understand that the woman satirist might in fact mediate between and transform both sides of the critical opposition femininity/politics which structures his thinking. She might be peculiarly well positioned both to feminize politics and politicize femininity. Like Lovemore himself most critics and theorists of eighteenth-century satire have been unwilling to concede the possibility of a female satire. Then, as now, satire is understood to be a masculine form, written by men for men (Swift, Pope, Defoe) and restricted to the fields of poetry and political journalism, with the honourable exceptions of Jonathan Swift's *A Tale of a Tub* (1704) and *Gulliver's Travels* (1726).[3]

Feminist critics, when they have turned their attention to satire, have tended to focus on its structuring misogyny in order to explore the way in which gender opposition is employed as a means of representing political conflict.[4] Thus, Felicity Nussbaum, in her ground-breaking book *The Brink of All We Hate*, argues that:

> Satire . . . helps men to survive their fears, to remain potent when threatened with impotence, both real and imagined. The formalized ritual of the anti-feminist satire within the tradition reassures the threatened male minority. The myth of satires against women includes the myth that women create chaos, and the imposition of form (satire) on formlessness provides meaning and rationality when the fear of meaninglessness and insanity arises.[5]

The chaotic, nature-inverting figure of Dulness in Pope's *Dunciad* and that of Swift's beautiful Celia whose charm is broken when she is revealed to excrete and decay like all other mortals are figures for perceived social decay and political corruption. Pope and Swift offer a vision of a symbolic order that, through the metaphor of feminization, is revealed to be on the brink of dissolution, only preserved by the heroic maintenance of an incorruptible masculine self on the part of the isolated male satirist. Domna Stanton in her discussion of the satiric myth of the 'précieuse' in seventeenth-century French literature points to the neurotic quality of masculine identity construction in satire, achieved through the creation and subsequent debunking of an image of phallic female power. The corpus of satire against the figure of the 'précieuse', the pretentiously 'learned' lady or Amazonian warrior of the French salon and Fronde wars, emerges, Stanton suggests:

> as a fiction which, within particular bounds of intelligibility and representibility (seventeenth-century concepts of discourse and literarity that determine the specific re-writings of the satiric genre) creates a substitute (the précieuse) for the displaced articulation of anxiety about women aroused in man, qua male writer. This anxiety, which is caused by the (dream) thought of losing the primary female love object, a metonym for the demise of the phallic order, is overcome by cathecting the superego (the Name-of-the-Father) and reducing the feared female to the status of harmless child, degrading her through the hostility of satires.[6]

These formulations of the workings of satire would suggest that the only position available to the female writer in satire is as a satirist of the satirist, an exposer of his use of 'woman' as metaphoric substitute for his own sense of loss of phallic primacy. This is a strategy that we can see at work in Manley's texts, most clearly in her creation of male fictional narrators who, like Lovemore, reveal more about their own anxieties in narrating their histories of 'dangerous' women than they do about their supposed subject. The Count de St Gironne, one of the few entirely fictional characters in Manley's *roman-à-clef, Memoirs of Europe*, embarks upon an extraordinarily virulent misogynist attack on women as the conclusion to his tale of the sufferings of Isabella (Elizabeth Somers) when her lover, Alarick (Philip Königsmarck), murders her husband. Gironne adopts the conventional logic of the male satirist, that woman/Eve contaminates or corrupts man/Adam by her fleshly presence, and man's response can be only to turn woman's ploys and artifices back upon her:

> they [women] have set us the pattern, but Man has prov'd so excellent an Imitator as to refine upon the Invention, and now we may pretend even to out-do 'em at their own Weapon: They may thank themselves for giving us a sample of their Artifice.[7]

In the light of the fact that Gironne's heroine, Isabella, is revealed in the course of the story to be almost wholly innocent, we cannot, I think, read Manley's representation of his misogyny as anything but an ironic sideswipe at her male contemporaries in the field of satire. However, Manley's literary ambitions went beyond simply exposing the tedious deployment of misogyny as a vehicle for political critique in the work of the male satirist. She, quite self-consciously I would suggest, set out to develop and 'authorize' a position for the female satirist other than that of meta-satirist, to turn the masculine into the 'manley' form, in particular through presenting the *roman-à-clef* or 'scandal chronicle' as a peculiarly feminine form of satire.

The neglect of Manley's scandal fiction in accounts of early eighteenth-century satire and, more generally, of an attention to the use of gender opposition in the construction of the satiric text (at least in conventional literary criticism) seems especially remarkable given the fact that in English political life of the first two decades of the eighteenth century the question of the efficacy of female power was particularly significant. Although her sister Mary had shared the government of England with her husband, William, Anne ruled alone and her female favourites were reputed to have more influence upon her than her husband. From Anne's accession in 1702 to 1709, Sarah Churchill, Duchess of Marlborough, more passionate in the Whig cause than her own husband, was the single most important figure in the Queen's government, and she was succeeded by another woman, albeit a Tory, Abigail Masham. The influence of these women may have been exaggerated but a government in which both a female ruler and her female favourites took an active part in public political life (Sarah Churchill even campaigned at St Albans in the 1705 general election despite the fact that as a woman she had no personal franchise) was unprecedented.[8] Anne's uncle, Charles II, had of course been notorious for his extra-marital sexual liaisons and his long-term mistress Barbara Villiers, Duchess of Cleveland (at one point patroness to Delarivier Manley herself and an ex-mistress of Sarah Churchill's husband) had been rumoured to exercise considerable influence, but never to the extent and with the autonomy of a Sarah Churchill. Indeed, in her first piece of scandal fiction, *The Secret History of Queen Zarah and the Zarazians* (1705), Manley explained English resentment of Sarah Churchill's dominance on precisely the grounds that they 'wou'd not bear to think of being rid with a *Side-Saddle*, having had their Backs gall'd so much in the Female Reign of *Rolando* [Charles II]'.[9] Manley was only one of many Tory propagandists and pamphleteers who attacked Sarah Churchill as 'the Phoenix of a Qu--n'.[10] A particularly influential pamphlet entitled *An Account of a Dream at Harwich. In a Letter to a Member of Parliament about the Camisars* and dated 21 September 1708 depicts Anne as a saintly 'guardian angel' by whose side stands Sarah, given 'permission for a determined time to fix her seat, with audacious impudence, hard by the angel, and with her darkness to obscure its light, intercepting every good influence'.[11]

Party politics in the early eighteenth century were, then, already anything but an exclusively masculine preserve. However, satire itself seems to have been viewed as a masculine prerogative. Dryden's essay, 'A Discourse Concerning the Original and Progress of Satire' (first published in 1693), was the formative statement for most satirists of the early eighteenth century, including Manley, although its attention is largely focused on verse, rather than prose, satire.[12] The 'Discourse Concerning Satire' famously divided satire into two main types, developed from two different etymological roots, and modelled upon the work of the two major classical satirists, Horace and Juvenal. Dryden determines that the proper etymological root of the term 'satire' is the Latin word '*satura*', signifying a mixture or combination as opposed to the Latin word '*satyrus*', a 'rural god, made up betwixt a man and a goat'.[13] Dryden goes on to identify Horace with the former definition and Juvenal with the latter, thus cementing the operative distinction between 'smiling' and 'savage' satire in early eighteenth-century concepts of the genre.

Dryden recognizes that Juvenal and Horace faced very different historical conditions for the production and reception of their satire. The privileged position of gentleman courtier which Horace occupied was unavailable to the exile, Juvenal. However, in making an aesthetic judgement of their respective merits, Dryden turns to sexual metaphor to give Juvenal the laurel:

> [Horace] may ravish other men; but I am too stupid and insensible to be tickled. . . . His urbanity, that is, his good manners, are to be commended, but his wit is faint; and his salt, if I may dare to say so, almost insipid. Juvenal is of a more vigorous and masculine wit; he gives me as much pleasure as I can bear; he fully satisfies my expectation; he treats his

subject home: his spleen is raised, and he raises mine: I have
the pleasure of concernment in all he says; he drives his reader
along with him; and when he is at the end of his way I would
willingly stop with him. If he went another stage, it would
be too far; it would make a journey of a progress, and turn
delight into fatigue.[14]

The foppish, emasculated gentleman lazily tickling his reader/lover
into laughing submission is no match for the consummate sexual
artistry of the angry misanthropist, whose powerful thrusts rapidly
bring the reader/lover to full satisfaction.

This conflict between urbanity and anger as modes of satiric
effect is replayed in the different political and aesthetic perspectives
of Swift and Addison and Steele, major rivals in the periodical press
from 1710 onwards. In the early decades of the eighteenth century
Addison and Steele became the major advocates for Horatian
smiling satire. A month before the publication of the second
volume of Manley's *Memoirs of Europe*, we find Isaac Bickerstaff
pontificating in the *Tatler* (no. 242, Thursday 26 October 1710) on
the most desirable qualities in a satirist, concluding:

> that Good-Nature was an essential Quality in a Satyrist. . . .
> Good-Nature produces a Disdain of all Baseness, Vice and
> Folly, which prompts them to express themselves with Smart-
> ness against the Errors of Men, without Bitterness towards
> their Persons.[15]

In direct opposition to this advocacy of smiling satire, Swift in
his *A Tale of a Tub* satirized concern for the individual reputation,
pointing out that a depersonalized criticism of contemporary ills
lets everybody off the hook. Such generalized satire, he writes, is
'but a *Ball* bandied to and fro, and every Man carries a *Racket* about
him to strike it from himself among the rest of the Company',
while the satirist who dares to name names 'must expect to be
imprisoned for *Scandalum Magnatum*: to have Challenges sent him;
to be sued for *Defamation*; and to be *brought before the Bar of the
House*'.[16]

Manley not only employed the kind of personalized satire Swift
advocated but she enjoyed a close political and personal association
with the man himself. She collaborated with him on a number of
political pamphlets from 1711 to 1714 and took over the editorship
of his newspaper *The Examiner* from 14 June to 26 July in 1711,

frequently acting as his 'front (wo)man' for the expression of more extreme Tory positions with which he did not wish to be publicly associated.[17] Moreover, she was a personal as well as political enemy of the Whig Richard Steele, since the point in 1702 when Steele, then a close personal friend, had refused to lend her money in order to escape to the country from an unhappy love affair.[18] It is clear that Manley knew Dryden's essay, since in her dedication to the second part of the New Atalantis she validates her practice of naming satirical targets by citing the former's defence of Juvenal.[19] Given these factors, we might be led to expect that Manley would have joined forces with Swift in identifying herself as a Juvenalian satirist. However, in this same dedication she goes on to claim a different model than Juvenal, the 'more vigorous and masculine wit'. Capitalizing on Dryden's brief discussion of the satirist Varro in his 'Discourse Concerning Satire', she claims: 'The New Atalantis seems . . . to be written like Varonian Satyrs, on different Subjects, Tales, Stories and Characters of Invention, after the Manner of Lucian, who copy'd from Varro.'[20]

Manley here explicitly echoes Dryden's comment 'that as [Varro's] subjects were various, so most of them were tales or stories of his own invention'.[21] By taking Varro as her model, then, Manley furthers her (false) claim that her novels are simply fictions, invented stories, rather than taken from the lives of contemporary persons. Dryden rejects Varro as a satiric model because his verses, already 'mixed' in genre, were frequently 'mixed with prose', but it is precisely this formal 'mixing' that Manley finds attractive as a classical precedent for her prose satire.[22] Dryden further criticizes Varro for breaking the formal convention that satire should only treat one subject in many diverse ways, making all 'underplots . . . subservient to the chief fable'.[23] The New Atalantis's structure of a series of loosely connected but distinct plots, then, again conforms to Dryden's description of Varronian technique. Varro's writings, Dryden informs us, were imitations of the work of Menippus, but tempered the latter's 'impudence and filthiness'.[24] Like that of Menippus, Varro's satire has, he tells us, been lost to posterity, surviving only in fragments. It was Varro's imitator, Lucian, who revived the tradition. Here too, Manley finds a useful precedent. The bawdiness of her work might be interpreted as the trace of the lost Menippus in the writings of Lucian.

Beyond providing a useful classical model for her satire, the model of Varro offers Manley a way out of the sexualized dichotomy of Horace and Juvenal that Dryden's essay established. By citing Varro, Manley successfully conveys her critical difference from her contemporaries in satire, without placing herself outside of the politically over-determined debate on the form in general. Here, then, as I have argued elsewhere with regard to *Rivella*, Manley finds a means of resisting masculine impositions of 'form'.[25] Her satire, she suggests, is, like Varro's, a hybrid form, which falls on neither side of the savage and smiling dichotomy. In adopting the pseudo-origin of the lost Varro, Manley seems to point to a rejection of the two models of 'masculine' authority in satire offered in the exclusively male opposition of Horace and Juvenal, to her own manl(e)y femininity as that literary contradiction, the female satirist.

Although, through this brief reference to classical origin, Manley succeeds in positioning herself within the contemporary critical debate on satire, the invocation of Varro is, I would argue, nothing more than an audacious trope. A far more immediate and pervasive model lay far closer to home in the distinctly feminocentric, seventeenth-century French *roman-à-clef* or *'chronique scandaleuse'*, already experimented with by English women writers in the shape of Lady Mary Wroth's *Urania* (1621) and Aphra Behn's *Love-Letters from a Nobleman to his Sister* (1685–7).

The formal origins of the *'chronique scandaleuse'* are notoriously difficult to determine. Peter Wagner describes it as a 'hybrid form, with literary, semi-literary, and sub-literary branches offering many degrees of fact and fiction', while Ronald Paulson concludes that '[a]t its best, [it] represents another form of anti-romance, a conscious effort to attain to the real in reaction to romance'.[26] Unlike the romance and the *'nouvelle'*, two other French forms that were popularized in England in the late seventeenth century, the scandal chronicle had a directly political and often incendiary purpose, and its authors display an attendant wariness with regard to their claims to veracity, in order to avoid legal reprisals or ostracism from the court.[27] Roger de Rabutin, Count de Bussy's *Histoire Amoureuse des Gaules* (1665) became the model for many scandal fictions in France and Britain, while his experiences as a result of its publication also acted as a warning to later authors. Bussy-Rabutin was imprisoned for fifteen months in the Bastille as a punishment for ridiculing King Louis XIV in his representation of the king's affair with Louise la Vallière. Later editions of the novel were accompanied by a letter from Bussy-Rabutin to the Duke de St Agnan which constructed an elaborate history of the theft of the original manuscript by a lady friend of whom he was enamoured and the subsequent publication and corruption of the text at her hands.

Bussy-Rabutin presents himself in the role of an amateur wit whose private musings have fallen into the wrong hands, claiming that as 'true Events are never extraordinary enough to give any great Interest, [he] had recourse to Invention, which [he] thought would be more pleasing'.[28] His prefatory letter supposedly establishes that the entire text is an 'invention'. The truth about the text is its falsity. A further level of inversion is introduced in Bussy-Rabutin's claim that his lady friend edited the text to make it even more scandalous and 'as everybody is most pleas'd with the highest Satyr, the true Copies were thought flat, and suppress'd as false'.[29] Bussy-Rabutin employs a familiar romance convention to construct his own fiction of the text's invention. Fiction is more 'pleasing' than fact. Its readers are more willing to believe it because it fulfils their own fantasies (in this case the female reader's desire for power over the processes of history and the male world, or her desire to believe all other women 'false').

Bussy-Rabutin's scandalous history about the sexual duplicities of power-hungry court ladies is put into circulation by just such another ambitious lady who 'exploits' the author's amorous disposition in order to win power and favour. The two 'heroines' of the novel, Madame d'Olonne and Madame de Châtillon, manipulate and manoeuvre their way to wealth, power and influence by the discriminating surrender of their bodies to men of power. Bussy-Rabutin, meanwhile, presents himself as a 'ladies' man', maligned by the world due to his weakness for the female sex but still gallant in their cause. He even presents a fictionalized version of himself as further vindication. The Count de Bussy, we are told:

> was gallant with the Ladies, and very well bred, and his Familiarity with those that were his best Friends amongst them, never made him lose that Respect he ow'd them: This manner of Behaviour made the World believe he had a Passion for them; and it is certain there was a little in all his greatest Intimacies.[30]

Under the cloak of gallantry, Bussy-Rabutin introduces the familiar misogyny of the satiric tradition. As author, character and man of gallantry, he mediates between the gender dichotomies of his own text in which men figure as dupes and women as seductresses. Only

Bussy-Rabutin himself, it appears, can take up both positions, at one moment the victim of female artifice, at another, able to turn the trick back upon the trickster.

Misogyny was not, however, the only means of identifying the tangled power relations of scandal narratives with 'feminine' art. Marie Catherine La Motte, Baronne d'Aulnoy, introduced a different frame from that of the man of gallantry as a vehicle for the narration of intrigues in the European courts, that of the female gossip. D'Aulnoy built her reputation as a writer on her 'travel' narratives about Europe. Forced to leave the country following the discovery of a conspiracy with her mother to instigate a prosecution for treason against her husband in the late 1660s, she was finally allowed to return to France in recognition of her assistance to the French secret service in Europe.[31] On her return, she published a series of narratives detailing the intrigues of the aristocracy of the European courts.[32] D'Aulnoy frequently addresses herself to a female cousin in France, on whose behalf she acts as 'spy', underpinning her narratives throughout with a claim to absolute veracity. D'Aulnoy here conducts a double bluff, employing the travel writer's conventional claim to truth to conceal the political focus of her account. Having no 'interest' to protect in her wanderings beyond that of providing a faithful account to her correspondents, d'Aulnoy presents herself as uniquely positioned to provide an impartial account. In her preface to the reader that accompanies the *Travels into Spain*, d'Aulnoy insists:

> I write nothing but what I have seen, or heard from Persons
> of Unquestionable Credit; And therefore shall conclude with
> assuring you, That you have here no Novel, or Story, devised
> at pleasure; but an Exact and most True Account of what I met
> with in my Travels.[33]

Here d'Aulnoy's narrative persona reminds us of the figure of Astrea, goddess of justice, who opens Manley's *New Atalantis*. Astrea has come to earth in order to review its present state on behalf of the young prince she has made her charge. The childless Princess of Inverness (Queen Anne) currently reigns in Atalantis, and Astrea is rearing the next heir (the Elector of Hanover, later to be George I) for his succession. 'I will go to the Courts', she declares:

> where *Justice*, is profess'd, to view the Magistrate, who
> presumes to hold the Scales in my Name, to see how

remote their profession is from their Practice; thence to
the *Courts* and *Cabinets* of *Princes*, to mark their *Cabal* and
disingenuity, to the *Assemblies* and *Alcoves* of the Young and
Fair to discover their Disorders, and the height of their
Temptations, the better to teach my young *Prince* how to
avoid them, and accomplish him.[34]

Astrea plans to visit regal and legal courts, observing both the
public (political) and private (sexual) world of 'courtship'. The
name of Astrea must have been peculiarly resonant for early
eighteenth-century readers of both satire and prose fiction, recalling
the eponymous heroine of the popular French romance by D'Urfé,
L'Astrée (1607), the poetic persona of Manley's best-known female
predecessor in British scandal fiction, Aphra Behn, and Juvenal's
notorious satire on women in which the departure of Astrea,
goddess of justice, signals the corruption of the entire sex. In
the context of Anne's independent sovereignty (unlike her sister,
Anne never accorded her husband anything more than the status
of consort), it may also have evoked memories of the last great
female reign, that of Elizabeth I and that queen's use of Astrea as
icon and symbol for her government.

In Manley's novel, the figure of Astrea re-enacts the transformation of a disempowered observer's perspective into a written
'witness' who seeks to bring about social and political change in
order to influence the 'masculine' sphere. Astrea's ability to make
herself and her companions invisible so that they may gain access
to every particular of the world she seeks to observe and judge,
is, of course, significant in this context. The lack of social and
political recognition afforded to women is, in the sphere of art,
converted into an asset by the female satirist's watchful pen. The
enforced invisibility of women in the world of politics is now
presented through the figure of Astrea as a supernatural gift: 'we
will make us Garments of the ambient Air, and be invisible, or
otherways, as we shall see convenient'.[35] Yet d'Aulnoy's claim to
moral objectivity, the traveller free of political 'interest', adapted
and expanded upon in Manley's supernatural Astrea, precisely
conceals political intent. The fiction of the innocent dispatch of
diverting love stories to another woman cloaks the 'truth', that
d'Aulnoy was acting as a government spy. Thus, the naïveté of
her preface to her *Memoirs of the Court of England* must surely be
interpreted as disingenuous:

The Acquaintance of so many Persons of Distinction gave
me opportunity of knowing a thousand diverting Stories, of
which I have composed these *Memoirs*, and, according to your
Desire, put them into as regular a Method as I could.[36]

The trope of concealing political commentary behind the claim to
women's exchange of amatory tales, was to become an important
one in the scandal fiction of Delarivier Manley. Thus Rivella
challenges her prosecutors by enquiring 'Whether the Persons in
Power were ashamed to bring a Woman to her Trial for writing
a few amorous Trifles purely for her own Amusement . . . ?'[37]
In the *New Atalantis*, the dual functions of the narrator, gossip and
moral observer, are split into different personae. Astrea remains,
throughout the *New Atalantis*, an auditor of and commentator
upon, rather than narrator of, the numerous stories of seduction
and betrayal of innocent virgins at the hands of cynical (Whig)
politicians that populate Manley's text. She appears as a muse to fictions that are largely mediated and controlled by the more mundane
figures of the 'gossip' in the shape of the allegorical Intelligence and
the midwife in the shape of Mrs Nightwatch, neither of whom are
discriminating tale-tellers, taking 'Truth with [them] when [they]
can get her', as Intelligence puts it.[38] Where Astrea's garments are
'ambient Air', Intelligence's are 'all Hieroglyphicks'.[39] Here too,
the insight of women into political intrigue is privileged by virtue
of a special access to knowledge. Mrs Nightwatch points out that
the dissemination of scandal is part of her job:

> without this indirect *Liberty*, we [midwives] should be but
> ill Company to most of our Ladies, who love to be amused
> with the failings of others, and would not always give us
> so favourable and warm a Reception, if we had nothing of
> Scandal to entertain them with.[40]

It is interesting to note that it is only in her scandal fiction that
Manley works with an explicitly feminine narrative persona. Her
political journalism, although it adopts the technique of ironically
undermining an opposing political view by pretending to be its
advocate, never employs the kind of complex gender inversion and
female narrative voice that marks out her scandal fiction from the
Tory propaganda of her male contemporaries.[41]

D'Aulnoy's scandal narratives also bring us closer to the erotic-
bathetic clichés of scandal fiction in Britain in the late seventeenth and

early eighteenth centuries. Unlike Bussy-Rabutin, d'Aulnoy presents the male aristocrat as the duplicitous villain, seducing and corrupting innocent ladies. Women tend to be presented as innocent 'readers' of masculine fiction-making, unable to judge the verity of their lovers' claims to fidelity and passion. D'Aulnoy frequently provides an apologia for feminine 'weakness' in succumbing to the complexity of the male seducer's rhetoric. In contrast to her faithless seducers, d'Aulnoy undertakes to act as guardian of women's secrets. She has no qualms about naming her male characters, but she introduces the *Memoirs of the Court of England* with the explanation that she has:

> concealed some of the Ladies Names . . . while [she has] nam'd others, hoping that what [she] speak[s] in their Favour, will counterballance what the Malice of their Enemies should say against them.[42]

Women, it appears, are less guilty than men in affairs of sexual intrigue, and thus more deserving of protection. D'Aulnoy's early use of the seduction and betrayal motif of the '*histoire galante*' was to be developed by her female followers in Britain into a full-blown use of gender polarities to signify political conflict.[43]

The importance of d'Aulnoy's fictions to the development of Manley's distinctive form of scandal writing cannot be underestimated. First, they extrapolated a special position for the woman in relation to the ambiguities of fact and fiction so central to the formation of early prose narrative and second, they established politico-sexual intrigue as a narrative realm in which the woman writer had a privileged authority and interest. Both projects were to preoccupy Manley throughout her career in scandal. The influence of d'Aulnoy's work upon Manley's is nowhere better illustrated than in a close reading of their respective seduction scenes. Here Manley simultaneously adopts and subverts d'Aulnoy's amatory conventions, increasingly destabilizing the fact/fiction, nature/art dichotomies that d'Aulnoy habitually employs to structure her narratives.

The second letter of d'Aulnoy's *Travels into Spain* is largely taken up with the tragic love story of a hermit she meets at Mass. The hermit, Don Lewis, has retired from the world as penance for his responsibility in the death of his best friend's wife at the hands of her husband, the Marques de Barbaran. The Marques interrupts Don Lewis in his seduction of his wife, who is under the mistaken apprehension she is making love with her husband, and promptly murders her. The details of this seduction scene are replayed again and again in Manley's fiction:

> *She was in a Ground-Room which lookt into the Garden; all was fast and shut close, save a little Window, whereby he saw on her Bed this charming Creature: She was in a profound Sleep, half undrest; he had the time to discover such Beauties as still augmented the force of his Passion. He approacht so softly to her, that she did not awake: It was already some moments that he had lookt on her with all the Transports of a Man amazed, when seeing her naked Breasts, he could not forbear kissing them. She arose on a sudden; she had not her Eyes open; the Chamber was dark, and she could not have believ'd Don Lewis could have been so bold . . . [C]alling him several times,* her dear Marquess and Husband, *she tenderly embrac'd him.* [44]

Manley takes these ingredients, the garden, the sleeping woman, the woman's body exposed to the lover's amorous gaze, and subtly reorganizes them into configurations that disturb the dichotomy established here between innocent woman and duplicitous male. Her description of the seduction of Diana de Bedamore (Frances Scudamore) near the end of the second volume of the *New Atalantis* is one such example. Don Thomasio Rodrigues (Thomas, Earl of Coningsby) draws Diana into an illicit liaison when she and her husband go to stay at his country seat. This time it is the wife who catches the couple *in flagrante delicto*. Once again the woman is sleeping in a garden when the man comes upon her, although there is no case of mistaken identity here:

> It was the Evening of an excessive hot Day, she got into a shade of *Orange* Flowers and *Jessamine*, the Blossoms that were fallen cover'd all beneath with a profusion of Sweets. . . . *Diana*, full of the uneasiness of Mind that Love occasion'd threw her self under the pleasing Canopy, apprehensive of no *Acteon* to invade with forbidden Curiosity, her as *numerous perfect Beauties*, as had the *Goddess*. Supinely laid on that repose of Sweets, the dazling Lustre of her Bosom stood reveal'd, her polish'd Limbs all careless and extended, show'd the *Artful Work of Nature. Rodriguez* (who only pretended to depart, and had watch'd her every Motion) with softly treading Steps, stole close to the *unthinking* Fair, and throwing him at his length beside her, fix'd his Lips to hers, with so happy a

Celerity, that his Arm was round her to prevent her rising, and himself in possession of her lovely Mouth, before she either saw or heard his Approach.[45]

Innocence and sexual knowledge become radically confused in this scene. Diana is not only the victim of her lover's importunities but her own desires, 'lull'd by the enchanting Poison Love had diffus'd throughout her form'.[46] Her lack of resistance is excused by the author on the grounds of that 'beauteous Frailty' in women, the combined effects of '*Love* and *Nature*'.[47] The rhetoric of this passage situates Diana as passive victim, indeed presents her to the reader's and her lover's gaze by analogy with the garden that frames her as a thing of nature to be exploited and shaped by man.

J.J. Richetti has argued that the scandal novel dramatized two basic conflicts, social and sexual, embodied in two key figures, 'the innocent persecuted maiden and the aristocratic *libertin*-seducer'.[48] Manley's mythology of persecuted innocence, he suggests, provides its 'predominantly female audience' with 'an opportunity for extended erotic fantasy, even while it guarantees the moral innocence of the heroine and the readers who are invited to identify with her'.[49] Yet, as April London points out, Manley leaves the reader of either sex no other position to occupy in this scene than that of Acteon, 'the secret observer of a hidden scene'.[50] Indeed, this is precisely the position that the female audience within Manley's *New Atalantis*, the invisible Astrea and her companion and sometime guide Intelligence, do occupy in the text. The satirical observing eye, then, comes perilously close to the voyeuristic gaze.

Manley repeatedly calls our attention to this troubled scenario. What 'interest' does the woman spectator, and by extension the female audience, have in watching this spectacle of the man amorously contemplating the inviting female body? Her satirical attack upon her one time protectress, the Duchess of Cleveland, in the *New Atalantis* demonstrates her subversion of gender dichotomies in the seduction scene. In this scene, narrated by Intelligence to the goddesses Virtue and Astrea, the roles of victim and seducer are repeatedly exchanged and reversed between two men and a woman. Fortunatus (the Duke of Marlborough), in love with Jeanatin (Sarah Jennings, later Duchess of Marlborough) is seeking to disentangle himself from a love affair with the Duchesse de l'Inconstant (the Duchess of Cleveland), without losing her financial and political patronage. He enlists the help of his friend, Germanicus (Henry Jermyn, Duke of Dover) who is enamoured of the Duchess. Germanicus substitutes for Fortunatus at a rendezvous, having prearranged for Fortunatus to interrupt them. The Duchess, expecting to find Fortunatus awaiting her on a day bed in a closet adjoining her bathing room, is instead greeted with the sight of the young Germanicus, feigning sleep.

Germanicus carefully 'frames' himself for consumption by the lover's gaze. The characteristic ingredients of the seduction scene are all in place:

> the Weather violently hot, the *Umbrelloes* were let down from behind the Windows, the Sashes open, and the Jessimine that covered 'em blew in with a gentle Fragrancy; *Tuberoses* set in pretty *Gilt* and *China Posts*, were placed advantageously upon Stands, the Curtains of the Bed drawn back to the *Canopy*, made of yellow Velvet embroider'd with white *Bugles*, the Panels of the Chamber Looking-Glass, upon the Bed were strow'd with a lavish Profuseness, plenty of *Orange* and *Lemon Flowers*, and to compleat the Scene, the young *Germanicus* in a dress and posture not very decent to describe.[51]

The same elements which serve to undermine Diana's virtue in the scene discussed above, a warm evening, a bed of flowers, a mind already prepared for love, are here used to seduce the viewer (the Duchess), although, according to the logic of this well-tried tableau, she should occupy the role of sexual aggressor.

Courtly intrigue now becomes comic farce since Germanicus is both impersonating and observing the role of the assailed virgin, as the looking-glass panels imply:

> he had thrown himself upon the Bed, pretending to Sleep, with nothing on but his Shirt and Night-Gown, which he had so indecently dispos'd, that slumbring as he appear'd. His whole Person stood confess'd to the Eyes of the Amorous Dutchess, his Limbs were exactly form'd, his Skin shiningly white, and the Pleasure the Ladies graceful entrance gave him, diffus'd Joy and Desire throughout all his Form; his lovely Eyes seem'd to be clos'd, his Face turn'd on one side (to favour the Deceit) was obscur'd by the Lace depending from the *Pillows* on which he rested.[52]

Germanicus thus neatly parodies the love-struck virgin of amatory fiction, winning erotic pleasure by presenting himself as an aesthetic object, but retaining the position of 'knower' and 'seducer' in that he is party to the trick that is being played.

The Duchess occupies a paradoxical position in this scene. She is given the prerogative of the male seducer, of initiating the sexual act and objectifying the lover's body, but is also a victim, duped by sexual passion into surrender and manipulated by amatory codes she does not control. Like d'Aulnoy's Marquesa, she is betrayed through a case of mistaken identity, succumbing first to Germanicus under the apprehension that he is Fortunatus:

> the Dutchess . . . was so blinded by [her desires], that at first she did not perceive the Mistake, so that giving her Eyes, time to wander over Beauties so inviting, and which encreased her Flame; with an amorous Sigh, she gently threw her self on the Bed close to the desiring Youth; the Ribbon of his Shirt-Neck not tied, the Bosom . . . was open, upon which she fix'd her charming Mouth, impatient and finding that he did not awake, she rais'd her Head, and laid her Lips to that part of his Face that was reveal'd; The burning Lover thought it was now time to put an end to his pretended Sleep, he clasp'd her in his Arms, grasp'd her to his Bosom, her own Desires help'd the Deceit.[53]

In order to confirm her villainy, however, Manley has her willingly offer herself to Germanicus once she discovers the deceit. The Duchess is thus presented to us as both victim and aggressor, the lustful 'gazer' of amatory convention, but also 'blinded' by her desires.

Manley departs from d'Aulnoy, not only in her destabilization of the gender dichotomies of the seduction scene, but also in the means she employs to establish the 'truth' of her texts. Whereas d'Aulnoy transforms the information she gleaned as a spy for the French government into tales of sexual intrigue for the consumption of the French gentility after the fact, Manley transforms contemporary sexual scandal into political allegory with the purpose of making and breaking political careers, at moments of intense party political crisis.[54] *Queen Zarah* appeared in the same year that the Godolphin ministry and the Whig Party won the election, their popularity enhanced by Marlborough's victory at Blenheim. The *New Atalantis* was instrumental in the propaganda war that resulted in the Tories overthrowing the Whig ministry in August 1710.[55] Sarah Churchill was concerned enough about the *New Atalantis* to have her counsellor, Maynwaring, read it and report back to her on its likely effects. Maynwaring in two letters in October 1709, the same month in which Manley was taken into custody, tried to assuage her fears, but an undercurrent of concern is evident:

> such weak slanderers as these, do not so much defame their enemies as they hurt their friends . . . Yet I am afraid it will be very difficult quite to cure the mischief; for so long as the people will buy such books, there will always be vile printers ready to publish them; and low indigent writers will never be wanting for such a work.[56]

Once the Tory Party had gained the ministry, Manley produced her *Memoirs of Europe* (1710), a panegyric to the two major Tory leaders, Robert Harley and Lord Peterborough, at a point when her party was seeking to consolidate its supremacy at court.

Manley trod a delicate path in seeking to protect herself from legal retribution and ensure that her allegorical structure was not so obscure that her readers could not recognize her fiction as the party political propaganda it was. As a result, she produced elaborate 'frames' to her texts, providing her rediscovered manuscripts from distant cultures with such far-fetched geneses that her reader could not fail to look nearer to home for their actual source. *Queen Zarah* (1705), the *New Atalantis* (1709) and *Memoirs of Europe* (1710) are all accompanied by prefaces that frame the texts as translations from long obsolete books that the author has stumbled upon by circuitous routes.

The *Memoirs of Europe* see the height of Manley's complex feigning of the foreign source. In this two-volume novel, she sets about evolving a representation of early eighteenth-century political history by analogy with historical events in eighth-century Europe, ostensibly anthologized from a sixteenth-century French translation of a Latin manuscript by Eginardus discovered by the author in her father's library. Manley's extraordinary achievement with historical analogy in this text has largely been ignored by her twentieth-century critics. Richetti, for instance, dismisses her scandal fiction as a whole as 'formally nothing more than a series of anecdotes, some swollen to novella length and complexity', which only deserves attention because of its 'embarrassing popularity'.[57] In the author's preface to the *Memoirs of Europe*, Manley uses the trope of linguistic translation to signify her act of historical translation, claiming that '*The* French *is so obsolete, that* [she has] *bestow'd much*

Pains and Application in the Work.[58] The 'translation' of content, from eighth-century political history to early eighteenth-century scandal, is encoded in the claim to translate language, obsolete French into contemporary English.

Manley offers her readers 'facts' (an account of eighth-century European politics, the history of an imagined island called Atalantis) which are in reality fictions created by the author feigning the role of translator. In turn, these fictions point to a different set of 'facts', contemporary political and sexual scandal, disclosing the supposed 'truth' of Whig degeneracy and corruption. Finally, of course, these 'facts' are themselves 'fictions', in that the stories she tells of Whig politicians are largely invented or hearsay, deployed in the service of Tory ideology.

Both Lennard Davis and Michael McKeon have pointed out the importance of a certain fact/fiction ambiguity in the history of the early modern novel.[59] The development of an elaborate machinery for ascribing sources, accompanied by repeated claims for its verity, was, of course, by no means exclusive to Manley's writing. Jonathan Swift in his *A Tale of a Tub* (1704) neatly satirizes both practices. His bookseller, in an address to the reader, declares:

> *If I should go about to tell the Reader, by what Accident, I became Master of these Papers, it would, in this unbelieving Age, pass for little more than the Cant, or Jargon of the Trade. I, therefore, gladly spare both him and my self so unnecessary a Trouble.*[60]

If the bookseller provides a means of satirizing the convoluted histories of the passage of material from distant land to publishing house, the modern author of *A Tale of a Tub* is employed to poke fun at the meaningless function of the truth claim in fictional texts. In 'The Epistle Dedicatory to Prince Posterity', the modern author insists:

> I profess to *Your Highness*, in the Integrity of my Heart, that what I am going to say is literally true this Minute I am writing: What Revolutions may happen before it shall be ready for your Perusal, I can by no means warrant.[61]

As Swift's satire proves, Manley was, in many ways, simply following narrative convention in constructing elaborate frames simultaneously to conceal and signify political intent.

However, Manley's use of narrative frames is but one aspect of a wider project in her scandal novels, the attempt to figure the possibility of female political agency through the allegorical use of the seduction plot as substitute for the political plot. Manley's repetitious tales of seduction can be seen as a series of attempts to destabilize the structuring oppositions of contemporary ideology (fact versus fiction, love versus politics, feminine versus masculine) in order to privilege the woman as commentator upon and actor in the political realm.

Indeed, both Manley's self-representation in *Rivella* and production of female and male narrative personae in the *New Atalantis* and *Memoirs of Europe* imply that by virtue of her liminal position in relation to the state, to politics and to citizenship (precisely as a '*feme covert*'), the eighteenth-century educated woman was peculiarly well-equipped to act as a satirist. Denied political subjecthood by virtue of their lack of a vote (and at no point does Manley make a plea for such a provision), but with a special access to the 'private' intrigue behind the public action by virtue of their enclosure in reproductive and family life, women, these texts imply, could achieve that position of 'disinterest' so frequently invoked by male counterparts as the central quality of the satirist.[62] As a woman, Manley could not receive remuneration in the form of public office for her activities on behalf of the Tory party. Swift, encountering Manley at the home of Lord Peterborough, comments: 'she was soliciting him to get some pension or reward for her service in the cause, by writing her Atalantis, and prosecution &c. upon it. I seconded her, and hope they will do something for the poor woman.'[63] The only evidence we have of financial remuneration offered to Manley is a letter in her own hand written in 1714 and thanking Robert Harley, Earl of Oxford, for a gift of fifty pounds, secured before he was deprived of office.[64] But Manley, in her biography, turns what must have been a galling poverty unexperienced by the male writers who had achieved less in the Tory cause, into an advantage in the field of satire. In *Rivella* Lovemore tells us that as a result of her experience of prosecution for the *New Atalantis*:

> she was become Misanthrope, a perfect Timon, or Man-Hater; all the World was out of Humour with her, and she with all the World, more particularly a Faction who were busy to enslave their Sovereign, and overturn the Constitution; . . . she was proud of having more Courage than had any of our [i.e. the male] Sex, and of throwing the first Stone, which

might give a Hint for other Persons of more Capacity to examine the Defects, and Vices of some Men who took a Delight to impose upon the World by the Pretence of publick Good, whilst their true Design was only to advance and gratify themselves.[65]

By a clever sleight of hand Manley here converts the politically interested activities of the party satirist into moral authority, aesthetic independence, or 'disinterest' through claiming the peculiar 'privilege' of her gender. As in the case of her invocation of Varro as a satiric model, Manley, through invoking women's alienation from politics as the very grounds of their ability to critique it, succeeds in signifying both female difference and her credentials as satirist. If Swift and Pope sought to locate this aesthetic and moral autonomy in a utopian picture of country retirement for the male Tory, and Addison and Steele in the moneyed mercantile 'gentleman' classes of London, a vigorous tradition in narrative prose from Aphra Behn through Marie d'Aulnoy and Delarivier Manley to Samuel Richardson found it in the voice of the late seventeenth- and eighteenth-century woman.

NOTES

(Place of publication for works printed before 1800 is London unless otherwise stated.)

1 This is a reference to Manley's brief imprisonment in October 1709 and trial before the Queen's Bench in February 1710 following the publication of the second volume of the *New Atalantis*.

2 Delarivier Manley, *The Novels of Mary Delariviere Manley 1704–1714*, ed. Patricia Köster, 2 vols, Gainesville, FL, Scholars' Facsimiles and Reprints, 1971, vol. 2, pp. 852–3. The attribution of the name 'Mary' to Manley appears to have been a nineteenth-century creation, as Köster herself has demonstrated in her article, 'Delariviere Manley and the DNB', *Eighteenth-Century Life*, 1977, vol. 3, pp. 106–11. I concur with Fidelis Morgan's argument that Manley's first name was taken from the French, Delariviere, and anglicized by dropping the final 'e'. See Fidelis Morgan, *A Woman of No Character: An Autobiography of Mrs Manley*, London, Faber & Faber, 1986, p. 15. Manley most commonly signed herself 'Dela'.

3 See in particular Ian Jack, *Augustan Satire*, Oxford, Clarendon, 1966, and P.K. Elkin, *The Augustan Defence of Satire*, Oxford, Clarendon, 1973.

4 For the most impressive example of this focus in feminist criticism and a radical re-reading of the question of Swift's 'misogyny', see Ellen Pollak, *The Poetics of Sexual Myth: Gender and Ideology in the*

Verse of Swift and Pope, Chicago and London, University of Chicago Press, 1985.

5 Felicity Nussbaum, *The Brink of All We Hate: English Satires on Women 1660–1750*, Lexington, University of Kentucky Press, 1984, p. 20.

6 Domna C. Stanton, 'The Fiction of Préciosité and the Fear of Women', *Yale French Studies*, 1981, vol. 62, pp. 118–19.

7 Manley, vol. 2, p. 143.

8 See Geoffrey Holmes and W.A. Speck (eds), *The Divided Society: Party Conflict in England 1694–1716*, London, Arnold, 1967, pp. 82–7.

9 Manley, vol. 1, p. 110.

10 ibid., p. 164.

11 Quoted in J.A. Downie, *Robert Harley and the Press: Propaganda and Public Opinion in the Age of Swift and Defoe*, Cambridge, Cambridge University Press, 1979, p. 110.

12 In *Essays of John Dryden*, ed. W.P. Ker, New York, Russell & Russell, 1961, vol. 2, pp. 15–114.

13 ibid., p. 45.

14 ibid., p. 84.

15 Joseph Addison and Richard Steele, *The Tatler*, ed. Donald F. Bond, Oxford, Clarendon, 1987, vol. 3, p. 241.

16 Jonathan Swift, *A Tale of a Tub to Which is Added the Battle of the Books and the Mechanical Operation of the Spirit*, ed. A.C. Guthkelch and D. Nichol Smith, 2nd edn, Oxford, Clarendon, 1958, pp. 52, 53.

17 See, for example, Swift's *Journal to Stella*, in which he comments that he persuaded Manley to write a pamphlet on the Marquis de Guiscard's attempt to stab Robert Harley, being himself 'afraid of disobliging Mr Harley or Mr St John in one critical point about it' (Jonathan Swift, *Journal to Stella*, ed. Harold Williams, 2 vols, Oxford, Clarendon, 1948, vol. 1, p. 245). Swift contributed the first page of Manley's *A True Narrative of What Pass'd at the Examination of the Marquis de Guiscard at the Cock-Pit the 8th March 1710/11*, 1711, in which she argued that Guiscard's real object was the murder of the queen.

18 See Morgan, p. 109.

19 Manley, vol. 1, p. 527.

20 ibid., p. 527.

21 Dryden, vol. 2, p. 66.

22 ibid., p. 67.

23 ibid., p. 102.

24 ibid., p. 66.

25 See my chapter, 'Seizing the Means of Seduction: Fiction and Feminine Identity in Aphra Behn and Delarivier Manley', in Isobel Grundy and Susan J. Wiseman (eds), *Women/Writing/History 1640–1740*, London, Batsford, forthcoming.

26 Peter Wagner, *Eros Revived: Erotica of the Enlightenment in England and America*, London, Secker and Warburg, 1988, p. 89; Ronald Paulson, *Satire and the Novel in Eighteenth-Century England*, London and New Haven, CN, Yale University Press, 1967, p. 221.

27 C.R. Kropf has drawn our attention to the importance of the libel laws in late seventeenth- and early eighteenth-century Britain to the construction of convoluted satirical forms, such as the scandal chronicle, developed in order to avoid prosecution. See his 'Libel and Satire in the Eighteenth Century', *Eighteenth Century Studies*, 1974–5, vol. 8, pp. 153–68.

28 Roger de Rabutin, Count de Bussy, *The Amorous History of the Gauls, Written in French by Roger de Rabutin, Count de Bussy, And now Translated into English*, 1725, sig. A5V.

29 ibid., n.p.

30 ibid., p. 187.

31 The facts of d'Aulnoy's biography are still unclear. A supposed auto-biography published in France in 1697 and translated as *The Memoirs of the Countess of Dunois: Author of the Lady's Travels into Spain* in 1699, was in fact the fictional creation of one Madame de Murat. See Melvin D. Palmer, 'Madame d'Aulnoy in England', *Comparative Literature*, 1975, vol. 27, p. 239. D'Aulnoy's twentieth-century biographer, Raymond Foulché-Delbosc, claims that d'Aulnoy never went to Spain and her 'travels' are literary hoaxes. See Foulché-Delbosc, 'Madame d'Aulnoy et l'Espagne', *Revue hispanique*, 1926, vol. 67, pp. 1–151.

32 Marie d'Aulnoy, *Mémoires de la cour d'Espagne* (1679–81), *Mémoires sur la cour de France* (1692) and *Mémoires de la cour d'Angleterre* (1695).

33 Marie d'Aulnoy, *The Ingenious and Diverting Letters of the Lady —'s Travels into Spain*, 2nd edn, 1692, sigs A3R–A3V.

34 Manley, vol. 1, pp. 280–1.

35 ibid., p. 282.

36 Marie d'Aulnoy, *Memoirs of the Court of England*, trans. 1707, p. 2.

37 Manley, vol. 2, p. 850.

38 ibid., vol. 1, p. 593.

39 ibid., p. 290.

40 ibid., p. 545.

41 Manley's two mock 'Whig' pamphlets are *The Duke of M—h's Vindication*, 1711, and *A Learned Comment Upon Dr Hare's Excellent Sermon*, 1711.

42 D'Aulnoy, *Memoirs*, p. 2.

43 For an example of a British scandal novel that continued in the vein of Bussy-Rabutin, however, see *The Amours of the Sultana of Barbary*, 1689, in which Charles II's mistress, Louise, Duchess de Querouaille (Indamora), and Barbara Villiers, Duchess of Cleveland (Homira), are portrayed as a pair of duplicitous viragos exploiting the king's sexual weakness in order to win political power and influence. The similarity between the pseudonym 'Homira' and Manley's use of the name 'Hilaria' to designate Cleveland in her *Rivella*, as well as the complex oriental key structure of this novel, which Manley employed in her *Memoirs of Europe*, makes it likely that it had some influence on her work.

44 D'Aulnoy, *Travels into Spain*, part 1, pp. 55–6.

45 Manley, vol. 1, pp. 759–60.

46 ibid., pp. 760–1.

47 ibid., p. 761.
48 J.J. Richetti, *Popular Fiction before Richardson: Narrative Patterns 1700–39*, Oxford, Clarendon, 1969, p. 124.
49 ibid., pp. 142, 146.
50 April London, 'Placing the Female. The Metonymic Garden in Amatory and Pious Narrative 1700–1740', in Cecilia Macheski and Mary Anne Schofield (eds), *Fetter'd or Free? British Women Novelists 1670–1815*, Athens, OH, Ohio University Press, 1985, p. 104.
51 Manley, vol. 1, p. 305.
52 ibid., pp. 305–6.
53 ibid., p. 306.
54 On the timeliness of Manley's interventions in party politics, see Paul Bunyan Anderson, 'Delariviere Manley's Prose Fiction', *Philological Quarterly*, 1934, vol. 13, pp. 168–88.
55 G.M. Trevelyan has described the *New Atalantis* as the most harmful publication to the Whig ministry in Britain in 1709. See his *England Under Queen Anne*, vol. 3 of *The Peace and the Protestant Succession*, London, Longman, 1934, p. 38.
56 Sarah Churchill, *Private Correspondence of Sarah, Duchess of Marlborough, Illustrative of the Court and Times of Queen Anne; With her Sketches and Opinions of her Contemporaries and the Select Correspondence of her Husband, John, Duke of Marlborough*, London, Colburn, 1838, vol. 1, p. 239. See also Maynwaring's comments in his previous letter (p. 236) and the Duchess's to the queen on the book, in which she upbraids Anne for her evident favouritism of Abigail Masham (pp. 244–5). Thanks to Rachel Weil for pointing out to me, however, that in her comments to the queen on the *New Atalantis* Sarah Churchill seems to have confused the novel with a Whig pamphlet entitled *The Rival Dutchess: or Court Incendiary*, 1708, which attacks Abigail Masham with the charge, among others, of lesbian activity and portrays her in conversation with Madame Maintenon. Neither this charge, nor Maintenon, appear in Manley's novel, but Sarah Churchill cites them with reference to the *New Atalantis* in her letter.
57 Richetti, pp. 120, 121.
58 Manley, vol. 2, n.p.
59 Lennard Davis, *Factual Fictions: The Origins of the English Novel*, New York, Columbia University Press, 1983, pp. 102–23; Michael McKeon, *The Origins of the English Novel 1600–1740*, London, Hutchinson, and Baltimore, Johns Hopkins University Press, 1987, pp. 25–65.
60 Swift, *Tale of a Tub*, p. 28.
61 ibid., p. 36.
62 Catherine Gallagher has identified this same logic at work with regard to the writings of Margaret Cavendish and Mary Astell in the context of her discussion of the particular attractions of a theory of absolutism for Tory feminists. See her 'Embracing the Absolute: The Politics of the Female Subject in Seventeenth-Century England', *Genders*, 1988, vol. 1, no. 1, pp. 24–39. On the importance of the term 'disinterest' to the formation of the cultural image of the modern critic in the

eighteenth century, see John Barrell, *English Literature in History 1730–80: An Equal, Wide Survey*, London, Hutchinson, 1983, and Terry Eagleton, *The Function of Criticism*, Oxford, Blackwell, 1984.

63 Swift, letter to Stella (Saturday 30 June 1711) in *Journal to Stella*, vol. 1, p. 306.

64 See Gwendolyn Needham, 'Mary de la Riviere Manley, Tory Defender', *Huntingdon Library Quarterly*, 1948–9, vol. 12, p. 283.

65 Manley, vol. 2, p. 845.

9

SPEAKING OF WOMEN: SCANDAL AND THE LAW IN THE MID-EIGHTEENTH CENTURY

Clare Brant

At evr'y Word a Reputation dies

Alexander Pope

And 'tis ever allowed that the losers may have right to speak

Laetitia Pilkington

Around the mid-eighteenth century, several women – Teresia Constantia Phillips, Laetitia Pilkington and Frances Anne, Viscountess Vane – published vindicatory texts. Their place in literary history where it has figured at all has been that given them by Samuel Richardson, who reviled them as a 'Set of Wretches, wishing to perpetuate their Infamy'.[1] Recent critics, however, have declined to see them as moral scarecrows and have looked instead for more productive ways of reading them. Chief among these is Felicity Nussbaum who analyses how 'women's representation escapes its policing to threaten patriarchal relations as the scandalous memoirs negotiate the culture's clashes over character, class and gender in published texts'.[2] Janet Todd treats them briefly as examples of female nonconformity whose attempts at rebellion failed because of their inability to respond to a historically rising tide of sentiment and moralizing which then swept them away.[3] Patricia Meyer Spacks provides a helpful frame by which to read them in her investigation of gossip as a significant and pejoratively gendered eighteenth-century discourse.[4] The increasingly accepted designation of these texts as 'scandalous memoirs' seems to represent a current consensus on their engagement with transgressive discourse (scandalous) and their generic role of producing a self in

242

historical relation to society (memoirs). The interpretation I wish to put forward in this chapter takes up both these concerns but develops them to explore the ways in which self-representations compete with social productions of identity, and how both relate in some surprising ways to the law as a regulating discourse. Agreeing with Nussbaum that the construction of a subject in these texts is more a matter of process than product, my focus is not only on gendered subjects and subjects in gender relations, but also on the interlocking and competing discourses within which subject positions are negotiated. This involves taking a fresh look at what might be meant by scandal, and comparing it to the law as a mechanism of definition and control.

The designation of 'scandalous memoirs' does, however, raise awkward issues. Though contemporaries lumped together Phillips and Pilkington as a pair,[5] and Phillips, Pilkington and Vane as a trio,[6] this is at least as much because they could all be labelled 'bad' women as because their writings shared literary characteristics. The texts are formatted differently: while both Phillips and Pilkington published serially, Vane's text mysteriously appeared in the middle of Smollett's novel *The Adventures of Peregrine Pickle* and may not be written by her.[7] Different kinds of signature are involved: Vane's text uses the mask of 'a Lady of Quality', and Phillips sets up odd dislocations by using a third-person voice which refers to her insistently as Mrs Muilman, though each number is signed in ink by her as Teresia Constantia Phillips. Recent critics have attached Charlotte Charke to the group, though as a determined cross-dresser her offences differ from the enthusiastically hetero-sexual transgressions of Phillips, Pilkington and Vane.

Without being over-nice about generic distinctions, it is worth pointing out how the convenience of genre can override original diversity. It is absolutely necessary to avoid calling these texts autobiographies, since autobiography is a term not found until the late eighteenth century and not available until the early nineteenth.[8] But in removing this anachronism, one is faced with a plethora of sub-genres. Phillips's text is titled an *Apology*, Pilkington's and Vane's are *Memoirs*, Charke's is a *Narrative*.[9] One could use 'vindication' as a synthesizing term, and one which, like autobiography, usefully conveys the sense of a mode rather than necessarily a genre. An objection to this is its implication that the texts do indeed vindicate, whereas publication gave these women either limited rehabilitation or none at all. Textual intervention on their own behalf did make some material difference to their circumstances – Phillips in particular reports that sales exceeded expectations in spite of obstructive booksellers. But that their extenuations did not take up a common format suggests that no genre was recognized as the best vehicle of expressing a common project, supposing that to be vindication.

The generic complications are nicely illustrated by a text which will feature in my argument: *Amelia, or, The Distress'd Wife: A HISTORY founded in REAL Circumstances* by Elizabeth Justice.[10] The *Monthly Review* uncertainly placed it as a *roman-à-clef*:

> As this is a piece of secret personal history, to which we have no key, we shall take no further notice of it, except that it is printed by a subscription, which, seems to have been meerly a charitable one, for the benefit of the writer, a woman, who gives her own history under the name of *Amelia*.[11]

More memoir than apology, it is not 'scandalous' in the usual sense; Justice, or 'Amelia', was much more sinned against than sinning. The text describes her courtship, her marriage and her separation from an impossible husband, one 'Mr Johnson', and how she repeatedly tried and repeatedly failed to get him to pay the alimony to which by law she was entitled. According to her, he prevaricated, procrastinated, denied and lied, not only defrauding her of money to pay his mistress but taking away her children too.[12] Desperate to escape penury, she went to Russia as a governess and on her return found a female benefactor with whom she lived as a companion. After this woman's death, she tried various forms of work again (including sleuthing) while being dogged by debts and ill-health. The book was apparently a last-ditch attempt to make money respectably – an attempt endorsed by the *Monthly Review*'s notice of its subscription.

Amelia is of particular interest because its author is relatively obscure, not in the public eye as the others variously were. She also avails herself less of literary models whereas Vane's text, for example, inclines to romance and Charke's to rogue biography.[13] But despite the class, educational and economic differences of these women and the different situations which give rise to their writings, their texts all show an interest in an extra-textual process of representation and in particular to what one might call the choric. This term covers a number of processes and products, including collective discourses such as hearsay, gossip and scandal (and, in other contexts, news), and social constructions of identity such as character, which may be individuated or gendered or both, as in the case of reputation. It refers to plural originators of discourse (here, more often spoken rather than written), but without suggesting that those voices are necessarily in unison or can be named. As the medium through which third parties circulate first persons, it may be read as an interface between private and public spheres, though since one of its functions is precisely to dissolve that distinction, it could more properly be described as a catalyst which facilitates extensions of the personal into the social and vice versa. Gender factors enter this economy at a number of points: its origin, propagation, exchange, dispersal and reception. Though women are not exclusively its objects and agents, the choric is often feminized to serve particular ends. By identifying women as talking subjects defined by talk the choric can more widely and immediately regulate them, and the supposed orality of women can be used both to restrict women's access to print and control representations of them within it.[14]

The most familiar aspect of the choric is reputation, an unfortunate familiarity in some ways because by focusing on the choric product one can overlook the process of its manufacture. Reputation thus comes to seem an unalterable artefact, a view expressed by Todd: 'Calumny murdered since for women reputation was identity. A woman became "even such a one" as she was represented and there was no possibility of change: representation was the reality'.[15] In biographical terms, women thus stigmatized did suffer the consequence of social rejection. But this does not explain why such women should risk further rejection by writing and publishing if, as Nussbaum argues, publication was itself cause for scandal. Fallen women affirm the value of reputation to insure themselves against further abuse; platitudinously invoking those precepts they had hitherto fallen foul of secures for their texts a nominal didactic justification. Thus Pilkington:

I think the story may be instructive to the female part of my readers, to teach them that reputation

> *Is the immediate jewel of their soul*
> *And that the loss of it*
> *Will make them poor indeed! – Othello.*[16]

But she immediately adds a rider: 'However numerous my mistakes in life have been, they have still had most surprising additions made to them.' Charke makes the same point in describing herself as 'a hapless Wretch, whose real Errors were sufficient without the Addition of MALICIOUS SLANDERS',[17] and Phillips also distinguishes between 'the blameable Part of her Conduct' and 'Offences she had never been guilty of' from which she aims to 'disculpate her Character'.[18] All three refuse to see reputation as separable from the choric. Their texts try to arrest not the process by which the choric commodifies them (they submit to that) but the ways in which it exaggerates and distorts its material in order to expand its own regulatory significance. Some part at least of a bad reputation cannot be fixed if the choric is busy aggrandizing it. Loss of reputation can be mitigated because the flux of the choric makes it open to challenge, even at the risk of inscribing fixity through a text.

The misrepresentation which these texts argue is contingent on reputation is frequently related to scandal. Scandal is not just a matter of events, but the discourses through which those events are constructed as transgressive. The texts offer a rich vocabulary of distinctions: there are infringements, intemperances, imprudences, indiscretions, errors, follies, faults and offences which may be met negatively by objections, censures and reproaches, or positively by approbation, applause and acquittal. The largest category, however, is that which covers misrepresentation: its fictions, prejudices, inventions, imputations, insinuations, traducings, defamations, malice, slander and abuse. This selection is taken from Vane's text, which gives least space to the issue. One could add others.

Verbal diversity is one way in which these women writers unsettle reputation. The effect of differentiating terms such as lies, untruths and falsehoods is not to suggest logocentric shades of meaning but to emphasize the signifying power of language. It also breaks up the metonymic operation whereby reputation reduces the whole woman to a single speech figure, which in turn determines others. As Phillips puts it, 'she who *offendeth in one Point*, is immediately denounced guil[t]y of all'.[19]

Reputation appears to invest exclusively in chastity as its synec-doche because the choric can guarantee that investment. Chastity is not the only valuable part of a woman's reputation, Phillips argued,[20] but it could seem that way as long as continence was what was talked about or was *supposed* to be what was talked about, and as long as the choric imposed gender difference on representations of sexual activity. As Phillips complained, 'Infidelity in the Men is softened into Gallantry; but in the Ladies, hardened into *Infamy*.'[21] Pilkington points out that men used the choric to absolve themselves: 'Is it not monstrous that our seducers should be our accusers?', she asks.[22] Such accusations depend on making men rhetorically absent from the scene of the crime; reputation turns male agency into female responsibility. Conversely male presence, particularly the social and economic protection of a husband, becomes a rhetorical shield against scandal. Had her husband provided for her, says Vane, 'I should never have given the world the least cause to scandalize my reputation'.[23] Pilkington points out how masculine presence, or its possessive substitute reputation, frees female agency: 'Women whose characters are unblemished or who have their husbands with them as guardians to it may do a thousand things which those who have fallen on evil days and evil tongues in prudence must avoid.'[24]

Vane's and Pilkington's hints about provision and agency suggest that reputation serves another agenda besides the sexual. Spacks has observed that

> Reputation for women, the literature suggests, is sexual reputa-
> tion. A man's good name concerns behavior in many situations;
> a woman's sexual conduct is definitive. Detraction and tattling
> alike victimize women more seriously than they do men partly
> because of the special fragility of sexual reputation.[25]

The literature does indeed suggest reputation for women is sexual, but in doing so that suggestion distracts from other factors. The 'special fragility' is not a matter of women's intrinsic moral frailty (though some ideologues argued that) but of the tenuous economic security available to dependent women. An overt stress on relations as sexual makes covert their economic components. Calling a woman a whore accuses her of sexual licence; it also implies she is a working girl. A study by Anna Clark of insults to working women later in the century shows how defamation threatened their economic independence.[26] Women in charge of small businesses went to court to clear their names not just for their own satisfaction but to protect their livelihoods, a concern recognized in law. Clark quotes Polly Morris's study of Somerset defamation showing how 'Sexual language was used by men to discipline women who challenged their supremacy, and it referred, increasingly, to emerging definitions of femininity that denied the contemporary variety of material roles.'[27] Clark herself concludes 'Sexual reputation thus became a marker of class status, but one which limited the lives of women not men.'[28] Since upper and middle class women were less likely to earn a living through work, the scandalizing of reputation made them more vulnerable economically when relationships through which they had been funded failed.

While reputation helped to restrict economic options for non-working-class women, the process of forming it through scandal appeared to provide women of all classes with an occupation as agents of the choric. Gossip and scandal count as idle talk – idle in the senses of being non-productive and dependent on leisure. So Vane discusses an incident of locking a lord into her bedroom in order to counter 'a thousand idle stories'.[29] The two meanings run together, carrying class, gender and even racial inflections. Pilkington alleges that Dublin has 'the least sin and most scandal of any city in the world', and offers an explanation: 'In London almost everyone in the middling state of life has some employment or diversion to kill their time; and here it is the reverse – we are all gentry, wherefore the females have no amusement but that of SLANDER.'[30] The Irish, like women an economically disadvantaged group, convert their material unproductiveness into rhetorical productions which in turn are read as representations of vacancy.

Class and gender factors associated with leisure combine to give force to a much-used tropological site of scandal production: the tea-table. Tea was a luxury commodity; keys to caddies were rarely entrusted to servants. Tea acts as synecdoche for socially closed feminine talk, a class- and gender-bounded paradigm simultaneously characterized as trivial and harmful. Spacks discusses masculine anxiety about it in terms of its unregulatable and domestic nature, intensified by fears of all-female assemblies.[31] As segregated forums of talk, women's tea-tables could compete with men's coffee-houses: hence the masculine interest in belittling them, and hence too perhaps a feminine interest in representing them as places of relaxation from which faction was excluded. But though what Lady Mary Wortley Montagu describes as 'tea-table chat'[32] could be represented as irrelevant because feminine, the presence of men was as likely to confirm as change its choric function. 'Amelia' writes in a letter from Petersburgh, 'As to Scandal, here is enough of it; but the Gentlemen rival the Ladies of the Talent always allowed them, of a little Tittle-tattle'.[33] In mixed company, etiquette required women to perform tea-making duties by which their status in the household could be placed. One of the family honours of which Richardson's *Clarissa* is deprived is that of making tea. Distinctions among visitors could be precisely expressed through a politics of preference: 'Amelia's' suitor, for example, faints when she hands tea to another man first. Through the elaborations of tea ceremonies men kept women serviceable, defined their status relative to one another, and further imposed a heterosexual erotics on the activity, reinforced by metaphors which link the fragility of china to women and their reputations.[34]

In these representations, women act as passive or willing agents of patriarchal order. In contrast, disrupting this ideal norm unleashes anarchy of mythic proportions. Pilkington, attacking female scandalmongers, begs men 'never to believe anything that is said of me by a *woman*, as it is more than four to one it is a lie'. She cites masculine mythologizing in support of this, first Milton, then various satirists:

I know a very ingenious gentleman who, whenever he sees a parcel of females seated at their tea, names the chamber *Pandemonium*; and Doctor Young, in one of his *Satires*, says:

> *Tea, how I tremble at the dreadful stream!*
> *As Lethe fatal to the love of fame;*
> *What devastations on thy banks are seen!*
> *What shades of mighty names that once have been?*

And I really cannot remember ever to have seen a set of ladies tippling this liquor but scandal straight ensued.[35]

Interestingly Pilkington uses a comestible trope for her own text: 'for truly I mean to give both pleasure and offence: Lemon and Sugar is very pretty.'[36] This recipe for literary success stresses the text as a confection more tasteful than scandal. The gendered connection between scandal and tea is so persistently reinforced that by the late eighteenth century a dictionary of cant offered the entry '*Scandal broth*, tea'.[37] The trope proves useful because it evokes the dynamic nature of scandalous talk. Women were not passively imbibing scandal with their tea: they were dishing it out as well as taking it.

In this context, a well-known zeugma from *The Rape of the Lock* looks less innocent:

Here Thou, Great *Anna*! whom three Realms obey,
Dost sometimes Counsel take – and sometimes *Tea*.[38]

Pope is not bathetically comparing conceptual and material aspects of the body politic, but differentiating statecraft and slander as social discourses. The subsequent lines make it clear that the decorum being violated by this feminized court (both sexes are present but a woman presides) is that of a properly passive speech relation. When great Anna takes counsel, she listens: in listening, one party uses silence to show deference to another. When she takes tea, she participates in scandal which Pope figures as disconnected speech acts: one courtier speaks, another describes, a third interprets. This babel erases its auditors and makes their absence the silence of consent. Where counsel as a discourse is authorized by a position of receptivity (advice has to be heard, whether it is accepted or rejected), scandal acts out agreement in its listeners by showing consumers as producers (everyone joins in). This collectivity also increases its currency, a plurality Pope counters by invoking singularity: 'At ev'ry Word a Reputation dies.'[39]

Pope makes scandal murderous and motiveless. A number of women writers who identify choric agency as feminine suggest possible motives. One is self-defence: Pilkington in one of her terrorizing sallies addressed to 'fair ladies' remarks 'it does not a little surprise me that every person who suffers a panic lest their own reputations should be attacked has not a little compassion for that of another.'[40] She also considers the problem that fellow victims do not recognize each other as such: 'women who have suffered most in their own reputations are generally most cruel in their censures on others.'[41] But she does not consider how women might mitigate appearances for themselves by turning choric attention to others, nor how by participating in the choric they might claw back tolerance and perhaps approval from scandalmongers whose concerns they demonstrate they share. Like gossip, scandal employs paradigms of likeness and difference in order to establish and regulate race, class and gender boundaries. Women who attack other women challenge the power of reputation to totalize women as a group, even though by gesturing towards individual difference they confirm the gendered social grounds on which favourable representation depends.

The violence of scandal is most often said to arise from feminine envy and its attendant malice. Women writers often specify the gender of their detractors in such instances. Charke blames the malice of her stepmother for her father's displeasure; 'Amelia' attributes to envy the stories of women who say she has never been to Russia. Envy emphasizes difference in two ways – first, circumstantially, in that the woman envied has something which envious women lack. This may be a material benefit which cannot be verified through the text: her beauty, or experience of travel, or financial security. But the text may invoke it as a substantive proof of the author's truth-telling. Because that proof belongs to the realm of life beyond the text, it stands as corroborative evidence available to the choric to check.

If envy depends on difference and that difference makes other women malicious, the writer is therefore not malicious and her text acquires neutrality on this point. This leads into a second kind of difference through which representations of envy produce strangely ungendered moments for women writers. When other women are plurally envious, the writer takes on a first-person voice in which gender is temporarily suspended.[42] But such a moment is typically associated with a larger politics of representation:

> Neither can I really imagine what I had done to merit all the cruel and scandalous aspersions thrown on me, especially by the ladies: it would be infinite vanity to suppose envy had any share in their gentle breasts, or that the praises I received from the other sex, on account of my writings, awaked their displeasure against me. For though
>
> > *They had no title to aspire*
> > *Yet, when I sank, they rose the higher.*[43]

Pilkington implies that choric praise or approving talk generates feminine envy or disapproving talk, manifesting a feminine desire to regain control of the choric. Envious women reintroduce sexuality in order to police representations of women. 'Amelia' illustrates this too:

> Mrs. *Tomlinson*'s Pride was piqued, that *Amelia* should be thus caressed. and that she must be by every Set of Company ding'd with the Perfections of the Woman; for that was what she us'd to call *Amelia*, to lessen her in the Esteem of her Friends. She declared that she was surprized that so worthy and good a Lady as Mrs. *Sweet* was, should talk of taking her into her House; for that she had never been in *Russia*, only Sailing the World round with a Captain of a Ship.[44]

Women are exposed as 'envious' for trying to hijack the choric, disrupting its representations of a particular woman in order to produce rival versions. Moreover, these particular women are women engaged in making representations – in Pilkington's case, her writings; in 'Amelia's', her stories about Russia (which she then turns into a book, encouraged by a dream in which a nodding ghost with a truncheon urges her to write). Scandal arises to counter the use of less overtly gendered terms in choric discussion of women, an intervention open to counter-challenge through the figure of feminine envy.

Sometimes feminine expressions of envy are projected as emanating from a ghostly female body – Phillips talks of female spleen, Vane of women's weakness. But the texts tend to represent choric women as discursive figures even as they also personalize them as named individuals. A similar doubling appears in references to servants as originators and purveyors of scandal, despite class reluctance to individuate servants more than is necessary to place their reportage. Pilkington warns darkly against making servants confidantes, and points to the way scandal treats class barriers as permeable: 'so true is it that either good or evil fame proceeds from our domestics.'[45] Phillips learns important information about her enemy Tartufe's treatment of the unfortunate Delia from her maid, who she discovers was employed by Delia. 'Amelia' trusts a woman called Margaret as a servant despite stories told against her; ironically imputing these to feminine envy, 'Amelia' finds herself targeted for scandal through this servant who is bribed by Amelia's husband to tell lies of her. (Another servant overhears and warns her.) The attribution of effective choric agency to servants undoubtedly expresses class anxieties, in that public discussion of household affairs can constitute class treachery in employers' eyes, but it also carries gender inflections since many of the servants are women.

Besides gendering class, scandal also puts class inflections on gender. The key term here is 'impudence'. The etymological register of this word (*im* + *pudens*, ashamed, modest) points to sexual embarrassments but also to language: the discourse of modesty is marked by verbal restraint and that of shame by silence. Its use in the eighteenth century as a term for class infringement still carries these associations; hence its use by objects of scandal who invoke rank as protection against accusations of transgressions. Phillips reports that Tartufe's response to her version of his maltreatment of Delia is 'very concise, and to the Purpose, *viz.* "That all this *impudent* Creature has said of him is *utterly false*, and *scandalous*"'.[46] Damage to reputation causes gender and class dislocations, and one can be figured through the other. Pilkington finds herself attacked by women on class grounds:

> Ladies, let me entreat you will drop that nasty paw word 'impudent' . . . . But a woman who has suffered in reputation knows not what to do; 'tis all impudence, though her betters have more; for that in the Captain is but a choleric word, in the soldier is flat blasphemy.[47]

The uncertainty of class for women so distanced from the respectability they were born into is reinforced by scandal.

The complex and connected forms of class and gender fit into a discursive spectrum in which scandal is propagated by both general and particular agents. The texts name many individuals as sources of scandal, but they also employ collective or absent figures. The 'World' may be referred to as the origin of a point of view, or there may be no location at all. Peregrine Pickle, for example, has heard the Lady of Quality's story 'indistinctly related, with numberless errors and misrepresentations',[48] but he doesn't say from whom. Vane reports within the story that a 'Mr B— told me, that before he saw me, he heard I was a fool; but finding (as he was pleased to say) that I had been egregiously misrepresented, he courted my friendship';[49] neither he nor she name the agents. Phillips takes every opportunity to trace abuse back to her machinating husband, but sometimes generalizes: 'we are told, the Enemies of Mrs *Muilman* give out, that her Books are not only intended to introduce but to traduce the Characters of the Generality of her Acquaintance.'[50] Charke disembodies her detractors with references to 'False and evil Tongues' and the 'Tongue of Slander'.[51] 'Amelia' hears stories of her husband's ill-doing from 'designing malicious People'.[52]

Use of these general figures may imply only that a text cannot name all its writer's detractors, or within its scope give sources for all manifestations of scandal, however much serial publication might allow it to extend its exposure of misrepresentations. But just as specifying women as choric agents yields rhetorical rewards, so representing scandal in impersonal terms assists a text's own intervention in the choric. First, its exemplification of persecution rather than paranoia is made credible by distinguishing between general scandal and scandal which leads to a narrative – an important factor in texts of uncertain or open genre. Second, representing agency as impersonal reflects the exclusionary practices of scandal. Scandal generally depends on the physical absence of the person being talked about; the text's omission of names projects that absence onto the persons doing the talking. These disappearing acts enhance the text's power over naming by making it seem strategic: not naming becomes a kind of forbearance. This virtue, however, has distinct rewards since naming then acts to register authenticity. Anonymous letters of abuse, of which Pilkington gives an example, are rendered inauthentic by their lack of signature. But this is a period in which anonymity and scurrility were profitable parts of print culture. Pilkington herself occasionally wrote blackmail letters for selected clients, and Charke takes lodgings vacated by a person to whom she delightfully refers as 'a celebrated Dealer in murdered Reputations, Wholesale and Retale [sic]'.[53] The value of a name was not simply rhetorical but commercial too.

Despite the different kinds of signature used by these texts, they all act to claim and proclaim themselves as property. Phillips denounces 'Hirelings . . . who, by scrawling a few unintelligible Characters upon Paper, would impose on the Public, by fixing her Name to the Trash they expose to Sale.' She is more indignant about their anonymity than their inventions: 'untill they have learned to sign their Names (if they have any) we shall think ourselves under no Obligation to take Notice of their Marks.'[54] Signature, the mark of literacy, also prevents fraud; it becomes the means of limiting the circulation of representations by others. Nussbaum has suggested literary conditions as the market forces operating on self-representations: 'Female subjectivity is for sale.'[55] But the texts are also competing with choric constructs and their material powers. The texts' commercial potential can be realized because print reaches a larger audience, but the difference of medium does not necessarily create a different discursive field.[56] Though Pilkington writes a number of poems into her Memoirs, choric prototypes are more valuable assets than literary ones: 'I went on with my story to Mr Cibber, who at last in flowing spirits, cried: "Z—ds! write it out just as you relate it, and, I'll engage it will sell."'[57]

Personalizing discourse is one way in which the texts express resistance to the social appropriation of personal knowledge which scandal exemplifies. Phillips's third-person narrator is introduced with ironic credentials:

> I have (as the World calls it) *known* Mrs *Muilman* about these twenty Years, which means no more, than that I was once in a Room with her; and have seen her several Times in public Places. The rest of my knowledge I had from common Fame, a Circumstance no way advantageous to her Character; for, I believe it will easily be admitted, that, among the Numbers whom those who call themselves the World pretend to be acquainted with and characterize, there is scarce one in a Million whose general Character is justly represented or understood, either as to Virtue or Vice.[58]

Such pretences of acquaintance are the harder to resist because the texts do include many named individuals; as the historical relation of a writer's dealings with people, the texts make personal acquaintance a central concern. This creates awkwardness. Friendship can be evoked as a protective frame to the text, but this does not easily transfer to the text's entry into the public and publicizing medium of print. 'Amelia's' preface explains she has been urged by her friends to write her history, but she puzzles over how to make it accessible to strangers: 'But in what Words shall I address myself, on this Occasion, to those to whom I have not the Favour of being Personally known?' Being known attracts detraction as well as support and can aggravate the choric divisions which gave rise to the book. 'Amelia' hesitates over writing the account of her travels which will prove she is no liar, because 'tho' Truth was to be her Subject, it would be read by her Enemies as well as her Friends; and she should only put herself in the Way of being called a Fool'.[59] Reader reaction could be loudly hostile: Phillips reports that 'the best name a certain noble Lord can give her, in a public Chocolate-House, is *Damned impudent B—h, &c. how dare she attack People of high Rank*; the *B—h ought to be duck'd*, &c.'[60] Not all readers were such implacable critics: Phillips also says that publication has converted into friends some who 'led away by common Fame, were heretofore her most inveterate Enemies'.[61] But she seems to uphold choric neutrality as best, begging her readers 'to think of her as of an Acquaintance dead'[62] – presumably because there is less ill spoken of the dead.

That some readers know the writer personally and some know of her through scandal leads to another awkwardness when the writer appeals to her acquaintances as witnesses. For example, one of Phillips's quarrels with her husband was supposedly witnessed by a lady who 'was an astonished Spectator of all this scene, and is now alive to attest the Truth of it; tho', for some Reasons, we forbear to give her Name'.[63] Phillips's veiling shows how etiquette complicates the issue of naming such people: to name them is to draw them into the choric spectrum. Since her text protests against social appropriation of personal information, an appeal to personal information contradicts the principle of choric restriction it supposedly upholds.

Choric interest in the writer leads to audience participation in her text. In serial publications, a text is able to articulate reader response to its earlier parts as it goes along. Readers collaborate, sending Pilkington their poems to print in her next number. Charke's readers urge her after her first number to expand her account of herself, a request she gratifies, whereas she refuses to yield to a fine lady's objections and to desist from her practice of naming benefactors and acknowledging obligations. Phillips includes a letter from a gentleman praising the spirit of her account of Tartufe's amours, and Pilkington comments on a pamphlet called *The Parallel* which compared the first instalments of her text with Phillips's.[64] The fictional surround of Vane's text draws the reader into the hyperbole of romance; after hearing her story, doubtful male auditors change their minds and acclaim her. Such a response may satirically play on the incorporation of ideal reactions by didactic novelists, but the reader can still take on a character as a lover, to be 'agitated, thrilled and transported' by her story.[65]

Attentiveness to readers and the issue of naming, however, have more than a literary significance. They connect in highly specific ways to writers' various legal embroilments. To cast these texts as self-defences and overlook the ways in which they are shaped within and against legal discourse is to miss a vital dimension. Just as the texts stress scandal as a discursive system, so they explore the law as an alternative – one which, unlike scandal, is supposed to do them justice. For if scandal involves the deregulation of representation, the law is its regulatory opposite. Itself a regulated discourse, it in theory functions to regulate personal relations through social forms. The law, moreover, can be used to control scandal in that some forms of scandal are open to legal restraint. Scandal is actionable when it falls within the legal definition of libel.

That the law in theory was available as an instrument of

justice with which to counter misrepresentation does not mean it functioned thus in practice. Far from it. But an idea of justice can survive its failings in practice – indeed, faith in its principles can be increased because they should transcend any temporal or material corruptions. So Phillips complains, 'in a Country where the best Laws that ever were made subsist, they are so *corruptly* executed, that they are become our greatest Oppressions'.[66] As a force which shapes, is shaped by and expresses ideologies, the law, like medicine, manifests and empowers economic, class and patriarchal systems. As Phillips puts it in the guise of 'a LADY, labouring under the Iron Hand of Injustice', she has lived to know that 'even the fixed Ideas of Right and Wrong which are always held invariable, [can be] altered and perverted, to ruin and oppress an unhappy, helpless Woman'.[67]

'The eighteenth-century legal system – if system it can be called – was . . . a dense, complex and bewildering jungle', observes Lawrence Stone.[68] There were, for example, three competing systems which had jurisdiction over marriage, separation and divorce, and each worked by different rules.[69] One certainty among the confusions is women's lamentable position under the law, though three factors mitigate this a little. One is that statutory concepts do not always govern people in practice. Evidence about marriage practices, for example, shows that the confusions which pre-dated Hardwicke's Marriage Act of 1753 survived that Act's attempts to reorder them. A second mitigation is the paradox that systems of power provide to those they oppress some means to challenge that oppression. Third, the *idea* of law can function as a practice; the threat of court action can regulate as efficiently as an actual prosecution.[70] In its capacity as a discourse of control, in and out of court, the law was available to be used by women even though particular laws were likely to be used against them.

A sketch of how the law affected the writers under discussion, in terms of their histories rather than their texts, must necessarily be brief. The complications of Phillips's case were peculiar and labyrinthine.[71] After she was seduced and abandoned, she married a man (called 'Delafield' in the text) so he as her husband would take on liability for her debts. When a Dutch merchant called Muilman proposed to her, she explained the situation; he promised to fix it so she could marry him without bigamy. This he supposedly did. Later, apparently under pressure to marry a richer woman, he tried to get Phillips to agree she was still married to Delafield. Phillips refused, and for the next sixteen years they engaged in suit and countersuit while he remarried and she had numerous affairs. Eventually Phillips ran out of money and gave up. Her *Apology* gives her version of events in great detail, with an often savage commentary on the operations of the law.

Elizabeth Justice was also embroiled in legal action over the maintenance which her deserting husband refused to pay. Despite the courts' support, she no sooner got her due than he fell into arrears again. Using the law cost her almost as much as she was owed, and the point of her book's subscription is to raise money and thereby 'avoid the Necessity of entering into a Second Law-Suit'. Pilkington, Charke and Vane all faced problems in which separation from their husbands involved them in either wrangling over maintenance or divorce (Pilkington and Vane) or the difficulties of keeping money subsequently acquired (Charke). Pilkington and Charke also illustrate how imprisonment for debt intertwined legal, economic and gender issues, as did prostitution and blackmail. They both also have specific connections to slander. Charke's book was partly a plea to her father to rescind the punishment of exclusion from his presence, a plea he ignores. Charke's familial indictment invokes paradigms of Christian rather than worldly justice, but in pointing to her stepmother's slanders she asserts her innocence within a legal discourse. For Pilkington, the violent ending of her marriage and her subsequent endeavours to support herself generated a set of grievances against the clergy and numerous individuals which she satisfied in print. Her denunciations, however, made her vulnerable to charges of libel.

Since mid-eighteenth-century women did not appeal to natural rights as later women did,[72] injustices against women sanctioned by the law could only be remedied by law. As one anonymous writer asked in 1735, 'what shall restrain the *Strong* from oppressing the *Weak*, if the Laws of our Country do not, they being in such a State the only established Rules of Society?'[73] The same writer pointed out that women's ignorance of the law left them unaware of its possible use.[74] But knowledge did not ensure comprehension since the specialization of legal language kept it baffling. As Pilkington put it,

there are so many loop-holes [in the law] that even persons
conversant with it may be deceived: how then should a female
be on her guard, against the professors of a certain kind of
unintelligible jargon, whose skill is to puzzle the cause, or a
science where

> Endless tautologies and doubts perplex
> Too harsh a study for our softer sex![75]

One effect of these texts is to make the law intelligible to other
women, and pass on information about its practices. 'Amelia'
comments that her husband 'knew the Quirks of the Law';[76] her
narrative educates readers in some of them.

Ironically, the abuse by husbands of their legal powers over
wives may have prompted women to turn to the law as a higher
patriarchal authority. As 'Amelia' tells her husband, 'Dear Sir, do
not imagine that all Law centers in you'.[77] On the other hand,
men who have power are best placed to abuse it. Pilkington
attacks clergymen who seduce women for being 'the first to
persecute with Ecclesiastical Courts, and Spiritual Authority, that
very person whom they themselves first taught the way to sin'.[78]
Legal practices could include harassment: Phillips describes being
discomfited by a lawyer's use of 'mean, low *Ribaldry* to put her out
of Countenance'.[79] Legal discourse is permeated by others; legal
personnel are not immune to choric effects: 'the Judge, like *other
People* at that Time, had imbibed all the Prejudices that common
Fame had stir'd up against her.'[80] Just as what goes on in court
is absorbed by the choric, so court exchanges made use of choric
constructs. Phillips articulates a widespread complaint that

> to the very great Scandal of Courts of Justice, there are some
> Council who take the Liberty to say everything that comes
> into their Heads, true or false, to asperse the Character of
> the Party they are emply'd against, in order to prejudice the
> Court, or Jury, against them, and Custom has given them the
> Privilege of doing this with Impunity.[81]

'Custom' includes what people were used to hearing from the choric.

None the less, legal discourse seemed to provide subject positions
less assailable by scandal for, as Phillips observed, 'calling her
Names, and inventing lewd Falshoods, and scandalous Stories of
her does not refute one single Circumstance we have asserted'.[82]
The comparatively strict definitions of evidence and mechanisms

of assessment in ideal law were mimicked by texts which provided copies of documents and letters, named witnesses and showed how accusations either arose from interested parties or were scandalous in the sense of being choric and hence inaccurate. Legal idioms were used figuratively to indicate commitment to truth-telling. Charke declares

> I was questioned, not long since, whether it was possible for me to have run through the strange Vicissitudes of Fortune I have given an account of, which I solemnly declare I am ready to make Oath of the Truth of every Circumstance; and if any particular Person or Persons require it, will refer them to Hundreds now living, who have been Witnesses of every Article contained in my History.[83]

This rhetorical commitment to law gains credibility by being set against a cultural stereotype of masculine language as devious (familiar from fictional tales of male perfidy in love). The greater agency of men is also demonstrated as put to bad use, with cases being cited of men suborning servants, stealing evidence, bribing and even murdering witnesses. Phillips points to the literary implications of these proto-gothic scenes, announcing a programme of comic relief to vary the reader's diet of 'Astonishment . . . Surprise and Horror'.[84] For Phillips especially the interaction of choric scandal with aspersion in court commits her to elaborating narrative and commentary in resistance. A simple denial is not enough: 'it will not be sufficient to tell the World the Fact is not so, – that Mr B—neither is, nor ever was, ruin'd: No, that Answer would have no weight.'[85] Uncertainly searching for a subject position, she becomes a character by becoming a character witness.

Yet in practice these women were defeated by the law even when the law approved their stories. Partly this was a matter of money; 'Amelia' remarked ruefully how 'the Law went on heavily without the valuable thing call'd Money'.[86] Phillips calculated that her husband had spent four times as much on going to law as it would have cost him to offer her a decent settlement; she claimed her legal costs amounted to £20,000.[87] Financial constraints did limit women's use of the law. Writing, on the other hand, could not only make them money, but could also substitute for the courts a protected space in which they could stage a fair hearing. Even if the choric then turned that hearing into hearsay, texts could act out triumphant court-room dramas. Pilkington, accused by readers of her first volume of literary theft in her use of quotations, as well as of libelling lords and clerics, answers both charges in a mock-legal dialogue with herself in which she cannot lose:

> *I.* Well, upon my word, Mrs Pilkington, I am weary of your argument; you seem resolved to get the better of me, and that my readers may always be assured I do, when I am both plaintiff and defendant.[88]

Women's charges against socially more powerful men could win conviction in texts as they could not in courts. Phillips says of the three men her text particularly indicts, 'Such have been the principal Offenders we have thought proper to bring before the Bar of the Public; and have the Satisfaction to find our Prosecution of them justified by the Verdict of that impartial Tribunal.'[89] A conventional eighteenth-century trope of readers as judges takes on the ideological weight of legal procedures; a legal frame of restraint masks a fantasy of control.

One particular part of the law acts as a site of gender control: libel. As a hinge between the law and scandal, libel covers the use of verbal violence to challenge reputations rather as a duel uses violence to settle them. The legal commentator Blackstone begins his discussion of criminal libel by declaring, 'Of a nature very similar to duels are *libels*'[90] – because both tend to breach the peace. Women could not fight duels, though some did resort to physical force: Charke, incensed by a lie that she had donned the disguise of a highwayman and robbed her father, found out its fabricator and beat him up.[91] Libel's substitution for violence made it a figure for women's unruliness; at the same time, it represented order since it fixed discourse into definable transgressions. Pilkington complains of being read as disorderly and threatened with libel: 'When I, in plain English, set down undeniable facts, they menace me with law.'[92] Equally, what looks like plain English could thinly conceal legal menace: 'where a villainous Odium could not be thrown a ridiculous one was sure to be cast, even on the innocent Actions of my Life.'[93] Charke's summary of family hostility uses a distinctly legal idiom, echoing Blackstone: 'A SECOND way of affecting a man's reputation is by printed or written libels, pictures, signs and the like; which set him in an odious or ridiculous light, and thereby diminish his reputation.'[94] That Charke uses terms for written libel about what are evidently slanders or verbal libel may show no more than the vagueness of her knowledge of the law. Alternatively, her

imprecision may be a protection against a countercharge of libel, in
that by mixing her terms she cannot be accused of accusing others
of slander.

Eighteenth-century libel law is much more explicitly class than
gender inflected. Yet working-class women did use it to protect
their reputations and consequently their livelihoods; Pilkington
and Charke who at different times each kept a shop may have
picked up a working knowledge of the law by working. But for
women distanced by class from employment, livelihoods and libels
were more bound up with the economics of sexual relations. Pope
connects sexual and verbal looseness in a couplet on Lady Mary
Wortley Montagu:

> From furious *Sappho* scarce a milder Fate
> P–x'd by her Love, or libell'd by her Hate.[95]

But aristocratic men did not work either. Phillips neatly fends off
a 'menace of prosecution' from Tartufe by denying libel since he
has no livelihood for her to threaten: 'pray, what Damage has he
to complain of? Surely, at his Time of Life, he has done farming
his Person out for the Use of the Fair.'[96] That he could only win
by proving himself a prostitute shows how libel law occasionally
allowed sexual politics to disarm class privilege. But class privileges
did pose unconquerable difficulties because of a clause concerning
scandalum magnatum.[97] Both Phillips and Pilkington skirted round
this, Phillips in her reproach to a duchess who had slandered her,
and Pilkington in her attacks on the clergy (her detested husband
was a clergyman). Their argument was slippery: that they could
not be guilty of injuring high and reputable characters when
those characters had, by behaving in low and disreputable ways,
forfeited the privileges due to rank. This secured them moral high
ground from which they could point out the aristocracy's failings
in terms of social responsibility rather than personal grievance.
Blackstone's comments on civil libel declare that 'words spoken in
a friendly manner, as by way of advice, admonition, or concern'
were not slanderous, and such a position of rebuke could also
gain literary status for writers by laying claim to the dignity of
satire disassociated from its conventional modes of geniality or
savagery.[98]

Satire, scandal and libel are connected as discourses by their common interest in controlling representation. Economies of power in
each are marked by different moral functions, but one can have

some sense of how they work by looking at masculine representations of women's vindicatory writings. Two are particularly relevant to the writers discussed: Henry Fielding's *Amelia* (1751) and Smollett's *The Adventures of Peregrine Pickle* (1751). *Amelia* responds explicitly to 'the Apologies with which certain gay Ladies have lately been pleased to oblige the World', and can be read as a reaction against their discourse of protest, particularly that of Phillips who in her last number criticized Fielding at length.

Conventional fictions of femininity are used defensively, but the novel invests as much in the impossibility of feminine self-representation as in resistance to it. Difference from other women which in women's texts is expressed in moments of complex alienation is simplified by Fielding into a comedy of ignorance. For example, as Miss Mathews tells her story to Captain Booth in prison, she bursts out against the hypocrisy of a rival: 'But such are the Friendships of Women!'[99] This provokes Booth to smothered laughter which she does not notice. The supposed joke lies in her ignorance of an ironical reading – that she is differentiating herself as a subject within a discourse which always lumps women together. This fulfils the chapter heading's prophecy, *'that it is possible for a Woman to appear to be what really she is not'* – that is, different. The heading also promises the usual warning that respectable appearances are not to be trusted, which events bear out: Miss Mathews looks genteel but declares herself to be a maenadic murderer. But even this is a misrepresentation since the man she has stabbed lives, news to which she reacts with abuse. Phillips's and other women writers' concern with legal discourse as a defence against misrepresentation is turned into a disproportionate obsession with words as Miss Mathews insists that bribing a witness to testify on her behalf would trouble her more than committing twenty murders. Her refusal or inability to see that murder is a worse crime than perjury acts as a trope for a feminine failure to understand principles of justice. Since women cannot distinguish serious crime, the text argues, it follows that any use they may make of the law cannot be taken seriously.

Mathews appeared good but is bad; multiple reversals unfold as the unlucky woman turns murderess and the murderess turns into the familiar figure of an unruly woman. She appeared startling because a woman can appear to be what she is not; what she really is, after all, is ordinary. The misrepresentations which women writers make such efforts to expose, analyse and challenge are turned into the changeability of women whose metamorphoses are the products of their own instability not choric flux. Booth is all agog to hear Mathews's story when the narrator holds up proceedings, suggesting that critics may be as surprised as Booth that

> a Lady, in whom we had remarked a most extraordinary Power of displaying Softness, should the very next Moment after the Words were out of our Mouth, express Sentiments becoming a *Dalila, Jezebel, Medea, Semiramis, Parysatis, Tanaquil, Livilla, Messalina, Agrippina, Brunichilde, Elfrida,* Lady *Macbeth, Joan* of *Naples, Christina* of *Sweden, Katherine Hays, Sarah Malcolm, Con. Phillips,* or any other Heroine of the tender Sex, which History sacred or prophane, antient or modern, false or true, hath recorded.[100]

This list of defiant female characters collapses historical and fictional difference into the literary predictability of the virago. Possibly parodying the serial publication of memoirs, the text defers Mathews's story not to intensify suspense but to show its absence.

Later on, Booth gets a letter from Mathews (both 'warm' and 'upbraiding') which he pretends not to have received. A second letter, 'full of bitterness and upbraiding', reveals that Colonel James is Booth's rival for her. In both cases, an 'absent' text – that is, a letter supposedly passed between characters but not given to the reader – stands as a signifier for the vindicatory female text. Its non-contents generate negative definitions of the writer: 'this dreadful Woman', 'a Whore'.[101] Gender stereotyping is made efficient by being predicated on unreadable female texts. Mathews then alienates James from Booth by implying Booth has traduced him. The colonel writes a letter to Booth which is not given, but it is explained:

> The cold and distant Stile of this Letter . . . greatly puzzled and perplexed poor *Booth*; and it was so long before he was able to solve it, that the Reader's Curiosity will perhaps be obliged to us for not leaving him so long in the dark as to this Matter.[102]

Female misrepresentations of men can be controlled through explication of the masculine texts they generate, however mysterious those at first appear. In the process, women's critiques are evaded, displaced into their effects on male bonding. Homosociality crowds out heterosexuality. Interestingly, Mathews's letter retracting her slurs – 'Know, then, cruel Wretch, that poor *Booth* loved you of all Men breathing'[103] – is given. The implication is that women tell the truth – when admitting they have lied.

In *Peregrine Pickle*, the explicit reaction to the Lady of Quality's memoirs is admiring and approving. But what happens next in the novel is distinctly odd. Pickle has 'a strange whim' to persuade his friend Cadwallader to dress up as a magician and tell fortunes. Pickle brings him customers whose secrets he has already either found out or played a part in making. Cadwallader then uses this information to give revelatory answers to questions, to the amazement and confusion of his auditors. Pickle and Cadwallader refine the scheme so as to keep better control of it, using it to ridicule, judge and shame people of fashion until Pickle grows bored with it.

The Cadwallader episode can be read many ways but its emphasis on gender, class and transgression reflects significantly on Vane's narrative with its gendered plots of misrepresentation. Sexual plots and women's reputations are mediated through masquerade exchanges[104] which force masculine control into a culturally marginal and fantastic space: Cadwallader is disguised as an Oriental necromancer. A kind of anarchy breaks out, exemplified by the first two cases. In the first, a lady and her maid personate each other and ask about their amours. Their uncertain identities and class reversals make them embody misrepresentation, but even that is transparent and pointless: 'the fictitious chambermaid' and 'the counterfeit lady' are alike in their credulity and lust. The second case concerns a woman, also disguised, who has had an affair with a black servant and admits to a string of other lovers. The two men vow after her departure to punish severely 'the shameless and insatiable termagant who had so impudently avowed her own prostitution'.[105] Miscegenation and licence act as tropes for women's histories; female lack of self-control justifies exclusively masculine jurisdiction and control. The prophetic discourse of fortune-telling becomes reflexively historicist – that is, predictions are made on the basis of what has already happened, a reversal which mirrors the inversions let loose by airing women's secrets. The key to control is manipulation of the choric, illustrated by Cadwallader telling a story of a man said to have vomited three black crows, which is traced back through each stage of misrepresentation. This example of 'Chinese whispers' demonstrates choric embellishment and distortion, but as in *Amelia* explication is masculine. Disorder may be invented and abandoned at will. This suggests masculine fantasy rather than carelessness, a strange exoticizing of the systems of judicial and choric control present in women's vindications, but one which still depends upon controlling women.

An adversarial system of law figures the struggle over representation; for women, the supposed equity of subjects under the law offsets cultural bias towards their gender, a bias reflected and intensified in masculine texts which stage representations of women as subjects. In legal settings, both actual and metaphorical, women could articulate the ways in which representation was unfairly gendered because, as Pilkington put it, 'And 'tis ever allowed that the losers may have right to speak.'[106]

The stress these women's texts put on choric and legal discourse emphasizes the collective context of representation, and the inseparability of personal from social constructs. As Pilkington put it, 'I should be glad to know how I could prosecute my own history without intermingling that of others; I have not lived in deserts where no men abide, nor in a cave like Echo.'[107] Abstracting these others into an Other can be valuable in the analysis of literary economy.[108] But self-representation can equally be seen as a series of assertions made in different discourses taking place in a field of voices – discourses, moreover, which are culturally specific and historically fluctuating. Feminist readings of autobiography have tended to suggest the text as voice: the writer speaks up and speaks out. This may suppose a model of silence into which women writers project texts. In the mid-eighteenth century, some women's texts provide a wealth of evidence to show that if they are silenced, it is in the sense of being drowned out rather than made mute. For silence is a matter of hearing nothing as well as saying nothing, and writing is in the case of these texts not an issue of breaking silence but of stilling tongues.

NOTES

(Place of publication for works printed before 1800 is London unless otherwise stated.)

1 Samuel Richardson, *Selected Letters of Samuel Richardson*, ed. John Carroll, Oxford, Oxford University Press, 1964, p. 173.
2 Felicity Nussbaum, *The Autobiographical Subject: Gender and Ideology in Eighteenth-Century England*, Baltimore and London, Johns Hopkins University Press, 1989, p. 180.

3 Janet Todd, *The Sign of Angellica: Women, Writing and Fiction, 1660–1800*, London, Virago, 1989, pp. 128–31.

4 Patricia Meyer Spacks, *Gossip*, Chicago and London, University of Chicago Press, 1986.

5 *The Parallel; or Pilkington and Phillips compared . . . by an Oxford Scholar*, 1748.

6 'The Heroines: or Modern Memoirs', in the *London Magazine*, 1751, vol. 20, p. 136.

7 See the introduction to Tobias Smollett, *The Adventures of Peregrine Pickle in which are included Memoirs of a Lady of Quality*, ed. James L. Clifford, rev. Paul-Gabriel Bouce, Oxford, Oxford University Press, 1983.

8 See Nussbaum, pp. 1–2.

9 Teresia Constantia Phillips, *An Apology for the conduct of Mrs Teresia Constantia Phillips*, 3 vols, 1748; Laetitia Pilkington, *Memoirs of Mrs Laetitia Pilkington 1712–1750 Written by Herself*, 1st edn 1748–54, ed. Iris Barry, London, Routledge, 1928; [Lady Vane], *Memoirs of a Lady of Quality* in Smollett, pp. 432–539; Charlotte Charke, *A Narrative of the Life of Mrs. Charlotte Charke*, 1st edn 1755, London, Constable, 1929.

10 Elizabeth Justice, *Amelia, or, The Distress'd Wife: A HISTORY founded on REAL Circumstances. By a Private GENTLEWOMAN*, 1751. I have preferred to keep the persona and refer to the writer subsequently as 'Amelia'.

11 *Monthly Review*, 1751, vol. V, pp. 72–3.

12 His particular vice was second-hand books, in pursuit of which he spent all their money. 'Amelia' says he was at one point in danger of being hanged for robbing the Cambridge University Library.

13 As a prelude to the statement of modesty common in women's writings, she says two Cambridge gentlemen were supposed to help her write the book, but pulled out of the project.

14 See Spacks, and Kathryn Shevelow, *Women and Print Culture: The Construction of Femininity in the Early Periodical*, London and New York, Routledge, 1989.

15 Todd, p. 130.

16 Pilkington, p. 25. Given the financial hardships such women faced, 'poor' is more than metaphorical.

17 Charke, p. 25.

18 Phillips, vol. II, p. 242.

19 ibid., vol. III, p. 313.

20 ibid., p. 23.

21 ibid., vol. II, p. 190.

22 Pilkington, p. 103.

23 Vane, p. 486.

24 Pilkington, p. 245.

25 Spacks, p. 32.

26 Anna Clark, 'Whores and Gossips: Sexual Reputation in London 1770–1825', in Arina Angerman, Geerte Binnema, Annemieke Kennen, Vefie Poels and Jacqueline Zirkzee (eds), *Current Issues in Women's History*, London and New York, Routledge, 1989, pp. 231–48.

27 Polly Morris, 'Defamation and Sexual Slander in Somerset, 1733–1850', unpublished Ph.D. thesis, University of Warwick, 1985, p. 134; in Clark, p. 240.
28 ibid., p. 245.
29 Vane, p. 496.
30 Pilkington, pp. 158, 316–17.
31 Spacks, pp. 152–5.
32 Lady Mary Wortley Montagu, *The Complete Letters of Lady Mary Wortley Montagu*, ed. Robert Halsband, Oxford, Oxford University Press, 3 vols, 1965–7, vol. II, p. 194.
33 Justice, p. 178.
34 For example:

> Whether the Nymph shall break *Diana*'s Law,
> Or some frail *China* Jar receive a Flaw.

Alexander Pope, *The Rape of the Lock*, 1714, canto II, 105–6, in *The Poems of Alexander Pope*, ed. John Butt, London, Methuen, 1963, reprinted 1977, p. 225.
35 Pilkington, p. 317.
36 ibid., p. 345.
37 Humphry Tristram Potter, *A New Dictionary of all the Cant and Flash Languages*, 2nd edn, 1795.
38 Pope, canto III, 7–8, p. 227.
39 ibid., canto III, 16.
40 Pilkington, p. 346.
41 ibid., p. 108.
42 Nussbaum, especially ch. 8.
43 Pilkington, p. 108.
44 Justice, p. 209.
45 Pilkington, pp. 130, 213.
46 Phillips, vol. II, p. 198.
47 Pilkington, p. 424.
48 Smollett, p. 432.
49 Vane, p. 478.
50 Phillips, vol. III, pp. 8–9.
51 Charke, pp. 17, 217.
52 Justice, p. 47.
53 Charke, p. 122.
54 Phillips, vol. III, p. 316.
55 Nussbaum, p. 156.
56 I do not mean to play down the considerable problem of how to relate lives to texts, or to suggest that textuality makes no difference. Sermons and plays are examples of texts which may not address but do not exclude the possibility of their being spoken or heard. Vane's text is more deaf to aural concerns, explained by its fictional context and its possible polishing by others.
57 Pilkington, p. 210. I do not mean to suggest one should take this at face value but the implications are important.
58 Phillips, vol. I, p. 13.

59 Justice, p. 212. She does write the book but it is short.
60 Phillips, vol. III, p. 32.
61 ibid., vol. II, p. 244.
62 ibid., vol. I, p. 316.
63 ibid., p. 203.
64 Pilkington, p. 315; Charke, pp. 142, 188; Phillips, vol. II, p. 108; Pilkington, p. 335.
65 Smollett: not in the Oxford edition, but see the Everyman edition, London, Dent, 2 vols, 1930, vol. II, p. 65.
66 Phillips, vol. III, p. 229.
67 ibid., Appendix, p. 2.
68 Lawrence Stone, *Road to Divorce: England 1530–1987*, Oxford, Oxford University Press, 1990, p. 27. For further information, see Bridget Hill, *Women, Work and Sexual Politics in Eighteenth-Century England*, Oxford, Blackwell, 1989, especially ch. 11.
69 Stone, pp. 24–5.
70 ibid., p. 25. Stone suggests that people went to court to get out-of-court settlements.
71 Lawrence Stone, *Broken Lives*, Oxford, Oxford University Press, forthcoming, takes Phillips as a case study.
72 See Carole Pateman, *The Disorder of Women: Democracy, Feminism and Political Theory*, Cambridge, Polity, 1989, ch. 1 on the appeal to natural rights of Wollstonecraft and others.
73 *The Hardships of the English Laws in relation to Wives*, 1735, in Vivien Jones (ed.), *Women in the Eighteenth Century: Constructions of Femininity*, London and New York, Routledge, 1990, pp. 217–18.
74 Hill, p. 201.
75 Pilkington, p. 151.
76 Justice, p. 191.
77 ibid., p. 107.
78 Pilkington, p. 73.
79 Phillips, vol. II, p. 286.
80 ibid., p. 69.
81 ibid., vol. II, pp. 286–7.
82 ibid., vol. III, p. 311.
83 Charke, pp. 209–10.
84 Phillips, vol. II, p. 247.
85 ibid., vol. I, p. 311.
86 Justice, pp. 107–8.
87 Phillips, vol. III, pp. 216, 229.
88 Pilkington, p. 342.
89 Phillips, vol. III, p. 315.
90 William Blackstone, *Commentaries on the Laws of England*, 4 vols, 1769, vol. IV, p. 150.
91 Charke, pp. 95–6. 'Amelia' also hints at duels as a solution to slander: 'Poor *Amelia* with a Change of Colour replies, I have heard that long since, which makes me wish to be a Man, she then should not say it twice' - Justice, p. 212.
92 Pilkington, p. 315.

93 Charke, p. 115.
94 Blackstone, vol. III, p. 125.
95 Alexander Pope, *The First Satire of the Second Book of Horace Imitated*, 1733, ll. 83–4, p. 616.
96 Phillips, vol. II, p. 227.
97 Blackstone, vol. III, p. 123:

> Words spoken in derogation of a peer, a judge, or other great officer of the realm, which are called *scandalum magnatum*, are held to be still more heinous; and, though they be such as would not be actionable in the case of a common person, yet when spoken in disgrace of such high and respectable characters, they amount to an atrocious injury.

98 ibid., p. 125. A *Tatler* paper in which Richard Steele criticizes the prevalence of libels denigrating great men suggests that literati were aware of the threat posed to high-culture satire by competition from libel.
99 Henry Fielding, *Amelia*, Wesleyan edition, ed. Martin C. Battesin, Oxford, Oxford University Press, 1983, p. 52.
100 ibid., pp. 44–5.
101 ibid., pp. 172, 177.
102 ibid., p. 185.
103 ibid., p. 225.
104 For a full account of the theory and practice of eighteenth-century masquerade, see Terry Castle, *Masquerade and Civilization*, Stanford, Stanford University Press, 1986.
105 Smollett, Everyman edition, vol. II, p. 148.
106 Pilkington, p. 33.
107 ibid., p. 345.
108 A frame used by William Ray in his study of the dynamics of self and narrative in eighteenth-century English and French fictions: *Story and History*, Oxford, Blackwell, 1990.

BIBLIOGRAPHY

PRIMARY SOURCES

Manuscripts

Bodleian MS North c.4, fol. 146.
Wroth, Lady Mary. *The Countess of Montgomery's Urania*, MS continuation, Newberry Library, Chicago, call no. Case MS f. Y1565.W95.

Books

Note: Place of publication for works printed before 1800 is London unless otherwise stated.

Addison, Joseph and Richard Steele. *The Tatler*, ed. Donald F. Bond, Oxford, Clarendon, 1987.
Agrippa, Cornelius. *A Treatise of the Nobilitie and Excellencye of Womankynde*, trans. David Clapham, 1542.
Amours of the Sultana of Barbary, The, 1689.
Anger, Jane (pseud.). *Jane Anger her Protection for Women*, 1589.
Astell, Mary. *The Christian Religion, as Profess'd by a Daughter of the Church of England*, 1705.
Astell, Mary. *A Serious Proposal to the Ladies, For the Advancement of their True and Greatest Interest. By a Lover of Her Sex*, 1694.
Astell, Mary. *A Serious Proposal to the Ladies, Part II. Wherein a Method is offer'd for the Improvement of their Minds*, 1697.
Aulnoy, Marie, Baronne d'. *The Ingenious and Diverting Letters of the Lady—'s Travels into Spain*, 2nd edn, 1692.
Aulnoy, Marie, Baronne d'. *Memoires de la cour d'Anglettere*, 1695.
Aulnoy, Marie, Baronne d'. *Memoires de la cour d'Espagne*, 1679–81.
Aulnoy, Marie, Baronne d'. *Memoires sur la cour de France*, 1692.
Aulnoy, Marie, Baronne d'. *Memoirs of the Court of England*, 1707.

B., F. *Vercingetorixa: or, the Germane Princess Reduc'd to an English Habit*, 1663.

Behn, Aphra. *A Discovery of New Worlds* (trans. of B. de Fontenelle), 1688.

Behn, Aphra. *The Emperor of the Moon*, 1687.

Behn, Aphra. *Oroonoko and Other Stories*, ed. Maureen Duffy, London, Methuen, 1986 (1st pub. 1688).

Behn, Aphra. *Poems Upon Several Occasions*, 1694.

Blackstone, William. *Commentaries on the Laws of England*, 4 vols, 1769.

Carleton [Anon]. *The Arraignment, Tryal and Examination of Mary Moders*, 1663.

Carleton [Anon]. *The Deportment and Carriage of the German Princess*, 1673.

Carleton [Anon]. *An Elegie on the Famous and Renowned Lady*, 1673.

Carleton [Anon]. *An Exact and True Relation of . . . Mary Carleton*, 1673.

Carleton [Anon]. *The Female-Hector, or, the Germane Lady Turn'd Mounsieur*, 1663.

Carleton [Anon]. *The Great Tryall and Arraignment of the Late Distressed Lady*, 1663.

Carleton [Anon]. *The Lawyers Clarke Trappan'd by the Crafty Whore of Canterbury*, 1663.

Carleton [Anon]. *The Life and Character of Mrs Mary Moders*, 2nd edn, 1732.

Carleton [Anon]. *Memories of the Life of the Famous Madam Charlton*, 1673.

Carleton [Anon]. *The Memoires of Mary Carleton*, 1673.

Carleton [Anon]. *News From Jamaica*, 1671.

Carleton [Anon]. *Some Luck, Some Wit*, 1673.

Carleton [Anon]. *A True Account of the Tryal of Mrs Mary Carlton*, 1663.

Carleton [Anon]. *A Vindication of a Distressed Lady*, 1663.

Carleton [Anon]. *The Westminster Wedding*, 1663.

Carleton, John. *The Replication, Or Certain Vindicatory Depositions*, 1663.

Carleton, John. *The Ultimum Vale of John Carleton*, 1663.

Carleton, Mary. *The Case of Madam Mary Carleton*, 1663.

Carleton, Mary. *An Historicall Narrative of the German Princess*, 1663.

Cary, Mary [Rande]. *The Little Horns Doom and Downfall*, followed by *A New and More Exact Mappe of New Jerusalems Glory when Jesus Christ and his Saints with him shall Reign on Earth a Thousand Years, and Possess all Kingdoms*, 1651.

Cary, Mary [M.R.]. *Twelve Humble Proposals To the Supreme Governours of the three Nations now assembled at Westminster*, 1653.

Cavendish, Lady Jane and Lady Elizabeth Brackley. '*The Concealed Fansyes*, by Lady Jane Cavendish and Lady Elizabeth Brackley', ed. N.C. Starr, *PMLA* 46, 1931: 802–38.

Cavendish, Margaret. *CCXI Sociable Letters*, 1664, New York, Scolar, 1969.

Cavendish, Margaret. *The Life of William Cavendish, Duke of Newcastle, to Which is Added the True Relation of my Birth, Breeding and Life*, ed. C.H. Firth, 2nd edn, London, Routledge, 1906.

Cavendish, Margaret. *Observations upon Experimental Philosophy*, followed by *The Description of a New World called the Blazing-World*, 1668 (first pub. 1666).

Cavendish, Margaret. *Orations of Divers Sorts*, 1662.

Cavendish, Margaret. *Philosophical and Physical Opinions*, 2nd edn, revised and expanded, 1663 (first pub. 1655).

Cavendish, Margaret. *Playes Written by the Thrice Noble, Illustrious and Excellent Princess, the Lady Marchioness of Newcastle*, 1662.

Cavendish, Margaret. *Plays, Never Before Printed*, 1668.

Cavendish, Margaret. *Poems and Fancies*, 1653.

Cavendish, Margaret. *Poems and Phancies*, 2nd imp. 1664.

Cavendish, Margaret. *The World's Olio*, 1655.

Charke, Charlotte. *A Narrative of the Life of Mrs. Charlotte Charke*, London, Constable, 1929 (first pub. 1755).

Churchill, Sarah. *Private Correspondence of Sarah, Duchess of Marlborough, Illustrative of the Court and Times of Queen Anne with her Sketches and Opinions of her Contemporaries and the Select Correspondence of her Husband, John, Duke of Marlborough*, London, Colburn, 1838.

Cotton, Charles. *Erotopolis: or the Present State of Bettyland*, 1684.

D'Urfé, Honoré. *L'Astrée*, 1607–27, trans. 1620.

Davidson, Clifford (ed.). *Torquato Tasso's Aminta Englisht. The Henry Reynolds Translation*, Fennimore, WN: John Westburg & Associates, 1972.

Defoe, Daniel. *Moll Flanders*, ed. David Blewett, London, Penguin, 1989.

Dekker, Thomas and Thomas Middleton. *The Roaring Girl*, ed. Paul A. Mulholland, Manchester, Manchester University Press, 1987.

Dod, John and Richard Cleaver. *A Godly Forme of Householde Governmente*, 1614.

Dryden, John. *Essays of John Dryden*, ed. W.P. Ker, New York, Russell & Russell, 1961.

E., T. *The Lawes Resolutions of Womens Rights*, 1632.

Elyot, Sir Thomas. *Defence of Good Women*, 1542.

Exact Diurnall of the Parliament of Ladyes, An, 1647.

F.B. *See* B., F.

Fehrenbach, R.J. 'A Letter Sent by the Maydens of London (1567)', *English Literary Renaissance* 14, 1984: 285–304.

Ferguson, Moira (ed.). *First Feminists: British Women Writers 1578–1799*, Bloomington, Indiana University Press, 1985.

Fifth and Last Part of the Wandring Whore, The, 1661.

Flecknoe, Richard. *A Relation of Ten Years Travells in Europe, Asia, Affrique and America*, 1654.

Fone, B.R. (ed.). *An Apology for the Life of Colley Cibber, with a historical view of the stage during his own times*, Ann Arbor, University of Michigan Press, 1968.

Gallant She-Souldier, The, 1655.

Goodman, Nicholas. *Hollands Leaguer*, 1632.

Gosynhill, Edward. *Mulierum Paen*, 1542.

Gosynhill, Edward. *Scholehouse of Women*, 1542.

Green, M.A.E. (ed.). *Letters of Queen Henrietta Maria*, London, 1857.

Greer, Germaine, Jeslyn Medoff, Melinda Sansone and Susan Hastings (eds). *Kissing the Rod: An Anthology of Seventeenth-Century Women's Verse*, London, Virago, 1988.

Haec Vir, or the Womanish Man, 1620.

Hey Hoe for a Husband, or, the Parliament of Maides, 1647.

Hic Mulier, or the Man-Woman, 1620.

Howard, Edward. *The Six Days Adventure or the New Utopia. A Comedy*, 1671.

Jonson, Ben. *The New Inn*, ed. M. Hattaway, *The Revels Plays*, Manchester, Manchester University Press, 1984.

Jonson, Ben. *Poems*, ed. Ian Donaldson, Oxford, Oxford University Press, 1978.

Justice, Elizabeth. *Amelia, or, The Distress'd Wife: A HISTORY founded in REAL Circumstances. By a Private GENTLEWOMAN*, 1751.

Kirkman, Francis. *The Counterfeit Lady Unveiled*, 1673.

Lanyer, Aemilia. *The Poems of Shakespeare's Dark Lady: Salve Deus, Rex Judeorum by Emilia Lanyer*, ed. A.L. Rowse, London, Cape, 1976.

Latham, R. and W. Matthews (eds). *The Diary of Samuel Pepys*, 11 vols, London, Bell, 1970–83.

Life and Death of Mrs Mary Frith. Commonly called Mal Cutpurse, The, 1662.

Life of Long Meg of Westminster, The, 1635, reprinted in *Miscellanea Antiqua Anglicana; or a Select Collection of Curious Tracts*, vol. I, London, 1816.

Lord, E. *Translation of the Orpheus of Angelo Politian and the Aminta of Torquato Tasso*, London, 1931.

Manley, Delarivier. *The Duke of M—h's Vindication*, 1711.

Manley, Delarivier. *A Learned Comment Upon Dr Hare's Excellent Sermon*, 1711.

Manley, Delarivier. *The Novels of Mary Delarivier Manley 1704–1714*, ed. Patricia Koster, 2 vols, Gainesville, FL, Scholars' Facsimiles and Reprints, 1971.

Manley, Delarivier. *A True Narrative of What Pass'd at the Examination of the Marquis de Guiscard at the Cock-Pit the 8th March 1710/11*, 1711.

Motteville, Françoise Bertaud de. 'A Short History of the Troubles in England', in *Memoirs for the History of Anne of Austria*, trans. from the French, 5 vols, 1725–6.

Mulde Sacke, or the Apology of Hic Mulier, 1620.

Munda, Constantia. *The Worming of A Mad Dogge*, 1617.

[Murat, Madame de.] *The Memoirs of the Countess of Dunois: Author of the Lady's Travels into Spain*, 1699.

Neville, Henry. *The Parliament of Ladies*, 1647.

Pallavicino, F. *The Whores Rhetorick Calculated to the Meridian of London and Conformed to the Rules of Art in Two Dialogues*, 1683.

Parliament of Women . . . with the Merry Laws, The, 1646.

Parliament of Women: or, a Compleat History, The, 1684.

Phillips, Teresia Constantia. *An Apology for the Conduct of Mrs Teresia*

Constantia Phillips, London, 3 vols, 1748–9.

Pilkington, Laetitia. *Memoirs of Mrs Laetitia Pilkington 1712–1750 Written by Herself*, ed. Iris Barry, London, Routledge, 1928 (1st edn. 1748–54).

Porter, Thomas. *A Witty Combat*, 1663.

Rabutin, Roger de, Count de Bussy. *The Amorous History of the Gauls, Written in French By Roger de Rabutin, Count de Bussy, And now Translated into English*, 1725.

Relation of the Life of Christina Queen of Sweden, A, 1656.

Rival Duchess, or Court Incendiary, The, 1708.

Roxburghe Ballads, The, ed. William Chappell and Joseph Woodfall Ebsworth, 9 vols, Hertford, Stephen Austin & Sons, 1871–99.

Shepherd, Simon (ed.). *The Women's Sharp Revenge: Five Women's Pamphlets from the Renaissance*, London, Fourth Estate, 1985.

Shirley, James. *The Dramatic Works and Poems of James Shirley*, ed. W. Gifford and A. Dyce, 6 vols, London, 1833.

Sowernam, Ester. *Ester hath Hang'd Haman*, 1617.

Speght, Rachel. *A Mouzell for Melastomus*, 1617.

Speght, Rachel. *Mortalities Memorandum*, 1621.

Stretzer, T. *A New Description of Merryland, Containing a Topographical, Geographical and Natural History of that Country*, 1740.

Swetnam, Joseph. *The Arraignment of Lewd, Idle, Froward and Unconstant Woman*, 1615.

Swetnam, Joseph. *The Schoole of the Noble and Worthie Science of Defence*, 1617.

Swift, Jonathan. *A Tale of a Tub to Which is Added the Battle of the Books and the Mechanical Operation of the Spirit*, ed. A.C. Guthkelch and D. Nichol Smith, 2nd edn, Oxford, Clarendon, 1958 (first pub. 1704).

Tattle-well, Mary and Joan Hit-Him-Home. *The Womens Sharpe Revenge*, 1640.

Trapnel, Anna. *The Cry of a Stone: or a Relation of Something Spoken in Whitehall, by Anna Trapnel, being in the Visions of God*, 1654.

Travitsky, Betty. 'The "Wyll and Testament" of Isabella Whitney', *English Literary Renaissance* 10, 1980: 76–94.

[Vane, Frances Anne, Viscountess.] *The Adventures of Peregrine Pickle in which are included Memoirs of a Lady of Quality*, ed. James L. Clifford, rev. Paul-Gabriel Boucé, Oxford, Oxford University Press, 1983.

Virgins Complaint, The, 1643.

Whately, William. *A Bride-Bush, or a Directory for Married Persons*, 1619.

Whitelocke, Bulstrode. *A Journal of the Swedish Embassy in the Years 1653 and 1654*, 2 vols, 1772.

Widowes Lamentation, The, 1643.

Womans Champion, The, 1662.

Wroth, Lady Mary. *The Countesse of Mountgomeries Urania*, London, John Marriott & John Grismand, 1621.

Wroth, Lady Mary. *Lady Mary Wroth's Love's Victory: The Penshurst Manuscript*, ed. Michael G. Brennan, London, Roxburghe Club, 1988.

Wroth, Lady Mary. *Pamphilia to Amphilanthus*, ed. G.F. Waller, *Salzburg*

Studies in English Literature, Elizabethan & Renaissance Studies no. 64, 1977.

Wroth, Lady Mary. *The Poems of Lady Mary Wroth*, ed. Josephine A. Roberts, Baton Rouge and London, Louisiana State University Press, 1983.

SECONDARY SOURCES

History and social history

Amussen, Susan Dwyer. *An Ordered Society: Gender and Class in Early Modern England*, Oxford, Blackwell, 1988.

Bray, Alan. *Homosexuality in Renaissance England*, London, Gay Men's Press, 1982.

Burke, Peter. *Popular Culture in Early Modern Europe*, Aldershot, Wildwood, 1978.

Capp, Bernard. 'Popular Literature', in Barry Reay (ed.), *Popular Culture in Seventeenth-century England*, London, Routledge, 1985: 198–243.

Clark, Alice. *Working Life of Women in the Seventeenth Century*. New introduction by Miranda Chaytor and Jane Lewis, London, Routledge, 1982 (first pub. 1911).

Clark, Stuart. 'Inversion, Misrule and the Meaning of Witchcraft', *Past and Present* 87, 1980: 98–127.

Darnton, Robert. 'Don Juanism from Below', in Jonathan Miller (ed.), *The Don Giovanni Book: Myths of Seduction and Betrayal*, London, Faber, 1990: 20–35.

Davis, Natalie Zemon. 'Women on Top', in *Society and Culture in Early Modern France*, Cambridge, Polity, 1987: 124–51 (first pub. 1965).

Ezell, Margaret. *The Patriarch's Wife: Literary Evidence and the History of the Family*, Chapel Hill, North Carolina University Press, 1987.

Fildes, Valerie (ed.). *Women as Mothers in Pre-Industrial England*, London, Routledge, 1990.

George, Margaret. *Women in the First Capitalist Society: Experiences in Seventeenth-Century England*, Brighton, Harvester, 1988.

Higgins, Patricia. 'The Reactions of Women, With Special Reference to Women Petitioners', in Brian Manning (ed.), *Politics, Religion and the English Civil War*, London, Arnold, 1973: 179–222.

Hill, Bridget. *Women, Work and Sexual Politics in Eighteenth-Century England*, Oxford, Blackwell, 1989.

Holmes, Geoffrey and W.A. Speck (eds). *The Divided Society: Party Conflict in England 1694–1716*, London, Arnold, 1967.

Ingram, Martin. *Church Courts, Sex and Marriage in England, 1570–1640*, Cambridge, Cambridge University Press, 1988.

Ingram, Martin. 'Ridings, Rough Music and Mocking Rhymes in Early Modern England', in Barry Reay (ed.), *Popular Culture in Seventeenth-Century England*, London, Routledge, 1985: 166–97.

Jones, Vivien (ed.). *Women in the Eighteenth Century*, London and New York, Routledge, 1990.

Kent, Joan. 'Attitudes of Members of the House of Commons to the Regulation of "Personal Conduct" in Late Elizabethan and Early Stuart England', *Bulletin of the Institute for Historical Research* 46, 1973: 41–71.

Ladurie, Emmanuel Le Roy. *Carnival in Romans: A People's Uprising at Romans 1579–1580*, Harmondsworth, Penguin, 1979.

Lévi-Strauss, Claude. *The Elementary Structures of Kinship*, Boston, Massachusetts University Press, 1969.

Pateman, Carole. *The Sexual Contract*, Cambridge, Polity, 1988.

Prior, Mary (ed.). *Women in English Society 1500–1800*, London, Methuen, 1985.

Quaife, G.R. *Wanton Wenches and Wayward Wives: Peasants and Illicit Sex in Early Seventeenth-Century England*, London, Croom Helm, 1979.

Roper, Lyndal. *The Holy Household: Women and Morals in Reformation Augsberg*, Oxford, Oxford University Press, 1989.

Sharp, Buchanan. 'Popular Protest in Seventeenth-Century England', in Barry Reay (ed.), *Popular Culture in Seventeenth-Century England*, London, Routledge, 1985: 271–308.

Sharp, J. A. 'Plebeian Marriage in Stuart England; Some Evidence from Popular Literature', *Transactions of the Royal Historical Society*, 36, 1986: 69–90.

Smith, Hilda. 'Gynecology and Ideology in Seventeenth-Century England', in Berenice A. Carroll (ed.), *Liberating Women's History*, Urbana, Illinois University Press, 1976, 97–114.

Spufford, Margaret. *Small Books and Pleasant Histories: Popular Fiction and its Readership in Seventeenth-Century England*, Cambridge, Cambridge University Press, 1981.

Stone, Lawrence. *Broken Lives*, Oxford, Oxford University Press, forthcoming.

Stone, Lawrence. *Road to Divorce: England 1530–1987*, Oxford, Oxford University Press, 1990.

Thomas, Keith. *Rule and Misrule in the Schools of Early Modern England*, Reading, Reading University Press, 1976.

Thompson, E. P. 'Rough Music: Le Charivari Anglais', *Annales ESC* 27, 1972: 285–312.

Thompson, Roger. *Women in Stuart England and America: A Comparative Study*, London, Routledge & Kegan Paul, 1974.

Todd, Barbara J. 'The Remarrying Widow: A Stereotype Reconsidered', in Mary Prior (ed.), *Women in English Society 1500–1800*, London, Methuen, 1985: 54–92.

Trevelyan, G. M. *England under Queen Anne*, vol. 3 of *The Peace and the Protestant Succession*, London, Longman, 1934.

Underdown, David. *Revel, Riot and Rebellion: Popular Politics and Culture in England 1603–1660*, Oxford, Oxford University Press, 1985.

Underdown, David. 'The Taming of the Scold: The Enforcement of Patriarchal Authority in Early Modern England', in Anthony Fletcher and John Stevenson (eds), *Order and Disorder in Early Modern England*, Cambridge, Cambridge University Press, 1985: 116–36.

Warnicke, Retha M. *Women of the English Renaissance and Reformation*, Westport, CN, Greenwood, 1983.

Winkler, John J. *The Constraints of Desire: The Anthropology of Sex and Gender in Ancient Greece*, London and New York, Routledge, 1989.
Wrightson, Keith. *English Society 1580–1680*, London, Hutchinson, 1982.

Theory and criticism

Albinski, Nan Bowman. *Women's Utopias in British and American Fiction*, London, Routledge, 1988.
Anderson, Linda. 'At the Threshold of the Self: Women and Autobiography', in Moira Monteith (ed.), *Women's Writing: A Challenge to Theory*, Brighton, Harvester, 1986: 54–71.
Anderson, Paul Bunyan. 'Delariviere Manley's Prose Fiction', *Philological Quarterly* 13, 1934: 168–88.
Armstrong, Nancy. *Desire and Domestic Fiction*, New York, Oxford University Press, 1987.
Bakhtin, Mikhail. *Rabelais and his World*, trans. Helene Iswolsky, Bloomington, Indiana University Press, 1984.
Ballaster, Rosalind. 'Seizing the Means of Seduction: Fiction and Feminine Identity in Aphra Behn and Delarivier Manley', in Isobel Grundy and Susan J. Wiseman (eds), *Women/Writing/History 1640–1740*, London, Batsford, forthcoming.
Barker, Francis. *The Tremulous Private Body*, London and New York, Methuen, 1984.
Barr, Marleen S. (ed.) *Future Females: A Critical Anthology*, Bowling Green, OH, Bowling Green State University Popular Press, 1981.
Barr, Marleen S. and Nicholas D. Smith (eds). *Women and Utopia: Critical Interpretations*, Landham, MD, University Press of America, 1983.
Barrell, John. *English Literature in History 1730–80: An Equal, Wide Survey*, London, Hutchinson, 1983.
Bartkowski, Frances. *Feminist Utopias*, Lincoln, University of Nebraska Press, 1989.
Beer, Gillian. *The Romance*, London, Methuen, 1970.
Beilin, Elaine V. '"The Onely Perfect Vertue": Constancy in Mary Wroth's *Pamphilia to Amphilanthus*', *Spenser Studies* 2, 1981: 229–45.
Beilin, Elaine V. *Redeeming Eve: Women Writers of the English Renaissance*, Princeton, Princeton University Press, 1987.
Belsey, Catherine. *The Subject of Tragedy: Identity and Difference in Renaissance Drama*, London, Methuen, 1985.
Benstock, Shari (ed.) *The Private Self: Theory and Practice of Women's Autobiographical Writings*, London and New York, Routledge, 1988.
Bentley, G. E. *The Jacobean and Caroline Stage*, 7 vols, Oxford, Clarendon, 1941–68.
Berg, Christine and Philippa Berry. 'Spiritual Whoredom: An Essay on Female Prophets in the Seventeenth Century', in Francis Barker *et al.* (eds), *1642: Literature and Power in the Seventeenth Century*, Colchester, University of Essex, 1981: 37–54.
Bernbaum, Ernest. *The Mary Carleton Narratives 1663–1673*, Cambridge, MA, Harvard University Press, 1914.
Blain, Virginia, Patricia Clements and Isobel Grundy (eds). *The Feminist*

Companion to Literature in English: Women Writers from the Middle Ages to the Present, London, Batsford, 1990.

Bloch, R. Howard. 'Medieval Misogyny', *Representations* 20, 1987: 1–24.

Brown, Laura. 'The Romance of Empire: Oroonoko and the Trade in Slaves', in Laura Brown and Felicity A. Nussbaum (eds), *The New Eighteenth Century*, London and New York, Methuen, 1987: 41–61.

Browne, Alice. *The Eighteenth Century Feminist Mind*, Brighton, Harvester, 1987.

Castle, Terry. *Masquerade and Civilization*, Stanford, CA, Stanford University Press, 1986.

Cave, Terence. *The Cornucopian Text*, Oxford, Clarendon, 1979.

Chandler, F.W. *The Literature of Roguery*, London, Archibald Constable, 1907.

Cixous, Hélène and Catherine Clément. *The Newly Born Woman*, trans. Betsy Wing, Minneapolis, University of Minnesota Press, 1986 (first pub. in French 1975).

Clark, Anna. 'Whores and Gossips: Sexual Reputation in London 1770–1825' in Arina Angerman *et al.* (eds), *Current Issues in Women's History*, London and New York, Routledge, 1989.

Clark, Sandra. '*Hic Mulier, Haec Vir*, and the Controversy over Masculine Women', *Studies in Philology*, 82, 1985: 157–83.

Cohen, Alfred. 'The Fifth Monarchy Mind: Mary Cary and the Origins of Totalitarianism', *Social Research* 31, 1964: 195–213.

Cohen, Walter. 'Political Criticism of Shakespeare', in Jean E. Howard and Marion F. O' Connor (eds), *Shakespeare Reproduced: The Text in History and Ideology*, London, Methuen, 1987, 18–46.

Cotton, Nancy. *Women Playwrights in England c.1363–1750*, London and Toronto, Associated University Presses, 1980.

Crawford, Patricia. 'Women's Published Writings 1600–1700', in Mary Prior (ed.), *Women in English Society 1500–1800*, London, Methuen, 1985: 211–82.

Cropper, Elizabeth. 'The Beauty of Woman: Problems in the Rhetoric of Renaissance Portraiture', in Margaret W. Ferguson, Maureen Quilligan and Nancy J. Vickers (eds), *Rewriting the Renaissance: The Discourses of Sexual Difference in Early Modern Europe*, Chicago, University of Chicago Press, 1986: 175–90.

Davis, J.C. *Utopia and the Ideal Society. A Study of English Utopian Writing 1516–1700*, Cambridge, Cambridge University Press, 1981.

Davis, Lennard. *Factual Fictions; The Origins of the English Novel*, New York, Columbia University Press, 1983.

Day, Gary. 'Looking at Women: Notes Towards a Theory of Porn', in Gary Day and Clive Bloom (eds), *Perspectives on Pornography: Sexuality in Film and Literature*, London, Macmillan, 1988, pp. 83–100.

De Lauretis, Teresa. 'The essence of the triangle or, taking the risk of essentialism seriously: feminist theory in Italy, the U.S., and Britain', *differences* 1(2), 1989: 3–37.

De Lauretis, Teresa. 'Feminist Studies/Critical Studies: Issues, Terms and Contexts', in *Feminist Studies/Critical Studies*, London, Macmillan, 1986, pp. 1–19.

BIBLIOGRAPHY

De Lauretis, Teresa. *Technologies of Gender: Essays on Theory, Film, and Fiction*, Bloomington and Indianapolis, Indiana University Press, 1988.

Dekker, Rudolf, and Van de Pol, Lotte. *The Tradition of Female Transvestism in Early Modern Europe*, London, Macmillan, 1989.

Derrida, Jacques. 'Signature Event Context', in *Margins of Philosophy*, trans. Alan Bass, Brighton, Harvester, 1982: 307–30.

Diamond, Elin '*Gestus* and Signature in Aphra Behn's *The Rover*', *English Literary History* 56, 1989: 519–41.

Docherty, Thomas. *On Modern Authority: The Theory and Condition of Writing 1500 to the Present*, Brighton and New York, Harvester & St Martin's Press, 1987.

Downie, J.A. *Robert Harley and the Press: Propaganda and Public Opinion in the Age of Swift and Defoe*, Cambridge, Cambridge University Press, 1979.

Dugaw, Dianne. *Warrior Women and Popular Balladry 1650–1850*, Cambridge Studies in Eighteenth Century English Literature and Thought 4, Cambridge, Cambridge University Press, 1990.

Dworkin, Andrea. *Pornography: Men Possessing Women*, London, Women's Press, 1982.

Eagleton, Terry. *The Function of Criticism*, Oxford, Blackwell, 1984.

Edwards, Philip, Gerald Eades Bentley, Kathleen McLuskie and Lois Potter. *The Revels History of Drama in English, Vol. IV 1613–1660*, London and New York, Methuen, 1981.

Elkin, P.K. *The Augustan Defence of Satire*, Oxford, Clarendon, 1973.

Fabricant, Carol. 'Binding and Dressing Nature's Loose Tresses: The Ideology of Augustan Landscape Design', *Studies in Eighteenth-Century Culture* 8, 1983: 109–35.

Faller, Lincoln B. *Turned to Account: The Forms and Functions of Criminal Biography in the Late Seventeenth- and Early Eighteenth-Century England*, Cambridge, Cambridge University Press, 1987.

Ferguson, Margaret W., Maureen Quilligan and Nancy J. Vickers (eds). *Rewriting the Renaissance: The Discourses of Sexual Difference in Early Modern Europe*, Chicago, University of Chicago Press, 1986.

Findley, Sandra and Elaine Hobby. 'Seventeenth-Century Women's Autobiography', in Francis Barker *et al.* (eds), *1642: Literature and Power in the Seventeenth Century*, Colchester, University of Essex, 1981: 11–36.

Fitz, Linda. '"What Says the Married Woman?" Marriage Theory and Feminism in the English Renaissance', *Mosaic*, 13, 1980: 1–22.

Foster, H. (ed.) *Vision and Visuality*, Seattle, Bay Press, 1988.

Foucault, Michel. *The History of Sexuality Vol. 1: An Introduction*, trans. Robert Hurley, Harmondsworth, Penguin, 1984 (first pub. in French 1977).

Foucault, Michel. *The Order of Things; An Archaeology of the Human Sciences*, London, Tavistock, 1970 (first pub. in French 1966).

Foulché-Delbosc, Raymond. 'Madame d'Aulnoy et l'Espagne', *Revue hispanique* 67, 1926: 1–151.

Foxon, David. *Libertine Literature in England 1660–1745*, New York, University Books, 1963.

Franklin, W. *Discoverers, Explorers, Settlers: The Diligent Writers of Early America*, Chicago and London, Chicago University Press, 1979.

Fraser, Antonia. *The Weaker Vessel: Woman's Lot in Seventeenth-Century England*, London, Weidenfeld and Nicolson, 1984.

Fraser, Nancy. *Unruly Practices. Power, Discourse and Gender in Contemporary Social Theory*, Minneapolis, University of Minnesota Press, 1989.

Friedman, Susan Stanford. 'Women's Autobiographical Selves', in Shari Benstock (ed.), *The Private Self: Theory and Practice of Women's Autobiographical Writings*, London and New York, Routledge, 1988.

Gallagher, Catherine. *The Industrial Reformation of English Fiction*, Chicago, University of Chicago Press, 1985.

Gallagher, Catherine. 'Embracing the Absolute: The Politics of the Female Subject in Seventeenth-Century England', *Genders* 1(1), 1988: 24–39.

Gallagher, Catherine. 'Who was that Masked Woman? The Prostitute and the Playwright in the Comedies of Aphra Behn', *Women's Studies* 15, 1988: 23–42.

Gibson, R.W. and J. Max Patrick. 'Utopias and Dystopias 1500–1750', in *St. Thomas More: A Preliminary Bibliography of his Works and of Moreana to the Year 1750*, New Haven, CN, Yale University Press, 1961.

Gilbert, O.P. *Women in Men's Guise*, trans. J. Lewis May, London, Bodley Head, 1932.

Goreau, Angeline. 'Two English Women in the Seventeenth Century: Notes for an Anatomy of Female Desire', in Philippe Ariés and André Béjin (eds), *Western Sexuality: Practice and Precept in Past and Present Times*, trans. Anthony Forster, Oxford, Blackwell, 1985.

Goreau, Angeline. *The Whole Duty of a Woman: Female Writers in Seventeenth-Century England*, New York, Dial, 1985.

Graham, Elspeth, Hilary Hinds, Elaine Hobby and Helen Wilcox (eds). *Her Own Life: Autobiographical Writings by Seventeenth-Century Englishwomen*, London, Routledge, 1989.

Grant, Douglas. *Margaret the First: A Biography of Margaret Cavendish, Duchess of Newcastle*, London, Rupert Hart-Davies, 1957.

Griffin, Susan. *Pornography and Silence*, London, Women's Press, 1982.

Grundy, Isobel and Susan J. Wiseman (eds). *Women/Writing/History 1640–1740*, London, Batsford, 1992.

Habermas, Jurgen. *The Structural Transformation of the Public Sphere: An Inquiry into a Category of Bourgeois Society*, trans. Thomas Burger with the assistance of Frederick Lawrence, Cambridge, Polity, 1989.

Hannay, Margaret Patterson. 'Mary Sidney: Lady Wroth', in Katharina M. Wilson (ed.), *Women Writers of the Renaissance and Reformation*, Athens and London, University of Georgia Press, 1987: 548–65.

Hannay, Margaret Patterson (ed.). *Silent But For the Word: Tudor Women as Patrons, Translators, and Writers of Religious Works*, Kent, OH, Kent State University Press, 1985.

Haraway, Donna. 'A Manifesto for Cyborgs: Science, Technology, and Socialist Feminism in the 1980s', in Elizabeth Weed (ed.), *Coming to Terms. Feminism, Theory, Politics*, London, Routledge, 1989 (first pub. 1985).

Harbage, Alfred. *Cavalier Drama*, New York, Russell & Russell, 1964 (first pub. 1936).

Henderson, Katherine Usher, and Barbara F. McManus (eds). *Half Humankind: Contexts and Texts of the Controversy about Women in England 1540–1640*, Urbana and Chicago, Chicago University Press, 1985.

Hill, Bridget (ed.). *The First English Feminist: Reflections upon Marriage and other Writings by Mary Astell*, London, Gower/Temple Smith, 1986.

Hobby, Elaine. *Virtue of Necessity. English Women's Writing 1649–88*, London, Virago, 1988.

Holstun, James. *A Rational Millennium. Puritan Utopias of Seventeenth-Century England and America*, New York and Oxford, Oxford University Press, 1987.

Hotson, Leslie. *The Commonwealth and Restoration Stage*, Cambridge, MA, Harvard University Press, 1928.

Howe, E. *Women and Drama: The First English Actresses*, Cambridge, Cambridge University Press, forthcoming.

Humm, Maggie. 'Is the Gaze Feminist? Pornography, Film and Feminism', in Gary Day and Clive Bloom (eds), *Perspectives on Pornography: Sexuality in Film and Literature*, London, Macmillan, 1988, pp. 69–82.

Hutson, Lorna. *Thomas Nashe in Context*, Oxford, Clarendon, 1989.

Irigaray, Luce. *This Sex Which Is Not One*, trans. Catherine Porter with Carolyn Burke, Ithaca, Cornell University Press, 1985.

Jack, Ian. *Augustan Satire*, Oxford, Clarendon, 1966.

Jackson, Rosemary. *Fantasy: The Literature of Subversion*, London, Methuen, 1981.

Jameson, Fredric. 'Of islands and trenches: naturalizations and the production of utopian discourse', *diacritics* 7(2), 1977: 2–21.

Jardine, Lisa. *Still Harping on Daughters: Women and Drama in the Age of Shakespeare*, Brighton, Harvester, 1983.

Jed, Stephanie H. *Chaste Thinking: The Rape of Lucrece and the Birth of Humanism*, Bloomington, Indiana University Press, 1989.

Jones, Ann Rosalind. 'Counterattacks on "the Bayter of Women": Three Pamphleteers of the Early Seventeenth Century', in Anne M. Haselkorn and Betty S. Travitsky (eds), *The Renaissance Englishwoman in Print: Counterbalancing the Canon*, Amherst, Massachusetts University Press, 1990: 45–62.

Jones, Ann Rosalind. 'Surprising Fame: Renaissance Gender Ideologies and Women's Lyric', in Nancy K. Miller (ed.), *The Poetics of Gender*, New York, Columbia University Press, 1986.

Jones, Kathleen. *A Glorious Fame: The Life of Margaret Cavendish Duchess of Newcastle, 1623–1673*, London, Bloomsbury, 1988.

Jordan, Constance. 'Feminism and the Humanists: The Case of Sir Thomas Elyot's *Defence of Good Women*' in Margaret W. Ferguson, Maureen Quilligan and Nancy J. Vickers (eds), *Rewriting the Renaissance: The Discourses of Sexual Difference in Early Modern Europe*, Chicago, University of Chicago Press, 1986: 242–58.

Kahn, Victoria. *Rhetoric, Prudence and Scepticism in the Renaissance*, Ithaca, Cornell University Press, 1985.

Kappeler, Susanne. *The Pornography of Representation*, Cambridge, Polity, 1986.

Kelly, Joan. 'Early Feminist Theory and the *querelle des femmes*', in

Women, History and Theory: The Essays of Joan Kelly, Chicago, Chicago University Press, 1984.

Kolodny, Annette. *The Lay of the Land: Metaphor as Experience and History in American Life and Letters*, Chapel Hill, University of North Carolina Press, 1975.

Köster, Patricia. 'Delariviere Manley and the DNB', *Eighteenth-Century Life*, 1977, 3: 106–11.

Kropf, C.R. 'Libel and Satire in the Eighteenth Century', *Eighteenth Century Studies* 8, 1974–5: 153–68.

Laqueur, Thomas. 'Orgasm, Generation, and the Politics of Reproductive Biology', *Representations* 14, 1986: 1–41.

Le Doeuff, Michèle. *The Philosophical Imaginary*, trans. Colin Gordon, London, Athlone Press, 1989.

Le Doeuff, Michèle. 'Utopias: Scholarly', trans. Susan Rotenstreich, *Social Research* 49(2) 1982: 441–66.

Lefanu, Sarah. *In the Chinks of the World Machine. Feminism and Science Fiction*, London, Women's Press, 1988.

Levin, Carole and Jeanie Watson (eds). *Ambiguous Realities; Women in the Middle Ages and the Renaissance*, Detroit, Wayne State University Press, 1987.

Lewalski, Barbara. 'Of God and Good Women: the Poems of Aemilia Lanyer', in Margaret Patterson Hannay (ed.), *Silent But for the Word: Tudor Women as Patrons, Translators and Writers of Religious Works*, Kent, OH, Kent State University Press, 1985.

London, April. 'Placing the Female: The Metonymic Garden in Amatory and Pious Narrative 1700–1740', in Cecilia Macheski and Mary Anne Schofield (eds), *Fetter'd or Free? British Women Novelists 1670–1815*, Athens, OH, Ohio University Press, 1985.

MacCarthy, Brigid M. *Women Writers: Their Contribution to the English Novel 1621–1744*, Cork, Cork University Press, 1944.

Macheski, Cecilia and Mary Anne Schofield (eds). *Fetter'd or Free? British Women Novelists 1670–1815*, Athens, OH, Ohio University Press, 1985.

Mack, Phyllis. 'Women as Prophets during the English Civil War', *Feminist Studies* 8(1) 1982: 18–45.

McKeon, Michael. *The Origins of the English Novel 1600–1740*, London, Hutchinson, and Baltimore, Johns Hopkins University Press, 1987.

Maclean, Ian. *Woman Triumphant: Feminism in French Literature 1610–1652*, Oxford, Oxford University Press, 1977.

Main, C.F. 'The German Princess; or, Mary Carleton in Fact and Fiction', *Harvard Library Bulletin*, 1956, 10: 166–85.

Manuel, Frank E. and Fritzie P. Manuel. *Utopian Thought in the Western World*, Oxford, Blackwell, 1979.

Marcus, Steven. *The Other Victorians: A Study of Sexuality and Pornography in Mid-Nineteenth-Century England*, New York, Median, 1964.

Marin, Louis. *Utopics: Spatial Play*, trans. Robert A. Vollrath, London, Macmillan, 1984.

Marks, Elaine and Isabelle de Courtivron (eds). *New French Feminisms*, Amherst, University of Massachusetts Press, 1980.

Masson, G. *Queen Christina*, London, Secker & Warburg, 1968.

Maus, K.E. '"Playhouse Flesh and Blood": Sexual Ideology and the Restoration Actress', *English Literary History* 46, 1979: 595–617.

Mendelson, Sara Heller. *The Mental World of Stuart Women: Three Case Studies*, Brighton, Harvester, 1987.

Moi, Toril. *Sexual/Textual Politics*, London, Methuen, 1985.

Morgan, Fidelis. *A Woman of No Character: An Autobiography of Mrs Manley*, London, Faber, 1986.

Needham, Gwendolyn. 'Mary De La Riviere Manley: Tory Defender', *Huntington Library Quarterly* 12, 1948–9: 253–88.

Nelson Paulissen, May. *The Love Sonnets of Lady Mary Wroth, A Critical Introduction, Salzburg Studies in English Literature, Elizabethan and Renaissance Studies* 104, 1982.

Nicolson, Marjorie Hope. *Voyages to the Moon*, New York, Macmillan, 1948.

Novak, Maximillian E. '"Appearances of Truth": The Literature of Crime as a Narrative System 1660–1841', *Yearbook of English Studies* 11, 1981: 29–48.

Nussbaum, Felicity. *The Autobiographical Subject: Gender and Ideology in Eighteenth-Century England*, Baltimore and London, Johns Hopkins University Press, 1989.

Nussbaum, Felicity. *The Brink of All We Hate: English Satires on Women 1660–1750*, Lexington, University Press of Kentucky, 1984.

Nussbaum, Felicity. 'Eighteenth-Century Women's Autobiographical Commonplaces', in Shari Benstock (ed.), *The Private Self: Theory and Practice of Women's Autobiographical Writings*, London, Routledge, 1988.

Nussbaum, Felicity. 'Heteroclites: The Gender of Character in the Scandalous Memoirs', in Laura Brown and Felicity A. Nussbaum (eds), *The New Eighteenth Century*, London, Methuen, 1987: 144–67.

O'Faolain, Julia and Lauro Martines (eds). *Not in God's Image*, London, Women's Press, 1973.

Oman, Carola. *Henrietta Maria*, London, Hodder & Stoughton, 1936.

Ong, Walter. 'Latin Language Study as a Renaissance Puberty Rite', *Studies in Philology* 56, 1959: 103–24.

Palmer, Melvin D. 'Madame d'Aulnoy in England', *Comparative Literature* 27, 1975: 237–53.

Paloma, Dolores. 'Margaret Cavendish: Defining the Female Self', *Women's Studies* 7, 1980, 55–66.

Parker, Patricia. *Literary Fat Ladies: Rhetoric, Gender, Property*, London, Methuen, 1987.

Pateman, Carole. *The Disorder of Women: Democracy, Feminism and Political Theory*, Cambridge, Polity, 1989.

Patterson, Annabel. *Censorship and Interpretation: The Conditions of Writing and Reading in Early Modern England*, Madison, University of Wisconsin Press, 1984.

Paulson, Ronald. *Satire and the Novel in Eighteenth-Century England*, London and New Haven, CN, Yale University Press, 1967.

Pearson, Jacqueline. *The Prostituted Muse: Images of Women and Women Dramatists 1642–1737*, Brighton, Harvester, 1988.

Perry, Ruth. *The Celebrated Mary Astell. An Early English Feminist*, Chicago, University of Chicago Press, 1986.

Pollak, Ellen. *The Poetics of Sexual Myth: Gender and Ideology in the Verse of Swift and Pope*, Chicago and London, University of Chicago Press, 1985.

Poovey, Mary. *Uneven Developments: The Ideological Work of Gender in Mid-Victorian England*, London, Virago, 1988.

Pugh, Simon. *Garden-Nature-Language*, Manchester and New York, Manchester University Press, 1988.

Quilligan, Maureen. 'Lady Mary Wroth: female authority and the family romance', in George M. Logan and Gordon Teskey (eds), *Unfolded Tales: Essays on Renaissance Romance*, Ithaca, and London, Cornell University Press, 1989.

Ray, William. *Story and History*, Oxford, Blackwell, 1990.

Reynolds, Myra. *The Learned Lady in England from 1650 to 1760*, Gloucester, MA, Peter Smith, 1964.

Ricoeur, Paul. *Lectures on Ideology and Utopia*, ed. George H. Taylor, New York, Columbia University Press, 1986.

Riley, Denise. *'Am I That Name?' Feminism and the Category of 'Women' in History*, London, Macmillan, 1988.

Roberts, Josephine A. 'An Unpublished Literary Quarrel Concerning the Suppression of Mary Wroth's *Urania* (1621)', *Notes and Queries* n. s. 24, 1977: 532–5.

Rogers, Katharine M. and William McCarthy. *The Meridian Anthology of Early Women Writers. British Literary Women from Aphra Behn to Maria Edgeworth 1660–1800*, New York, Meridian, 1987.

Rose, Mary Beth. 'Gender, Genre, and History: Seventeenth Century English Women and the Art of Autobiography', in *Women in the Middle Ages and the Renaissance: Literary and Historical Perspectives*, Syracuse, NY, Syracuse University Press, 1986: 245–78.

Rosinsky, Natalie M. *Feminist Futures: Contemporary Women's Speculative Fiction*, Ann Arbor, UMI Research Press, 1984.

Salzman, Paul. 'Contemporary References in Lady Mary Wroth's Urania', *Review of English Studies* 19, 1978: 178–81.

Salzman, Paul. *English Prose Fiction 1558–1700: A Critical History*, Oxford, Clarendon, 1985.

Sarahson, Lisa T. 'A Science Turned Upside Down: Feminism and the Natural Philosophy of Margaret Cavendish', *Huntington Library Quarterly* 47, 1984: 299–307.

Sargent, Lyman Tower. *British and American Utopian Literature 1516–1985: An Annotated, Chronological Bibliography*, New York, Garland, 1988.

Scott, Joan Wallach. 'Gender: A Useful Category of Historical Analysis', in *Gender and the Politics of History*, New York, Columbia University Press, 1988.

Shepherd, Simon. *Amazons and Warrior Women: Varieties of Feminism in Seventeenth-Century Drama*, Brighton, Harvester, 1981.

Shevelow, Kathryn. *Women and Print Culture: The Construction of Femininity in the Early Periodical*, London and New York, Routledge, 1989.

Showalter, Elaine. 'Towards a Feminist Poetics', in Mary Jacobus (ed.),

Women Writing and Writing About Women, London, Croom Helm, 1979: 22–41.

Singleton, Robert R. 'English Criminal Biography 1651–1722', *Harvard Library Bulletin* 18, 1970: 63–83.

Smith, Hilda. *Reason's Disciples: Seventeenth-Century English Feminists*, Urbana, University of Illinois Press, 1982.

Smith, Joan. *Misogynies*, London, Faber, 1989.

Smith, Nigel. *Perfection Proclaimed*, Oxford, Clarendon, 1989.

Spacks, Patricia Meyer. *Gossip*, Chicago and London, University of Chicago Press, 1986.

Spencer, Jane. *The Rise of the Woman Novelist from Aphra Behn to Jane Austen*, Oxford, Blackwell, 1986.

Spender, Dale. *Mothers of the Novel: 100 Good Women Writers before Jane Austen*, London, Pandora, 1986.

Stallybrass, Peter. '"Drunk With The Cup Of Liberty": Robin Hood, the Carnivalesque and the Rhetoric of Violence in Early Modern England', in Nancy Armstrong and Leonard Tennenhouse (eds), *The Violence of Representation: Literature and the History of Violence*, London and New York, Routledge, 1990: 45–76.

Stallybrass, Peter. 'Patriarchal Territories: The Body Enclosed', in Margaret W. Ferguson, Maureen Quilligan and Nancy J. Vickers (eds), *Rewriting the Renaissance: the Discourses of Sexual Difference in Early Modern Europe*, Chicago, University of Chicago Press, 1986: 123–42.

Stallybrass, Peter and Allon White, *The Politics and Poetics of Transgression*, London and New York, Methuen, 1986.

Stanton, Domna C. (ed.) *The Female Autograph: Theory and Practice of Autobiography From the Tenth to the Twentieth Century*, Chicago and London, University of Chicago Press, 1987.

Stanton, Domna C. 'The Fiction of Préciosité and the Fear of Women', *Yale French Studies* 62, 1981: 118–19.

Staves, Susan. *Players' Scepters: Fictions of Authority in the Restoration*, Lincoln, NB, and London, University of Nebraska Press, 1979.

Swift, Carolyn Ruth. 'Female Identity in Lady Mary Wroth's Romance *Urania*', *English Literary Renaissance* 14(3) 1984: 328–46.

Swift, Carolyn Ruth. 'Female Self-Definition in Lady Mary Wroth's *Love's Victorie*', *English Literary Renaissance* 19(2) 1989: 171–88.

Theweleit, Klaus. *Male Fantasies: Volume I: Women, Floods, Bodies, History*, trans. Stephen Conway, Cambridge, Polity, 1987 (first pub. in German 1977).

Thomas, Keith. 'Women and the Civil War Sects', *Past and Present* 13, 1955: 42–64.

Thomas, P. *A Long Time Burning: The History of Literary Censorship in England*, London, Routledge & Kegan Paul, 1969.

Thompson, Roger. *Unfit for Modest Ears: A Study of Pornographic, Obscene and Bawdy Works Written or Published in England in the Second Half of the Seventeenth Century*, London, Macmillan, 1979.

Todd, Janet. 'Marketing the Self: Mary Carleton, Miss F. and Susannah Gunning', *Studies on Voltaire and the Eighteenth Century* 217, 1983: 95–106.

Todd, Janet. *The Sign of Angellica: Women, Writing and Fiction 1660–1800*, London, Virago, 1989.

Tomlinson, Sophie 'She that Plays the King: Henrietta Maria and the Threat of the Actress in Caroline Culture' in Gordon McMullan and Jonathan Hope (eds), *The Politics of Tragicomedy: Shakespeare and After*, London, Routledge, 1991.

Travitsky, Betty. 'The Lady Doth Protest: Protest in the Popular Writings of Renaissance Englishwomen', *English Literary Renaissance* 14(3) 1984: 255–83.

Travitsky, Betty (ed.). *The Paradise of Women: Writings by Englishwomen of the Renaissance*, New York, Columbia University Press, 1989.

Turner, Victor. *The Ritual Process: Structure and Antistructure*, Chicago, Chicago University Press, 1965.

Valverda, M. *Sex, Power and Pleasure*, London, Women's Press, 1985.

Veevers, Erica. *Images of Love and Religion: Queen Henrietta Maria and Court Entertainments*, Cambridge, Cambridge University Press, 1989.

Vickers, Nancy. '"The blazon of sweet beauty's best": Shakespeare's *Lucrece*', in Patricia Parker and Geoffrey Hartman (eds), *Shakespeare and the Question of Theory*, London, Methuen, 1985: 95–115.

Vickers, Nancy. 'Diana Described: Scattered Woman and Scattered Rhyme', in Elizabeth Abel (ed.), *Writing and Sexual Difference*, Brighton, Harvester, 1982.

Wagner, Peter. *Eros Revived: Erotica of the Englightenment in England and America*, London, Secker & Warburg, 1988.

Warner, Marina. *Monuments and Maidens: The Allegory of the Female Form*, London, Weidenfeld & Nicolson, 1985.

Weaver, Elissa. 'Spiritual Fun: A Study of Sixteenth-Century Tuscan Convent Theatre', in Mary Beth Rose (ed.), *Women in the Middle Ages and the Renaissance: Literary and Historical Perspectives*, Syracuse, NY, Syracuse University Press, 1986.

Williams, Raymond. 'Utopia and Science Fiction', *Science Fiction Studies* 5(3) 1978: 203–14.

Wiseman, Susan J. 'Gender and Status in Dramatic Discourse: Margaret Cavendish, Duchess of Newcastle' in Isobel Grundy and Susan J. Wiseman (eds), *Women/Writing/History 1640–1740*, London, Batsford, 1992.

Wittig, Monique. *Across the Acheron*, trans. David Le Vay, London, Peter Owen, 1987.

Woodbridge, Linda. 'New Light on *The Wife Lapped in Morel Skin* and *The Proud Wife's Paternoster*', *English Literary Renaissance* 13, 1983: 3–35.

Woodbridge, Linda. *Women in the English Renaissance*, Brighton, Harvester, 1984.

Wright, Louis B. *Middle-Class Culture in Elizabethan England*, Chapel Hill, University of North Carolina Press, 1935.

Zurcher, Amelia. '"Dauncing in a Net": Representation in Lady Mary Wroth's *Urania*', unpublished M.Phil. thesis, Oxford University, 1989.

INDEX